U.S. Coast Guard Cutters & Craft of World War II

BY ROBERT L. SCHEINA

FOREWORD BY ADMIRAL JOHN B. HAYES, USCG (RET)

NAVAL INSTITUTE PRESS   ANNAPOLIS, MARYLAND

Copyright © 1982
by the United States Naval Institute
Annapolis, Maryland

Library of Congress Cataloging in Publication Data

Scheina, Robert L.
  U.S. Coast Guard cutters and craft of
World War II.

  Includes index.
  1. United States. Coast Guard—Lists of
vessels. 2. United States. Coast Guard—History
—World War, 1939–1945. I. Title.

VA61.S33	1983	359.9′7′0973	82-12398

ISBN 0-87021-717-8

Unless otherwise indicated, all photographs are
courtesy of the U. S. Coast Guard.

Printed in the United States of America

Contents

Foreword

Franklin Delano Roosevelt once said, "There is nothing I love so much as a good fight." Coast Guardsmen must agree with him, for they have played a significant role in most armed conflicts that the United States has been engaged in since 1790, when the service was established as the Revenue Marine. In this book, Dr. Scheina documents the Coast Guardsmen's contributions to World War II, not in an attempt to elevate them above the accomplishments of others, but to give the reader a better appreciation of the Coast Guard's rich heritage. An astute and capable historian, he draws out the thread of Coast Guard involvement from the complex tapestry of World War II, so that we can fully admire the special abilities of this unique, seagoing, armed service.

Throughout the war, Coast Guardsmen crewed their own cutters. They also manned U.S. naval vessels and participated in a wide variety of missions, from ocean convoy escort and antisubmarine warfare to operating landing craft for amphibious assaults in the Atlantic and Pacific theaters. Their skill in contributing to these missions is the result of many years of experience. Coast Guard expertise in small boat operations, recognized worldwide, has its roots in the Life-Saving Service, which was organized in 1848 and could claim such highly decorated heroes as Surfman Joshua James. Deep-water operations date back even further, to the career of our first commissioned officer, Hopley Yeaton, and the establishment of the Revenue Marine by Secretary of the Treasury Alexander Hamilton in 1790.

As is true of many of its missions, the Coast Guard's search and rescue is as significant in time of war as it is in peacetime. Its coastal and high-seas search-and-rescue network is second to none. From the very start of World War II, it accounted for the retrieval of over 25,000 persons whose vessels fell victim to the war at sea. During the Normandy Invasion alone, Coast Guardsmen rescued over 1,400 allies from landing craft that had succumbed to enemy fire.

The Coast Guard maintains the United States' fleet of polar icebreakers, which currently support scientific exploration in both the Arctic and Antarctic. The service also operates a number of smaller cutters with hulls reinforced for domestic ice-breaking under less severe conditions. Ice-breaking capabilities in World War II made Greenland operations a Coast Guard show: keeping icebound inland waters open allowed many U.S. warships to enter the conflict far sooner than otherwise could have been expected. In any future global strife, the ability to operate on the frigid rim of the North Atlantic and in the polar zones may prove to be even more crucial than it was forty years ago.

During World War II the Coast Guard acquired the commercial-vessel safety program when it absorbed the Bureau of Marine Inspection and Navigation. Coast Guard expertise in marine safety, port safety and security, and aids to navigation, along with the domestic ice-breaking capability already mentioned, will be crucial to moving vital cargos quickly and safely in any future war or national emergency.

Coast Guard Selective Reserve strength for 1982 is established at 12,000, but this valuable component of the service is a mere fraction of its World War II counterpart. With the rapid expansion of our fighting forces during World War II, the Coast Guard Reserve grew to over 170,000; Reservists operated 351 Navy and 288 Army ships and small craft. Today the primary mobilization role of the Coast Guard Reserve is port security. Their small boat and cutter skills, honed through augmentation of Regular Coast Guard units, are every bit as vital as those of their forerunners.

Throughout its history, the Coast Guard has been a constantly evolving organization. A conglomerate of roles, acquired in piecemeal fashion, has been molded through the crucible of time into a highly effective multi-mission organization of maximum value to the country. Wartime tasking being developed in conjunction with the Navy includes new roles in mine countermeasures, control of naval shipping, and expanded responsibilities for maritime coastal defense.

Such a many-faceted organization as the Coast Guard, emerging from a diverse background and enjoying an abundant heritage, cannot be fathomed without the sure illumination of the historian's pen. To live without a knowledge of history is to experience only the threshold of reality; to live with history is to serve alongside shipmates gone before. For those who would avail themselves of it, Dr. Scheina's book fills in one more piece of the Coast Guard story . . . and we should thank him for that.

ADMIRAL JOHN B. HAYES, USCG (RET)
Former Commandant

Preface

This book presents key dates, characteristics, and an operational sketch for each Coast Guard cutter and craft that served during World War II. Ships manned by the Coast Guard but administratively controlled by another government agency are listed in appendices. The World War II era is defined as beginning in early 1939 and ending with the capitulation of Japan on 2 September 1945. Adhering to this precise closing date excludes an influx of ships that more accurately belong to the postwar era, including units acquired at the close of the war for the short-lived Air-Sea Rescue Agency. The *Gladwyne* (PF 62), for example, is listed only in appendix A, since she did not commission in the Coast Guard as a WPF until 15 April 1946. The *Gladwyne* and other units like her belong in a work dealing with postwar cutters.

This book presents the individual ships of each type from the latest wartime acquisition to the earliest. Each ship is identified by its visual call sign (similar to the hull number of the U.S. Navy's classification system).

Before World War II, the Coast Guard used its own system of cutter designation. When it was created on 28 January 1915 by the amalgamation of the Revenue Cutter Service and the Life-Saving Service, its cutters were divided into three groups: cruising cutters, station ships, and harbor cutters. From 1921 through 1931, it classified them as first- or second-class cruising cutters, harbor cutters, and launches; and after 1931, it used the categories of cruising cutters, harbor cutters, and patrol boats. Classes were defined by their length in feet. Those units 100 feet or over were *named* and called cutters; those under 100 feet were *numbered* and called craft. As with all Coast Guard administrative rules, there were exceptions. Finally, a system of visual call signs was adopted by the Coast Guard in 1941 and published in the *U.S. Coast Guard Call Sign Book, 1941* (part II, visual). Most large cutters were assigned an identification number, which was preceded by a *W*. The use of a *W* to identify Coast Guard cutters may be traced well back into the 1930s, but why the letter was chosen is unclear.

When Coast Guard ships began to operate under the Navy's control in 1941, the latter service identified them by its own type designations. Types with appropriate Navy equivalents were given those designations; large cruising cutters, for example, were classed as gunboats (PG). Special designations were given to types unique to the Coast Guard; for example, the buoy tender was designated an AGL. To distinguish Coast Guard–owned from Navy-owned vessels, the Navy added the prefix *G*, but this identification was not adopted by the Coast Guard. Therefore, the Navy identified a Coast Guard gunboat (PG) as a GPG. Toward the end of the war, however, the Navy reassigned the *G* prefix to vessels being lent to Greece, and assigned Coast Guard cutters the identifying letter *W*, a designation the Coast Guard had been using for some time. This identification is still in use today, although in 1967 the Coast Guard changed some of the Navy designations to ones used exclusively by the Coast Guard.

On 7 February 1942 the Commandant proposed to the Chief of Naval Operations that cutters be numbered sequentially from 700, beginning with the *Alexander Hamilton* (see 327-foot cutters, page 13) and ending with the *Myrtle* as 913. However, on 16 February the Commandant requested that this proposed numbering system not be implemented; instead, he recommended that visual signal calls, without the letter *W*, be painted on the hulls of Coast Guard cutters that required designating numbers. The Coast Guard married the Navy's classification lettering to the visual call sign in the spring of 1942. This system was *loosely* applied to Coast Guard cutters for the remainder of the war.

Another set of numbers is also frequently associated with cutters. Beginning in the late nineteenth century, the Revenue Cutter Service, and subsequently the Coast Guard, assigned building numbers to cutters. When used in the text, these are shown *under* the visual call sign and are preceded by a building number (bn). Ships acquired in a completed state did not, of course, receive a building number.

For the Coast Guard, the visual call sign was little more than a point of reference for administrative purposes. Any attempt to interpret the mission, capability, or size of the ships by a particular visual call sign would be an error. For example, weather station duty was regularly performed by WPGs, WAGs, and WAGLs. The capabilities of ships within each visual call sign category range from the first-line to the hopelessly obsolete. The fact that Coast Guard records casually move a cutter from one visual call sign to another and then back again without administrative paperwork underscores the informality of the system. For example, Coast Guard records refer to the *Mayflower* as being a WPG and a WAG indiscriminately. When determining the visual call sign of a variously classified cutter, therefore, the author tried to use common sense. Most Coast Guard cutters in service in 1939, but disposed of by early 1941, did not receive visual call signs; in these cases, call signs have been assigned by the author and enclosed in brackets—for example, [WAGL]. Many training ships, in particular, lacked visual call signs, for they commissioned into the Coast Guard from the U.S. Maritime Service when the Coast Guard took over its administration on 1 September 1938. These training ships are given [WIX] visual call signs by the author.

Within each class of ships, data that might change with age, upkeep, or mission has been dated. Hull weights (i.e., displacements) are expressed in tons. Electronics and armament cited are representative examples and not a comprehensive listing for the war. Under electronics, only radars and sonars have been listed. Other more common hardware, such as echo sounders and gyro compasses, are not included.

To my knowledge, this book is the first attempt to gather data for all World War II Coast Guard cutters and craft within one cover. Care has been taken to check data against original sources to assure accuracy. For example, all commissioning dates for the 327-foot cutters were checked against the logs, and in each case a message from the cutter to headquarters announcing the commissioning has been located to verify the date. The sources, however, were often meager; I would appreciate receiving additions or corrections.

To those family, friends, and colleagues who have helped make a difficult task easier, thank you.

I am especially indebted to Commander George Wildes, USCG (Ret), Mr. William Wilkinson, and Mr. John P. Young for their generous sharing of time and resources. Commander Wildes has long been a student of Coast Guard cutters; he freely gave of his time and talent in order to make this a better book. When the work was in its final stages, Commander Wildes spent many hours at the Coast Guard Academy library researching missing data. Mr. William Wilkinson is the foremost authority on Coast Guard small craft; he has devoted years to a study of their design. Mr. Wilkinson prepared numerous tables and design histories in the craft section, and he reviewed the entire text. He has kindly granted me permission to use copyrighted materials. Mr. John Young has developed an expertise on cutters through years of research. He spent many hours reviewing the manuscript and provided pages of additions and refinements.

A special debt is owed to my wife, Linda, and daughter, Robyn, for sacrificing family time so that I might write this book. Linda patiently typed the manuscript, a most difficult task given the nature of the work. Other colleagues have given of their special skills and knowledge to make this a better book. To all the following people, thank you very much: A. Davidson Baker III; Christian Beilstein; Robert Bennett; Robert Browning; Bernard Cavalcante; Robert Cressman; Charles Dragonette; John Fisher; Norman Friedman; Charles "B. W." Haberlein; Agnes Hoover; Kohji Ishiwata; John Jedrlinic; Paul Johnson; Philip Lundeberg; Dorothy Maddox; Jeffrey Moore; H. E. "Pete" Musgrove; Dennis Noble; T. Michael O'Brien; John Reilly, Jr.; Walter Remick; Jurgen Rohwer; Anthony Stolze; Kenneth Sutherland; Nicholas Tiberio; Susan Urbanski; John Wager; Richard White; Richard Wright.

Introduction

The World War II histories of Coast Guard cutters and craft have become lost among those of U.S. naval ships. This is understandable. The number of Coast Guard ships was small when compared with the number operated by the Navy, and the Coast Guard served as part of the Navy from 1 November 1941 until 1 January 1946, making it difficult to distinguish the relatively few Coast Guard cutters from the many naval ships. Many of the large cutters had been assigned to the Navy piecemeal prior to 1 November, adding to the confusion. However, the size of the Coast Guard fleet was impressive when compared with any but the largest of the World War II navies. The Coast Guard war fleet was, in fact, larger than either the French or Russian navy.

During the war, the Coast Guard operated 400 cutters and more than 4,000 small craft. Over 2,000 units of all sizes were newly constructed, at a cost of about $160 million, and thousands of crafts were taken into the service to meet emergencies of the war. In addition, the Coast Guard manned almost 300 vessels for the Navy and a slightly smaller number for the Army—including transports over 700 feet long requiring 900-man crews. During the war, the Coast Guard expanded from 10,000 to 170,000 full-time personnel. In addition, 50,000 temporary Reservists served.

The Coast Guard served the war effort in two ways. First, it used its own cutters and craft to carry out its normal missions under conditions of war. Second, its personnel were used to man Navy and Army ships. This task was an accident of timing as much as it was a result of long-range planning. Coast Guard personnel became available for reassignment in early 1941 and again beginning in mid-1943—and at these times, the Navy needed crews. Ships manned by Coast Guard personnel for a sister service operated under that service's control.

Search and rescue, ice operations, aids to navigation, weather stations, and merchant marine training—all peacetime missions of the service that required cutters and craft—were primary responsibilities of the Coast Guard during the war.

Search and rescue took place under greatly varying circumstances. Early in the war, when German U-boats were taking a heavy toll on shipping close in to the East Coast, small craft from the service's lifeboat stations rescued hundreds of torpedoed sailors. Standard 36-foot motor lifeboats were the primary rescue vehicles, but these craft were soon joined by thousands of Coast Guard and Coast Guard Reserve craft brought into the service to meet this emergency. The U-boat threat in coastal waters abated by early 1943, thus freeing Coast Guard personnel assigned to these craft for other tasks.

The responsibility of search and rescue on the high seas, however, belonged to cutters assigned to convoys as escorts—and these cutters rescued 15,000 victims on the high seas. The Coast Guard, in fact, sustained its two largest cutter losses—the *Alexander Hamilton* (29 Jan 42) and the *Escanaba* (13 Jun 43)—while assisting distressed merchantmen. The antisubmarine warfare role of the service has also received much publicity, and not without reason: one Coast Guard class alone, the 327-foot cutters, sank four U-boats. However, cutters assigned to convoy duty had a primary search-and-rescue responsibility, an extension of the peacetime role; the fact that the 327s were excellent submarine killers was simply a bonus. During World War II cutters were not technologically specialized, and a first-class gunboat could, without much difficulty, be modified to make an excellent submarine killer.

Search and rescue also took place during amphibious landings. Sixty Coast Guard 83-foot patrol boats were used during the Normandy Invasion, and thirty of these craft were sent to the Pacific to rescue those in distress during the landings.

Ice operations were the domain of the Coast Guard during the war. Officially tasked with ice operations in 1936, the service and two of its predecessors (the Revenue Cutter Service and the Lighthouse Service) had been performing ice-breaking for many years prior to this. All major cutters designed for the Coast Guard from the early 1930s through World War II had been either ice-breaking or ice-going cutters (except for the 327s, which had a naval-designed hull). In fact, the *Storis* and the "Wind" class were specifically designed to operate in Greenland waters, where the Coast Guard conducted successful operations during the war.

The Coast Guard was further tasked with extending the navigation season on the Great Lakes. Early in the war, a few Great Lakes merchantmen with ice-breaking capabilities were taken into the service. The introduction of the new 180-foot buoy tenders, all built on the Lakes between 1942 and 1944, greatly increased the number of ice-breaking ships available to the service. Those commissioned during the winter and spring would break ice on the Lakes until they could work their way out.

The wartime extension of aids to navigation has gone almost unnoticed. Traditional aids, such as buoys and day markers, were placed and serviced in remote sites in Greenland and across the Pacific. Further, the Coast Guard built and maintained the LORAN (long-range) navigation system, the first worldwide electronics navigation system and one of the Allies' closely guarded secrets. These new tasks required a fleet of tenders, which had to be dependable and self-sufficient. The new 180-foot tenders were assigned to these tasks, while the older tenders were retained to service domestic aids.

Weather stations were mid-ocean sites manned by cutters whose purpose was to provide an emergency landing site for the fledgling international air traffic and to issue weather reports for air and sea traffic. This latter function became increasingly important, for with Europe at war, merchant ships had to maintain radio silence and could no longer provide weather data. When weather patrols began in 1940, 327-foot cutters, the newest and best cutters the service had, were used. In 1941, however, these cutters were reassigned to tasks that were given higher priority. Because ships were in short supply, old merchantmen were acquired by the Navy and loaned to the Coast Guard for weather-station duty. One, the *Muskeget,* was lost on or about 9 September 1942 with all hands. In late 1943, Coast Guard–manned, naval patrol frigates began to take over this duty.

The Coast Guard was also assigned the administration of ships belonging to the U.S. Merchant Service on 1 September 1938. Thus, numerous training ships were commissioned into the Coast Guard, where they remained until 31 August 1942, when responsibility was returned to the Maritime Commission.

Beginning in early 1941, when the United States began to expand its amphibious force, the Navy drew on Coast Guard personnel both for special talents and to fill shortages. A joint-service exercise was held in the Caribbean that year: the First Army Division was embarked in civilian-manned Army transports; the First Marine Division was on board naval transports. Because of the skills they developed during peacetime, several hundred Coast Guard surfmen from lifeboat stations had been assigned to man the landing craft for this exercise. Thirty to fifty, in fact, were assigned to each transport. Following the exercise, the Army transports were turned over to the Navy without crews. Since the Navy was short of trained personnel, and the Coast Guard had just turned over to Great Britain ten 250-foot cutters under lend-lease, the Coast Guard crews from the 250s were used as the nucleus for the crews of the Navy's newly acquired transports. Coast Guardsmen were further used throughout the war to man small amphibians and to train members of the other services in their use.

In the days immediately following Pearl Harbor, the Coast Guard was tasked to patrol the extensive coastal waters and to prevent enemy landings. Thousands of privately owned motor boats, yachts, and small fishing craft were taken into the service as Coast Guard reserve craft (CGR). Many of these craft were manned by their owners, who enrolled in the Coast Guard as temporary Reservists. Summer and winter, day and night, in fair weather and foul, for over two years the patrol was maintained. As an adjunct to such patrolling, the Coast Guard developed an extensive port security program and a beach patrol. The need for these coastal defense programs abated in mid-1943, and at about the same time, the Navy needed personnel to man its growing fleet. Thus, many Coast Guardsmen who had been involved in coastal defense were retrained and used to man the numerous Navy and Army ships commissioned in 1943, 1944, and 1945. By V-J Day, the Coast Guard manned 299 naval ships, requiring 54,000 men, and 278 Army vessels, requiring 7,000 men.

Abbreviations

AA	antiair		EM	emergency manning
ABHD	Advanced Base Harbor Defense		f	future
ALASKASEAFRON	Alaska Sea Frontier		fl	full load
A/N	aids to navigation		gal	gallons
AS DEVLANT	Antisubmarine Development Detachment, Atlantic Fleet		Gov.	government
			GULFSEAFRON	Gulf Sea Frontier
ASW	antisubmarine warfare		HAWAIIANSEAFRON	Hawaiian Sea Frontier
ATS	Army Transport Service		HEW	Department of Health, Education and Welfare
bn	building number (assigned to cutters)		IOC	initial operational capability
BHP	brake horsepower		kts	knots
BNSI	Bureau of Navigation and Steamboat Inspection		kVa	kilovolt-amperes
bp	between perpendiculars		loa	length overall
BSA	Boy Scouts of America		LORAN	long-range aid to navigation
CARIBSEAFRON	Caribbean Sea Frontier		LS	lightship
cal.	caliber		MARAD	Maritime Administration
CG	Coast Guard		max	maximum
CINC	Commander in Chief		mb	molded beam
CINCLANT	Commander in Chief Atlantic Fleet		mg	machine gun
CINCPAC	Commander in Chief Pacific Fleet		mi	nautical miles
CNO	Chief of Naval Operations		Mk	Mark
comm.	commissioned		MMA	Merchant Marine Academy
COTCLANT	Commander Operational Training Command Atlantic Fleet		NA	not available
			NAOTC	Naval Air Operational Training Center
COM4THFLEET	Commander Fourth Fleet		NOWESTSEAFRON	Northwest Sea Frontier
COM7THFLEET	Commander Seventh Fleet		NPS	National Park Service
COM12THFLEET	Commander Twelfth Fleet		NSF	National Science Foundation
CZ	Panama Canal Zone		oa	overall
d	draft		PASEAFRON	Panama Sea Frontier
dc	depth charge		pdr	pounder
Dept I	Department of the Interior		PHILSEAFRON	Philippine Sea Frontier
DESLANT	Destroyers Atlantic Fleet		pos	possibly
dis	displacement		psi	pounds per square inch
Div	division		PWA	Public Works Administration
EA	emergency acquisition		R & D	research and development
EASTSEAFRON	Eastern Sea Frontier		RCS	Revenue Cutter Service
			RN	Royal Navy
			SAR	search and rescue
			SERVLANT	Service Force Atlantic Fleet

NOTE: Each of the states in the Union is abbreviated to its appropriate two-letter code assigned by the U.S. Post Office.

SERVPAC	Service Force Pacific Fleet	USAT	United States Army Transport
SHP	shaft horsepower	USLHS	United States Lighthouse Service
SNAME	Society of Naval Architects & Marine Engineers	USN	United States Navy
t	tons	USSB	United States Shipping Board
TF	task force	VCNO	Vice Chief of Naval Operations
trans	transferred	WESTSEAFRON	Western Sea Frontier
TVA	Tennessee Valley Authority	wl	waterline
USA	United States Army	WSA	War Shipping Administration
USAAF	United States Army Air Force	WW I	World War I
USAF	United States Air Force	WW II	World War II

Gunboats (WPG)

The cutters grouped together as gunboats varied considerably in their potential to carry out the missions traditionally assigned to the gunboat type.

Those designed and built for the Coast Guard, particularly the 327s, 165As, and 240s, were extensively employed in convoy duty. The fact that these units sank four U-boats—U-175, U-225, U-606, and U-626—has received much more attention than accounts of their dangerous, high-seas rescues of U-boat victims have. Two of these cutters, the *Alexander Hamilton* and *Escanaba*, were engaged in rescue activities when they themselves were sunk by U-boats.

The gunboats that were acquired as emergency measures, however, ranged from the useless to the indispensable. The *Bodkin* was never commissioned due to her poor state, and convoy members requested that the cutter *Gresham* be left home because she was so slow and leaked fuel oil badly. And yet, the *North Star* was indispensable, at least until the "Wind" class (WAGs) came into service in 1944, for the Germans had established weather stations, important to U-boat activities, in this remote area, and icebreaking gunboats were essential in order to rout them out. At the beginning of World War II, the United States possessed only three ships which were marginally capable of operating off the east coast of Greenland—the USS *Bear* and the cutters *North Star* and *Northland*.

WPG—GUNBOATS

255-FOOT CUTTERS ("INDIAN TRIBES" CLASS, *OWASCO* CLASS)

Name	Visual Call Sign	Builder	Keel Laid	Launched	Commissioned	Disposition
Owasco (ex-*Oneida*)	WPG 39 (bn CG-105)	Western Pipe & Steel Co., San Pedro, CA	17 Nov 43	18 Jun 44	18 May 45	*Decomm* 27 Jun 73; sold 7 Oct 74
Winnebago	WPG 40 (bn CG-106)	Western Pipe & Steel Co., San Pedro, CA	1 Dec 43	2 Jul 44	21 Jun 45	*Decomm* 27 Feb 73; sold 7 Oct 74
Chautaqua	WPG 41 (bn CG-107)	Western Pipe & Steel Co., San Pedro, CA	22 Dec 43	14 May 44	4 Aug 45	*Decomm* 1 Aug 73
Sebago (ex-*Wachusett*)	WPG 42 (bn CG-108)	Western Pipe & Steel Co., San Pedro, CA	7 Jun 43	28 May 44	20 Sep 45	*Decomm* 29 Feb 72; *trans* MARAD 14 Apr 72
Iroquois	WPG 43 (bn CG-109)	Western Pipe & Steel Co., San Pedro, CA	19 Jun 44	22 Oct 44	9 Feb 46	*Decomm* 13 Jan 65; sold 1 Jun 65
Wachusett (ex-*Huron*)	WPG 44 (bn CG-110)	Western Pipe & Steel Co., San Pedro, CA	3 Jul 44	5 Nov 44	23 Mar 46	*Decomm* 30 Aug 73; sold 18 Nov 74
Escanaba (ex-*Otsego*)	WPG 64 (bn CG-111)	Western Pipe & Steel Co., San Pedro, CA	25 Oct 44	25 Mar 45	20 Mar 46	*Decomm* 28 Jun 73
Winona	WPG 65 (bn CG-112)	Western Pipe & Steel Co., San Pedro, CA	8 Nov 44	22 Apr 45	19 Apr 46	*Decomm* 31 May 74
Klamath	WPG 66 (bn CG-113)	Western Pipe & Steel Co., San Pedro, CA	13 Dec 44	2 Sep 45	19 Jun 46	*Decomm* 1 May 73; sold 18 Nov 74
Minnetonka (ex-*Sunapee*)	WPG 67 (bn CG-114)	Western Pipe & Steel Co., San Pedro, CA	26 Dec 44	21 Nov 45	11 Jul 46	*Decomm* 31 May 74
Androscoggin	WPG 68 (bn CG-115)	Western Pipe & Steel Co., San Pedro, CA	30 Dec 44	16 Sep 45	26 Sep 46	*Decomm* 27 Feb 73; sold 7 Oct 74
Mendota	WPG 69 (bn CG-116)	Coast Guard Yard, Curtis Bay, MD	5 Jul 43	29 Feb 44	2 Jun 45	*Decomm* 1 Nov 73
Pontchartrain (ex-*Okeechobee*)	WPG 70 (bn CG-117)	Coast Guard Yard, Curtis Bay, MD	5 Jul 43	29 Feb 44	28 Jul 45	*Decomm* 19 Oct 73

Cost
$4,239,702 each (hull & machinery)

Hull

Displacement (tons)	2,010 fl (1945)
Length	255' oa
Beam	43' mb
Draft	16' max (1945)
Tons per Immersed Inch	15.0

Machinery

Main Engines	1 Westinghouse 3,200 kVa electric motor driven by a turbine
Main Boilers	2 Foster-Wheeler, 2 drum-top fired Express-type, 635 psi, 750°F superheat
SHP	4,000 total (1945)
Propellers	Single

Performance

Max Sustained	19.0 kts, 5,800 mi radius (1945)
Cruising	16.0 kts, 10,000 mi radius (1945)
Economic	12.0 kts, 12,200 mi radius (1945)

Logistics

Fuel Oil (95%)	105,000 gal
Complement	18 officers, 2 warrants, 256 men (1945)

Electronics (1945)

Detection Radar	*Mendota & Pontchartrain:* SC-4, SF-1; all other units: SR, SU
Fire Control Radar	All units: Mk 26
Sonar	All units: QJA

Armament (1945)

4 5"/38 (twin); 8 40mm/60 (2 quad); 4 20mm/80; 2 dc tracks; 6 Y-guns; 1 Hedgehog

Design

"The bow and the stern for each other yearn, and the lack of interval shows. . . ." Myths have long shadowed the design history of the 255-foot class. These cutters were to have been much longer ships, and two theories persist as to why they were shortened: the first is that these cutters were built to replace the ships given to Great Britain under lend-lease, and Congress stipulated that the Coast Guard had to build these replacement cutters to the same size and character as those provided to the British; the second is that their length was determined by the maximum length that could pass through the locks of the Welland Canal from the Great Lakes to the St.

Lawrence River. The Great Lakes shipbuilding industry brought pressure to bear on Congress to ensure that it had the potential to bid on the contracts. The first theory seems to be correct, but the second cannot be ruled out.

The Coast Guard had prepared a design for a 316-foot cutter that was to have been an austere 327. This design was cut down into the 255-foot ship. To accomplish this, everything was squeezed down and automated to a degree not before achieved in a turbo-electric driven ship.

The machinery design of the 255s was compact and innovative, but overly complex. It had pilothouse control, variable rate (10 to 1) burners, and automatic synchronizing between the turbogenerator and the motor. Westinghouse engineers developed a system of synchronization and a variable frequency drive for main propulsion auxiliary equipment, which kept the pumps and other items at about two-thirds the power required for constant frequency operation. The combined boiler room/engine room was a break with tradition.

The turbo-alternators for ship service power exhausted at 20 psi gauge pressure instead of into a condenser. This steam was used all over the ship before finally going to a condenser. Space heating, galley cooking, laundry, freshwater evaporating, fuel and feed water heating were all taken from the 20 psi back pressure line.

The 255-foot class was an ice-going design. Ice operations had been assigned to the Coast Guard early in the war, and almost all new construction was either ice-going or ice-breaking.

The hull was designed with constant flare at the waterline for ice-going. The structure was longitudinally framed with heavy web frames and an ice belt of heavy plating, and it had extra transverse framing above and below the design waterline. Enormous amounts of weight were removed through the use of electric welding. The 250-foot cutters' weights were used for estimating purposes. Tapered bulkhead stiffeners cut from 12" I-beams went from the main deck (4" depth of web) to the bottom (8" depth of web). As weight was cut out of the hull structure, electronics and ordnance were increased, but at much greater heights. This top weight required ballasting the fuel tanks with seawater to maintain stability both for wind and damaged conditions.

The superstructure of the 255s was originally divided into two islands in order to accommodate an aircraft amidships, but this requirement was dropped before any of the units became operational. Construction of this class received a low priority, and none of the cutters served in the war. Following completion of the preliminary design by the Coast Guard, the work was assigned to George G. Sharp of New York to prepare the contract design.

The number of units—13 of them—had an interesting origin. Three were to have been replacements for overaged cutters—the *Ossipee, Tallapoosa,* and *Unalga;* ten units were to be replacements for the 250-foot class transferred to Great Britain under lend-lease. For economy, all 13 were built to the same design.

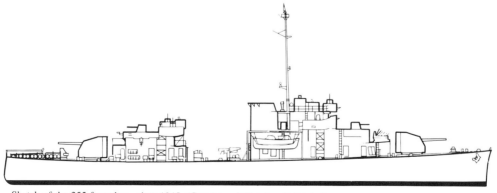

Sketch of the 255-foot class, circa 1945. (Courtesy of Christian Beilstein.)

The *Owasco*, 18 Jul 45. This overhead view clearly shows a massive armament for a ship this size, plus a tubby length-to-beam ratio. The *Owasco*s had about the same displacement as a *Fletcher*-class destroyer, but they were 122 feet shorter and 3 feet wider.

The *Pontchartrain*, 3 Aug 45, running trials. Many demands were placed on this design and, as a result, these cutters were uncomfortable seaboats. An SC-4 air-search radar antenna sits atop the mast, and below that is an SF-1 antenna in a radome.

The *Owasco*, 21 Feb 46. Many of the units completed in 1946 were never given their full wartime armament. The after 5″ gunhouse and much ASW armament were never fitted. This class was fitted with Mk 26 fire-control radar. The 255s, the 327s, and the 269s (''Wind'' class) were the only CG cutters to be fitted with fire-control radars during WW II. (Courtesy of the National Archives.)

EMERGENCY ACQUISITION

Name	Visual Call Sign	Builder	Launched	Commissioned	Disposition
Cobb (ex-*Governor Cobb*)	WPG 181	Delaware River Co., Chester, PA	21 Apr 06	23 Oct 06 (completed); 20 Jul 43 (CG)	*Decomm* 31 Jan 46; *sold* 6 Mar 47

Cost
  Acquisition $1; conversion $2,500,000

Hull
  Displacement (tons)   3,500 fl (1945)
  Length   300'8" oa
  Beam   55" mb
  Draft   19' max (1945)

Machinery
  Main Engines   3 Parsons LP impulse turbine, center turbine high pressure, outboard turbines low pressure
  Main Boilers   6 Scotch, 180 psi
  SHP   5,000
  Propellers   Triple

Performance
  Max Speed   15.7 kts (1945)
  Cruising   14.7 kts, 3,300 mi radius (1945)
  Economic   9.5 kts, 4,370 mi radius (1945)

Logistics
  Fuel Oil (95%)   185,000 gal
  Complement   9 officers, 114 men (1945)

Aircraft
  None assigned; HNS-1 and HOS-1 operated from cutter, 1944–45

Electronics (1945)
  Detection Radar   SA, SL
  Sonar   QCL-8

Armament (1945)
  2 5"/38 (single); 6 20mm/80 (single); dc tracks; 4 Y-guns; 2 Mousetraps

Design

The *Governor Cobb* was the first turbine-propelled commercial ship built in the United States. Eastern Steamship Co. awarded the contract to W. & A. Fletcher Co., Hoboken, NJ; the Fletcher yard constructed the turbines under license from Parsons of England. Fletcher sublet the hull contract to the Chester, PA yard. General Ship Repair Co. of Baltimore converted the *Cobb* to a helicopter test ship. The ship's name was shortened to the *Cobb* by the Coast Guard on 2 Aug 43.

Cobb

Built for Eastern Steamship Co.; served as a training ship during WW I under U.S. Shipping Board control; leased to P & O Steamship Co. for Key West–to–Havana service; 1937 sold to Romance Line; May 37 failed inspection by BNSI and laid up; 5 Jun 42 taken over by the WSA at Philadelphia; 1943 assigned to EASTSEAFRON—stationed at New York, NY; 20 Jul 43 commissioned in CG after conversion; suffered numerous breakdowns and machinery failures; 29 Jun 44 first flight operation conducted; operated in Long Island Sound area during WW II; mid 1944–45 assigned to Groton Training Station—stationed at New London, CT, and used for training.

The *Governor Cobb*, recently completed. Her original configuration differs markedly from her appearance while in the CG. She was the first American-built ship to have geared turbines. (Courtesy of The Mariners Museum.)

The *Cobb* at sea, 29 Jun 44. The helicopter over the stern is an HNS-1, and the one astern is an HOS-1. The CG led the development of the helicopter during WW II. All American and British helicopter pilots were trained by the CG at Brooklyn Air Station. Early wartime helicopters were oriented toward ASW. As the U-boat threat abated, search and rescue evolved as the helicopter's primary mission.

The first day of landings on board the cutter *Cobb*, 29 Jun 44. The first landing on board a ship took place on 7 May 43, when Colonel Frank Gregory, USAAF, landed an XR-4 on board the tanker *Bunker Hill*. The first landing on board the *Cobb* was made by the pioneer aviator Commander Frank Erickson, USCG.

EMERGENCY ACQUISITION

Name	Visual Call Sign	Builder	Keel Laid	Commissioned	Disposition
Mayflower (ex-*Butte*; ex-*Mayflower*; f-*Malla*)	WPG 183	J & G Thompson, Clydebank, Scotland	1896	24 Mar 98 (Navy); 20 Oct 43 (CG)	*Decomm* 1 Jul 46; *sold* 8 Jan 47

Cost
  Acquisition $1; conversion $2,500,000

Hull
  Displacement (tons)   2,690 max (1943); 2,850 max (1945)
  Length   320'7" oa; 288' less bow sprit; 276' wl
  Beam   37 mb
  Draft   17'2" max (1943); 19'10" max (1945)

Machinery
  Main Engines   2 triple-expansion steam, 4-cyl, double-acting
  Main Boilers   2 Navy Express Thornycroft, 180 psi
  SHP   2,400
  Propellers   Twin

Performance
  Max Speed   12.0 kts, 4,800 mi radius (1943)
  Economic   9.0 kts, 5,000 mi radius (1945)

Logistics
  Fuel Oil (95%)   136,000 gal
  Complement   9 officers, 2 warrants, 142 men (1945)

Electronics (1945)
  Detection Radar   SC-2, SG, SG-1, SL, SQ-2 (portable set), SN (portable set)

Sonar   QCL-8

Armament (1943)
  1 5"/51 (single); 2 3"/50 (single); 6 20mm/80 (single); 2 dc tracks; 4 Y-guns, Hedgehog

Design:
The *Mayflower* was designed by George Watson as a luxurious steam yacht for Ogdon Goelet, New York Yacht Club. She was acquired by the Navy on 19 Mar 98 from his estate for employment as an auxiliary gunboat during the Spanish-American War. The *Mayflower* served as a presidential yacht from 1905 until 1929. She was seriously damaged by fire on 24 Jan 31 at the Philadelphia Navy Yard. She was stricken from the Navy list 23 Mar 31 and sold on 19 Oct 31 as a hulk. The *Mayflower* was reacquired by the WSA on 31 Jul 42 and transferred to the Coast Guard on 6 Sep 43. Norfolk Shipbuilding & Drydock Co., VA, converted the *Mayflower* to wartime configuration from 1 Oct 42 to 12 Aug 43.

Mayflower

31 Jul 42 name changed from the *Mayflower* to the *Butte*—15 Aug 43 original name reinstated; Oct 43–mid 44 assigned to EASTSEAFRON—stationed at New York, NY, and used principally as an escort; mid 44–Aug 45 assigned to CINCLANT (COTLANT)—stationed at Norfolk, VA, and used for radar training; mid 45 assigned to Boston, MA.

The *Mayflower*, circa 1900. She was one of many ships purchased by the Navy to fight in the Spanish-American War. The *Mayflower* was later used as a presidential yacht by Presidents T. Roosevelt, Taft, Wilson, Harding, and Coolidge. (Courtesy of the U.S. Navy.)

The *Mayflower*, 1 Mar 44. From mid-1944 to the close of the war, this cutter was used for radar training. Mounted on the prow is a Hedgehog ASW launcher. This weapon, first developed by the British, consisted of an array of spigot launchers from which contact-fused depth bombs were projected over the bow. In the absence of a hit, there would be no explosion, thus the sound contact would not be lost. The Hedgehog was so named because of the resemblance of her launchers to the animal when its spines bristle up. (Courtesy of A. D. Baker III.)

EMERGENCY ACQUISITION

Name	Visual Call Sign	Builder	Keel Laid	Launched	Commissioned	Disposition
Gresham	WPG 85	Globe Iron Works Co., Cleveland, OH	17 Jan 96	12 Sep 96	30 May 97 (RCS); 25 Mar 43 (CG)	*Decomm* and *sold* 19 Jan 35; *decomm* and turned over to WSA 7 Apr 44; *sold* 1945

Cost
  Original cost $148,800; reacquisition WSA loan; conversion $95,000

Hull
  Displacement (tons)   906 at mean draft (1897); 1,090 fl (1943)
  Length   205'6" oa; 188' bp
  Beam   32' mb
  Draft   10'10" mean (1897); 12'6" max (1943)

Machinery
  Main Engines   1 vertical, inverted-cylinder, direct-acting, triple-expansion steam
  Main Boilers   4 single-ended, fire tube
  SHP   2,500
  Propellers   Single

Performance
  Max Speed   8.0 kts (1943)

Logistics
  Fuel   Coal

Electronics (1943)
  Detection Radar   SF
  Sonar   QCL-8

Armament
  1916   4 6-pdrs. (rapid-fire)
  1942   2 3"/50 (single); 4 20mm/80 (single); 2 dc tracks; 4 dc projectors

Design
  The *Gresham* was designed for service on the Great Lakes by the Revenue Cutter Service, a predecessor of the Coast Guard. During the Spanish-American War, she had to be cut in two in order to pass through the locks controlling access to the Lakes. She never returned to the Lakes. She was sold for scrapping 22 Apr 35; due to wartime needs, however, the *Gresham* was reacquired on 21 Jan 43.

Gresham

Mar 43 renovated by General Ship Repair Co., Baltimore, MD; Mar 43–Apr 44 assigned to EASTSEAFRON—stationed at New York, NY, and used for coast escort; found to be in very poor condition and removed from service.

The *Gresham*, 1898, cut in two so that she could be removed from the Great Lakes in order to serve in the Spanish-American War. She never returned to the Great Lakes.

The *Gresham* in 1943. The plow-bow reveals her age; by this time, she was slower than the speed maintained by most convoys—8 knots was a strain. Because of her poor condition, the *Gresham* was decommissioned before the end of the war.

EMERGENCY ACQUISITION

Name	Visual Call Sign	Builder	Launched	Commissioned	Disposition
Bodkin (ex-*Burke*; ex-*Nokomis*; ex-*Nokomis II*)	WPG 182	Pusey & Jones Co., Wilmington, DE	May 1914	3 Dec 17 (USN); not applicable (CG)	Work suspended 15 Jul 43; WSA for scrapping 21 Jul 44

Cost
  Acquisition WSA loan; conversion $150,000

Hull
Displacement (tons)	1,000 fl (1942)	Beam	31'7" mb
Length	243' oa	Draft	10'6" (1942)

Machinery
Main Engines	Wood River Iron Works steam triple expansion
Main Boilers	2 Babcock & Wilcox watertube boilers, 250 psi
SHP	2,000
Propellers	Twin

Performance
Max Speed	16.0 kts (1942)

Logistics
Fuel	Coal
Complement	9 officers, 109 men (1945)

Design

The *Bodkin* is the former yacht *Nokomis II* taken over by WSA and renamed the *Burke*. During WW I she served in the U.S. Navy as the *Nokomis*. Name changed to the *Bodkin* on 1 Jun 43.

Bodkin

Material condition at time of acquisition was very poor; conversion at Coast Guard Yard, Curtis Bay, MD, was suspended due to the decline in German submarine activity on East Coast; was to have been assigned to EASTSEA-FRON and stationed at New York, NY.

The *Bodkin*, 24 May 43, at the Coast Guard Yard, Curtis Bay, MD. Because of her poor condition and the decreasing number of U-boat successes, the *Bodkin* never commissioned in the CG. (Courtesy of the Smithsonian Institution.)

The *Bodkin* as the USS *Nokomis* during WW I. She was acquired by the CG early in WW II. As the U-boat threat abated in early 1943, and as new frigate and destroyer-escort construction became available, work was suspended on the *Bodkin*. (Courtesy of the U.S. Navy.)

EMERGENCY ACQUISITION

Name	Visual Call Sign	Builder	Launched	Commissioned	Disposition
Sea Cloud (ex-*Hussar*)	WPG 284	Friederich Krupp Germaniawerft, A. G., Kiel, Germany	1931	1931 (as yacht); 4 Apr 42 (CG)	Turned over to Navy 9 Apr 43; *decomm* 4 Nov 44; returned to owner by Navy

Cost
  Acquisition Navy Charter; conversion $318,101
Hull
  Displacement (tons)   3,077 fl (1945)
  Length   316' oa
  Beam   49'2" mb
  Draft   19' (1942)
Machinery
  Main Engines   2 diesels
  BHP   1,600
  Propellers   Twin
Performance
  Cruising   12.0 kts, 20,000 mi radius (1942)

Logistics
  Diesel Fuel   590 tons
  Complement   11 officers, 175 enlisted men (1942)
Electronics
  Detection Radar   Not fitted (1943); SA (1944)
Armament (1942)
  2 3"/50 (single); 5 20mm/80 (single); dc tracks
Design
  The *Sea Cloud* was launched as the four-masted bark *Hussar*. She was acquired in 1935 by Joseph E. Davies, U.S. ambassador to the Soviet Union and Belgium prior to WW II, and named the *Sea Cloud*.

Sea Cloud

Apr 42–Apr 43 assigned to EASTSEAFRON—stationed at Boston, MA, and used on weather patrol duty; Jul 42–Apr 44 used for integration experiment—some of the crew and a few officers were black; 6 Jun 42 rescued 8 survivors from the schooner *Maria da Gloria*; 1980 the reconditioned *Sea Cloud* began cruises for a German owner under Panamanian flag; during some of the intervening years she had served as Rafael Trujillo's yacht, the *Angelita*.

The *Sea Cloud* prior to WW II. She is considered by many to be one of the handsomest yachts ever built. One can still sail on board the *Sea Cloud* in 1980: she is operating as a sail cruise ship in the Caribbean and Mediterranean. (Courtesy of the U.S. Naval Academy.)

The *Sea Cloud*, Jul 44, at Argentia. She is in naval service and wears hull number 99. Note the ship's wheel lashed to the side of the weather balloon hangar.

EMERGENCY ACQUISITION

Name	Visual Call Sign	Builder	Launched	Commissioned	Disposition
North Star	WPG 59 (f-IX-148)	Berg Shipbuilding Co., Seattle, WA	1932	14 May 41 (CG)	*Decomm* 13 Jan 44; *trans* to Navy 15 Jan 44

Cost
  Acquisition loan from Dept. of Interior; conversion $350,000

Hull
  Displacement (tons)   1,780 fl (1941); 2,200 fl (1943)
  Length   225' oa
  Beam   41' max
  Draft   16'6" mean (1943)

Machinery
  Main Engines   1 McIntosh Seymour diesel
  BHP   1,500
  Propellers   Single

Performance
  Max Speed   13.0 kts (1941)
  Cruising   11.0 kts, 9,000 mi radius (1941)

Logistics
  Diesel fuel   60,000 gal
  Complement   17 officers, 116 men (1941)

Aircraft
  1 J2F (1941–43)

Electronics (1942)
  Detection Radar   SK

Armament (1942)
  2 3"/50 (single); 6 20mm/80 (single); dc tracks

Design
  The *North Star* was constructed for the Department of the Interior for service off Alaska. Constructed of wood, the *North Star* was equipped with a semi-icebreaker bow. Due to the elasticity of wood, many believed that the wooden-hulled *North Star* would be more advantageous in ice waters than a steel ship. She was the only named cutter (excepting tenders) with a wooden hull.

North Star

1941 used to evacuate Little America and Palmer Islands prior to CG service; 1941–43 permanently stationed at Boston, MA; 1 Jul 41 assigned to Navy for duty and assigned to newly established Northeast Greenland Patrol; 12 Sep 41 assisted the *Northland* in seizing the Norwegian trawler *Boskoe*—first U.S. naval capture of WW II; 1941–44 assigned to CINCLANT—stationed at Boston, MA, and operated principally in Greenland waters; Jul 43 trapped and damaged by ice; 23 Jul 43 attacked by German plane off Jan Mayen Island; 31 Aug 43 investigated German camp at Sabine Island; 15 Dec 43 designated IX 148.

The *North Star*, 11 Jul 42. The most prominent feature is a J2F Grumman carried on her quarterdeck. Note the 55-gallon drums (for aviation fuel) carried amidships. Many believed that her wooden hull provided an elasticity advantageous in ice operations.

The *North Star*, 12 May 43, mounts a new radar, and new life rafts have replaced the old-style life rafts. A wartime CG study showed that those abandoning ship who chose the life raft over the life boat were much less likely to survive.

EMERGENCY ACQUISITION

Name	Visual Call Sign	Builder	Launched	Commissioned	Disposition
Nourmahal	WPG 72 (first CG tour); WPG 122 (second CG tour)	Friederich Krupp Germaniawerft, A.G., Kiel, Germany	1928	17 Jun 28 (as yacht); 21 Aug 40 (CG); 29 Dec 43 (acquired from Navy); 12 Jan 44 (officially stricken from Navy List)	*Trans* to Navy 16 Jun 43; *decomm* 30 May 46

Cost
1ˢᵗ acquisition chartered for $1; 2ⁿᵈ acquisition chartered from Navy; conversion $206,363

Hull
Displacement (tons) 3,200 fl (1945)
Length 263'10" oa
Beam 41'6" mb
Draft 18'5" max (1945)

Machinery
Main Engines 2 Sulzer Bros. 6-cyl, 2 cycle diesels
BHP 3,200
Propellers Twin

Performance
Max Sustained 13.7 kts, 12,700 mi radius (1945)
Economic 8.0 kts, 23,500 mi radius (1945)

Logistics
Diesel Fuel 138,700 gal
Complement 9 officers, 98 men (1941); 9 officers, 1 warrant, 101 men (1945)

Electronics
Detection Radar None (1941); SF (1945)

Armament
1941 2 4"/50 (single); 6 .50 cal. AA; 8 .30 cal. AA; 2 dc tracks
1944 2 4"/50 (single); 6 20mm/80 (single); 8 .30 cal. AA; 2 dc tracks, 4 dc projectors; 2 Mousetraps

Design
The *Nourmahal* is a former yacht belonging to William Vincent Astor. She was converted for weather-station service between 22 Sep and 1 Dec 41. Although possessing a steel hull, the *Nourmahal*'s interior wood finishings presented a fire hazard. She had been acquired by the Navy 3 Mar 42.

Nourmahal

1941–43 assigned to EASTSEAFRON—stationed at New York, NY, and used principally for escort duty; 1943–45 assigned to CINCLANT—stationed at Boston, MA (1943–Sep 44) and Norfolk, VA (Sep 44–1945)—used principally for weather-station duty.

The *Nourmahal*, circa 1942, during her first "tour" with the CG. She is not yet fitted with radar. Light machine guns were later replaced with 20mms as they became available.

327-FOOT CUTTERS ("SECRETARY" CLASS, *CAMPBELL* CLASS, *BIBB* CLASS, *HAMILTON* CLASS)

Name	Visual Call Sign	Builder	Keel Laid	Launched	Commissioned	Disposition
Bibb (ex-*George M. Bibb*)	WPG 31; WAGC 31 (bn CG-71)	Charleston Navy Yard, Charleston, SC	15 Aug 35	14 Jan 37	10 Mar 37	Active
Campbell (ex-*George W. Campbell*)	WPG 32; WACG 32 (bn CG-65)	Philadelphia Navy Yard, Philadelphia, PA	1 May 35	3 Jun 36	16 Jun 36	*Decomm* 1 Apr 82
Duane (ex-*William J. Duane*)	WPG 33; WAGC 6 (bn CG-67)	Philadelphia Navy Yard, Philadelphia, PA	1 May 35	3 Jun 36	1 Aug 36	Active
Alexander Hamilton (ex-*Hamilton*; ex-*Alexander Hamilton*)	WPG 34 (bn CG-69)	New York Navy Yard, New York, NY	11 Sep 35	6 Jan 37	4 Mar 37	Sank 30 Jan 42
Ingham (ex-*Samuel D. Ingham*)	WPG 35; WAGC 35 (bn CG-66)	Philadelphia Navy Yard, Philadelphia, PA	1 May 35	3 Jun 36	17 Sep 36	Active
Spencer (ex-*John C. Spencer*)	WPG 36; WAGC 36 (bn CG-70)	New York Navy Yard, New York, NY	11 Sep 35	6 Jan 37	1 Mar 37	*Decomm* special status Engineering Training School 23 Jan. 74; *decomm* 15 Dec 80; *sold* 8 Oct 81
Taney (ex-*Roger B. Taney*)	WPG 37; WAGC 37 (bn CG-68)	Philadelphia Navy Yard, Philadelphia, PA	1 May 35	3 Jun 36	24 Oct 36	Active

Cost
  $2,468,460 each
Hull
  Displacement (tons)   2,350 trial (1936); 2,750 fl (1945)
  Length   327' oa; 308' wl
  Beam   41' mb; 41' wl; 41'2" max
  Draft   12'6" mean (1936); 15' max (1945)
  Block Coefficient   0.510
  Tons per Immersed Inch   21.5
Machinery
  Main Engines   2 Westinghouse double-reduction geared turbines
  Main Boilers   2 Babcock & Wilcox sectional express, air-encased, 400 psi, 200°F superheat
  SHP   5,250 total (1936); 6,200 total (1945)
  Propellers   Twin, 3 blades
Performance
  Max Speed   19.5 kts (1945)
  Max Sustained   19.0 kts, 4,200 mi radius (1945)
  Cruising   13.0 kts, 7,000 mi radius (1945)
  Economic   11.0 kts, 9,500 mi radius (1945)
Logistics
  Fuel Oil (95%)   136,520 gal
  Complement   12 officers, 4 warrants, 107 men (1936)
    16 officers, 5 warrants, 200 men (1941)
    24 officers, 2 warrants, 226 men (1945)
Aircraft (*See* Design remarks)
  Alexander Hamilton   V143 (JF-2) (1938)
  Bibb   V172 (SOC-4) (1938–39)
  Duane   1 SOC-4 (1941)

  Spencer   V159 (J2F-1) (1937)
    V144 (JF-2) (1938)
  Taney   V135 (JF-1) (1937–41)
Electronics
  Special Equipment   British high-frequency direction finder (early 1942)
  Detection Radar   *Bibb:* SC-4, SGa (1945)
    Campbell: British prob. 271, SC, SG (1943); SC, SG (1945)
    Duane: SC-3, SGa (1945)
    Ingham: SC-2, SGa (1945)
    Spencer: SC-4, SGa (1945)
    Taney: SK, SG-1 (1945)
  Fire-Control Radar   All units: Mk 26 (1945)
  Sonar   All units: QC series (1945)
Armament
  1936   All units: 2 5"/51 (single); 2 6 pdrs.; 1 1 pdr.
  1940   *Campbell, Taney:* 2 5"/51 (single); 4 3"/50 (single)
  1941   *Duane:* 3 5"/51 (single); 3 3"/50 (single); dc tracks; 1 Y-gun
  1942   *Hamilton:* 3 5"/51 (single); 3 3"/50 (single); dc tracks; 1 Y-gun
  1945   *Bibb, Campbell, Taney:* 2 5"/38 (single); 6 40mm/60 (twin); 4 20mm/80 (single)
    Ingham, Spencer: as above, except 8 20mm/80 (twin) instead of 4
    Duane: 14 40mm/60 (2 quad & 3 twin); 8 20mm/80 (single)

Design
  The 327s were designed to meet changing missions of the service as it emerged from the Prohibition era. Because the air passenger trade was expanding both at home

and overseas, the Coast Guard believed that cutter-based aircraft would be essential for future high-seas search and rescue. Also, during the mid-1930s narcotics smuggling, mostly opium, was on the increase, and long-legged, fairly fast cutters were needed to curtail it. The 327s were an attempt to develop a 20-knot cutter capable of carrying an airplane in a hangar. A preliminary Coast Guard design effort married these desires to the basic qualities of the 250-foot cutters. The resulting design was 316′ × 46′6″ × 16′ on 2,350 tons displacement—a very broad, deep cutter. The design was a single-screw ship costing $1,500,000—not quite half the cost of the final product. Concurrently, the Navy was developing a 20-knot, 2,000-ton design. After comparison, the Coast Guard selected the Navy design and heavily modified it. The final 327 design was based on the *Erie*-class gunboats: the machinery plant and hull below the waterline were identical. This standardization cut costs of designing and building. In fact, on 23 Jan 46 the Coast Guard requested the USS *Charleston* from the Navy on the basis ''of her construction along the lines of the 327 ft. cutters. . . .'' This request was withdrawn due to manpower shortage.

Thirty-two preliminary designs based upon the *Erie* class were drawn up before one was finally selected. The healthy sheer forward and the high slope in the deck in the wardrooms was known as the ''Hunnewell Hump.'' Commander (Constructor) F. G. Hunnewell, USCG, was head of the Construction and Repair Department at that time.

There is ample evidence that all of the class carried aircraft prior to 1941. Specific examples are cited in the Aircraft section. In 1941 the CG invited bids for three new cutters. Shaft horse power was raised to 6,500, but in most respects, these ships were to have been similar to the 327s. Because of wartime demands, the money allocated was used instead to construct three 255s.

All units carried full names until May–June 1937. At that time, names were shortened to surnames only. On 11 Jan 42, the Navy requested that the *Hamilton* resume her full name so she would not be confused with the USS *Hamilton* (DMS 18, ex-DD 141). CG Operational Memorandum No. 17 of 12 Jan 42 directed that ''the Coast Guard Cutter HAMILTON be referred to in all correspondence as ALEXANDER HAMILTON.'' The Coast Guard used her full name after this date.

Although assigned to the Greenland area during the war, this class was not ideally suited to icy waters. Propeller blades, which protruded past the sides of the cutters and near the surface, were on occasion ''trimmed off'' by ice. The 327s did, however, possess unique qualities above and beyond their weapons and sensors, which made them excellent convoy escorts. As Captain A. G. Shepard, USN, observed, ''They are considerably more roomy, so that they can carry a large number of survivors. They are better sea boats than destroyers, and lend themselves better to boat operations and rescues. In connection with picking up people, their hospital accommodations are superior to those of destroyers.'' As the U-boat threat abated, 327s were converted into Amphibious Force Flagships. Their Command and Control capabilities were greatly improved when they were fitted with 35 radio receivers and 25 transmitters.

Conversion to AGC

Bibb	Charleston Navy Yard, SC	17 Oct 44–29 Jan 45
Campbell	Boston Navy Yard, MA	4 Jan–28 Mar 45
Duane	Norfolk Navy Yard, VA	16 Jan–6 Mar 44
Ingham	Charleston Navy Yard, SC	1 Aug–21 Oct 44
Spencer	Norfolk Navy Yard, VA	26 Jun–11 Sep 44
Taney	Boston Navy Yard, MA	10 Oct 44–29 Jan 45

Alexander Hamilton

1937–39 home ported in Oakland, CA; 1939 transferred to Norfolk, VA; 12 Oct 39–27 Jan 40 made 4 cruises as part of Destroyer Div. 18 on Grand Banks Patrol; 28 Feb 40–4 May 41 used on weather ocean station; 11 Sep 41 assigned to Navy for duty; 27 Dec 41 assigned to Cdr TF 24.6.2; 29 Jan 42 torpedoed approximately 17 miles off Reykjavik, Iceland by U-132: 1 officer and 19 men killed, 6 later died of burns; 30 Jan 42 capsized; hulk sunk by DD gunfire.

Bibb

1938 cadet cruise from CG Academy; 1939 3 months with Navy on maneuvers and Grand Banks Patrol; Feb 40–41 on first weather patrol approximately 600 miles east of Bermuda; 11 Sep 41 transferred to Navy by Executive Order; 1941–43 assigned to CINCLANT (DESLANT) and operated in the North Atlantic; 26 Sep 42 rescued 61 survivors from the freighter *Penmar*; 7 Feb 43 rescued 202 survivors from the SS *Henry S. Mallory* and 33 survivors from the *Kalliopi*; 9 Mar 43 rescued 3 survivors from the SS *Coulmore*, and 2 survivors from the SS *Bonneville* and SS *Melrose*; 9 May 43–Oct 44 served as convoy escort to Mediterranean; 1945 operated in Pacific as AGC; Apr–Aug 45 at Okinawa as flagship for Commander Mine Craft, Pacific Fleet.

Campbell

1936–41 stationed at Stapleton, NY; Sep 39 assigned to Destroyer Div. 18 as part of Grand Banks Patrol; May 40 wartime armament installed at New York Navy Yard, NY; Oct 40–25 Apr 41 stationed at Lisbon, Portugal under direction of Navy; 1 Jul 41 assigned to the Navy for duty; 1941–43 assigned to CINCLANT (DESLANT) and operated as escort in North Atlantic; Feb 43 rescued 50 survivors from the SS *Neilson Alonzo*; 22 Feb 43 rammed and sank U-606, 47° 44′N, 33° 43′W—engine room flooded and power lost; under repairs until 19 May 43; 1943–45 escorted convoys to Mediterranean; 1945 operated as AGC in Pacific.

Duane

1936–40 stationed at Oakland, CA; Sep 39 assigned to Destroyer Div. 18 as part of Grand Banks Patrol; 1940 reassigned to Boston, MA; Feb 40–41 operated on first weather station approximately 1,200 miles east of Bermuda; Aug 40 aircraft from cutter surveyed Greenland's west coast; 14 Jun 41 rescued 46 survivors from the SS *Tresillian*; 11 Sep 41 assigned to Navy for duty; 1941–43 assigned to CINCLANT (DESLANT) and operated as escort in North Atlantic; 3–6 Feb 42 assisted in USAT *Dorchester* rescue; 10 Apr 42 grounded in Cape Cod Channel—slight damage; 17 Apr 43 assisted the *Spencer* in sinking U-175—rescued 22 from crew; 1943 assigned to CINCLANT (8th Fleet) and escorted convoys to Mediterranean; late 43–early 44 operated in Caribbean; 1944–45 operated in Mediterranean as AGC; Aug 44 served as flagship for Commander 8th Amphibious Force for invasion of South France.

Ingham

1937–40 stationed at Port Angeles, WA; 1940–41 reassigned to Boston, MA; Mar 40 on weather station 1,200 miles east of Bermuda; 1941 stationed at Lisbon, Portugal; 1 Jul 41 assigned to Navy for duty; 1942–43 assigned to CINCLANT (DESLANT) and operated as escort in North Atlantic; 26 Sep 42 rescued 8 survivors from the SS *Tennessee*; 15 Dec 42 sank U-626, 56° 46′N, 27° 12′W; 7 Feb 43 rescued 33 survivors from the SS *Henry R. Mallory*, SS *Robert E. Hopkins*, and SS *West Portal*; Feb 43 rescued survivors from the SS *Jeremiah Van Rensseler*; 18 Mar 43 rescued all hands from the SS *Matthew Luckenbach*; mid 43–mid 44 escorted convoys to Mediterranean; late 44–45 operated as AGC in Pacific; 13–18 Feb 45 served as flagship of Mariveles-Corregidor Attack Group; 18 Mar 45 served as flagship for Tigbauan landings, Panay, Philippines; 29 Mar 45 served at Negros Island landings, Philippines; Jul 45 served as flagship for Balut Island Attack Unit, Philippines landings.

Spencer

1937–40 stationed at Cordova, AK; 1940–41 reassigned to Stapleton, NY; 1940 used on weather patrol; 11 Sep 41 assigned to Navy for duty; 1941– mid 43 assigned to CINCLANT (DESLANT) and operated as escort in North Atlantic; 12 May 42 rescued 52 survivors from the SS *Cristales* and SS *Mont Parnes;* 21 Feb 43 sank U-225—51° 25′N, 27° 28′W; 8 Mar 43 rescued 35 from the SS *Guido;* 17 Apr 43 sank U-175 (losing 1 enlisted man to gunfire), 48° 50′N, 21° 20′W—and rescued 19 of crew; mid 43–late 43 escorted convoys to Mediterranean; late 43–early 44 operated in Caribbean; early 44–mid 44 returned to Mediterranean; late 44–45 operated as AGC in Pacific; 7 Dec 44 grounded at San Pedro Bay, Leyte—moderate damage; 31 Jan 45 served as flagship for 8th Amphibious Group at Nasugbu landing, Luzon, Philippines; 26–28 Feb 45 served as flagship Task Group 78.2 for Puerto Princessa landing,

Palawan, Philippines; Apr–May 45 served as flagship for Parang and Malabang landing, Mindanao, Philippines; Jun 45 employed as fighter direction ship for Brunei, North Borneo, landing; Jul 45 served as flagship for Task Group 78.2 Balikpapan, Borneo, landing.

Taney

1936–41 stationed at Honolulu, HI; Mar 40 cruised to Howland, Jarvis, and Baker Islands; 1 Jul 41 assigned to Navy for duty; 7 Dec 41 stationed at Honolulu Harbor, pier 7, during Japanese attack; 1941–early 44 assigned to HAWAIIANSEAFRON and operated as escort in Pacific; early 44–late 44 escorted convoys to Mediterranean; 1945 operated in Pacific as AGC; Apr 45 served as combat information center for Okinawa operations.

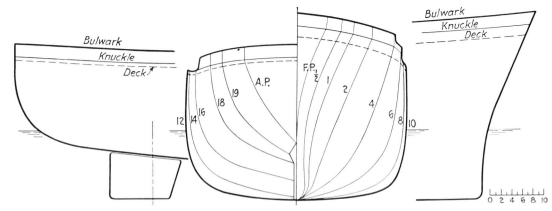

Lines of the cutter *Alexander Hamilton*. (Courtesy of SNAME, *Transactions* XLV [1937]: 98.)

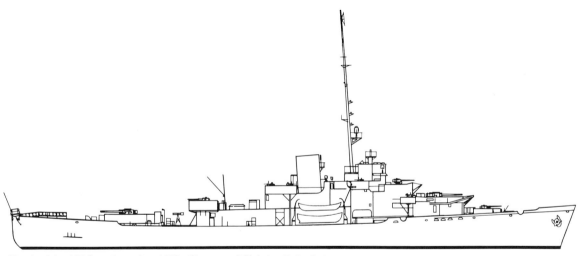

Sketch of the 327-foot class, circa 1943. (Courtesy of Christian Beilstein.)

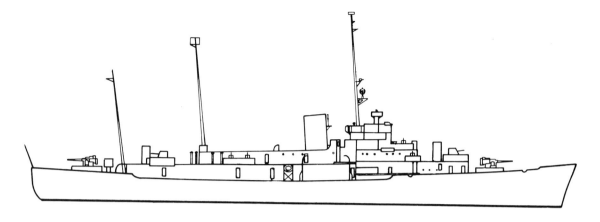

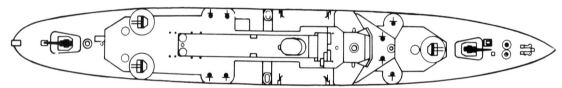

Sketch of the 327-foot class, circa 1945. The *Duane*'s armament varied considerably from the armament shown in this drawing. (Courtesy of Christian Beilstein.)

CG aircraft V172 (an SOC-2) is being lowered onto the *Bibb* in 1938. One preliminary design incorporated a main-deck hangar by extending the superstructure aft. This concept was abandoned before construction began. All of the 327s carried an aircraft at one time or another.

The *Duane*, spring 1941, in Godthaab Fjord, Greenland. Her mission was to survey the east coast of Greenland in order to identify sites for airfields. This was probably the last time a 327-footer carried an aircraft. (Courtesy of A. D. Baker III.)

The *Campbell*, prior to Mar 41. Armament has been increased to two 5″/51s forward, a 3″/50 before the bridge, and three 3″/50s aft. One 3″/50 sits between the "goalposts," and two are farther aft. The *Campbell* mounts no ASW armament at this time. On 22 Feb 43 she rammed and sank U-606. Her bow had to be reconstructed, and she ended up with a length of 326′; she was the only 326-footer in the CG.

A midship view of the *Alexander Hamilton* taken 30 minutes after she was torpedoed off Iceland. Boats are being lowered in order to transfer the wounded to fishing craft. The remainder of the crew did not abandon the cutter until an hour later.

The *Ingham*, circa 1943, on patrol in the North Atlantic. All units except the *Alexander Hamilton* and *Taney* received a similar camouflage pattern.

The *Ingham*, circa 1944, wearing an unusual camouflage scheme. A second radar has been added to the mast, and a light mainmast is now fitted.

The *Spencer*, 29 Apr 44. Note the construction of the aft 3″ gun tubs. The sides folded in and the bottom up, reducing the maximum beam of the cutter. (Courtesy of A. D. Baker III.)

The *Bibb* in 1944. The forward 5″/51 has been replaced with a 3″/50. There is a Hedgehog mounted on the bow. The mast, carrying both an SG radar and a lookout position, bears testimony to the changing times.

The *Taney*, 10 Apr 44, convoying in the Atlantic. She mounts a unique armament of 5″/38s. None of her sisters received this configuration. The *Taney* was in nearby Honolulu Harbor during the 7 Dec 41 Japanese attack on Pearl Harbor. Over the years, the cutter has received much publicity for this reason, even though all of her sisters had more active wartime careers.

The *Ingham* after conversion to an AGC. As amphibious force flagships, all 327s except the *Duane* carried single 5″/38s fore and aft, plus a variety of 40mm/60s and 20mm/80s.

The *Duane* as an AGC, 24 Jul 44. Ship is "dressed" for a visit by King George VI in Naples Harbor. An SC-3 radar antenna is atop the mainmast, and an SGa atop the foremast.

165-FOOT (A) CUTTERS

Name	Visual Call Sign	Builder	Keel Laid	Launched	Commissioned	Disposition
Algonquin	WPG 75 (bn CG-56)	Pusey & Jones Co., Wilmington, DE	14 Oct 33 (contracted)	25 Jul 34	20 Oct 34	*Decomm* 18 Apr 47; *sold* 13 Jul 48
Comanche	WPG 76 (bn CG-57)	Pusey & Jones Co., Wilmington, DE	14 Oct 33 (contracted)	6 Sep 34	1 Dec 34	*Decomm* 29 Jul 47; *sold* 10 Nov 48
Escanaba	WPG 77 (bn CG-55)	Defoe Works, Bay City, MI	10 Nov 31 (contracted)	17 Sep 32	23 Nov 32	*Sank* 13 Jun 43
Mohawk	WPG 78 (bn CG-58)	Pusey & Jones Co., Wilmington, DE	14 Oct 33 (contracted)	1 Oct 34	19 Jan 35	*Decomm* 8 Jan 48; *sold* 1 Nov 48
Onondaga	WPG 79 (bn CG-59)	Defoe Works, Bay City, MI	23 Oct 33 (contracted)	2 Aug 34	11 Sep 34	*Decomm* 24 Jul 47; *sold* 7 Dec 54
Tahoma	WPG 80 (bn CG-60)	Defoe Works, Bay City, MI	23 Oct 33 (contracted)	5 Sep 34	22 Oct 34	*Decomm* 1 Jul 53; *sold* 17 Oct 55

Cost

$525,550 each

Hull

Displacement (tons)	1,005 fl (1934); 1,050 fl (1945)
Length	165′ oa; 150′ wl
Beam	36′ mb; 36′ wl
Draft	12′3″ mean (1936); 14′ max (1945)
Block Coefficient	0.538
Tons per Immersed Inch	9.73

Machinery

Main Engines	1 Westinghouse double-reduction geared turbine (*Algonquin, Comanche, Mohawk*); 1 DeLaval double-reduction geared turbine (*Escanaba, Onondaga, Tahoma*)
Main Boilers	2 Foster-Wheeler (*Algonquin, Comanche, Mohawk*); 2 Babcock & Wilcox (*Escanaba, Onondaga, Tahoma*); all units: 310 psi, 200°F superheat
SHP	1,500 total (1934)
Propellers	Single, 4 blades

Performance

Max Speed	12.5 kts, 2,000 mi radius (1945)
Max Sustained	12.0 kts, 2,500 mi radius (1945)
Cruising	11.0 kts, 3,100 mi radius (1945)
Economic	10.0 kts, 3,300 mi radius (1945)

Logistics

Fuel Oil (95%)	41,500 gal
Complement	6 officers, 56 men (1934); 7 officers, 1 warrant, 90 men (1945)

Electronics

Detection Radar	None (late 1942); SF (1945)
Sonar	*Algonquin, Comanche:* QCL-2 (1945); *Mohawk, Onondaga, Tahoma:* QCJ-3 (1945)

Armament

1934	All units: 2 3″/50
1942	All units except *Onondaga:* 2 3″/50 (single); 2 20mm/80 (single; 2 dc tracks; 4 Y-guns; 2 Mousetrap; *Onondaga:* 2 3″/50 (single)

Design

The 165-foot cutter units were the first Coast Guard cutters to employ geared-turbine drive. They were constructed from PWA funds. The hull design was derived from the *Tallapoosa* type of 1915. The 165As were the first flush-deck type with good freeboard. These cutters were designed for light ice-breaking. The plating doubled around the bow, the cutaway forefoot, short length, and medium draft made these cutters good ice boats. They had a heavy steel belt around the vessel at the waterline and relatively short bilge keels, so in a seaway they had a tendency to roll considerably. Also, while in Greenland service they were handicapped by their short cruising range.

Algonquin

1934–37 stationed at Woods Hole, MA; 1937–40 at Portland, ME—used for ice-breaking in Hudson and on Maine coast; Jul 41 assigned to the Navy for duty; 1941–45 assigned to CINCLANT (DESLANT)—stationed at Portland, ME, and used principally for escort duty in Greenland waters; 21 Mar 43 rescued 22 from the SS *Svend Foyne*, which had struck an iceberg; 1944–45 deployed on weather patrol.

Comanche

1934–40 stationed at Stapleton, NY, and used for ice-breaking on Hudson; May 40 transported first American Consul to Ivigtut, Greenland—this had been arranged one month after Germany invaded Denmark; 1 Jun 41 assigned to newly established South Greenland Patrol; 1 Jul 41 assigned to the Navy for duty; 1941–45 assigned to CINCLANT (DESLANT)—stationed at Boston, MA, and used principally for escort duty in Greenland waters; 4 Apr 42–8 May 42 conducted Greenland survey; 18 Jul 42 established Ice Cap Station, Comanche Bay—named for cutter; 3 Feb 43 rescued 97 survivors from the transport *Dorchester*—first rescue in which "retriever method" was used (where a Coast Guardsman was lowered over the side in a rubber suit to retrieve survivors in water); 15–16 Dec 43 rescued 29 from the USAT *Nevada*; 1944–45 served on weather patrol.

Escanaba

1932–40 stationed at Grand Haven, MI, and used for ice-breaking on Great Lakes; 1941 assigned to Greenland Patrol; 1941–45 assigned to CINCLANT (DESLANT)—stationed at Boston, MA, and used principally for escort duty in Greenland waters; 15 Jun 42 rescued 20 from the USS *Cherokee*; 3 Feb 43 rescued 132 from the SS *Dorchester*—first rescue in which "retriever method" was used—16 CG enlisted men lost their lives as passengers on board the *Dorchester*; 13 Jun 43 sunk by enemy—101 lost and 2 survivors, 60° 51′ N, 52° 00′ W.

Mohawk

1935–40 used for icebreaking in Hudson and Chesapeake; May 1940 towed the *Tusitala* to St. Petersburg, FL; 1941–45 assigned to CINCLANT (DESLANT)—stationed at Boston, MA, and used principally for escort duty in Greenland waters; 22 Nov 42 rescued 25 from the SS *Barberry*; 15 Jul 43 helped refloat the USAT *Fairfax*; May–Aug 44 used on weather patrol; 20 Dec 44 struck growler, causing moderate damage.

Onondaga

1941–45 assigned to NOWESTSEAFRON and ALASKASEAFRON—stationed at Ketchikan, AK, and used for escort and patrol duty; 3 Jun 42 attacked by Japanese carrier planes in Dutch Harbor, AK—no casualties.

Tahoma

1934–42 stationed on Great Lakes, at Cleveland, OH, and Sault Ste. Marie, MI—used for ice-breaking; 1942–45 assigned to CINCLANT (DESLANT)—

stationed at Boston, MA, and deployed in Greenland waters; 20 Jul 43 assisted the USAT *Fairfax*; 1 May–14 Aug 45 deployed on ice and weather patrol.

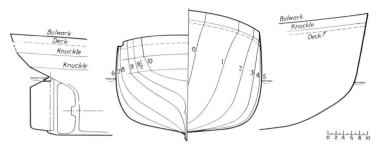

Lines of the cutter *Algonquin*. (Courtesy of SNAME, *Transactions* XLV [1937]: 99.)

The *Algonquin* in 1937. The compactness of this short, oceangoing cutter is apparent. Prewar armament consisted of two 3″/50s, mounted on the forecastle. Early in their careers, the 165As were used extensively for domestic ice-breaking. However, their design was not ideal for this work. The 110-foot tugs proved to be better at light ice-breaking.

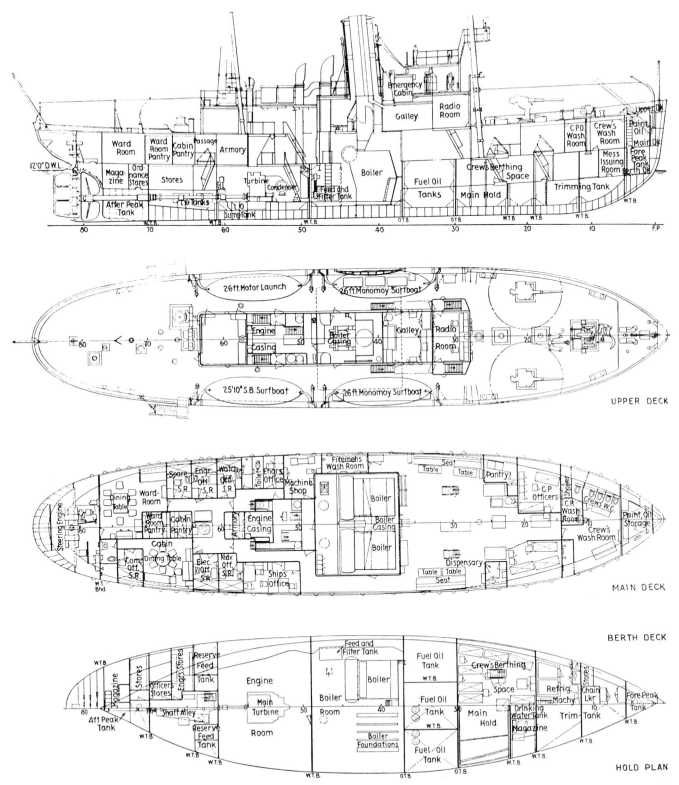

Inboard profile and deck plans of the cutter *Algonquin*. (Courtesy of *Marine Engineering/Log;* copied from *Marine Engineering and Shipping Age* [March 1935]: 32.)

The *Tahoma* on 14 Jul 42. The cutter has been rearmed and numerous structural changes have been made. Her foremast has been moved aft of the bridge structure, and the mainmast has been eliminated. No radar has yet been fitted. Bow bulwarks have been cut down to improve the field of fire for guns.

The *Mohawk* during late 1942. On 20 Dec 44, this cutter struck a growler (a small iceberg) while going to the assistance of a distressed merchantman and received moderate damage.

250-FOOT CUTTERS ("LAKE" CLASS)

Name	Visual Call Sign	Builder	Keel Laid	Launched	Commissioned	Disposition
Chelan	[WPG] (bn CG-45)	Bethlehem Shipbuilding Corp., Quincy, MA	14 Nov 27	19 May 28	5 Sep 28	*Trans* to G.B. 2 May 41
Pontchartrain	[WPG] (bn CG-46)	Bethlehem Shipbuilding Corp., Quincy, MA	29 Nov 27	16 Jun 28	13 Oct 28	*Trans* to G.B. 30 Apr 41
Tahoe	[WPG] (bn CG-47)	Bethlehem Shipbuilding Corp., Quincy, MA	5 Dec 27	12 Jul 28	8 Nov 28	*Trans* to G.B. 30 Apr 41
Champlain	[WPG] (bn CG-48)	Bethlehem Shipbuilding Corp., Quincy, MA	23 May 28	11 Oct 28	24 Jan 29	*Trans* to G.B. 12 May 41
Mendota	[WPG] (bn CG-49)	Bethlehem Shipbuilding Corp., Quincy, MA	20 Jun 28	27 Nov 28	23 Mar 29	*Trans* to G.B. 30 Apr 41
Itasca	[WPG] (bn CG-50)	General Engineering & Drydrock Co., Oakland, CA	NA	16 Nov 29	12 Jul 30	*Trans* to G.B. 30 May 41
Sebago	[WPG] (bn CG-51)	General Engineering & Drydock Co., Oakland, CA	NA	1930	2 Sep 30	*Trans* to G.B. 12 May 41
Saranac	[WPG] (bn CG-52)	General Engineering & Drydock Co., Oakland, CA	NA	12 Apr 30	2 Oct 30	*Trans* to G.B. 30 Apr 41
Shoshone	[WPG] (bn CG-53)	General Engineering & Drydock Co., Oakland, CA	NA	11 Sep 30	10 Jan 31	*Trans* to G.B. 20 May 41
Cayuga	[WPG] (bn CG-54)	United Drydock, Inc., Staten Island, NY	NA	7 Oct 31	22 Mar 32	*Trans* to G.B. 12 May 41

Cost
$900,000 each (hull & machinery)

Hull

Displacement (tons)	1,662 trial (1929); 2,075 fl (1929)
Length	250' oa; 239' wl; 236' bp
Beam	42' mb
Draft	12'11" mean (1929); 16' max (1929)
Block Coefficient	.490

Machinery

Main Engines	1 General Electric motor driven by generator driven by a turbine
Main Boilers	2 Babcock & Wilcox watertube boilers, 250 psi, 250° superheat

SHP	3,350
Propellers	Single, 4 blades

Performance

Max Speed	17.3 kts (trials, 1929)

Logistics

Fuel Oil (95%)	90,000 gal
Complement	8 officers, 4 warrants, 85 men (1940)

Electronics

Detection Radar	Not fitted (1941)

Armament

1929	1 5"/51; 1 3"/50; 2 6 pdrs.
1941	2 3"/50 (single); 1 Y-gun; dc tracks

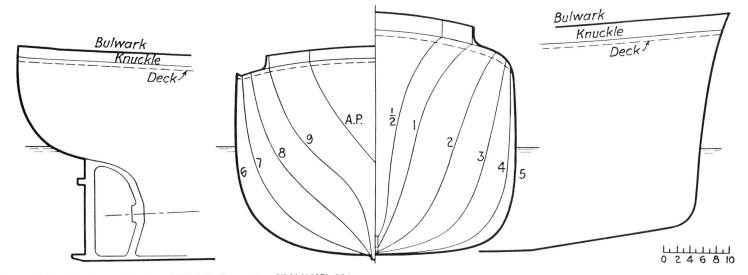

Lines of the cutter *Itasca*. (Courtesy of SNAME, *Transactions* XLV [1937]: 98.)

Design

The 250-foot class was designed by the Coast Guard. Captain Q. B. Newman, USCG, designed its innovative turbine-electric-drive power plant, which developed an amazing 3,000 shp. These were the first ships to have alternating current, synchronous motor for propulsion. The whole ship ran off the main turbine. The auxiliary generators were tied into the main generator electrically, after sufficient speed was attained. At that point, no steam was required to drive the turbines on the auxiliary generators. The propulsion plant achieved remarkable efficiency. The first five cutters were contracted on 6 Jul 27. This class had a slightly raked stem and a cruiser stern. These features were an attempt to improve sea qualities over the 240-foot class, particularly for service on ice patrol. In Dec 40 Chief of Naval Operations, Admiral Harold Stark, USN, informally told Commandant Russell Waesche, USCG, that he would request four units of this class for naval use in the Caribbean. However, President Franklin Roosevelt decided to make all ten available to Great Britain under lend-lease, and they were transferred. To replace these cutters, the Coast Guard was authorized to build the 255-foot cutter class.

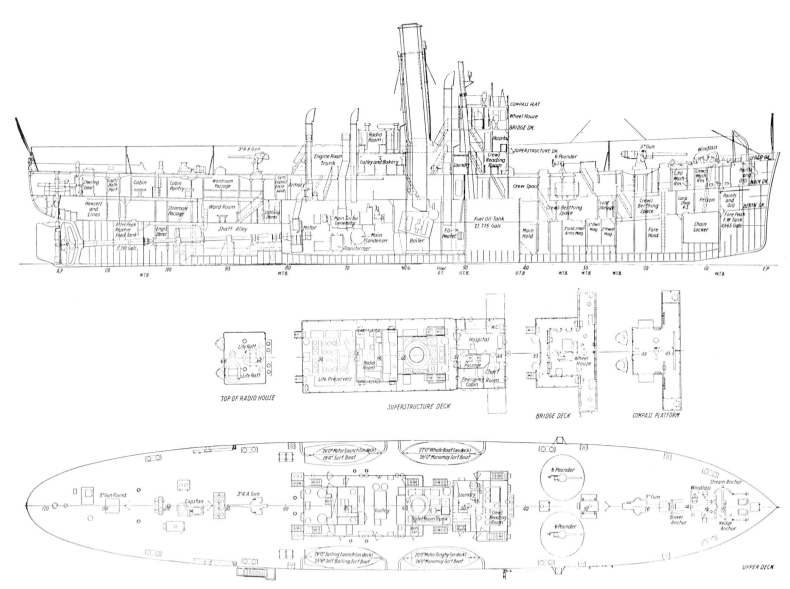

Inboard profile and deck plans of the ''Lake''-class cutters. (Courtesy of *Marine Engineering/Log;* copied from *Marine Engineering and Shipping Age* [June, 1929]: 308–9.)

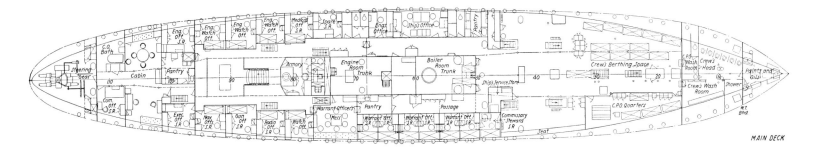

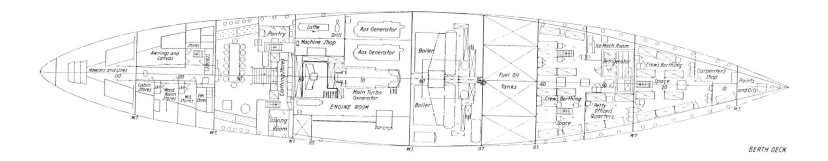

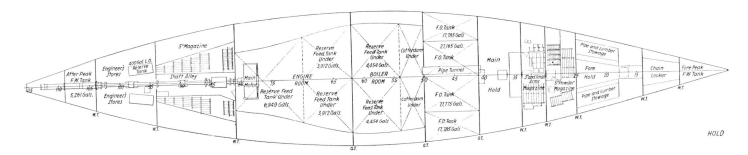

Inboard profile and deck plans of the "Lake"-class cutters. (Courtesy of *Marine Engineering/Log;* copied from *Marine Engineering and Shipping Age* [June, 1929]: 308–9.)

250-FOOT CUTTERS ("LAKE" CLASS)

Name	British Hull Number	British Name	Fate
Chelan	Y 60	*Lulworth*	Ret 12 Feb 46; *sold* 23 Oct 47
Pontchartrain	Y 00	*Hartland*	Lost 8 Nov 42; salvaged and scrapped 26 Oct 49
Tahoe	Y 59	*Fishguard*	Ret 27 Mar 46; *sold* 24 Oct 47
Champlain	Y 21	*Sennen*	Ret as *Champlain,* WPG 319 27 Mar 46; *sold* 25 Mar 48
Mendota	Y 87	*Culver*	Sank by U-105 31 Jan 42
Itasca	Y 92	*Gorleston*	Ret as *Itasca,* WPG 321 23 Apr 46; *sold* 4 Oct 50
Sebago	Y 04	*Walney*	Sank 8 Nov 42
Saranac	Y 43	*Banff*	Ret as *Sebec,* WPG 164 27 Feb 46; *comm* and renamed *Tampa* 27 May 47; *decomm* 10 Aug 54; *sold* 16 Feb 59
Shoshone	Y 56	*Languard*	Scrapped at Colombo, Ceylon (Sri Lanka) 1949–50
Cayuga	Y 88	*Totland*	Ret as *Mocoma,* WPG 163 1946; *recomm* 20 Mar 47; *decomm* 8 May 50; *sold* 15 Jul 55

Cayuga

1936 served in naval squadron 40-T during Spanish Civil War; Sep 40 operated in Greenland waters; 17 Mar–17 May 41 embarked on South Greenland Survey Expedition composed of State, Treasury, Navy, and War representatives whose purpose was to recommend installation sites.

Champlain

1940 stationed at New York, NY.

Chelan

1940 International Ice Patrol.

Itasca

Jan 40 "goodwill cruise" to Mexico and Central America; 1940 employed on Bering Sea Patrol and used as "floating court."

Mendota

1940 stationed at Norfolk, VA.

Pontchartrain

5 Dec 40 rescued crew of tug *Edwin Duke*.

Saranac

Used for 1940 cadet cruise.

Sebago

Used for 1940 cadet cruise.

Shoshone

1939 attached to Governors Island, NY, as an auxiliary training ship; 1940 employed on Bering Sea Patrol.

Tahoe

1940 stationed at New Bedford, MA.

The *Mendota* in 1937. During the 1930s, disposition of armament varied with the class. The *Mendota* mounts a 3"/50 and two 6-pdrs forward, and a 5"/51 aft. Most class members carried the 5"/51 forward and the 3"/50 aft during this decade.

The *Saranac*, 1941. Although still painted in peacetime white, depth-charge tracks have been added, as well as a 3″/50 and machine guns for protection against aircraft. These were the first major warships to have alternating-current, sychronous motors for propulsion. (Courtesy of the National Archives.)

The *Tahoe*, 1941, ready to be transferred to Great Britain as the USS *Fishguard*. Another view shows clearly that the *Tahoe* is still flying the U.S. flag and has her CG call signal—NRUD—flying from the starboard yard of her mainmast. Commandant Waesche, not wanting to give up ten relatively new cutters, suggested that perhaps it would be better to transfer aging cutters like the *Tallapoosa* and the *Unalga*. Secretary Morgenthau stated that such an offer might result in the transfer of the 327s instead. The commandant withdrew his ''generous'' alternate proposal.

The HMS *Hartland* (ex-*Pontchartrain*) burns in Oran Harbor, 8 Nov 42. She was lost while attempting to force the boom at the harbor's entrance. A sister ship, the *Walney* (ex-*Sebago*), was also lost in this action.

The *Mocoma* (ex-HMS *Totland,* ex-*Cayuga*), 13 May 46, lies at Curtis Bay, MD, in a state of disrepair. Three of the ten units transferred to Great Britain were lost in wartime action.

216-FOOT CUTTER

Name	Visual Call Sign	Builder	Keel Laid	Launched	Commissioned	Disposition
Northland	WPG 49	Newport News Shipbuilding & Dry Dock Co., Newport News, VA	16 Aug 26	5 Feb 27	7 May 27	*Decomm* 27 Mar 46; *sold* 3 Jan 47

Cost
  $865,730

Hull
  Displacement (tons)   1,785 trial (1927); 2,150 max (1945)
  Length   216′7″ oa; 200′ wl
  Beam   38′9″ mb; 39′ wl
  Draft   13′8″ trial (1927); 16′9″ max (1945)
  Block Coefficient   .611

Machinery
  Main Engines   1 double-armature electric motor driven by 2 generators driven by 2 6-cyl diesels

SHP   1,000
Propellers   Single, 4 blades

Performance
  Max Speed   11.7 kts on trial (1927)
  Max Sustained   11.0 kts, 10,280 mi radius (1927)
                  11.5 kts, 9,300 mi radius (1945)
  Cruising   10.0 kts, 12,000 mi radius (1945)
  Economic   8.2 kts, 18,800 mi radius (1927)
             8.6 kts, 15,000 mi radius (1945)

Logistics
  Diesel Fuel   63,600 gal

Complement	17 officers, 90 men (1927); 16 officers, 2 warrants, 102 men (1945)
Aircraft	
1941	1 SOC-4
1942–44	1 J2F-5
Electronics (1945)	
Detection Radar	SC-1, SF
Sonar	QCJ-3
Armament	
1927	2 6-pdrs., 1 1-pdr.
1941	2 3"/50 (single)
1945	2 3"/50 (single); 4 20mm/80 (single); 2 dc tracks; 2 Y-guns

Design

The *Northland* was designed to be the replacement for the famous Arctic-cutter *Bear*. She was structurally reinforced to withstand hull pressure of 100 psi and lined with cork for warmth. Welding as opposed to riveting was used extensively in her hull for added strength—an innovative feature for 1926. Captain Q. B. Newman, USCG, designed her diesel-electric power plant. As completed, her two masts carried yards to support sails. She was designed with a single screw, and the Coast Guard initially believed it advisable to provide an auxiliary means of power should the *Northland* sustain machinery damage in her icy environment. Her sails were removed and masts trimmed in 1936. Bilge keels were not fitted due to their susceptibility to ice damage. The two flaws in the design were the ship's relatively low power and the rather poor form of her bow entrance.

Northland

1927–38 stationed on West Coast, used extensively for Bering Sea Patrol; 26 Oct 38 assigned to Maritime Commission for Byrd Antarctic Expedition—9 Aug 39 assignment canceled due to war in Europe; 1939 assigned to maritime training; 18 Jun 40 ordered to East Coast for Greenland Patrol; 1 Jul 41 assigned to newly established Northeast Greenland Patrol; 12 Sep 41 took the Norwegian trawler *Boskoe* into ''protective custody'' and captured 3 German radiomen ashore; 1941–45 assigned to CINCLANT (DESLANT)—stationed at Boston, MA, and used extensively in Greenland waters, making 8 cruises in all; 22 Jul 42 rescued 25 survivors from 2 B-17s and 4 P-38s which made forced landings on ice cap; 23 Nov 42 landing party from cutter rescued 3 Canadian airmen stranded on Greenland Ice Cap; 26–27 Nov 42 plane from cutter rescued 2 Army airmen stranded on Greenland Ice Cap—2 Coast Guardsmen and cutter J2F-5 plane lost; 1–15 Apr 43 on weather station; 28 Jul–31 Aug 43 destroyed German weather station on Sabine Island, Greenland; Sep 43 propeller crushed in ice; Nov 43 installed a direction finder station on Jan Mayen Island in the Arctic Ocean; 21 Apr 44 sustained moderate damage from ice in dense fog; Jul 44 discovered the burned-out German trawler *Coburg*; 24–31 Jul 44 destroyed German weather station, Cape Sussie, Greenland; 1 Sep 44 pursued and caused to scuttle the German trawler *Kehdingen*—captured enemy crew of 28 and received moderate hull damage from ice; 2 Sep 44 J2F-5 aircraft from cutter bombed but missed surfaced U-boat.

The *Northland* under full sail. This cutter was built to replace the venerable *Bear*. Her CG designers wished to give her some emergency propulsion should her single screw be damaged by ice, so she was fitted with sail.

The *Northland* in full dress, 4 Jul 28, at Nome, AK. Yards are still carried. She had been designed to operate as a gunboat in Alaskan waters and was used frequently on the annual Bering Sea Patrol. During WW II she was used in Greenland waters and proved to be underpowered for heavy ice-breaking; however, the *Northland* was the best icebreaker the U.S. possessed in the early years of WW II.

The *Northland* receiving a towline from the cutter *Eastwind*, 1944. Note the rafts suspended just forward of the bridge.

240-FOOT CUTTERS (*TAMPA* CLASS)

Name	Visual Call Sign	Builder	Launched	Commissioned	Disposition
Haida	WPG 45 (bn CG-37)	Union Construction Co., Oakland, CA	27 Sep 20	19 Apr 21	26 Oct 21	*Decomm* 13 Feb 47; *sold* 20 Jan 48
Modoc	WPG 46 (bn CG-39)	Union Construction Co., Oakland, CA	20 Apr 21	1 Oct 21	14 Jan 22	*Decomm* 1 Feb 47; *sold* 30 Jun 47
Mojave	WPG 47 (bn CG-38)	Union Construction Co., Oakland, CA	20 Apr 21	7 Sep 21	12 Dec 21	*Decomm* 3 Jul 47; *sold* 14 Feb 48
Tampa	WPG 48 (bn CG-36)	Union Construction Co., Oakland, CA	27 Sep 20	19 Apr 21	15 Sep 21	*Decomm* 1 Feb 47; *sold* 22 Sep 47

Cost
$775,000 each

Hull
Displacement (tons)   1,506 trial (1921); 1,955 fl (1945)
Length   240' oa; 220' wl
Beam   39' mb; 39' wl
Draft   13'2" trial (1921); 17'9" max (1945)
Block Coefficient   .477
Tons per Immersed Inch   13.25

Machinery
Main Engines   1 General Electric 2,040 kVa electric motor driven by a turbo-generator
Main Boilers   2 Babcock & Wilcox, cross-drum type, 200 psi, 750°F superheat
Propellers   Single, 4 blades

Performance
Max Speed   16.2 kts on trial (1921)
Max Sustained   15.5 kts, 3,500 mi radius (1945)
Cruising   14.0 kts, 3,700 mi radius (1945)
Economic   9.0 kts, 5,500 mi radius (1945)

Logistics
Fuel Oil (95%)	87,400 gal
Complement	*Haida:* 14 officers, 2 warrants, 80 men (1945); all others: 10 officers, 2 warrants, 110 men (1945)

Electronics (1945)
Detection Radar	*Haida:* SA, SL; all others: SF-1, SC-3
Sonar	*Haida* and *Modoc:* QCJ-3; *Mojave* and *Tampa:* QCL-2

Armament
1921	2 5″/51 (single); 2 6 pdrs.; 1 1 pdr.
1942	2 5″/51 (single); 1 3″/50 (single); 2 .50 cal. mgs; 4 Y-guns; 2 dc tracks
1945	2 3″/50 (single); 4 20mm/80 (single); 2 dc tracks; 4 Y-guns; 2 Mousetraps

Design

The 240-foot cutters followed the traditional cutter hull form, having a plumb bow and counter stern. These features proved particularly undesirable while on International Ice Patrol. Heavy seas coming up under the counter caused severe shocks. The wardroom in this class was well forward; thus, the deck sloped upward. This feature was known as the "Honeywell Hill," in honor of the principal architect of the class.

Haida

Stationed at Port Townsend, WA; Seattle, WA; Cordova, AK; Juneau, AK—used extensively for Bering Sea Patrol and served as a "floating court"; 1941–44 assigned to NOWESTSEAFRON—stationed at Juneau, AK, and used for escort and patrol duty; 1944–45 assigned to CINCPAC—stationed at Juneau, AK, and used for weather patrol.

Modoc

1922–41 stationed at Wilmington, NC—participated in many international ice patrols; 24 May 41 witnessed air attack on the German battleship *Bismarck*—sighted the *Prince of Wales;* 1 Jun 41 assigned to newly established South Greenland Patrol; 1 Jul 41 assigned to Navy for duty; 1941–44 assigned to CINCLANT (DESLANT)—stationed at Boston, MA, and used for escort duty in Greenland waters; 21 Mar 43 rescued 28 survivors from the tanker *Svend Foyne,* which had collided with iceberg; 13 Feb 44 towed stranded trawler HMS *Strathella;* Jan 44–Jun 45 operated with Ocean Escort Group.

Mojave

1938–41 stationed in Florida waters; Apr–May 1941 used on weather station; 1941–44 assigned to CINCLANT (DESLANT)—stationed at Boston, MA, and used for escort duty in Greenland waters; 27 Aug 42 rescued 293 survivors from the Army transport *Chatham;* Jan 1944–45 operated with Ocean Escort Group; 25 May–14 Aug 45 used on ice patrol.

Tampa

1936–41 stationed in New Orleans, LA; 1941–44 assigned to CINCLANT (DESLANT)—stationed at Boston, MA, and used for escort duty in Greenland waters; 3 Jun 42 refloated the SS *Montrose.*

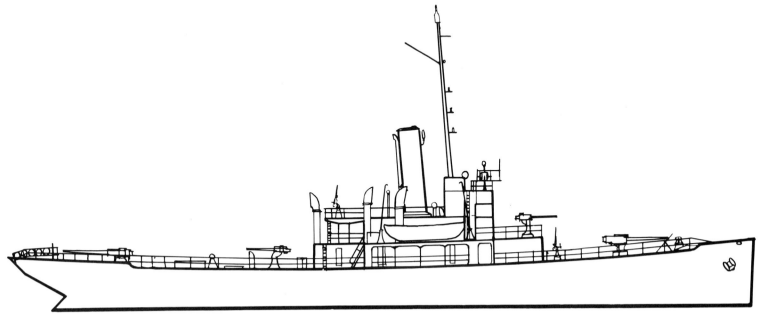

Sketch of the 240-foot class, circa 1943. (Courtesy of Christian Beilstein.)

The *Haida* early in her career. She was extensively employed in Alaskan waters prior to WW II. She is painted in traditional cutter colors: a white hull and superstructure, a buff stack, mast, and ventilators, and black funnel caps. Wooden decks were a natural wood finish, and steel decks were gray.

The crowded quarterdeck of the *Modoc*. Note the extensive armament of K-guns, depth-charge tracks, 3″/50 and 5″/51 guns, and 5″ powder tanks in their ready-service box.

The *Mojave* in 1943. The counter stern design, which made this cutter a rough sea boat, is visible. She rescued 293 survivors from the Army transport *Chatham* on 27 Aug 42.

165-FOOT CUTTER

Name	Visual Call Sign	Builder	Keel Laid	Launched	Commissioned	Disposition
Tallapoosa	WPG 52 (bn CG-27)	Newport News Shipbuilding & Dry Dock Co., Newport News, VA	16 Nov 14	1 May 15	12 Aug 15	*Decomm* 8 Nov 45; *sold* 22 Jul 46

Cost
  $225,000

Hull
  Displacement (tons)   912 trial (1915); 964 fl (1945)
  Length   165'10" oa; 150' wl
  Beam   32' mb
  Draft   11'9" trial (1915); 12'4" max (1945)
  Block Coefficient   .585

Machinery
  Main Engines   1 triple-expansion steam
  Main Boilers   2 Babcock & Wilcox
  SHP   1,000
  Propellers   Single, 4 blades

Performance
  Max Speed   12.0 kts on trial (1915)
  Max Sustained   10.4 kts, 4,300 mi radius (1945)
  Economic   8.5 kts, 6,000 mi radius (1945)

Logistics
  Fuel Oil (95%)   51,000 gal

Complement   5 officers, 2 warrants, 67 men (1945)
Electronics (1945)
  Detection Radar   SF-1, SA
  Sonar   WEA-2A
Armament
  1941   2 3"/50 (single); 1 3"/23; 2 dc tracks
  1945   2 3"/50 (single); 2 20mm/80 (single); 2 Mousetraps; 4 K-guns; 2 dc tracks

Design
  The *Tallapoosa* was designed for long continued cruises, and she was initially stationed in the Gulf of Mexico. Near sister *Ossipee* was designated a WPR—a river gunboat.

Tallapoosa

Pre–WW II used for general patrol duty and Bering Sea Patrol; 1941–45 assigned to EASTSEAFRON—stationed at Savannah, GA, and used for patrol duty.

The *Tallapoosa*, Jun 35, in Latuya Bay, AK. She possessed an unusually large cruising radius for a cutter constructed in 1915. The *Tallapoosa* was designed to operate in the Gulf of Mexico. Understandably, Commandant Waesche tried to give ten old cutters such as the *Tallapoosa* rather than the 250-foot class to Great Britain under lend-lease.

The *Tallapoosa*, 7 Apr 44. This angle affords an excellent view of her armament. The *Tallapoosa* mounts 3"/50s fore and aft, two 20mm/80s elevated forward of the aft 3"/50, two Mouse-trap ASW rocket launchers on the forecastle, four K-guns on the poop deck, and two long depth-charge tracks on the stern. (Courtesy of A. D. Baker III.)

190-FOOT CUTTER

Name	Visual Call Sign	Builder	Keel Laid	Launched	Commissioned	Disposition
Unalga	WPG 53	Newport News Shipbuilding & Dry Dock Co., Newport News, VA	10 Aug 11	10 Feb 12	23 May 12	*Decomm* 10 Oct 45; *sold* 19 Jul 46

Cost
  $250,000
Hull
  Displacement (tons)   1,180 fl (1912); 1,181 fl (1945)
  Length   190' oa
  Beam   32'6" mb
  Draft   14'1" (1912); 14'6" max (1945)
Machinery
  Main Engines   1 triple-expansion steam
  Main Boilers   2 Babcock & Wilcox
  SHP   1,000
  Propellers   Single
Performance
  Max Speed   12.4 kts, 2,500 mi radius (1945)
  Economic   7.9 kts, 4,200 mi radius (1945)
Logistics
  Fuel Oil (95%)   53,000 gal
  Complement   5 officers, 67 men (1945)
Electronics (1945)
  Detection Radar   SF-1, SA-2
  Sonar   QCL-5
Armament
  1941   2 3"/50 (single); 2 dc tracks
  1943   2 3"/50 (single); 2 20mm/80 (single)

Design
  The *Unalga* was designed for extended cruises in Alaskan waters. Initially she was coal-fired.

Unalga

Pre–WW II used for Bering Sea Patrol; 1941–Sep 43 assigned to CARIBSEAFRON—stationed at San Juan, PR, and used as an escort; Sep 43–Oct 45 assigned to CINCLANT (COTCLANT)—stationed at Newport, RI, and used for training.

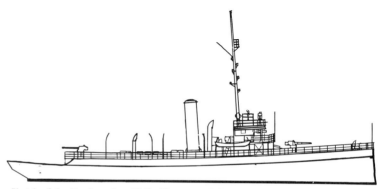

Sketch of the *Unalga*, circa 1943. (Courtesy of Christian Beilstein.)

The *Unalga* at San Juan, PR, during the war. In 1941 the two 3"/50s were mounted abreast on the forecastle. The decks could not support a centerline gun, so in 1944 the forecastle was strengthened: one gun was put on the centerline forward and the other on the centerline aft.

Submarine Chasers (WPC and WSC)

Only three classes were rated as submarine chasers by the Coast Guard. The important ones, the 165Bs and 125s, had been designed and built for the Coast Guard to combat smuggling during Prohibition. Both designs were very sturdy. In fact, the *General Greene* was used for the International Ice Patrol in 1941 due to the shortage of large cutters (240s or 250s). The remaining class of submarine chasers, the SC 1 class, was a Navy WW I design. The units from this class saw little service.

WPC—SUBMARINE CHASERS (LARGE)

165-FOOT (B) CUTTERS

Name	Visual Call Sign	Builder	Keel Laid	Launched	Commissioned	Disposition
Argo	WPC 100 (bn P-8)	John H. Mathis Co., Camden, NJ	15 Mar 32 (contracted)	12 Nov 32	6 Jan 33	*Decomm* 30 Oct 48; *sold* 2 Nov 55
Ariadne	WPC 101 (bn P-11)	Lake Union Dry Dock & Machine Works, Seattle, WA	15 Nov 33 (contracted)	23 Mar 34	9 Oct 34	*Decomm* 23 Dec 68; *sold* 26 Sep 69
Atalanta	WPC 102 (bn P-10)	Lake Union Dry Dock & Machine Works, Seattle, WA	23 Nov 33 (contracted)	16 Jun 34	20 Sep 34	*Decomm* 1 Aug 50; *sold* 7 Dec 54
Aurora	WPC 103 (bn P-2)	Bath Iron Works, Inc. Bath, ME	21 Jan 31 (contracted)	28 Nov 31	21 Dec 31	*Decomm* 17 Jan 68; *sold* 16 Dec 68
Calypso	WPC 104 (ex-AG 35; bn P-3)	Bath Iron Works, Inc., Bath, ME	21 Jan 31 (contracted)	1 Jan 32	16 Jan 32; *recomm* 20 Jan 42	*Decomm* and *trans* to USN 17 May 41; *decomm* 18 Jul 47; *sold* 2 Nov 55
Cyane	WPC 105 (bn P-12)	Lake Union Dry Dock & Machine Works, Seattle, WA	15 Nov 33 (contracted)	30 Aug 34	25 Oct 34	*Decomm* 1 Aug 50; *sold* 7 Dec 54
Daphne	WPC 106 (bn P-4)	Bath Iron Works, Inc., Bath, ME	21 Jan 31 (contracted)	27 Jan 32	12 Feb 32	*Decomm* 1 Aug 50; *sold* 7 Dec 54
Dione	WPC 107 (bn P-13)	Manitowoc Shipbuilding Corp., Manitowoc, WI	10 Nov 33 (contracted)	30 Jun 34	5 Oct 34	*Decomm* 8 Feb 63; *sold* 24 Feb 64
Galatea	WPC 108 (bn P-9)	John H. Mathis Co., Camden, NJ	15 Mar 32 (contracted)	16 Dec 32	3 Feb 33	*Decomm* 15 Mar 48; *sold* 1 Jul 48
Hermes	WPC 109 (bn P-5)	Bath Iron Works, Inc., Bath, ME	21 Jan 31 (contracted)	23 Feb 32	7 Mar 32	*Decomm* 2 Nov 48; *sold* 16 May 58
Icarus	WPC 110 (bn P-6)	Bath Iron Works, Inc., Bath, ME	21 Jan 31 (contracted)	19 Mar 32	1 Apr 32	*Decomm* 21 Oct 46; *sold* 1 Jul 48
Nemesis	WPC 111 (bn P-18)	Marietta Manufacturing Co., Point Pleasant, WV	17 Nov 33 (contracted)	7 Jul 34	10 Oct 34	*Decomm* 20 Nov 64; *sold* 9 Feb 66
Nike	WPC 112 (bn P-17)	Marietta Manufacturing Co., Point Pleasant, WV	17 Nov 33 (contracted)	7 Jul 34	24 Oct 34	*Decomm* 5 Nov 64; *sold* 9 May 66
Pandora	WPC 113 (bn P-15)	Manitowoc Shipbuilding Corp., Manitowoc, WI	10 Nov 33 (contracted)	30 Jun 34	1 Nov 34	*Decomm* 1 May 59; *sold* 4 Nov 59

Name	Visual Call Sign	Builder	Keel Laid	Launched	Commissioned	Disposition
Perseus	WPC 114 (bn P-7)	Bath Iron Works, Inc., Bath, ME	21 Jan 31 (contracted)	11 Apr 32	27 Apr 32	*Decomm* 26 Jun 59; *sold* 4 Nov 59
Thetis	WPC 115 (bn P-1)	Bath Iron Works, Inc., Bath, ME	21 Jan 31 (contracted)	9 Nov 31	1 Dec 31	*Decomm* 1 Jul 47; *sold* 1 Jul 48
Triton	WPC 116 (bn P-16)	Marietta Manufacturing Co., Point Pleasant, WV	17 Apr 34	7 Jul 34	20 Nov 34	*Decomm* 12 Jun 67; *sold* 16 Jan 69
Electra (f-*Potomac*)	WPC 187 (bn P-14)	Manitowoc Shipbuilding Corp., Manitowoc, WI	5 Mar 34	30 Jun 34	25 Oct 34	*Trans* to USN 12 Nov 35; *ret* to CG 21 Nov 45; *decomm* 23 May 46

Cost
  $258,000 each

Hull
  Displacement (tons)   337 fl (1934); 350 fl (1945)
  Length   165' oa; 160'9" wl
  Beam   25'3" mb; 23'9" wl
  Draft   7'8" trial (1931); 7' max (1934); 10' max (1945)
  Block Coefficient   0.378
  Tons per Immersed   6.23
    Inch

Machinery
  Main Engines   2 Winton, 6-cyl, Model 158 diesels
  BHP   1,340
  Propellers   Twin, 3 blades

Performance
  Max Speed   16.0 kts on trial (1931)
  Max Sustained   14.0 kts, 1,750 mi radius (1945)
  Cruising   11.0 kts, 3,000 mi radius (1945)
  Economic   6.0 kts, 6,417 mi radius (1945)

Logistics
  Diesel (95%)   7,700 gal
  Complement   5 officers, 39 men (1938); 7 officers, 68 men (1945)

Electronics (1945)
  Detection Radar   *Cyane:* SL
    Atalanta, Aurora, Daphne, Hermes, Nemesis: SF-1
    All others: SF
  Sonar   *Calypso:* QCJ-3
    Ariadne, Atalanta, Aurora, Cyane, Dione, Galatea, Icarus, Nemesis: QCN-1
    All others: QCO

Armament
  1932 and 1938   1 3"/23 (single); 2 1-pdrs.
  1941   1 3"/23 (single); 1 Y-gun; 2 dc tracks
  1945   2 3"/50 (single); 2 20mm/80 (single); 2 dc tracks; 2 Y-guns; 2 Mousetraps

Design
  The 165-foot (B) cutters were a follow-on to the 125-foot cutters, both classes being designed to enforce Prohibition. As of 1982, three units still serve in the Dominican Navy.

Argo

Jul–Aug 40 cadet practice cruise; Oct–Nov 40 rearmed by Merrill-Stevens, Jacksonville, FL; 1941–45 assigned to EASTSEAFRON—stationed at New-port, RI; 14 Jan 42 rescued 6 survivors from the tanker *Norness;* 7 Jan 44 rescued 23 survivors of the USS *St. Augustine;* Jun 45 assigned to Air-Sea Rescue duty, 1st District.

Ariadne

1940 used on Bering Sea Patrol; 1941–45 assigned to WESTSEAFRON—stationed at Alameda, CA, as an escort.

Atalanta

1934–39 stationed at Seattle, WA, and used on Bering Sea Patrol; Sep–Oct 42 rearmed at Lake Drydock Co., Seattle, WA; 1942–45 assigned to NO-WESTSEAFRON—stationed at Seattle, WA.

Aurora

1940 used on Bering Sea Patrol; 1941–45 assigned to NOWESTSEAFRON and employed as an escort ship and on antisubmarine patrol between Seattle, WA, and Alaskan waters—stationed at Juneau, AK.

Calypso

Oct–Nov 40 rearmed by Merrill-Stevens Co.; 17 May 41–20 Jan 42 transferred to Navy Department to escort the USS *Potomac*—presidential yacht; 1941–45 assigned to EASTSEAFRON—stationed at Norfolk, VA; 15 Feb 42 rescued 42 survivors from the SS *Buarque;* 7 Mar 42 rescued 54 survivors from the freighter *Arabutan;* 7 May 42 rescued 13 survivors from the SS *Pipestone County;* 15 Sep 43 rescued 60 survivors from the USS *Plymouth;* Jun 45 assigned to Air-Sea Rescue duty, 5th District.

Cyane

1941–45 assigned to NOWESTSEAFRON—stationed at Ketchikan, AK.

Daphne

1941–45 assigned to WESTSEAFRON—stationed at Alameda, CA; Oct–Nov 42 rearmed.

Dione

1941–45 assigned to EASTSEAFRON—stationed at Norfolk, VA; Jun 45 assigned to Air-Sea Rescue duty, 5th District.

Electra

12 Nov 35 transferred to USN, renamed the *Potomac* and used as a presidential yacht 1935–46.

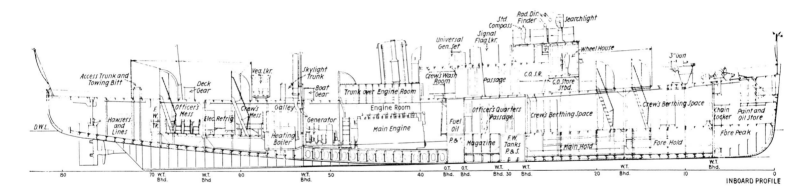

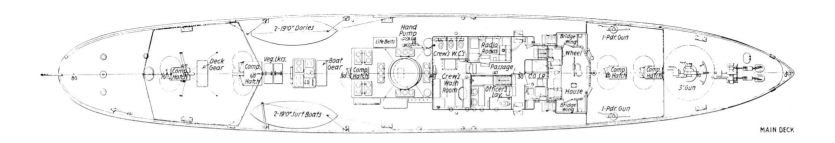

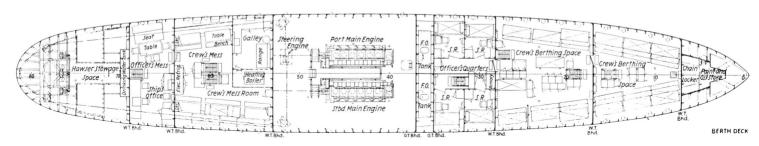

Inboard profile and arrangement plans of the 165-foot patrol boats.   (Courtesy of *Marine Engineering/Log;* copied from *Marine Engineering and Shipping Age* [September, 1932]: 384.)

Galatea

1 Jul 41 assigned to the Navy for duty; 1941–45 assigned to EASTSEA-FRON—stationed at Key West, FL; Jun 45 assigned to Air-Sea Rescue duty, 6th District.

Hermes

Fall 41 deployed on Bering Sea Patrol; 1941–45 assigned to WESTSEA-FRON—stationed at San Pedro, CA; 26 Jan 43 rescued 11 survivors from the SS *Lewis Cass.*

Icarus

Dec 40 rearmed by Merrill-Stevens Co., Jacksonville, FL; 1941–45 assigned to EASTSEAFRON—stationed at Staten Island, NY; 9 May 42 sank U-352,

34°12′N, 76°35′W—rescued 32 survivors; Jun 45 assigned to Air-Sea Rescue duty, 3rd District.

Nemesis

1941–45 assigned to EASTSEAFRON—stationed at St. Petersburg, FL; 21 May 42 rescued 28 survivors from the tanker *Faja de Oro;* 7 Jun 42 rescued 27 survivors from the SS *Suwied;* Feb 43–Jun 45 used on escort duty between Key West, FL, and New York, NY; 11 Jan 45 rammed the SS *Felipe de Neve* off Point Judith Light and received considerable damage; Jun 45 assigned to Air-Sea Rescue duty, 1st District.

Nike

1941–45 assigned to EASTSEAFRON—stationed at Gulfport, MS; 3 Feb 42 rescued 40 survivors from the freighter *San Gil;* 5 Feb 42 rescued 37 survivors from the tanker *China Arrow;* 14 May 42 rescued 9 survivors from the tanker *Portrero del Llano;* Jun 45 assigned to Air-Sea Rescue duty, 1st District.

Pandora

1 Apr 39 stationed at Key West, FL; Jan 40 took "Goodwill Cruise" to Mexico and Central America; 1 Jul 41 assigned to the Navy for duty; 1941–45 assigned to EASTSEAFRON—stationed at Key West, FL; Jun 45 assigned to Air-Sea Rescue duty, 4th District.

Perseus

1940 employed on Bering Sea Patrol; 1941–45 assigned to WESTSEAFRON; Nov–Dec 41 temporarily stationed at Cordova, AK; Dec 41–May 42 temporarily stationed at Juneau, AK; 1942–45 stationed at San Diego, CA.

Thetis

1 Jul 41 assigned to the Navy for duty; 1941–45 assigned to EASTSEA-FRON—stationed at Key West, FL; 13 Jun 42 sank U-157, 24°13'N, 82°03'W; 7 Jan 44 rescued 7 survivors from the USS *St. Augustine;* Jun 45 assigned to Air-Sea Rescue duty, 3rd District.

Triton

1 Jul 41 assigned to the Navy for duty; 1941–45 assigned to EASTSEA-

FRON—stationed at Key West, FL; Jun 45 assigned to Air-Sea Rescue duty, 6th District.

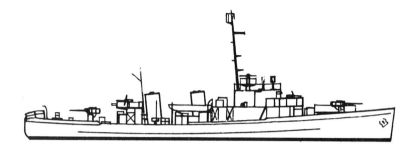

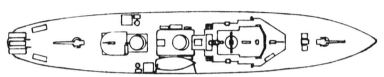

Sketch of the 165B class, circa 1943. (Courtesy of Christian Beilstein.)

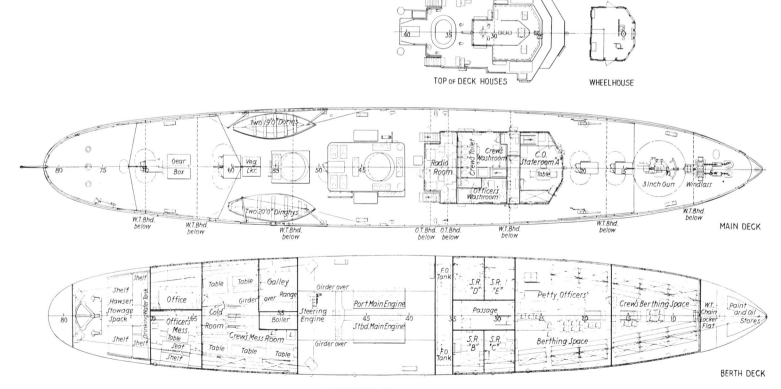

Accommodation plan of the *Thetis.* (Courtesy of SNAME, *Transactions* XLV [1937]: 90.)

The *Ariadne* running trials in 1934. Some units had one stack and others had two. The 165Bs were built as follow-ons to the 125s. Both classes were designed to operate off the coast in search of "motherships," which supplied fast, short-legged rum runners. Prior to WW II, both masts on the 165Bs were heightened. (Courtesy of the National Archives.)

The presidential yacht *Potomac* was the former cutter *Electra*. She had a Navy crew while serving as the presidential yacht. Her aft stack was modified to include an elevator for President Franklin D. Roosevelt. Note the presidential seal on the face of the bridge and the presidential flag flying from the main mast. FDR stands between two naval officers forward of the stack. (Courtesy of the *Courier Gazette*, Rockland, ME.)

The *Perseus*, 11 Jun 44. As was true of most CG cutters, these units were heavily armed, considering their displacements. The links connecting the tillers were arranged for adjustment to determine the position of the rudders with the boat underway.

The *Belleville* in 1943. The Mousetrap launchers are in a raised position. The CG operated SC 1–class units as both WPCs and WIXs. The units designated WPCs required constant maintenance.

WSC—SUBMARINE CHASERS (SMALL)

EMERGENCY ACQUISITION NAVY SC 1 CLASS

Name	Visual Call Sign	Builder	Commissioned	Disposition
Boone (ex-SC 229)	WPC 335	New York Yacht, Launch, & Engine Co., Morris Heights, NY	23 Jan 18 (Navy); 14 Aug 42 (CG)	*Decomm* 6 Jun 45; *trans* to WSA 8 Mar 46
Blaze (ex-SC 231)	WPC 336	New York Yacht, Launch, & Engine Co., Morris Heights, NY	8 Feb 18 (Navy); 18 Aug 42 *(trans)*; 15 Jan 43 (CG)	*Decomm* 25 Sep 44; *trans* to WSA 8 Mar 46
Bowstring (ex-*Sea Rover*; ex-SC 238)	WPC 365	New York Yacht, Launch, & Engine Co., Morris Heights, NY	12 Mar 18 (Navy); 7 Jul 43 (CG)	*Decomm* 22 Dec 44; *trans* to WSA 6 Jan 45
Belleville (ex-*Liberty II*; ex-SC 258)	WPC 372	George Lawley & Sons, Neponset, MA	28 Nov 17 (Navy); 20 Mar 43 (CG)	*Decomm* 30 Jun 45; *trans* to WSA 2 May 46

Cost
  See Design remarks

Hull
Displacement (tons)	85 fl (1917); 167 fl (1943)
Length	110′ oa
Beam	14′9″ max
Draft	5′8″ max (1917)

Machinery
Main Engines	3 Standard Motor Construction Co., 6-cyl gasoline
SHP	600
Propellers	Triple

Performance
Max Speed	18.0 kts in design (1918)
Max Sustained	14.0 kts, 680 mi radius (1942)
Cruising	11.0 kts, 760 mi radius (1942)

Logistics
Gasoline	NA
Complement	2 officers, 25 men (1917)

Electronics
Detection Radar	None

Armament
1917	1 3″/23 (single); 2 .30 cal mg; 1 DCP (early Y-gun)
1943	1 3″/23 (single); 2 .30 cal mg; 2 Mousetraps; 2 dc tracks

Design
  Designed by Captain A. Loring Swasey, USN, hundreds of these wooden craft were produced during WW I to meet the German submarine threat. They became known as the "Splinter Fleet." Many survived and saw service in both the Coast Guard and the Navy during WW II. Coast Guard units were designated WIX as well as WSC.

	Acquisition	Conversion
Belleville	$10,000	$99,714
Blaze	Navy loan	$27,799
Boone	Navy loan	$90,000
Bowstring	$26,750	$75,000

Boone

1942–43 assigned to EASTSEAFRON—stationed at Norfolk, VA, and used for patrol; 1943–Mar 44 assigned to GULFSEAFRON—stationed at Miami, FL, and used for patrol; Mar 44–Jun 45 assigned to the AS *Devlant*—stationed at New York, NY, and used for R & D.

Blaze

Early 43 assigned to GULFSEAFRON—stationed at Miami, FL, and used for patrol; 1943–Sep 44 assigned to Coast Guard Training Station, St. Augustine, FL; Sep 44–1945 in storage in unseaworthy condition.

Belleville

Mar 43–1945 assigned to GULFSEAFRON—stationed at Miami, FL (Mar 43–Apr 44) and New Orleans, LA (Apr 44–Jun 45).

Bowstring

Mar 43–1945 assigned to GULFSEAFRON—stationed at Miami, FL (Mar 43–Apr 44) and New Orleans, LA (Apr 44–Jun 45); general patrol duty—Mar 43–25 Apr 44 at Miami, FL; 25 Apr 44–Jun 45 at New Orleans, LA.

125-Foot Cutters ("Buck & a Quarter" Class)

Name	Visual Call Sign	Builder	Keel Laid	Launched	Commissioned	Disposition
Active	WSC 125	American Brown Boveri Electric Corp., Camden, NJ	NA	30 Nov 26	13 Jan 27	Decomm 2 Apr 62; sold 6 Sep 63
Agassiz	WSC 126	American Brown Boveri Electric Corp., Camden, NJ	31 Jul 26	30 Nov 26	20 Jan 27	Decomm 13 Oct 69; trans to MMA 16 Oct 69
Alert	WSC 127	American Brown Boveri Electric Corp., Camden, NJ	27 May 26 (contracted)	30 Nov 26	27 Jan 27	Decomm 10 Jan 69; sold 6 Oct 69
Bedloe (ex-Antietam)	WSC 128	American Brown Boveri Electric Corp., Camden, NJ	26 May 26 (contracted)	30 Nov 26	25 Jul 27	Lost at sea 14 Sep 44
Bonham	WSC 129	American Brown Boveri Electric Corp., Camden, NJ	NA	30 Nov 26	29 Jan 27	Decomm 20 Apr 59; sold 30 Dec 59
Boutwell	WSC 130	American Brown Boveri Electric Corp., Camden, NJ	NA	27 Jan 27	21 Feb 27	Decomm 7 May 63; sold 16 May 64
Cahoone	WSC 131	American Brown Boveri Electric Corp., Camden, NJ	NA	27 Jan 27	21 Feb 27	Decomm 11 Mar 68; sold 12 Dec 68
Cartigan	WSC 132	American Brown Boveri Electric Corp., Camden, NJ	NA	27 Jan 27	3 Mar 27	Decomm 12 Oct 68
Colfax (ex-Montgomery)	WSC 133	American Brown Boveri Electric Corp., Camden, NJ	27 May 26 (contracted)	22 Mar 27	7 Apr 27	Decomm 9 Nov 54; sold 5 Jan 56
Crawford	WSC 134	American Brown Boveri Electric Corp., Camden, NJ	27 May 26 (contracted)	27 Jan 27	21 Feb 27	Decomm 15 Aug 47; donated to Woods Hole Ocean. Inst., MA 28 Nov 55
Diligence	WSC 135	American Brown Boveri Electric Corp., Camden, NJ	NA	27 Jan 27	22 Feb 27	Decomm 30 Sep 61; sold 30 Jan 63
Dix	WSC 136	American Brown Boveri Electric Corp., Camden, NJ	27 May 26 (contracted)	27 Jan 27	5 Mar 27	Decomm 13 Jan 48; sold 16 Jun 48
Ewing	WSC 137	American Brown Boveri Electric Corp., Camden, NJ	NA	15 Mar 27	26 Mar 27	Decomm 23 Jun 67; sold 23 Jan 69
Faunce	WSC 138	American Brown Boveri Electric Corp., Camden, NJ	27 May 26 (contracted)	15 Mar 27	1 Apr 27	Decomm 13 Jan 48; sold 16 Jun 48
Frederick Lee	WSC 139	American Brown Boveri Electric Corp., Camden, NJ	NA	15 Mar 27	4 Apr 27	Decomm 15 Dec 64; sold 19 May 66
General Greene	WSC 140	American Brown Boveri Electric Corp., Camden, NJ	NA	14 Feb 27	7 Apr 27	Decomm and trans to Newburyport, MA as a museum 15 Nov 68
Harriet Lane	WSC 141	American Brown Boveri Electric Corp., Camden, NJ	27 May 26 (contracted)	30 Nov 26	4 Jan 27	Decomm 29 Apr 46; sold 16 Jun 48
Jackson	WSC 142	American Brown Boveri Electric Corp., Camden, NJ	27 May 26 (contracted)	14 Feb 27	14 Mar 27	Sank 14 Sep 44
Kimball	WSC 143	American Brown Boveri Electric Corp., Camden, NJ	NA	25 Apr 27	7 May 27	Decomm 31 Dec 68; sold 24 Feb 70
Legare	WSC 144	American Brown Boveri Electric Corp., Camden, NJ	NA	14 Feb 27	17 Mar 27	Decomm 5 Mar 68; sold 29 Nov 68
Marion	WSC 145	American Brown Boveri Electric Corp., Camden, NJ	NA	15 Mar 27	6 Apr 27	Decomm 15 Feb 62; sold 8 Mar 63
McLane	WSC 146	American Brown Boveri Electric Corp., Camden, NJ	NA	22 Mar 27	8 Apr 27	Decomm 31 Dec 68; sold 14 Nov 69
Morris	WSC 147	American Brown Boveri Electric Corp., Camden, NJ	NA	4 Apr 27	19 Apr 27	Decomm 7 Aug 70; trans to BSA 5 Nov 71
Nemaha	WSC 148	American Brown Boveri Electric Corp., Camden, NJ	27 May 26 (contracted)	4 Apr 27	19 Apr 27	Decomm 21 Jul 47; sold 14 Jun 48
Pulaski	WSC 149	American Brown Boveri Electric Corp., Camden, NJ	27 May 26 (contracted)	4 Apr 27	20 Apr 27	Decomm 4 Dec 46; sold 14 Jul 48
Reliance	WSC 150	American Brown Boveri Electric Corp., Camden, NJ	27 May 26 (contracted)	18 Apr 27	26 Apr 27	Decomm 8 Aug 47; sold 16 Jun 48
Rush	WSC 151	American Brown Boveri Electric Corp., Camden, NJ	27 May 26 (contracted)	18 Apr 27	27 Apr 27	Decomm 21 Aug 47; sold 16 Jun 48
Tiger	WSC 152	American Brown Boveri Electric Corp., Camden, NJ	NA	18 Apr 27	3 May 27	Decomm 12 Nov 47; sold 14 Jun 48
Travis	WSC 153	American Brown Boveri Electric Corp., Camden, NJ	NA	18 Apr 27	29 Apr 27	Decomm 5 Jun 62; sold 15 Nov 62

Name	Visual Call Sign	Builder	Keel Laid	Launched	Commissioned	Disposition
Vigilant	WSC 154	American Brown Boveri Electric Corp., Camden, NJ	NA	25 Apr 27	3 May 27	*Decomm* 9 Nov 54; *sold* 3 Jan 56
Woodbury	WSC 155	American Brown Boveri Electric Corp., Camden, NJ	NA	2 May 27	11 May 27	*Decomm* 11 Dec 46; *sold* 6 Jul 48
Yeaton	WSC 156	American Brown Boveri Electric Corp., Camden, NJ	NA	2 May 27	10 May 27	*Decomm* 18 Jul 69; *sold* 16 Jul 70
Cuyahoga	WSC 157	American Brown Boveri Electric Corp., Camden, NJ	NA	27 Jan 27	3 Mar 27; *recomm* 17 May 41	*Decomm* and *trans* to Navy 27 May 33; lost in collision 20 Oct 78

Cost
$63,173 each

Hull
Displacement (tons) 232 trial (1926); 220 fl (1945)
Length 125' oa; 120' wl
Beam 23'6" mb
Draft 7'6" mean (1926); 9' max (1945)
Block Coefficient 0.334
Tons per Immersed Inch 4.45

Machinery
Main Engines *Pulaski:* 2 Superior-type PTD 250-hp diesels; *Cartigan, Faunce, Harriet Lane:* 2 Winton-type 8-138 diesels; *Active, Marion, Reliance, Tiger, Vigilant, Woodbury:* 2 Cooper-Bessemer-type EN-8 diesels; all others: 2 General Motors–type 268-A diesels
BHP Superior diesels: 500; Winton diesels: 600; Cooper-Bessemer diesels: 600; General Motors diesels: 800
Propellers Twin, 3 blades

Performance
Superior Diesels
Max Speed 10.2 kts (1945)
Max Sustained 9.0 kts, 3,100 mi radius (1945)
Economic 7.0 kts, 4,000 mi radius (1945)
Winton Diesels
Max Speed 12.0 kts (1945)
Max Sustained 11.0 kts, 2,400 mi radius (1945)
Economic 8.0 kts, 3,300 mi radius (1945)
Cooper-Bessemer Diesels
Max Speed 12.0 kts (1945)
Max Sustained 10.0 kts, 2,900 mi radius (1945)
Economic 7.0 kts, 4,000 mi radius (1945)
General Motors Diesels
Max Speed 13.0 kts (1945)
Max Sustained 12.0 kts, 2,500 mi radius (1945)
Economic 8.0 kts, 3,500 mi radius (1945)

Logistics
Fuel Oil (95%) 6,800 gal
Complement
1938 2 officers, 20 men
1945 *Ewing, Morris:* 5 officers, 36 men; all others: 5 officers, 41 men

Electronics
Detection Radar
1942 None
1945 *Cuyahoga:* SF-1; *Harriet Lane, Kimball, Yeaton:* SF; all others: SO-9
Sonar (1945) *Kimball, Yeaton:* WEA-2; *Ewing, Morris:* QBE-3A; *Active, Agassiz, Alert, Bonham, Boutwell, Crawford, Frederick Lee, Reliance, Rush, Tiger, Travis:* QCN-2; all others: QCO-1

Armament
1927 1 3"/23
1941 *Active, Colfax, Crawford, Ewing, Harriet Lane, Legare, McLane, Vigilant, Diligence, Woodbury:* 2 dc tracks; all others: 1 3"/23; 2 dc tracks
1945 *Alert, Bonham, Colfax, Crawford, Diligence, Dix, Ewing, Kimball, Legare, Marion, McLane, Morris, Reliance, Rush, Vigilant, Woodbury:* 1 3"/23 (single); 2 20mm/80 (single); 2 dc tracks; 2 Mousetraps; all others: 1 40mm/60 (single); 2 20mm/80 (single); 2 dc tracks; 2 Mousetraps

Design

To combat smuggling during Prohibition, the CG developed offshore patrol vessels for an outer ring and inshore patrol craft for an inner one. The 125-foot cutters were the first class to be designed for the outer patrol. They were designed to trail "mother ships" to intercept the illegal liquor when it was transferred to small, fast craft. They were re-engined prior to WW II. In mid-1941, in order to meet the need for more vessels equipped to service aids to navigation, the CG temporarily converted the following 125s for use as buoy tenders: the *Active, Colfax, Crawford, Ewing, Harriet Lane, Legare, McLane, Vigilant, Diligence,* and *Woodbury.* However, wartime needs soon caused these units to be reconverted to patrol craft. *See also* 165-foot (B) class and 75-footers.

Active

Sep 41–May 42 stationed at Stapleton, Staten Island, NY; Jun 42–1945 assigned to CINCLANT (DESLANT) and home ported at Boston, MA—served on Greenland Patrol sailing out of Grønnedal, Greenland; Jul 43–summer 44 used on Ocean Station "A"; mid 44–1945 used as an escort in the Caribbean, sailing out of Miami, FL.

Agassiz

1941–45 assigned to CARIBSEAFRON—stationed at Charleston, SC; 12 Mar 42 assisted in rescue of 11 survivors from the tanker *John D. Gill;* Jun 45 assigned to 5th District.

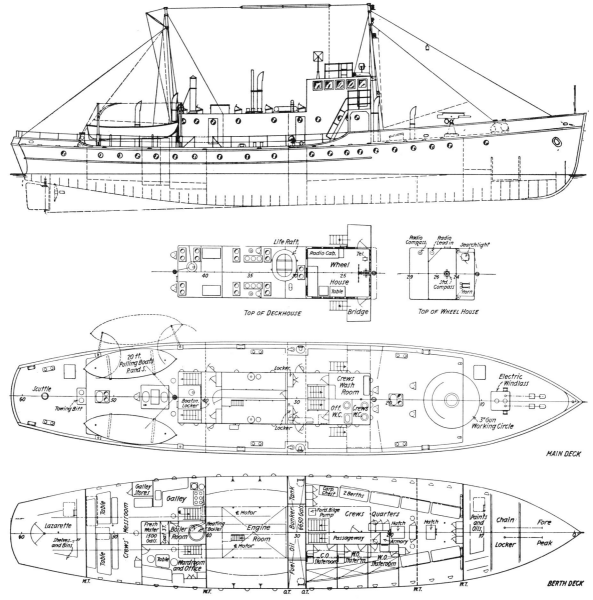

Profile and deck plans of the 125-foot class. Courtesy of *Marine Engineering/Log;* copied from *Marine Engineering and Shipping Age* [July, 1926]: 386.)

Alert

1937–40 served on Bering Sea Patrol; 1941–45 assigned to WESTSEA-FRON—stationed at Alameda, CA.

Bedloe

1940 rearmed at Hoboken, NJ; 1941–44 assigned to EASTSEAFRON—stationed at Stapleton, Staten Island, NY; 9 Mar 42 rescued 16 survivors from the tanker *Gulftrade*—cutter attacked by U-boat; 1 Jun 43 name changed from

the *Antietam* to the *Bedloe;* 14 Sep 44 lost in hurricane off Cape Hatteras, NC, while going to the assistance of a distressed merchantman—2 officers and 24 men lost, 12 survivors picked up after 58 hours by OS2U Kingfishers from CG Air Station, Elizabeth City, NC.

Bonham

1941–45 assigned to NOWESTSEAFRON—stationed at Sitka, AK, and Seattle, WA.

Boutwell

1941–45 assigned to GULFSEAFRON—stationed at Panama City, FL; 7 May 42 rescued 13 survivors from the SS *Pipestone County;* 13 Jul 42 rescued 44 survivors from the tanker *R.W. Gallagher.*

Cahoone

1941–45 assigned to WESTSEAFRON—stationed at San Pedro, CA.

Cartigan

Assigned to EASTSEAFRON—stationed at Boston, MA; early 1943 served as an icebreaker on Connecticut River; Jun 45 assigned to Air-Sea Rescue duty, 3rd District—stationed at Stapleton, Staten Island, NY.

Colfax

1 Apr 33 name changed from the *Montgomery* to the *Colfax;* 1941–45 assigned to CARIBSEAFRON—stationed at Philadelphia, PA; Jun 45 assigned to 4th District.

Crawford

1941–45 assigned to CARIBSEAFRON—stationed at San Juan, PR, and Philadelphia, PA; 5 Jun 44 rescued survivors from merchantman; 30 Jun 44 towed the torpedoed tanker SS *Unimak;* Jun 45 assigned to 10th District.

Cuyahoga

27 May 33–17 May 41 operated in Navy as escort to presidential yacht; 1941–45 assigned to CARIBSEAFRON—stationed at Norfolk, VA.

Diligence

1941–44 assigned to WESTSEAFRON—stationed at San Pedro, CA; Aug 44–1945 used for general A/N duty in 11th District.

Dix

1941–45 assigned to CARIBSEAFRON—stationed at Boston, MA; Aug 42 home ported at Willemstad, Curaçao—equipped as a minesweeper; Jun 45 assigned to 1st District—stationed at Provincetown, MA.

Ewing

1941–45 assigned to 11th District and SERVPAC—stationed at San Diego, CA; used as a training ship in ASW.

Faunce

1941–45 assigned to CINCLANT (DESLANT)—stationed at Boston, MA; used on Greenland Patrol.

Frederick Lee

1941–45 assigned to CINCLANT (DESLANT)—stationed at Boston, MA; used on Greenland Patrol; employed on weather station, operating out of Keflavik, Iceland; 21 Mar 43 rescued 20 survivors from the SS *Svend Foyne,* which had foundered after striking an iceberg.

General Greene

May 41 conducted an oceanographic survey off Newfoundland; 26 May 41 rescued 39 men from the SS *Marconi*—encountered four large warships speeding northward to engage the German battleship *Bismarck;* 1941–45 assigned

to EASTSEAFRON—stationed at Woods Hole, MA; 25 May 42 rescued 18 survivors from the SS *Peysander* off Nantucket Shoals; Jun 42 rescued 19 survivors from the SS *Mattawin;* Jun 45 assigned to Air-Sea Rescue duty, 1st District.

Harriet Lane

1941–45 assigned to EASTSEAFRON—stationed at Boston, MA; Jun 45 assigned to Air-Sea Rescue duty, 5th District.

Jackson

1941–44 assigned to EASTSEAFRON—stationed at Norfolk, VA; 1 Apr 42 unsuccessfully attempted to tow the torpedoed tanker *Tiger;* 14 Sep 44 lost in a hurricane off Cape Hatteras, NC, while going to the assistance of a distressed merchantman—2 officers and 19 men lost, 3 officers and 17 men rescued.

Kimball

1939 stationed at Hoffman Island, NY, for merchant-marine training; 1941–45 assigned to EASTSEAFRON—stationed at New York, NY; Jun 45 assigned to Air-Sea Rescue duty, 3rd District.

Legare

1941–45 assigned to CARIBSEAFRON—stationed at Norfolk, VA; Jun 45 assigned to 1st District.

Marion

1941–45 assigned to CARIBSEAFRON—stationed at Charlotte Amalie, VI; 14 Oct 43 rescued crew of the EM *Dow;* Jun 45 assigned to 10th District.

McLane

Dec 39 used for ice-breaking on Chesapeake Bay; 1941–45 assigned to NOWESTSEAFRON—stationed at Ketchikan, AK; 9 Jul 42, while working with Coast Guard–manned YP 251, attacked and reportedly sank a Japanese submarine, which many publications cite as RO-32—this submarine had been discarded as obsolete on 1 Apr 42; 4 Feb 43 party from cutter rescued 2 survivors ashore near Boca de Quadia, AK, from a Gillam Airlines Lockheed 10A; Feb 44 assisted Army tug ST 169 in distress in Chatham Strait; 18 Oct 44 rescued 3 survivors from fishing craft.

Morris

1940 employed on Bering Sea Patrol; Apr–Dec 40 stationed at Alameda, CA; Dec 41–Feb 42 stationed at Marshfield, OR; 1942–45 assigned to 11th District and SERVPAC, and used for training personnel in sound operations at San Diego, CA.

Nemaha

1941–45 assigned to NOWESTSEAFRON—stationed at Ketchikan, AK, and Seattle, WA.

Pulaski

1941–45 assigned to WESTSEAFRON—stationed at Alameda, CA.

Reliance

15 Dec 40 rearmed at Pearl Harbor, HI; 1941–45 assigned to HAWSEA-FRON—stationed at Honolulu, HI.

Rush

1941–45 assigned to CARIBSEAFRON—stationed at Norfolk, VA.

Tiger

1941–45 assigned to HAWSEAFRON—stationed at Honolulu, HI.

Travis

1941–45 assigned to CINCLANT (DESLANT)—stationed at Boston, MA; used on Greenland Patrol; 20 Dec 42 assisted the SS *Maltran*; 30 Nov 44 collided with the cutter *East Breeze* (ex-*Externsteine*) at 44°44′N, 60°53′W—towed into Halifax, Canada.

Vigilant

1941–45 assigned to GULFSEAFRON—stationed at Ft. Pierce, FL; 21 Feb 42 rescued 2 survivors from the tanker *Republic*; 22 Feb 42 rescued 2 survivors from the tanker *Cities Service Empire*—assisted survivors from the tankers *Pan Massachusetts* and *W. D. Anderson*.

Woodbury

1941–45 assigned to GULFSEAFRON—stationed at Galveston, TX; 16 Feb 42 rescued 40 from the tanker *E. H. Blum*.

Yeaton

1939 stationed at Hoffman Island, NY, for merchant-marine training—4 Apr 39 transferred to Maritime Commission, and 7 Aug 42 returned to CG; 1942–45 assigned to CARIBSEAFRON—stationed at Boston, MA; Jun 45 assigned to 3rd District.

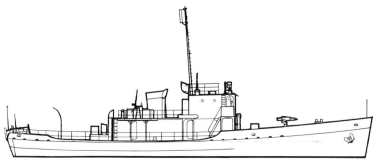

Sketch of the 125-foot class, circa 1943. (Courtesy of Christian Beilstein.)

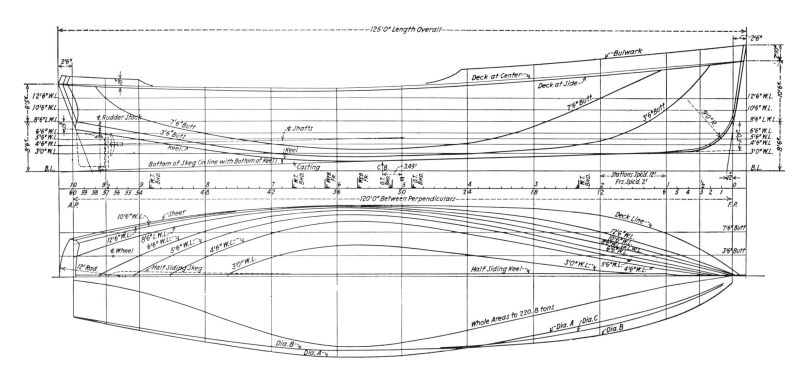

Lines of the 125-foot class. (Courtesy of *Marine Engineering/Log;* copied from *Marine Engineering and Shipping Age* [July, 1926]: 387.)

The *Marion*, 11 Jul 28, sailing from Boston on a scientific expedition to Labrador and Greenland. The 125s and the 165Bs were built to replace the ''fuelish'' destroyers that the CG had on loan from the USN to enforce Prohibition. (Courtesy of the National Archives.)

The *Active*, 1941. A rare photograph of a 125-foot unit outfitted for buoy tending. Following the war, a few were again fitted out as buoy tenders. Note the depth-charge tracks astern. (Courtesy of A. D. Baker III.)

The *Kimball* with a Mousetrap ASW weapon in a raised position on the forecastle. The 3"/23 can be seen directly behind the Mousetraps. The 125s and the follow-on design 165Bs were employed primarily in the sea frontiers.

The *Travis*, 16 Feb 44. Two units of this class—the *Bedloe* and the *Jackson*—were lost at sea during a hurricane on 14 Sep 44. The SE radar antenna mounted atop the mast had to be rotated by hand from the bridge area.

Miscellaneous Types (WAG, WAK, WAO)

Miscellaneous types fit into two categories: the icebreakers and the emergency acquisitions serving as weather ships. The "Winds," designed and built for the CG, were in reality ice-breaking gunboats. They were designed to operate off the east coast of Greenland. Only the *Mackinaw* was constructed for the purpose of aiding domestic navigation, although, admittedly, the "Winds" could serve this mission as well. The bizarre attempt to acquire the *Krassin* underscores the desperate need for icebreakers.

The emergency acquisitions served as weather ships, thereby freeing the more valuable gunboat cutters, which had been performing this mission before the war began. The *Asterion* and *Big Horn* retained their Navy designators—WAK and WAO; but, in reality, they served the same purpose as other emergency acquisitions. In late 1943, when Coast Guard–manned patrol frigates were assigned to weather stations, these miscellaneous types were used for training purposes.

WAG—MISCELLANEOUS AUXILIARIES

290-FOOT CUTTER

Name	Visual Call Sign	Builder	Keel Laid	Launched	Commissioned	Disposition
Mackinaw (ex-*Manitowoc*)	WAG 83 (bn CG-121)	Toledo Shipbuilding Co., Toledo, Ohio	20 Mar 43	4 Mar 44	20 Dec 44	Active

Cost
  $8,830,198 (hull & machinery)

Hull

Displacement (tons)	5,200 fl (1945)	
Length	290' oa	
Beam	74'4" mb	
Draft	19' max (1945)	
Tons per Immersed Inch	33.13	

Machinery

Main Engines	3 electric motors driven by 6 Westinghouse DC generators driven by 6 Fairbanks Morse, 10-cyl, 2-cycle diesels
SHP	12,000
Propellers	Twin aft, single forward (*see* Design remarks)

Performance

Max Speed	16.0 kts (1945)

Logistics

Diesel Fuel (95%)	457,375 gal
Complement	10 officers, 2 warrants, 132 men (1945)

Deck Gear

Cranes	Two 12 t

Electronics (1945)

Detection Radar	SL-1

Armament
  None

Design

Just prior to the United States' entry into World War II, Lieutenant Commander Edward Thiele, USCG (later engineer-in-chief) obtained details on icebreakers while vacationing in Europe. From these materials and details learned from the *Krassin*, the Coast Guard Naval Engineering Division prepared preliminary designs for the *Mackinaw* and the "Winds." The final designs were prepared by Gibbs & Cox of New York.

The *Mackinaw* and the "Winds" were very similar. According to Admiral Thiele, "the *Mackinaw* was nothing but a *Wind* class ship that was squashed down and pushed out and extended to meet the requirements of the [Great] Lakes." The draft of the lake-bound *Mackinaw* needed to be considerably less than that of her oceangoing near sisters. Compensation was made by making her a longer and much wider ship. In fact, the *Mackinaw* is "landlocked" to the Great Lakes because her beam is wider than the Welland Canal and her engine cooling system is directly open to the Great Lakes' fresh water. The *Mackinaw* and the "Winds" were built as Baltic-type icebreakers—they were fitted with bow propellers. Bow propellers work well in ice of uniform thickness, as found on the Great Lakes; however, they are a liability in polar ice. For this reason, the "Winds" bow propellers were removable.

There was one major difference in the construction of the *Mackinaw* and the "Winds." The *Mackinaw*'s hull was made of mild steel, since it was to operate against fresh water ice, whereas the hull of the "Winds" was a high tensile steel.

The *Mackinaw* and "Winds" were extremely strong. The frames (spaced about 16" apart) made up a truss similar to that found in an inverted hangar or gymnasium, and an inner shell was placed inside the truss. The volume between the inner and outer plating was divided into many tanks, which were used to store fuel and to carry ballast (seawater) for heeling.

The main engines of the *Mackinaw* consisted of six diesel generator sets, each driven by its own Fairbanks Morse 38D8-1/8 10-cylinder engines. These could be connected in several combinations to the two after DC electric propulsion motors or to the bow motor. In operation the *Mackinaw* could cruise on two or four generators driving the after screws. In ice, all six generators could be used to drive the two after shafts (4 generators) and the bow shaft (2 generators). In addition, heeling pumps and trimming pumps were installed to roll the ship or trim it to break free from the ice.

The *Mackinaw* was appropriated under 17X0908 and contracted on 16 Jul 42. Initially, she was to have been named the *Manitowoc*. However, the Navy had assigned this name to a patrol frigate which was under construction. The name of the icebreaker was, therefore, changed while under construction. Shortly after the war, her open quarterdeck was used as a helicopter landing area. See "Wind"-class Design remarks.

Mackinaw

Operated on Great Lakes from commissioning to close of war; 20 Jan–6 Feb 45, 25 Soviets on board received engineering training prior to manning a "Wind" class on lend-lease.

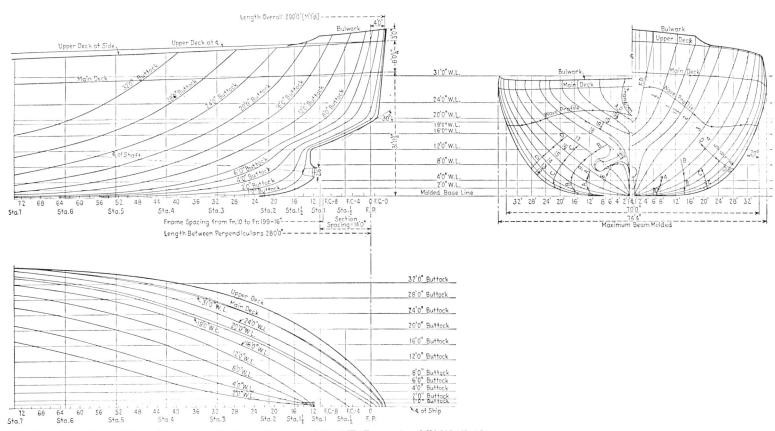

Bow lines, body plan, and lines of flow of the *Mackinaw*. (Courtesy of SNAME, *Transactions* LIV [1946]: 12.)

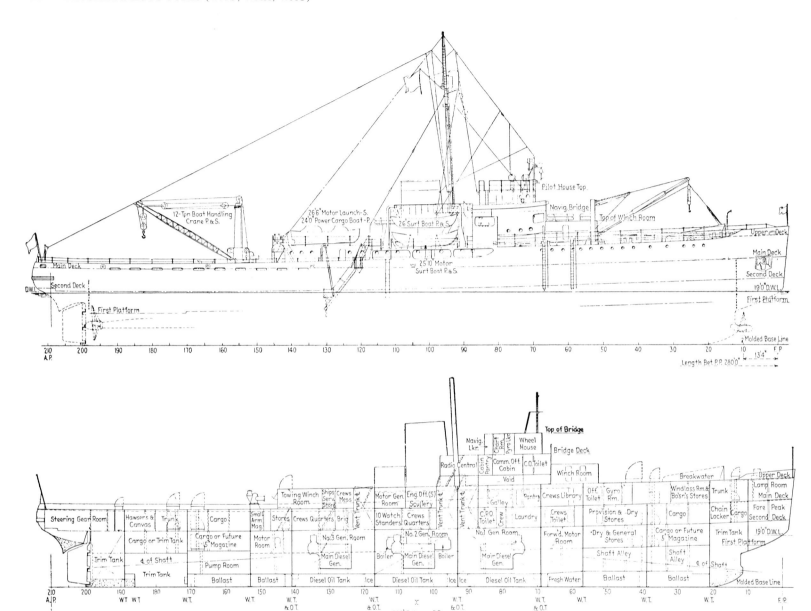

Bow lines, body plan, and lines of flow of the *Mackinaw*. (Courtesy of SNAME, *Transactions* LIV [1946]: 12.)

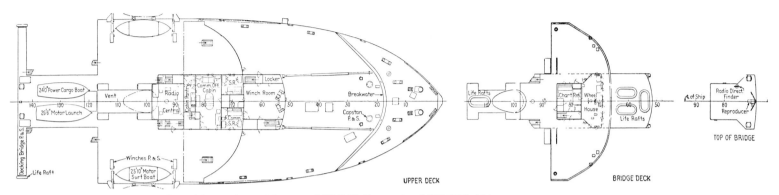

Bow lines, body plan, and lines of flow of the *Mackinaw*. (Courtesy of SNAME, *Transactions* LIV [1946]: 12.)

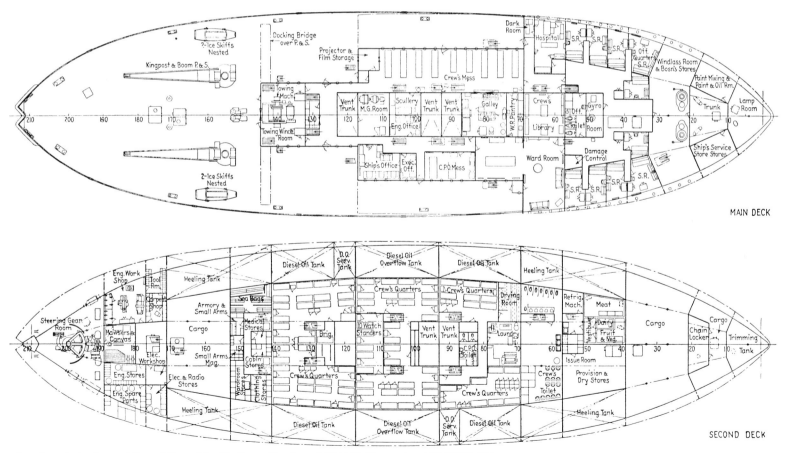

Bow lines, body plan, and lines of flow of the *Mackinaw*. (Courtesy of SNAME, *Transactions* LIV [1946]: 12.)

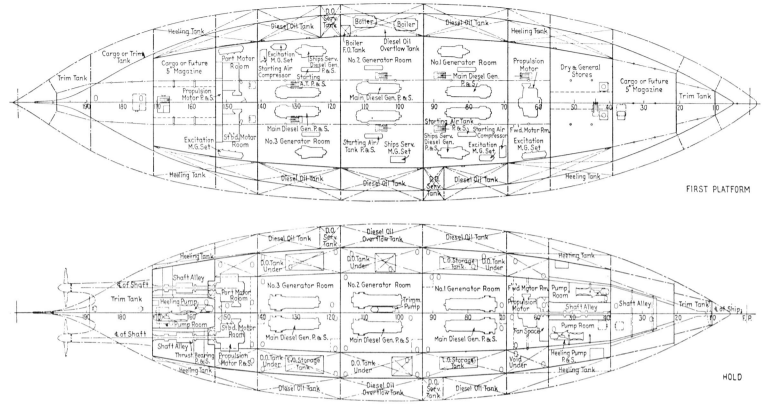

Bow lines, body plan, and lines of flow of the *Mackinaw*. (Courtesy of SNAME, *Transactions* LIV [1946]: 12.)

The *Mackinaw*, 10 Jan 45. Confined to the Great Lakes by her size, the *Mackinaw* is painted in peacetime color—white hull and superstructure, buff mast and stacks, and black funnel cap. This is a color scheme similar to that worn by steel ships of the U.S. Navy until 1909. The pre-1909 Navy ships had a buff-colored superstructure.

269-FOOT CUTTERS ("WIND" CLASS)

Name	Visual Call Sign	Builder	Keel Laid	Launched	Commissioned	Disposition
Northwind (I)	WAG 278 (bn CG-96)	Western Pipe & Steel Co., Los Angeles, CA	9 Jun 42	28 Dec 42	26 Feb 44	*Trans* to USSR 26 Feb 44
Eastwind	WAG 279 (bn CG-97)	Western Pipe & Steel Co., Los Angeles, CA	23 Jun 42	6 Feb 43	3 Jun 44	*Decomm* 13 Dec 68; *sold* 31 Jul 72
Southwind	WAG 280 (bn CG-98)	Western Pipe & Steel Co., Los Angeles, CA	20 Jul 42	8 Mar 43	15 Jul 44	*Trans* to USSR 23 Mar 45
Westwind	WAG 281 (bn CG-99)	Western Pipe & Steel Co., Los Angeles, CA	24 Aug 42	31 Mar 43	18 Sep 44	*Trans* to USSR 21 Feb 45
Northwind (II)	WAG 282 (bn CG-184)	Western Pipe & Steel Co., Los Angeles, CA	10 Jul 44	25 Feb 45	28 Jul 45	Active

Cost
$9,891,806 (*Northwind* [II]); $9,880,037 (all others)

Hull

Displacement (tons)	6,515 fl (1945)
Length	269' oa
Beam	63'6" mb
Draft	25'9" max (1945)
Tons per Immersed Inch	26.95

Machinery

Main Engines	3 electric motors driven by 6 Westinghouse DC generators driven by 6 Fairbanks Morse, 10-cyl 2-cycle diesels
SHP	12,000
Propellers	Twin aft, single forward (see Design remarks)

Performance

Max Speed	16.8 kts on trials (1944)
Economic	11.0 kts, 50,000 mi radius (1945)

Logistics

Diesel Fuel (95%)	427,869 gal
Complement	21 officers, 295 men (1945); 13 officers, 2 warrants, 160 men (peacetime)

Aircraft
1 J2F (1945)

Electronics (1945)

Detection Radar	SA-2, SL-1 for U.S. units; none for USSR units
Fire Control Radar	Mk 26
Sonar	QCJ-8

Armament

1945	U.S. units: 4 5"/38 (twin); 12 40mm/60 (quad); 6 20mm/80 (single); 2 dc tracks; 6 Y-guns; 1 Hedgehog
1945	Units transferred to USSR: 4 3"/30 (single); 8 40mm/60 (single); 6 20mm/80 (single); 2 dc tracks

Design
The "Wind"-class final design—modeled after the Swedish icebreaker *Ymer*—was prepared by Gibbs & Cox of New York. This class was to provide access to military bases in Greenland that would be inaccessible during most of the year without the use of a heavy icebreaker. All five were appropriated under 17X0908. All except the *Northwind* (II) were contracted on 15 Nov 41; she was contracted on 9 Oct 43. These ships were designed with a removable bow propeller. Under certain ice conditions, this bow propeller was advantageous for clearing the hull from ice and dredging broken ice forward; it was not used as a means of propulsion. The 3"/30s on board the units transferred to Russia were Army ordnance. Two units were also constructed for the Navy and were ultimately transferred to the CG: the *Edisto* on 25 Oct 65 and the *Burton Island* on 15 Dec 66. The *Edisto* was decommissioned on 15 Nov 74; the *Burton Island* was decommissioned on 19 May 78. *See* Design remarks under the *Mackinaw* for more details.

Eastwind

1944–45 assigned to CINCLANT—stationed at Boston, MA, and operated in Greenland waters throughout WW II; 4 Oct 44 captured German weather station, East Greenland, Little Koldewey Island—12 prisoners; 15 Oct 44 captured the German trawler *Externsteine*—17 prisoners—and the *Externsteine* was renamed the *East Breeze* and taken to Boston, MA, by a prize crew.

Northwind (I)

No U.S. WW II service—transferred to USSR.

Northwind (II)

No U.S. WW II service—completed too late.

Southwind

1944–45 assigned to CINCLANT—stationed at Boston, MA, and operated in Greenland waters; 15 Oct 44 assisted in capture of the German trawler *Externsteine*.

Westwind

Late 1944 was to have been assigned to NOWESTSEAFRON and stationed at Port Angeles, WA—transferred to USSR instead.

269-FOOT CUTTERS TRANSFERRED TO USSR

Name	Soviet Name	Fate
Northwind (I)	Severni Veter (later named Admiral Makarov)	Ret to USN 19 Dec 51—renamed the Northwind; 15 Apr 52 named the Staten Island to avoid confusion with sistership the Northwind; trans to CG 1 Feb 66; decomm 15 Nov 74; sold 14 May 75
Southwind	Kapitan Belusov (Kapitan Belousov)	Ret to USN 13 Apr 50—named the Atka; trans to CG 20 Oct 66; renamed the Southwind 15 Jan 67; decomm 31 May 74
Westwind	Severni Pulius (Severny Polyus)	Ret to CG 19 Dec 51; recomm 22 Sep 52; active

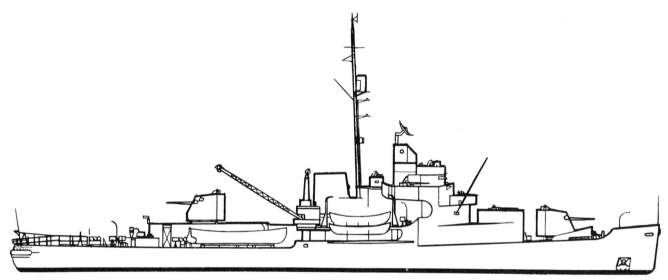

Sketch of the "Wind" class, circa 1944. Note the omission of the twin 5″/38 gun mounts and radar-equipped Mk 37 directors installed in the American Winds. (Courtesy of Christian Beilstein.)

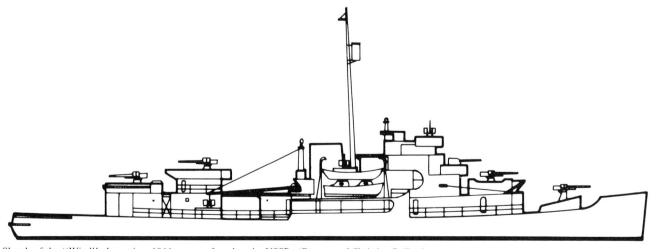

Sketch of the "Wind" class, circa 1944, as transferred to the USSR. (Courtesy of Christian Beilstein.)

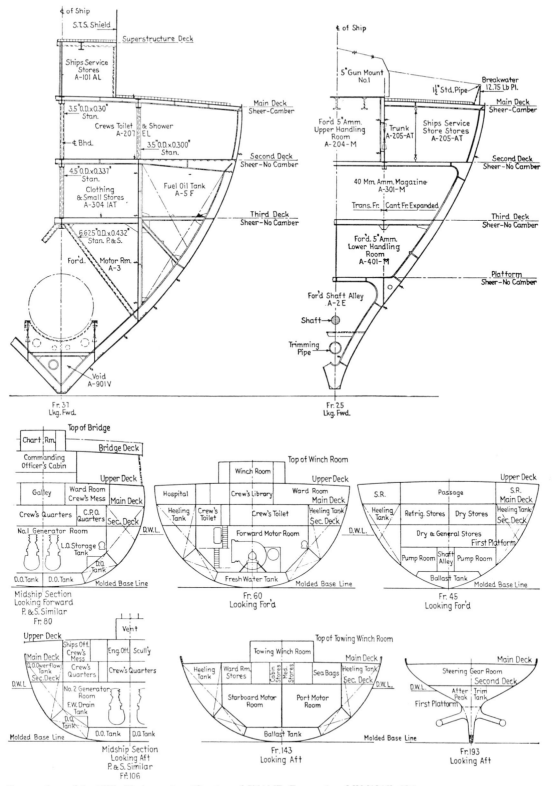

Type sections of the "Wind"-class cutter. (Courtesy of SNAME, *Transactions* LIV [1946]: 18.)

The *Westwind*, Jan 45. The stability of this design permitted a very heavy armament and allowed a J2F aircraft to be carried on the superstructure-deck-level amidships. She belonged to the first class of true ice-breakers built in the United States.

The *Northwind I* prior to transfer to the USSR. This cutter had already received much of her armament and electronics for CG service when the decision was made to give her to the USSR under lend-lease. Therefore, she had to be refitted. Note the reduced armament and lack of radar.

The *Northwind II* lies at anchor in New York Harbor, 26 Jun 46. Her aft twin 5"/38 has been removed and an HNS-1 helicopter is perched on a platform. During WW II, the CG was in charge of training all U.S. and British helicopter pilots.

EMERGENCY ACQUISITION, *MUSKEGET* CLASS

Name	Visual Call Sign	Builder	Launched	Commissioned	Disposition
Muskeget (ex-*Cornish*)	WAG 48 (ex-AG 48, ex-YAG 9)	Bethlehem Shipbuilding Corp., Sparrows Point, MD	Dec 22	1923 (mercantile); 3 Jan 42 (USN); 1 Jul 42 (CG)	Lost at sea about 9 Sep 42
Manhasset (ex-*Wilton*)	WAG 276 (ex-AG 47, ex-YAG 8)	Bethlehem Shipbuilding Corp., Sparrows Point, MD	1923	1923 (mercantile); 2 Jan 42 (USN); 8 Aug 42; (CG)	*Decomm* 15 Oct 45; *sold* 16 Oct 46

Cost
  Acquisition Navy loan; conversion $250,000 each

Hull
Displacement (tons)	3,170 fl (1942); 2,950 fl (1945)
Tonnage	1,827 gross (1923); 1,094 net (1923)
Length	250' oa; 233'6" bp
Beam	40'2" mb
Draft	24'3" max (1942)

Machinery
Main Engines	Hooven, Owens, Rentschler Co. triple-expansion steam
Main Boilers	2 Bethlehem Shipbuilding Corp. single-ended Scotch boilers, 190 psi
SHP	1,300
Propellers	Single

Performance
Max Speed	11.5 kts (1945); 9.0 kts, 15,000 mi radius (1945)

Logistics
Fuel Oil (95%)	198,000 gal
Complement	34 persons (merchant service, 1923); 14 officers, 12 warrants, 124 men (1945)

Electronics (1945)
Detection Radar	*Muskeget* none; *Manhasset* SF
Sonar	QCL-8

Armament (1945)
  1 4"/50 (single); 1 3"/50 (single); 4 20mm/80 (single); 2 dc tracks; 4 Y-guns; 2 Mousetraps

Design
  The *Muskeget* is the former freighter *Cornish*, operated by the Eastern Steamship Lines, Inc., Boston, MA, in coastwide cargo trade. She was acquired by the Navy on 29 Dec 41 and renamed the *Muskeget* on 30 May 42. Conversion work was completed on 29 Jun 42. The *Manhasset* is the former freighter *Wilton* built for the coastal cargo service out of Boston. She was loaned to CG by the U.S. Navy on 8 Aug 42 and transferred on 22 Oct. 43

Muskeget

1942 assigned to 1st District—stationed at Boston, MA; about 9 Sep 42 disappeared from Weather Station #2 (52°N by 42°30'W) without a trace; 9 Sep 42 U-755 attacked and presumably sank an American auxiliary, probably the *Muskeget*—all 121 men lost.

Manhasset

1942–45 assigned to 1st District—stationed at Boston, MA, and used for weather patrol; 19 Nov 42 disabled on station 42°20'N by 64°10'W—towed in by the *Wandank*.

The *Muskeget* on 17 Feb 42. On about 9 Sep of that year, she disappeared in the North Atlantic. After the war, the log of U-755 revealed that she had attacked and presumably sunk an American auxiliary on 9 Sep 42. (Courtesy of D. M. McPherson.)

Midship view of the *Manhasset*, 14 Sep 43. Like most weather ships, she is fitted with a weather balloon hangar aft the mainmast.

EMERGENCY ACQUISITION, "LAKE" CLASS

Name	Visual Call Sign	Builder	Launched	Commissioned	Disposition
Manasquan (ex-*Aetna;* ex-*Oscar J. Lingeman;* ex-*Lake Catherine*)	WAG 273 (ex-AG 36)	Toledo Shipbuilding Co., Toledo, OH	Jun 18	11 Oct 41 (USN); 2 Apr 42 (CG)	*Decomm* 22 Feb 45; *sold* 11 Mar 46
Menemsha (ex-*John Gehm;* ex-*Lake Orange*)	WAG 274 (ex-AG 39)	McDougall-Duluth, Duluth, MN	Oct 18	19 Sep 41 (USN); 20 Jan 42 (CG)	*Decomm* 24 Sep 45; *sold* 6 Mar 47
Monomoy (ex-*J. Floyd Massey, Jr.;* ex-*Lake Arline*)	WAG 275 (ex-AG 40)	Globe Shipbuilding Co., Duluth, MN	Oct 18	24 Dec 41 (USN); 22 Oct 43 (CG)	*Decomm* 12 Oct 45; *sold* 13 Feb 51

Cost

    Acquisition: all on loan from Navy; conversion: *Menemsha,* $500,000; *Monomoy* and *Manasquan,* $600,000

Hull

Displacement (tons)	3,900 fl (1918; 1945)
Tonnage	2,013 gross (1918; 1945); 1,178 net (1941)
Length	261' oa; 251 bp
Beam	43'6" max
Draft	16'5" max (1918; 1945)

Machinery

Main Engines	1 3-cyl triple expansion
Main Boilers	2 Scotch, 180 psi
SHP	1,200
Propellers	Single

Performance

Max Sustained	10.0 kts, 4,650 mi radius (1918)
Cruising	8.0 kts, 7,500 mi radius (1945)
Economic	7.0 kts, 8,500 mi radius (1945)

Logistics

Coal	862 tons (*Manasquan*); 1,100 tons (*Menemsha*)
Complement	8 officers, 97 men (1942)

Electronics (1945)

Detection Radar	*Menemsha:* SF-1
Sonar	NA

Armament (1945)

    1 5"/38 (single); 2 4"/50 (single); 2 20mm/80 (single)—*Menemsha:* 2 3"/50 (single); 8 20mm/80 (single)

Design

    The large "Lake" class was constructed on the Great Lakes as part of the WW I emergency shipbuilding program. Many of these ships were used to transport the North Sea Mine Barrage to Europe.

Manasquan

Late 1941–early 42 converted at the Bethelhem Steel Co. Atlantic Yards, Boston, MA; Jun–Jul 42 employed in LORAN tests; 1942–43 assigned to 1st District—stationed at Boston MA, and used for weather patrol; 12 Jun 43 collided at dock with the *Cactus,* causing considerable damage to the tender; mid-1943 rebuilt at Coast Guard Yard, Curtis Bay, MD, as a gunnery practice ship; 29 Aug 43–22 Feb 45 assigned to CG Academy, New London, CT, and used for training duty; 7 Oct 44 collided with the SS *Edward Pearce*—slight damage, but sonar destroyed.

Menemsha

Jan 42–Oct 43 assigned to 1st District—stationed at Boston, MA, and used on weather patrol extensively; 20 Aug 42 assisted in rescue of 5 survivors from the SS *Arletta;* mid-1943 rebuilt at Coast Guard Yard, Curtis Bay, MD, as a gunnery training ship; Oct 43–Sep 45 assigned to VCNO—stationed at Norfolk, VA, and employed for armed-guard training.

Monomoy

Late 1941 converted at Maryland Drydock Co., Baltimore, MD; 1942–43 assigned to 1st District—stationed at Boston, MA, and served as weather ship; Oct 43–Oct 45 assigned to VCNO—stationed at Norfolk, VA, and used for training.

The *Menemsha* under way, 13 Jan 44. A number of merchantmen of low military value were acquired and outfitted for duty as weather ships. Prior to the war, 327s—the newest and most important cutters—had been used on this duty. Ships like the *Menemsha* freed the 327s for escort duty.

The *Monomoy* in dry dock, 27 Aug 43. These ships had been built on the Great Lakes to meet the emergencies of WW I.

Name	Visual Call Sign	Builder	Launched	Commissioned	Disposition
Krassin (also cited as *Krasin* and *Leonid Krassin*)	[WAG]	Newcastle-on-Tyne, England	1917	Not applicable	Negotiations suspended 25 Nov 41

Cost
  NA
Hull
  Displacement (tons)   10,620 fl (1917); 8,730 normal (1917)
  Tonnage   5,105 gross (1917); 2,246 net (1917)
  Length   323'3" oa; 297' wl
  Beam   71' max; 70'6" wl
  Draft   30' max
  Block Coefficient   0.562
Machinery
  Main Engines   Reciprocating steam
  SHP   10,000
  Propellers   Triple
Performance
  Max Speed   15 kts (1941)
  Cruising   ? kts, 8,700 mi radius (1941)
Logistics
  Coal   3,750 tons
  Complement   190 Soviet service (1941)
Electronics
  Detection Radar   None
  Sonar   Planned
Armament (1941—planned)
  2 4"/50 (single)

Krassin

On 18 Jul 41 Secretary of the Treasury Morgenthau wrote to Acting Secretary of State Welles: "In order to meet the immediate needs of this country . . . it is recommended that negotiations be entered into with the Russian Government for the purchase of one or more of their modern ice breakers." Appended to the letter was a list of ships "in order of their desirability. . . ." They were the *Krasin* [sic], *Stephen Makarof*, *Krisjanie Valdemars*, and *Lenin*. The Secretary of State approached the Soviet ambassador. The ambassador pointed out that three of the ships were blockaded in the Baltic and not accessible, and that he would have to forward the inquiry to Moscow. On 1 Aug, Secretary Welles informed Secretary Morgenthau "that the Soviet Government would be pleased to place at the disposal of the American Government for a period of approximately eight months the Soviet ice breaker *Krassin*, which is at present near the Bering Straits." The letter also stated that the ship was in need of repairs.

  Eight months was not much time. The Coast Guard wished to employ the icebreaker on the east coast of Greenland. Subtracting the 80-day round-trip transit between Seattle and Ivigtut, Greenland, plus the overhaul, only 4 months' operational time would remain. Admiral Russell Waesche, commandant of the Coast Guard, advised that "the *Krasin* [sic] should be made available to the United States for at least a year, in order to obtain real service. . . ." Morgenthau wrote to Welles that the Coast Guard would accept the Soviet offer if the ship were made available for one year. In the fall of 1941, the *Krassin* arrived at Seattle, WA, and a Coast Guard party surveyed her. She then came around and was worked on at the Coast Guard Yard, Curtis Bay, MD. The attempt to lease the *Krassin* came to an abrupt end on 25 November. Secretary of War John Bell wrote:

> Day before yesterday the Russian Charge d'Affaires called on Secretary Morgenthau and said that the icebreaker was needed immediately by the Russians in the Archangel district. . . .
> Admiral Waesche said the Coast Guard had consulted with the Secretary and that in compliance with the wishes of the Russian Charge d'Affaires it had been decided to terminate all negotiations for use by the United States of the *Krassin*. . . .

Although the *Krassin* never served in the Coast Guard, the service did learn from studying her design.

The *Krassin* lies at Seattle, WA, awaiting transportation to the CG during 1941. Although she never served in the CG, the *Krassin* did influence the design of U.S. icebreakers.

WAK—CARGO SHIPS

EMERGENCY ACQUISITION

Name	Visual Call Sign	Builder	Launched	Commissioned	Disposition
Asterion (ex-*Evelyn*)	WAK 123 (ex-AK 63)	Newport News Shipbuilding & Dry Dock Co., Newport News, VA	Jun 1912	17 Sep 42 (USN); 12 Jan 44 (CG)	*Decomm* 20 Jul 44; *sold* 14 Mar 46

Cost
  NA

Hull
  Displacement (tons) 6,610 (1941)
  Tonnage 3,140 gross (1941); 2,443 net (1941)
  Length 328'2" oa
  Beam 46'1" max
  Draft Est. 20' max

Machinery
  Main Engines 1 3-cyl triple expansion
  Main Boilers 2 single-ended Scotch, 180 psi
  SHP 1,200
  Propellers Single

Performance
  Max Speed 11.0 kts (1944)

Logistics
  Fuel Oil (95%) 828 tons

Complement 141

Electronics
  Detection Pos, antenna concealed in crow's nest
  Sonar NA

Armament (1944)
  3 4"/50 (single; 2 concealed); 2 40mm/60 (single, concealed); 2 20mm/80 (single); 1 Hedgehog (concealed by fwd. hatch); 24 Y-guns; 4 K-guns

Design
  A freighter used in the sugar trade between the U.S. and Cuba, by A. H. Bull S. S. Co., New York.

Asterion

Employed by Navy as a "Q Ship" without success; turned over to CG; Jan–July 44 assigned to CINCLANT—stationed at Boston, MA, and used on weather patrol; decommissioned due to "age, condition of hull & machinery and lack of speed."

The *Asterion* as the "Q ship" *Evelyn*, 10 May 42. The CG took over the Q ships *Evelyn* and *Big Horn* and used them on weather stations. A Q ship was disguised as an unarmed or lightly armed merchantman, but, in fact, she concealed heavy armament and was therefore usually given increased buoyancy or watertight integrity. Q ships sailed alone in U-boat infested waters, hoping to lure a U-boat to the surface. Although the British had some success with them during WW I, U.S. Q ships employed in the world wars had uneventful careers.

WAO—OILERS

EMERGENCY ACQUISITION

Name	Visual Call Sign	Builder	Launched	Commissioned	Disposition
Big Horn (ex-*Gulfdawn*)	WAO 124 (CG); (ex-AO 45) (IX 207 post CG service)	Sun Shipbuilding & Dry Dock Co., Chester, PA	1936 (mercantile)	16 Apr 42 (USN); 17 Jan 44 (CG)	*Decomm & trans* to Navy 1 Feb 45

Cost
   Acquisition Navy loan; conversion $150,000
Hull
   Displacement (tons)   15,405 fl (1944)
   Tonnage   7,096 gross (1936)
   Length   425' bp
   Beam   64' max
   Draft   27'8" max (1944)
Machinery
   Main Engines   2 Westinghouse 2-cyl direct-drive turbines
   Main Boilers   Foster-Wheeler watertube, 450 psi
   SHP   3,300
   Propellers   Single
Performance
   Max Speed   12.5 kts (1944)
Logistics
   Fuel Oil (95%)   1,025 tons

Complement   239
Electronics
   Detection Radar   Possibly none
Armament (1944)
   2 3"/50 (single)—armament possibly much heavier due to Q Ship service (*see* Armament remarks on the *Asterion*)
Design
   The *Big Horn* was built for commercial service as a tanker, for Gulf Oil Corp., Philadelphia, Pa.

Big Horn

Jul 42–Jan 44 served as a Q Ship in eastern North Atlantic during naval service; 17 Jan 44–1 Feb 45 assigned to CINCLANT—stationed at Boston, MA, and used by CG as a weather ship.

The *Big Horn* while in the CG. She flies a naval jack at her bow. Although no radar is evident, it may be concealed—a holdover from her days as a Q ship. The Navy employed four Q ships in WW II: the *Atik, Evelyn, Big Horn,* and *Irene Forsyte;* it employed one—the *Charles Whittemore*—in WW I. U.S. Q ships did not sink any U-boats.

Tugs
(WAT and WYT)

The seventeen 110-foot tugs were the backbone of the tug force. Most were reinforced for light icebreaking and were fitted with fire monitors. Although designated as WYTs—harbor tugs—a number saw service in Greenland waters.

WAT—OCEANGOING TUGS

EMERGENCY ACQUISITION

Name	Visual Call Sign	Builder	Keel Laid	Launched	Commissioned	Disposition
Carrabasset	WAT 55 (ex-AT 35)	Staten Island Shipbuilding Co., Port Richmond, NY	6 Jan 19	12 Jun 19	30 June 20 (USN); 13 Oct 24 (CG)	*Decomm* 26 July 46

Cost
  Est. $220,845
Hull
  Displacement (tons)   1,133 max (1938); 1,511 max (1945)
  Length   155'10" oa; 153'8" bp
  Beam   30'6" mb
  Draft   17'7" max (1938); 20' max (1945)
Machinery
  Main Engines   1 triple-expansion steam
  Main Boilers   2 Scotch
  SHP   1,800
  Propellers   Single
Performance
  Max Sustained   13.0 kts, 3,200 mi radius (1945)
  Cruising   11.1 kts, 4,200 mi radius (1945)
  Economic   9.3 kts, 5,300 mi radius (1945)
                          6.6 kts, 6,050 mi radius (1938)
Logistics
  Fuel Oil (95%)   76,563 gal
  Complement   5 officers, 47 men (1938); 1 officer, 3 warrants, 39 men (1945)
Electronics
  Detection Radar   None (1942); SF (1945)
Armament
  1938   2 1-pdrs
  1945   1 3"/50; 2 20mm/80 (single)
Design
  This tug was built for the Navy as a member of the *Bagaduce* class; she is composite construction. She was transferred to the Treasury Department for use by the CG on 24 May 24.

Carrabasset

1941–45 assigned to EASTSEAFRON—stationed at Norfolk, VA.

The *Carrabasset*, 26 Nov 42. Radar has not yet been fitted. During the 1920s and 30s, the CG operated three oceangoing tugs in order to assist in distress. They were stationed at Port Angeles, WA, Eureka, CA, and Curtis Bay, MD. The *Carrabasset* operated out of Curtis Bay prior to WW II.

158-FOOT TUG

Name	Visual Call Sign	Builder	Keel Laid	Launched	Commissioned	Disposition
Shawnee	WAT 54	Union Construction Co., Oakland, CA	5 May 20	15 Nov 21	8 Mar 22	*Decomm* 21 Nov 46; *sold* 28 Nov 47

Cost
$355,000

Hull
Displacement (tons)   900 fl (1908 and 1945)
Tonnage   558 gross (1941)
Length   158′8″ oa
Beam   30′ mb
Draft   14′11″ max (1908 and 1945)

Machinery
Main Engines   1 triple-expansion steam
Main Boilers   2 Babcock & Wilcox
SHP   1,400
Propellers   Single

Performance
Max Sustained   12.0 kts, 2,340 mi radius (1945)
Cruising   10.0 kts, 2,930 mi radius (1945)
Economic   6.5 kts, 3,500 mi radius (1945)
   8.0 kts, 4,300 mi radius (1938)

Logistics
Fuel Oil (95%)   41,650 gal
Complement   1 officer, 3 warrants, 39 men (1945)

Electronics
Detection Radar   None (1941); SF-1 (1945)
Sonar   QCJ-3 (1945)

Armament
1938   2 1-pdrs.
1941   2 dc tracks
1945   2 20mm/80 (single); 4 Y-guns; 2 dc tracks

Design
Composite construction; the *Shawnee* was able to carry 14 dcs because aft gun was located so far forward.

Shawnee

1941–45 assigned to WESTSEAFRON—stationed at Eureka, CA.

The *Shawnee*, Jul 38. As completed, she had a tall slender stack, a heavy mainmast, and a lighter foremast forward of the bridge structure. (Courtesy of the Smithsonian Institution.)

EMERGENCY ACQUISITION

Name	Visual Call Sign	Builder	Keel Laid	Launched	Commissioned	Disposition
Redwing	[WAT] (ex-AM 48)	Baltimore Drydock & Shipbuilding Co., Baltimore, MD	5 Aug 18	7 Jun 19	17 Oct 19 (USN); 11 Oct 24 (CG)	*Trans* to Navy 29 Aug 41

Cost
  NA

Hull
  Displacement (tons)   1,210 fl (1941)
  Length   187'10" oa
  Beam   35'6'
  Draft   12' max (1941)

Machinery
  Main Engines   Steam

Performance
  Max Speed   14 kts (1941)
                12.8 kts (1938)
  Economic   8.0 kts, 6,550 mi radius (1938)

Logistics
  Fuel   Oil
  Complement   6 officers, 56 men (1938); 72 (1941)

Armament
  1938 and 1940   2 3"/23 (single); 2 1-pdrs
  1941   2 3"/50; minesweeping gear

Design
  A former Navy "Bird"-class minesweeper of composite construction.

Redwing

Stationed on West Coast throughout most of CG career; Jul–Aug 40 and May–Jun 41 used for special cruises in Bering Sea and Bristol Bay to study fishing.

The tug *Redwing*, 5 May 34, towing the disabled Norwegian merchantman *Childar* in the Columbia River Bay. She spent most of her career ready to assist ships in distress in the Strait of Juan de Fuca.

WYT—HARBOR TUGS

110-FOOT TUGS

Name	Visual Call Sign	Builder	Keel Laid	Launched	Commissioned	Disposition
Apalachee	WYT 71 (bn CG-118)	Ira S. Bushey & Sons, Brooklyn, NY	17 Nov 42	29 Apr 43	26 Nov 43	Active
Yankton	WYT 72 (bn CG-119)	Ira S. Bushey & Sons, Brooklyn, NY	26 Oct 42	29 Apr 43	26 Jan 44	Active
Mohican	WYT 73 (bn CG-120)	Ira S. Bushey & Sons, Brooklyn, NY	10 Nov 42	16 Jun 43	29 Feb 44	Active
Chinook	WYT 96 (bn CG-126)	Ira S. Bushey & Sons, Brooklyn, NY	10 Nov 42	16 Jun 43	24 Mar 44	Active
Ojibwa	WYT 97 (bn CG-127)	Ira S. Bushey & Sons, Brooklyn, NY	25 Jan 43	10 Sep 43	7 Apr 44	*Decomm* Apr 80; *sold* 22 Dec 80
Snohomish	WYT 98 (bn CG-128)	Ira S. Bushey & Sons, Brooklyn, NY	25 Jan 43	10 Sep 43	2 May 44	Active
Sauk	WYT 99 (bn CG-129)	Ira S. Bushey & Sons, Brooklyn, NY	25 Jan 43	10 Sep 43	25 May 44	Active

Cost
$622,677 each (hull & machinery)

Hull
Displacement (tons)   384 fl (1945)
Length   110' oa
Beam   26'5" mb
Draft   11'6" max (1945)

Machinery
Main Engines   1 electric motor driven by 2 Elliot Electric Co. generators driven by 2 Ingersoll Rand 8-cyl diesels
SHP   1,000
Propellers   Single

Performance
Max Speed   12.0 kts (1945)
Max Sustained   10.0 kts, 2,000 mi radius (1945)

Logistics
Diesel Fuel   *Apalachee* and *Ojibwa*: 10,000 gal; all others: 11,900 gal
Complement   2 warrants, 14 men (1945)

Electronics
Detection Radar   None (1944); SO-2 (1945)

Armament (1945)
2 20mm/80 (single)

Design
These 110-foot tugs were appropriated by 17X0908, contracted on 8 Jun 41. Based on the earlier 110-foot design, the design incorporated characteristics required for Greenland duty and fire-fighting.

Apalachee

Late 43–1945 assigned to 5th District—stationed at Baltimore, MD.

Chinook

1944–45 assigned to 1st District—stationed at Boston, MA.

Mohican

1944–45 assigned to 3rd District—stationed at New York, NY.

Ojibwa

1944–45 assigned to 1st District—stationed at Boston, MA.

Sauk

1944–45 assigned to 3rd District—stationed at New York, NY.

Snohomish

1944–45 assigned to 1st District—stationed at Boston, MA.

Yankton

1944–45 assigned to 4th District—stationed at Philadelphia, PA.

The *Ojibwa*, 2 Aug 44, armed only with a pair of 20mms. The seven units of this design, the last of the 110-foot tugs built, all served in East Coast districts during their brief wartime careers. (Courtesy of A. D. Baker III.)

110-FOOT TUGS

Name	Visual Call Sign	Builder	Keel Laid	Launched	Commissioned	Disposition
Kaw (ex-*Kennebec*)	WYT 61 (bn CG-87)	Coast Guard Yard, Curtis Bay, MD	9 May 42	6 Oct 42	1 Mar 43	*Decomm* 22 Jun 79
Manitou	WYT 60 (bn CG-86)	Coast Guard Yard, Curtis Bay, MD	20 May 42	29 Sep 42	15 Feb 43	*Decomm* 19 Nov 80

Cost
$587,209 each (hull & machinery)

Hull
Displacement (tons)   328 fl (1945)
Length   110' oa
Beam   26'5" mb
Draft   11'6" max (1945)

Machinery
Main Engines   1 electric motor driven by 2 Elliot Electric Co. generators driven by 2 Ingersoll Rand 8-cyl diesels
SHP   1,000
Propellers   Single

Performance
Max Speed   12.7 kts (1945)
Max Sustained   10.0 kts, 2,000 mi radius (1945)

Logistics
Diesel Fuel (95%)   *Kaw:* 8,140 gal; *Manitou:* 8,000 gal

Complement   2 warrants, 14 men (1945)

Electronics (1945)
Detection Radar   *Kaw:* SO-2; *Manitou:* SO-8

Armament (1945)
2 20mm/80 (single)

Design
These 110-foot tugs were appropriated under 17-20X1223, contracted on 31 May 41. They differed from the 110-foot *Arundel* type only in machinery installation.

Kaw

1943–45 assigned to 1st District—stationed at Portland, ME (Mar 43–Oct 44), and Sandwich, ME (Oct 44–1945); 1 Jan 45 assisted the cutter *Nemesis* following her collision with the SS *Felipe de Neve*.

Manitou

Feb 43–Mar 45 assigned to CINCLANT (DESLANT)—stationed at Boston, MA, and operated in Greenland waters; Mar 45 stationed at Philadelphia, PA.

The *Manitou* in Greenland waters. Radar has been "touched out" of the picture. Note metal frames used to prevent the AA guns from firing into the ship. The 110s possessed very good ice-breaking capabilities, and many tugs of this design served in Greenland waters.

EMERGENCY ACQUISITION

Name	Visual Call Sign	Builder	Launched	Commissioned	Disposition
Beverly (ex-*Maurice R. Shaw*; ex-*Cerberus*)	WYT 371	John H. Dialogue & Son, Camden, NJ	1905	6 Oct 42 (CG)	*Trans* to Navy 4 Aug 44

Cost
  Acquisition $30,000; alteration $81,172
Hull
  Tonnage   195 gross, 133 net
  Length   110′ oa; 102′9″ bp
  Beam   22′ max
  Draft   11′4″ max (1942)
Machinery
  Main Engines   1 Fairbanks Morse diesel
  BHP   450
  Propellers   Single
Performance
  Max Speed   10.0 kts (1942)
  Economic   6.5 kts, 12,000 mi radius (1942)

Logistics
  Diesel   10,000 gal
  Complement   3 warrants, 14 men (1942)
Electronics
  None
Armament
  None
Design
  Built for the U.S. Army Engineer Corps as the *Cerberus*, she was operated as the civilian tug *Maurice R. Shaw* out of Wilmington, DE, at the time of her acquisition. The *Beverly* had a steel hull and wood superstructure.

Beverly

1942–44 assigned to 1st District—stationed at Boston, MA.

EMERGENCY ACQUISITION

Name	Visual Call Sign	Builder	Launched	Commissioned	Disposition
Shearwater	[WYT]	NA	1909	17 Oct 41	*Sold* 17 Jul 42

Cost
  NA
Hull
  Tonnage   95 gross
  Length   85′ oa
  Beam   18′ max
  Draft   NA
Machinery
  Main Engines   NA
Performance
  Max Speed   NA

Logistics
  Complement   NA
Electronics
  NA
Armament
  NA
Design
  Obtained from Fish & Wildlife Service, Department of the Interior.

Shearwater

1941–42 stationed at Portland, ME.

110-FOOT TUGS

Name	Visual Call Sign	Builder	Launched	Commissioned	Disposition
Arundel	WYT 90 (bn CG-74)	Gulfport Works, Port Arthur, TX	24 Jun 39	6 Jul 39	Active
Mahoning	WYT 91 (bn CG-75)	Gulfport Works, Port Arthur, TX	22 Jul 39	7 Aug 39	Active
Naugatuck	WYT 92 (bn CG-73)	Defoe Boat Works, Bay City, MI	23 Mar 39	12 Apr 39	*Decomm* 15 Jan 79
Raritan	WYT 93 (bn CG-72)	Defoe Boat Works, Bay City, MI	23 Mar 39	11 Apr 39	Active

Cost
  $309,000 each
Hull
  Displacement (tons)   328 fl (1945)
  Length   110′ oa
  Beam   26′5″ mb
  Draft   12′ (1945)
Machinery
  Main Engines   1 Westinghouse electric motor connected to 2 Westing-
                         house generators driven by 2 General Motors 8-cyl die-
                         sels
  SHP   1,000
  Propellers   Single
Performance
  Max Speed   13.0 kts (1945)
  Max Sustained   12.0 kts, 1,600 mi radius (1945)
  Economic   10.0 kts, 3,500 mi radius (1945)
Logistics
  Diesel Fuel (95%)   7,740 gal
  Complement   2 warrants, 14 men (1945)
Electronics (1945)
  Detection Radar   SO-8

Armament
  1941–45   Some units: 1 20mm/80; others: mgs only
Design
  These units were a follow-on to the 110-foot *Calumet* type.

Arundel

Winter 1940 broke ice on Hudson River; 1941–45 assigned to CINCLANT
(DESLANT)—stationed at Boston, MA, and employed in Greenland waters.

Mahoning

Winter 1940 broke ice on Hudson River; 1941–45 assigned to 3rd District—
stationed at New York, NY.

Naugatuck

1941–45 assigned to 4th District—stationed at Philadelphia, PA.

Raritan

1 Jul 41 assigned to newly established South Greenland Patrol and to Navy
for duty; 1941–45 assigned to CINCLANT (DESLANT)—stationed at Boston,
MA, and employed in Greenland waters; Dec 42–1943 assisted in building
LORAN stations in Greenland; 1 Sep 45 assigned to 7th District—stationed
at Portsmouth, VA.

The *Arundel*, 1 Feb 43, in Kungnat Bay, Greenland. She is armed with two .50-cal machine guns.

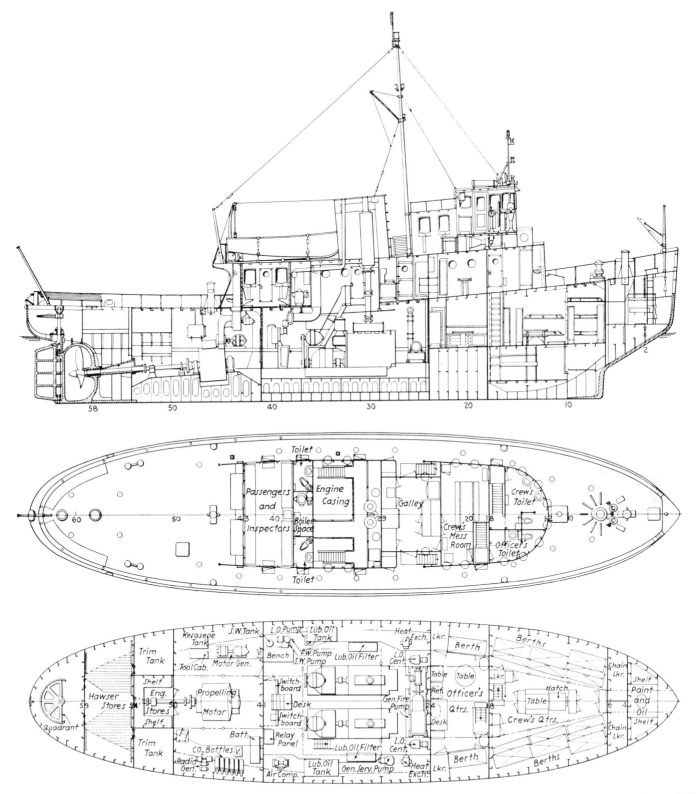

General arrangement of the 110-foot tugs, *Arundel* type. (Courtesy of *Marine Engineering/Log;* copied from *Marine Engineering and Shipping Age* [June, 1939]: 280.)

110-FOOT TUGS

Name	Visual Call Sign	Builder	Launched	Commissioned	Disposition
Calumet	WYT 86 (bn CG-61)	Charleston Navy Yard, SC	28 Sep 34	3 Dec 34	*Decomm* 29 Sep 67; *sold* 25 Nov 68
Hudson	WYT 87 (bn CG-62)	Portsmouth Navy Yard, NH	Oct 34	31 Oct 34	*Decomm* 11 Nov 68; *trans* to North Western College 8 Jul 70
Navesink	WYT 88 (bn CG-63)	Charleston Navy Yard, SC	28 Sep 34	5 Jan 35	*Decomm* 30 Oct 68; *sold* 21 May 70
Tuckahoe	WYT 89 (bn CG-64)	Charleston Navy Yard, SC	28 Sep 34	30 Jan 35	*Decomm* 14 Nov 68; donated to HEW 16 Apr 69

Cost
$236,000 each

Hull
Displacement (tons)   290 fl (1938 and 1945)
Length   110′6″ oa
Beam   24′ mb
Draft   12′6″ max (1945)

Machinery
Main Engines   1 General Electric motor connected to 2 General Electric generators driven by 2 McIntosh Seymour 6-cyl diesels
SHP   800
Propellers   Single

Performance
Max Speed   13.0 kts (1945)
Max Sustained   12.0 kts, 1,400 mi radius (1945)
Economic   10.0 kts, 1,500 mi radius (1938 and 1945)

Logistics
Diesel Fuel (95%)   3,800 gal
Complement   2 officers, 14 men (1938); 2 warrants, 14 men (1945)

Electronics (1945)
Detection Radar   *Hudson:* none; all others: SO-8
Sonar   *Tuckahoe:* WEA-2

Armament
1938   None
1945   2 20mm/80 (single); 2 dc tracks

Design

The design of the class proved so successful that the 3 subsequent classes were only slightly modified. In Jan 40 tests comparing the ice-breaking ability of the 110-foot tugs to the 165-foot (B) class cutters were conducted. The tugs proved to be far superior in breaking ability and maneuverability.

Calumet

1941–45 assigned to 5th District—stationed at Norfolk, VA; Sep 45 assigned to 12th District—stationed at San Francisco, CA.

Hudson

1941–43 assigned to the 3rd District—stationed at New York, NY; 1943–45 assigned to the 5th District—stationed at Baltimore, MD.

Navesink

1941–43 assigned to the 3rd District—stationed at New York, NY; 1943–45 assigned to the 5th District—stationed at Norfolk, VA.

Tuckahoe

1941–45 assigned to the GULFSEAFRON—stationed at New Orleans, LA; 14 May 42 rescued 9 survivors from the tanker *Portrero del Llamo;* 18 May 42 assisted in towing the torpedoed tanker *William C. McTarnahan.*

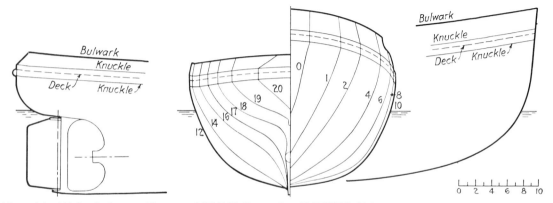

Lines of the 110-foot harbor tug. (Courtesy of SNAME, *Transactions* XLV [1937]: 98.)

The *Hudson* on 15 Aug 34. A diesel engine is being lowered into the tug.

120-FOOT CUTTER

Name	Visual Call Sign	Builder	Launched	Commissioned	Disposition
Manhattan	WYT 95 (bn CG-30)	Balboa Ships, Balboa, Canal Zone	15 Jun 18	15 Apr 21	*Decomm* 30 Jan 47; *sold* 28 Jul 47

Cost
 $220,465

Hull
 Displacement (tons)   406 fl (1938 and 1945)
 Length   120′3″ oa
 Beam   24′ mb
 Draft   11′9″ max (1938); 12′ max (1945)

Machinery
 Main Engines   1 triple-expansion steam
 Main Boilers   1 Babcock & Wilcox watertube
 SHP   600
 Propellers   Single

Performance
 Max Speed   10.0 kts (1945)

Cruising   9.0 kts, 1,000 mi radius (1945)
Economic   6.0 kts, 1,310 mi radius (1938 and 1945)

Logistics
 Fuel Oil (95%)   11,585 gal
 Complement   18 men (1938); 2 warrants, 17 men (1945)

Electronics (1945)
 Detection Radar   SO-8

Armament (1938)
 2 1-pdrs.

Design
 Steel hull.

Manhattan

1941–45 assigned to 3rd District—stationed at New York, NY.

The *Manhattan*, Dec 1918, in the Panama Canal Zone. (Courtesy of the Smithsonian Institution.)

92-FOOT TUG

Name	Visual Call Sign	Builder	Keel Laid	Launched	Commissioned	Disposition
Davey	WYT 81 (bn CG-19)	Pusey & Jones Corp., Wilmington, DE	27 Sep 07 (contracted)	14 Mar 08	14 Mar 08	*Decomm* 17 Jul 45

Cost
  $49,500

Hull
  Displacement   182 fl (1908)
  Length   92'6" oa
  Beam   19' mb
  Draft   10'2" max (1908)

Machinery
  Main Engines   Triple expansion
  Main Boilers   1 boiler
  SHP   275
  Propellers   Single

Performance
  Max Speed   10.5 kts (1908)
  Max Sustained   10.5 kts, 420 mi radius (1908)

Cruising   9.0 kts, 458 mi radius (1908)
Economic   8.0 kts, 420 mi radius (1945)

Logistics
  Fuel Oil (95%)   2,800 gal
  Complement   1 officer, 13 men (1908)

Electronics
  None

Armament
  None

Design
  Steel-hulled tug.

Davey

1941–45 assigned to the 8th District—stationed at New Orleans, LA.

The *Davey*, like many CG cutters of this era, was built by Pusey & Jones Corp., Wilmington, DE.

96-FOOT TUG

Name	Visual Call Sign	Builder	Keel Laid	Launched	Commissioned	Disposition
Winnisimmet	WYT 84 (bn CG-9)	Spedden Shipbuilding Co., Baltimore, MD	21 Oct 01 (contracted)	11 Oct 02	30 Jul 03	*Decomm* Oct 45; *sold* 22 Jul 46

Cost
  $49,000

Hull
  Displacement (tons)   178 fl (1945)
  Length   96'6" oa
  Beam   20'6" mb
  Draft   9' max (1945)

Machinery
  Main Engines   Reciprocating
  Main Boilers   1 Babcock & Wilcox watertube
  SHP   500
  Propellers   Single

Performance
  Max Speed   12.0 kts (1945)

Cruising   10.0 kts, 300 mi radius (1945)
Economic   8.0 kts, 680 mi radius (1945)

Logistics
  Fuel Oil (95%)   3,400 gal
  Complement   11 men (1945)

Electronics
  None

Armament
  None

Design
  Steel-hulled tug.

Winnisimmet

1941–45 assigned to the 5th District—stationed at Norfolk, VA.

The *Winnisimmet* in 1903. This harbor tug served on the Chesapeake Bay throughout her career.

110-FOOT TUG

Name	Visual Call Sign	Builder	Launched	Commissioned	Disposition
Golden Gate	WYT 94	Moran Brothers, Seattle, WA	3 Feb 96	17 Jun 97	*Decomm* 22 Nov 45; *sold* 8 Apr 47

Cost
  $80,000

Hull
  Displacement (tons) 250 fl (1945)
  Length   110' oa
  Beam   21' mb
  Draft   10'3" max (1945)

Machinery
  Main Engines   1 triple expansion
  Main Boilers   1 Babcock & Wilcox watertube
  SHP   500
  Propellers   Single

Performance
  Max Speed   11.0 kts (1897)
            10.0 kts (1945)
  Max Sustained   11.0 kts, 490 mi radius (1897)
  Cruising   9.0 kts, 320 mi radius (1945)
  Economic   8.0 kts, 535 mi radius (1897)
            8.0 kts, 400 mi radius (1945)

Logistics
  Fuel Oil (95%)   2,680 gal
  Complement   1 warrant, 21 men (1945)

Electronics
  None

Armament
  None

Design
  Steel construction.

Golden Gate

1941–45 assigned to 12th District—stationed at San Francisco, CA.

The *Golden Gate* as she appeared in 1897 for the Revenue Cutter Service. She served out her life (1897–1945) at San Francisco, CA.

95-FOOT TUG

Name	Visual Call Sign	Builder	Keel Laid	Launched	Commissioned	Disposition
Tioga (ex-*Calumet*)	WYT 74	David Bell, Buffalo, NY	27 Oct 92 (contracted)	Oct 94	18 Oct 94	*Decomm* 14 Oct 46; *sold* 22 Mar 47

Cost
  $38,500
Hull
  Displacement (tons)   190 fl (1945)
  Length   94'6" oa
  Beam   20'6" mb; 21'9" max
  Draft   9'6" max (1938 and 1945)
Machinery
  Main Engines   1 compound reciprocating
  Main Boilers   1 Babcock & Wilcox watertube
  SHP   NA
  Propellers   Single
Performance
  Max Speed   13.0 kts (1945)
  Cruising   11.0 kts, 225 mi radius (1945)

Economic   9.0 kts, 300 mi radius (1938 and 1945)
Logistics
  Fuel Oil (95%)   2,412 gal
  Complement   2 officers, 12 men (1938); 11 men (1945)
Electronics
  None
Armament (1938)
  None
Design
  Constructed with iron hull.

Tioga

1934 name changed from the *Calumet* to the *Tioga*; 1941–45 assigned to 5th District—stationed at Baltimore, MD.

88-FOOT TUG

Name	Visual Call Sign	Builder	Keel Laid	Commissioned	Disposition
Guthrie (ex-*James Guthrie*)	[WYT]	H. A. Ramsey Co., Baltimore, MD	18 Aug 81	13 May 82; *recomm* 8 Jul 95	*Decomm* 24 Oct 41; *sold* 24 Feb 42

Cost
  $17,900
Hull
  Displacement (tons)   149 fl (1895)
  Length   88' oa
  Beam   17'6" mb
  Draft   9' max (1895)
Machinery
  Main Engines   Steam
  SHP   300
  Propellers   Single
Performance
  Max Sustained   10.0 kts, 631 mi radius (1895)
  Cruising   8.0 kts, 850 mi radius (1895)
Logistics
  Coal (95%)   80 tons
  Complement   1 warrant, 10 men (1895)
Electronics
  None
Armament
  None
Design
  The *Guthrie* had an iron hull and wooden superstructure. On 25 Aug 93 she was ordered to be rebuilt by Spedden Co.; she recommissioned 8 Jul 95.

Guthrie

1939–41 stationed at Portland, ME.

The *Guthrie*, Jan 1928. Many of the older tugs were replaced during the war by new construction, such as the CG 64300 series.

67-FOOT TUG

Name	Visual Call Sign	Builder	Launched	Commissioned	Disposition
Guard	[WYT] (bn CG-24)	Mare Island Navy Shipyard, CA	20 Oct 13	9 Dec 13	*Decomm* and *sold* 17 Feb 43

Cost
  NA

Hull
  Displacement (tons)   52 fl
  Length   67'7" oa
  Beam   12'6"
  Draft   6'3" max

Machinery
  Main Engines   1 diesel
  Propellers   Single

Performance
  Max Speed   10.0 kts (1938)
  Economic   7.0 kts, 210 mi radius (1938)

Logistics
  Fuel (95%)   Oil
  Complement   2 officers, 8 men (1938)

Electronics
  None

Armament
  None

Design
  Constructed of wood.

Guard

1941–43 assigned to 13th District—stationed at Seattle, WA.

The *Guard*, prior to WW I. She served at Seattle, WA, until 1943, when she was decommissioned. Small tugs like her were used for boarding, harbor patrol, and assistance duties.

Aids-to-Navigation Types (WAGL, WARC, WAL)

In 1939 the Coast Guard acquired its buoy tender and lightship fleets when the USLHS was amalgamated into the service. For decades the USLHS had been constructing mostly one-of-a-kind tenders to meet the local needs of a district. In 1939, the USLHS was preparing a new, more versatile buoy tender design. This ship, the 180-footer, was to have a limited open-ocean, search-and-rescue capability as well as the traits common to the type. To these qualities in the design the Coast Guard added ice-breaking. The fact that this class was used for icebreaking, weather patrol, fire fighting, logistic support for LORAN construction and supply, and general A/N duty under-scores the success of the design. Thirty-nine units were constructed. Older tenders, which these new 180-footers were scheduled to replace, were retained until the close of the war. During World War II, all tenders were grouped together, regardless of whether they were riverine or coastal types. The few wartime emergency acquisitions were Great Lakes ships acquired because of their ice-breaking qualities, something in short supply early in the war.

Lightships substituted for lighthouses when the latter could not be con-structed. With the advent of war, most were made guardships, a few remained on station as lightships, and an isolated one or two was used for patrol.

WAGL—LIGHTHOUSE TENDERS

114-FOOT TENDER

Name	Visual Call Sign	Builder	Keel Laid	Launched	Commissioned	Disposition
Foxglove	WAGL 285 (bn CG-143)	Dubuque Boat & Boiler Works, Dubuque, IA	9 Nov 44	19 Jul 45	1 Oct 45	*Decomm* 8 Jul 77

Cost
  $191,595

Hull
  Displacement (tons) 385 fl (1945)
  Length 114' oa
  Beam 26' mb; 30' max
  Draft 6' max (1945)

Machinery
  Main Engines 3 Fairbanks Morse diesels
  BHP 600
  Propellers Triple

Performance
  Max Speed 9.0 kts (1945)
  Max Sustained 8.0 kts, 1,900 mi radius (1945)
  Economic 7.5 kts, 2,100 mi radius (1945)

Logistics
  Diesel Fuel (95%) 5,460 gal

Complement 1 officer, 21 men (1945)

Deck Gear
  Boom Capacity 3 tons
  Hoist Power Air

Electronics
  None

Armament
  None

Design
  Designed by the builder, the river tender *Foxglove* was appropriated under 17X0908 and contracted on 23 Jun 44.

Foxglove

Completed too late to serve in WW II; late 1945 assigned to 2nd District—stationed at St. Louis, MO.

The *Foxglove,* 18 Oct 45, commissioned too late to see service in WW II. (Courtesy of the National Archives.)

114-FOOT TENDER

Name	Visual Call Sign	Builder	Keel Laid	Launched	Commissioned	Disposition
Sumac	WAGL 311 (bn CG-179)	Peterson & Haecker, Ltd., Blair, NB	13 Mar 44	14 Oct 44	11 Nov 44	Active

Cost
  $356,372

Hull
  Displacement (tons)   350 fl (1944)
  Length   114'6" oa
  Beam   30'6" max
  Draft   9' max (1944)

Machinery
  Main Engines   3 Fairbanks Morse diesels
  BHP   960
  Propellers   Triple

Performance
  Max Speed   11.3 kts (1945)
  Max Sustained   11.3 kts, 3,320 mi radius (1945)
  Economic   9.0 kts, 5,350 mi radius (1945)

Logistics
  Diesel Fuel (95%)   26,260 gal
  Complement   1 officer, 23 men (1945)

Electronics
  None

Armament
  None

Design
  This 114-foot river tender was designed by A. M. Deering, Chicago, IL. She was appropriated under 17X0908 and contracted on 6 Sep 43.

Sumac

1944–45 assigned to 9th District—stationed at Burlington, IA, and Owensboro, KY; general A/N over 641 miles of Ohio River—Dam 44 to Cairo, IL, Cumberland and Tennessee rivers to Kentucky River.

The *Sumac,* 1 Mar 49, on the Ohio River.

73-FOOT TENDERS

Name	Visual Call Sign	Builder	Keel Laid	Launched	Commissioned	Disposition
Clematis	WAGL 286 (bn CG-125)	Peterson & Haecker, Ltd., Blair, NB	20 Jul 43	15 May 44	28 Jul 44	*Decomm* 17 Oct 76; *trans* TVA Feb 77
Shadbush	WAGL 287 (bn CG-124)	Peterson & Haecker, Ltd., Blair, NB	20 Jul 43	15 May 44	28 Jul 44	*Decomm* 24 Feb 76; *sold* Oct 76

Cost
$185,450 each (hull & machinery)

Hull
Displacement (tons)   80 fl (1945)
Length   73′6″ oa
Beam   18′10″ max
Draft   3′6″ max (1945)

Machinery
Main Engines   2 Buda diesels
BHP   150
Propellers   Twin

Performance
Max Speed   9.6 kts (1945)
Economic   6.4 kts, 3,300 mi radius (1945)

Logistics
Diesel Fuel (95%)   2,460 gal
Complement   0 officers, 8 men (1945)

Deck Gear
Boom Capacity   1.5 tons
Hoist Power   Electricity

Electronics
None

Armament
None

Design
Designed by Coast Guard with detail drawings by A. M. Deering, Chicago, IL, the *Clematis* and *Shadbush* were appropriated under 17X0908 and contracted on 24 Mar 43.

Clematis

1944–45 assigned to 8th District—stationed at Galveston, TX.

Shadbush

1944–45 assigned to 8th District—stationed at Mobile, AL.

The *Clematis* and the *Shadbush* (*right to left*), 18 Jul 44, at Blair, NB.

EMERGENCY ACQUISITION

Name	Visual Call Sign	Builder	Commissioned	Disposition
Franklin D. Roosevelt (ex-*Huck Finn*)	[WAGL]	Midland Barge Co., Midland, PA	1933 (Mercantile); 1944 (CG)	*Decomm* 3 Oct 44

Cost
  NA
Hull
  Tonnage   495 gross (1939); 603 registered (1939)
  Length   160' oa
  Beam   40' max
  Draft   8' max (1939)
Machinery
  Main Engines   2 8-cyl diesel engines
Performance
  NA
Logistics
  NA

Electronics
  Probably none
Armament
  NA
Design
  She was designed as a towboat and chartered from the Inland Waterways Corp. (Federal Barge Lines).

Franklin D. Roosevelt

1944 used for ice-breaking on the Great Lakes.

EMERGENCY ACQUISITION

Name	Visual Call Sign	Builder	Launched	Commissioned	Disposition
Tom Sawyer	[WAGL]	Midland, PA	1933	18 Dec 43 (CG)	*Ret* to owner 3 Apr 44

Cost
  Chartered
Hull
  Tonnage   603 gross, 495 net
  Length   148'8" oa
  Beam   40' max
Machinery
  Main Engines   Diesel
  BHP   1,180
Logistics
  Complement   20 men (1941, merchant service)

Electronics
  None
Armament
  None
Design
  Designed as a commercial vessel.

Tom Sawyer

1943–44 assigned to 9th District—stationed at St. Louis, MO; chartered and used for ice-breaking.

80-FOOT TENDER

Name	Visual Call Sign	Builder	Keel Laid	Launched	Commissioned	Disposition
Lantana	WAGL 310 (bn CG-144)	Peterson & Haecker Ltd., Blair, NB	21 Mar 43	18 Oct 43	6 Nov 43	Active

Cost
  $201,143 (hull & machinery)
Hull
  Displacement (tons)   273 fl (1943)
  Length   80' oa
  Beam   30' max
  Draft   6' max (1943)

Machinery
  Main Engines   3 Murphy diesels
  BHP   495
  Propellers   Triple
Performance
  Max Speed   9.0 kts (1943)
Logistics
  Diesel Fuel (95%)   12,424 gal

Complement   1 officer, 16 men (1945)

Electronics
  None

Armament
  None

Design
  The river tender *Lantana* was designed by A. M. Deering, Chicago, IL. She was

designed to accommodate an ice plow. The *Lantana* was contracted on 12 Jan 43 and appropriated under 17X0908.

Lantana

Late 1943–May 45 assigned to 9th District—stationed at Cape Girardeau, MO, and St. Louis, MO; general A/N duty for 203 miles on Mississippi River, Alton to Cairo, IL; May 45 to close of WW II stationed at Keokuk, IA.

The *Lantana* pushing a CG barge. Ships and craft constructed for the CG were each given a building number, as were barges and ice plows. Ships and craft purchased, borrowed, or chartered were not given one.

EMERGENCY ACQUISITION

Name	Visual Call Sign	Builder	Launched	Commissioned	Disposition
Blackrock (ex-*The Boys*)	WAGL 367	Morehead City, NC	1924	17 Jun 43 (CG); 23 Feb 45 (*recomm* in CG)	*Decomm* 31 Mar 44; *decomm* 24 Aug 54; *sold* 2 Nov 55

Cost
  Acquisition $56,079; conversion $86,698

Hull
  Displacement (tons)   230 fl (1942); 190 light (1942)
  Length   114′ oa; 112′ bp
  Beam   19′6″ mb
  Draft   8′ max (1942)

Machinery
  Main Engines   1 Atlas diesel
  BHP   300
  Propellers   Single

Performance
  Max Speed   12.0 kts, 2,948 mi radius (1942)
  Cruising   10.0 kts, 3,240 mi radius (1942)

Logistics
  Diesel Fuel (95%)   3,900 gal
  Complement   1 warrant, 14 men (1944)

Electronics
  None

Armament
  None

Design
  Constructed of wood, the *Blackrock* was a former fishing craft.

Blackrock

1943–44 assigned to CARIBSEAFRON—stationed at San Juan, PR, and used for general A/N duty; late 1944–45 assigned to 7th District—stationed at Portsmouth, VA.

The *Blackrock* during WW II. Her high freeboard and lack of a well deck indicate that she was not constructed as a buoy tender.

EMERGENCY ACQUISITION

Name	Visual Call Sign	Builder	Launched	Commissioned	Disposition
Jonquil (ex-*Lucinda Clark*)	WAGL 179	Harbor Point, MO	1937	6 Jan 43 (CG)	*Decomm* and *ret* to owner 1 Dec 43

Cost
  $75,000 (appraised value); conversion $3,974

Hull
  Tonnage   107 gross; 84 net (1941)
  Length   76′ oa; 73′ bp
  Beam   22′7″ mb
  Draft   4′8″ max (1943)

Machinery
  Main Engines   Semi-diesel
  BHP   360
  Propellers   Twin

Electronics
  None

Armament
  None

Design
  Built as a tow boat and leased by the Coast Guard.

Jonquil

1943 assigned to 9th District—stationed at St. Louis, MO, and Peoria, IL; used as an auxiliary icebreaker.

EMERGENCY ACQUISITION (162-FOOT CLASS)

Name	Visual Call Sign	Builder	Launched	Commissioned	Disposition
Almond (ex-*La Salle*)	WAGL 177	Toledo Shipbuilding Co., Toledo, OH	1922	11 Dec 42 (CG)	*Decomm* 29 Sep 45; *sold* 31 Jul 46
Arrowwood (ex-*Cadillac*)	WAGL 176	Great Lakes Engineering Works, River Rouge, MI	1928	15 Dec 42 (CG)	*Decomm* 29 Sep 45; *sold* 11 Jul 46

Cost
    Almond: acquisition $65,000; conversion $234,416
    Arrowwood: acquisition $70,000; conversion $234,416

Hull
Displacement (tons)	677 fl (1945)
Tonnage	636 gross (1941); 404 net (1941)
Length	161′10″ oa
Beam	56′ mb
Draft	13′6″ max (1945)

Machinery
Main Engines	1 compound reciprocating steam
Main Boilers	*Almond:* 2 Marine fire tube
	Arrowwood: 1 Marine fire tube
SHP	*Almond* 1,700; *Arrowwood* 1,500
Propellers	Single

Performance
Max Speed	10.0 kts (1945)
Max Sustained	9.0 kts, 1,220 mi radius (1945)
Economic	8.0 kts, 1,320 mi radius (1945)

Logistics
Coal	150 tons
Complement	1 officer, 3 warrants, 35 men (1942)

Electronics (1945)
Detection Radar	SO-1

Armament
    None

Design
    Former ferryboats, they were acquired because of their ice-breaking capabilities. They were converted to buoy tenders and fitted with fire-fighting apparatus by the Toledo Shipbuilding Co., Toledo, OH.

Almond

1942–45 assigned to 9th District—stationed at Ignace, MI, Chicago, IL, and Grand Haven, MI, and used for ice-breaking and general A/N duty.

Arrowwood

1942–45 assigned to 9th District—stationed at Cleveland, OH, and used for ice-breaking and general A/N duty.

The *Almond*, 24 Oct 42, being rebuilt. The *Almond* and *Arrowwood* were acquired because of their ice-breaking capabilities. Prior to the commissioning of the 180s, the CG was very short of ice-breaking cutters for the Great Lakes and Mississippi River systems. (Courtesy of the Smithsonian Institution.)

100-FOOT TENDERS (*COSMOS* TENDERS, *BLUEBELL* TENDERS)

Name	Visual Call Sign	Builder	Keel Laid	Launched	Commissioned	Disposition
Barberry	WAGL 294 (bn CG-101)	Dubuque Boat & Boiler Works, Dubuque, IA	20 Apr 42	14 Nov 42	3 Jan 43	*Decomm* 1 Sep 70; *donated* 23 Feb 71
Bluebell	WAGL 313 (bn CG-186)	Birchfield Boiler, Inc., Tacoma, WA	20 Mar 44	28 Sep 44	24 Mar 45	Active
Brier	WAGL 299 (bn CG-123)	Dubuque Boat & Boiler Works, Dubuque, IA	5 Aug 42	6 May 43	2 Jul 43	*Decomm* 9 Nov 67; *trans* to USN 10 Mar 68
Cosmos	WAGL 293 (bn CG-100)	Dubuque Boat & Boiler Works, Dubuque, IA	19 Feb 42	11 Nov 42	5 Dec 42	Active
Primrose	WAGL 316 (bn CG-180)	Dubuque Boat & Boiler Works, Dubuque, IA	26 Nov 43	18 Aug 44	23 Oct 44	Active
Rambler	WAGL 298 (bn CG-122)	Dubuque Boat & Boiler Works, Dubuque, IA	7 Dec 42	6 May 43	26 May 43	Active
Smilax	WAGL 315 (bn CG-181)	Dubuque Boat & Boiler Works, Dubuque, IA	26 Nov 43	18 Aug 44	1 Nov 44	Active
Verbena	WAGL 317 (bn CG-185)	Dubuque Boat & Boiler Works, Dubuque, IA	20 Mar 44	2 Oct 44	13 Nov 44	*Decomm* 1 Sep 77; *sold* Feb 78

Cost
  See Appropriations remarks

Hull
  Displacement (tons)   178 fl (1942)
  Length   100' oa
  Beam   24' mb
  Draft   5' max (1942)

Machinery
  Main Engines   2 Murphy 6-cyl diesels
  BHP   330
  Propellers   Twin

Performance
  Max Sustained   10.0 kts, 1,600 mi radius (1945)
  Cruising   8.0 kts, 2,400 mi radius (1945)
  Economic   6.5 kts, 3,000 mi radius (1945)

Logistics
  Diesel Fuel (95%)   4,000 gal
  Complement   0 officers, 16 men (1945)

Deck Gear
  Boom Capacity   5 tons
  Hoist Power   Air

Electronics
  None

Armament
  None

Design
  These 100-foot bay and sound tenders were designed by the Coast Guard with detail drawings by Dubuque Boat & Boiler Works, Dubuque, IA.

Appropriations

	Appropriations	Contract	Costs (hull & machinery)
Barberry	17-20X1223	17 Jan 42	$172,557
Bluebell	17X0908	22 Feb 44	173,399
Brier	17X0908	22 Mar 42	175,001
Cosmos	17-20X1223	17 Dec 41	172,260
Primrose	17X0908	7 Sep 43	194,230
Rambler	17X0908	23 Mar 42	175,001
Smilax	17X0908	7 Sep 43	194,238
Verbena	17X0908	1 Feb 44	186,287

Barberry

1943–45 assigned to 5th District—stationed at Morehead City, NC, and used for A/N duty.

Bluebell

1945 assigned to 13th District—stationed at Vancouver, WA, and used for A/N duty.

Brier

1943–45 assigned to 6th District—stationed at Charleston, SC, and used for A/N duty.

Cosmos

1942–45 assigned to 7th District—stationed at St. Petersburg, FL, and used for A/N duty.

Primrose

1944–45 assigned to 6th District—stationed at Charleston, SC, and used for A/N duty.

Rambler

1943–45 assigned to 8th District—stationed at New Orleans, LA (1943–44) and Mobile, AL (1944–45), and used for A/N duty.

Smilax

1944–45 assigned to 7th District—stationed at Ft. Pierce, FL, and used for A/N duty.

Verbena

1944–45 assigned to 5th District—stationed at Coinjock, NC, and used for A/N duty.

The *Smilax*, 18 Aug 44, being launched at Dubuque, IA. All units of this class served on coastal rivers. (Courtesy of the Smithsonian Institution.)

EMERGENCY ACQUISITION

Name	Visual Call Sign	Builder	Launched	Commissioned	Disposition
Chaparral (ex-*Halcyon*)	WAGL 178	Great Lakes Engineering Works, River Rouge, MI	1925	4 Dec 42 (CG)	*Decomm* 8 Feb 46

Cost
  Acquisition $55,000; conversion $234,416

Hull
  Tonnage   405 gross (1941); 273 net (1941)
  Length   161′ oa
  Beam   45′ max
  Draft   14′4″ max (1942)

Machinery
  Main Engines   1 triple-expansion steam
  Main Boilers   1 Marine fire tube
  SHP   800
  Propellers   Single

Performance
  Max Speed   9.0 kts (1945)

Logistics
  Fuel Oil (95%) Coal

Complement   14 men (commercial 1941); 2 officers, 1 warrant, 39 men (1945)

Electronics (1945)
  Detection Radar SO-1

Armament
  None

Design
  The *Chaparral* was the commercial ferryboat *Halcyon* and was acquired by CG on 19 Oct 42 because of her ice-breaking capabilities. She was converted to a buoy tender by the Toledo Shipbuilding Co., Toledo, OH.

Chaparral

1942–45 assigned to 9th District—stationed at Sault Ste. Marie, MI, and used as an auxiliary icebreaker.

115-FOOT TENDER

Name	Visual Call Sign	Builder	Keel Laid	Launched	Commissioned	Disposition
Fern	WAGL 304 (bn CG-134)	Peterson & Haecker Ltd., Blair, NB	1 Jul 42	6 Nov 42	19 Nov 42	*Decomm* 1 Sep 71; *sold* 19 Jun 72
Ice plow	(bn CG-136)	Peterson & Haecker Ltd., Blair, NB	Jun 42	23 Oct 42	7 Nov 42	*Sold* 19 Jun 72

Cost
  See Design remarks

Hull
  Displacement (tons)   350 fl (1942)
  Length   115' oa
  Beam   31' max
  Draft   8' max (1942)

Machinery
  Main Engines   3 Fairbanks Morse diesels
  BHP   960
  Propellers   Triple

Performance
  Max Speed   10.0 kts (1945)
  Max Sustained   9.0 kts, 3,100 mi radius (1945)
  Economic   4.0 kts, 3,500 mi radius (1945)

Logistics
  Diesel Fuel (95%)   16,940 gal
  Complement   1 officer, 23 men (1945)

Electronics
  None

Armament
  None

Design
  In May 1942 Coast Guard engineering was ordered to outline a contract for an ice-breaking river tender to be in service on the upper Mississippi complex by the end of the year. The *Fern*'s final design and the design of her ice plow were executed by Peterson & Haecker, Ltd., Blair, NB. The *Fern* was contracted within two weeks and delivered in November before the freeze-up. She was patterned on a conventional river towboat. Ice-breaking was achieved by means of a detachable ''Amsterdam'' type ice plow.

Appropriations

	Appropriations	Contract	Costs (hull & machinery)
Fern	17X0908	26 May 42	$256,369
Ice plow	17X0908	26 May 42	Total including plow

Fern
1942–45 assigned to 9th District—stationed at Peoria, IL, and Burlington, IA, and used for A/N for 291 miles on Mississippi River—Dubuque to Keokuk, IA, and Hennepin Canal, IL.

The *Fern* fitted with an ice plow, 18 Feb 43. Most river tenders retained their traditional black hulls, white superstructure, buff stack, and black funnel caps. They were not painted gray. The *Fern* was a ''pusher.'' Large stacks of buoy and maintenance equipment were transported on a barge. The tender provided propulsion and power to the barge's auxiliary.

230-FOOT TENDER

Name	Visual Call Sign	Builder	Keel Laid	Launched	Commissioned	Disposition
Storis (ex-*Eskimo*)	WAGL 38 (bn CG-82)	Toledo Shipbuilding Co., Toledo, Ohio	14 Jul 41	4 Apr 42	30 Sep 42	Active

Cost
$2,072,889 (hull & machinery)

Hull
Displacement (tons)   1,715 fl 1945)
Length   230' oa
Beam   43'2" m)
Draft   15' ma) (1945)
Tons per Immersed   17.7
Inch

Machinery
Main Engines   1 electric motor driven by generators driven by 3 Cooper-Bessemer-type GN-8, 8-cyl diesels
BHP   1,800
Propellers   Singl

Performance
Max Speed   13.0 kts, 10,900 mi radius (1945)
Max Sustained   12.5 kts, 11,300 mi radius (1945)
Cruising   10.0 kts, 15,500 mi radius (1945)
Economic   8.0 kts, 21,300 mi radius (1945)

Logistics
Diesel Fuel   108,430 gal
Complement   17 officers, 131 men (1945)

Deck Gear
Boom Capacity   20 tons

Hoist Power   Electricity
Aircraft (1945)
1 J2F
Electronics
Detection Radar   Bk (1943); SL (1945)
Sonar   QCL-2 (1945)
Armament (1945)
2 3"/50 (single); 4 20mm/80 (single); 2 dc tracks; 4 Y-guns; 2 Mousetraps

Design
The *Storis* was designed by the U.S. Coast Guard, with detail drawings by Toledo Shipbuilding Company, to be a supply ship for the Greenland area with a degree of ice-breaking capability. Contract was let 26 Jan 41 under appropriation 17-20X1222. Her design closely parallels the smaller 180-foot tenders of 1942–44. She was to be named the *Eskimo*. However, during her construction the State Department, concerned that the natives of Greenland might find the name offensive, requested that another name be selected. The *Storis* was the first tender fitted with a double-top lift boom.

Storis

1942–45 assigned to CINCLANT (DESLANT)—stationed at Boston, MA, and used extensively in Greenland waters; Aug 43 escorted convoy to Frobisher Bay, Canadian Arctic; 18 Dec 43 searched for survivors of the USAT *Nevada*; 7 Jul–31 Oct 44 searched for German trawlers off Northeast Greenland.

The *Storis*, 24 Sep 45, at Skjoldunden, Greenland. This tender was specifically designed to operate in northern waters. She was used for escort, patrol, and aids to navigation. Since WW II she has been a WAG (miscellaneous auxiliary), a WAGB (icebreaker), a WAGL (buoy tender), and a WMEC (medium-endurance cutter).

180-FOOT TENDERS, *IRIS* CLASS (180[C] CLASS)

Name	Visual Call Sign	Builder	Keel Laid	Launched	Commissioned	Disposition
Acacia (ex-*Thistle*)	WAGL 406 (bn CG-177)	Zenith Dredge Co., Duluth, MN	16 Jan 44	7 Apr 44	1 Sep 44	Active
Basswood	WAGL 388 (bn CG-149)	Marine Iron & Shipbuilding Corp., Duluth, MN	21 Mar 43	20 May 43	12 Jan 44	Active
Bittersweet	WAGL 389 (bn CG-172)	Zenith Dredge Co., Duluth, MN	16 Sep 43	11 Nov 43	11 May 44	Active
Blackhaw	WAGL 390 (bn CG-150)	Marine Iron & Shipbuilding Corp., Duluth, MN	16 Apr 43	18 Jun 43	17 Feb 44	Active
Blackthorn	WAGL 391 (bn CG-157)	Marine Iron & Shipbuilding Corp., Duluth, MN	21 May 43	20 Jul 43	27 Mar 44	Sank 28 Jan 80
Bramble	WAGL 392 (bn CG-171)	Zenith Dredge Co., Duluth, MN	2 Aug 43	23 Oct 43	22 Apr 44	Active
Firebush	WAGL 393 (bn CG-175)	Zenith Dredge Co., Duluth, MN	12 Nov 43	3 Feb 44	20 Jul 44	Active
Hornbeam	WAGL 394 (bn CG-152)	Marine Iron & Shipbuilding Corp., Duluth, MN	19 Jun 43	14 Aug 43	14 Apr 44	Active
Iris	WAGL 395 (bn CG-176)	Zenith Dredge Co., Duluth, MN	10 Dec 43	18 May 44	11 Aug 44	Active
Mallow	WAGL 396 (bn CG-173)	Zenith Dredge Co., Duluth, MN	10 Oct 43	9 Dec 43	6 Jun 44	Active
Mariposa	WAGL 397 (bn CG-174)	Zenith Dredge Co., Duluth, MN	25 Oct 43	14 Jan 44	1 Jul 44	Active
Redbud	WAGL 398 (bn CG-153)	Marine Iron & Shipbuilding Corp., Duluth, MN	21 Jul 43	11 Sep 43	2 May 44	*Trans* to Philippines 1 Mar 72
Sagebrush	WAGL 399 (bn CG-170)	Zenith Dredge Co., Duluth, MN	15 Jul 43	30 Sep 43	1 Apr 44	Active
Salvia	WAGL 400 (bn CG-169)	Zenith Dredge Co., Duluth, MN	24 Jun 43	15 Sep 43	19 Feb 44	Active
Sassafras	WAGL 401 (bn CG-154)	Marine Iron & Shipbuilding Corp., Duluth, MN	16 Aug 43	5 Oct 43	23 May 44	Active
Sedge	WAGL 402 (bn CG-166)	Marine Iron & Shipbuilding Corp., Duluth, MN	6 Oct 43	27 Nov 43	5 Jul 44	Active
Spar	WAGL 403 (bn CG-165)	Marine Iron & Shipbuilding Corp., Duluth, MN	13 Sep 43	2 Nov 43	12 Jun 44	Active
Sundew	WAGL 404 (bn CG-168)	Marine Iron & Shipbuilding Corp., Duluth, MN	29 Nov 43	8 Feb 44	24 Aug 44	Active
Sweetbrier	WAGL 405 (bn CG-167)	Marine Iron & Shipbuilding Corp., Duluth, MN	3 Nov 43	30 Dec 43	26 Jul 44	Active
Woodrush	WAGL 407 (bn CG-178)	Zenith Dredge Co., Duluth, MN	4 Feb 44	28 Apr 44	22 Sep 44	Active

Cost
  See Appropriations remarks
Hull
  Displacement (tons)   935 fl (1945)
  Length   180′ oa
  Beam   37′ mb
  Draft   12′ max (1945)
  Tons per Immersed   10.4
    Inch
Machinery
  Main Engines   1 electric motor connected to 2 Westinghouse generators driven by 2 Cooper-Bessemer diesels
  SHP   1,200
  Propellers   Single
Performance
  Max Sustained   13.0 kts, 8,000 mi radius (1945)

Cruising   12.0 kts, 12,000 mi radius (1945)
Economic   8.3 kts, 17,000 mi radius (1945)
Logistics
  Diesel Fuel   29,335 gal
  Complement   6 officers, 74 men (1945)
Deck Gear
  Boom Capacity 20 tons
  Hoist Power   Electricity
Electronics (1945)
  Detection Radar *Basswood:* SL-2; all others: SL-1
  Sonar   *Sundew:* QBE-3; *Hornbeam:* QCU and WEA-2; *Bramble:* WEA; *Acacia, Mallow, Redbud, Sweetbrier, Woodrush:* QCU; *Firebush, Iris, Mariposa, Salvia, Sedge, Spar:* QBE-3A; all others: WEA-2
Armament (1945)
  1 3″/50 (single); 4 20mm/80 (single); 2 dc tracks; 2 Mousetraps

Design

The preliminary design for the third set of 180-foot coastwise tenders was prepared by the Coast Guard, and the final design was prepared by Marine Iron & Shipbuilding Corp., Duluth, MN. *See* 180-foot tenders, *Cactus* class (180[A] class) for additional details.

Appropriations

	Appropriations	Contract	Cost (hull & machinery)
Acacia	17X0908	2 Mar 43	$927,156
Basswood	17X0908	2 Mar 43	896,402
Bittersweet	17X0908	2 Mar 43	926,769
Blackhaw	17X0908	2 Mar 43	871,771
Blackthorn	17X0908	2 Mar 43	876,403
Bramble	17X0908	2 Mar 43	925,464
Firebush	17X0908	2 Mar 43	926,446
Hornbeam	17X0908	2 Mar 43	864,296
Iris	17X0908	2 Mar 43	926,446
Mallow	17X0908	2 Mar 43	926,926
Mariposa	17X0908	2 Mar 43	926,446
Redbud	17X0908	2 Mar 43	926,926
Sagebrush	17X0908	2 Mar 43	925,134
Salvia	17X0908	2 Mar 43	923,995
Sassafras	17X0908	2 Mar 43	864,032
Sedge	17X0908	2 Mar 43	865,411
Spar	17X0908	2 Mar 43	865,941
Sundew	17X0908	2 Mar 43	861,589
Sweetbrier	17X0908	2 Mar 43	865,531
Woodrush	17X0908	2 Mar 43	926,156

Acacia

15 Mar 44 name changed from the *Thistle* to the *Acacia* "due to an Army hospital ship now in active service having been named THISTLE"; 10 Aug 44 general A/N duty 9th District; 5 Sep 44 stationed at Detroit, MI.

Basswood

Mar–Apr 44 general A/N and ice-breaking on Great Lakes; 1944–45 assigned to 14th District—stationed at Pearl Harbor, HI, and used for general A/N duty.

Bittersweet

1944–45 assigned to 17th District—stationed at Ketchikan, AK, and used for general A/N duty; 15 Jan 45 rescued 6 survivors from YP 73; 19 Mar 45 assisted in rescue of survivors of an Army C-47; Aug 45 escorted Soviet warships in the Bering Sea.

Blackhaw

Mar–Apr 44 general A/N and ice-breaking on Great Lakes; 1944–45 assigned to 6th District—stationed at Charleston, SC, and used for general A/N duty.

Blackthorn

Mar–Apr 44 general A/N and ice-breaking on Great Lakes; 1944–45 assigned to 11th District—stationed at San Pedro, CA, and used for general A/N duty; 28 Jan 80 sank in a collision with the SS *Capricorn* in Tampa Bay—23 men lost.

Bramble

Apr–mid 44 served on Great Lakes for training and ice-breaking; early 45 assigned to 11th District—stationed at San Pedro, CA, and used for general A/N duty; Mar 45 transferred to Juneau, AK.

Firebush

1944–45 assigned to 3rd District—stationed at Staten Island, NY, and used for general A/N duty.

Hornbeam

Mar–Apr 44 general A/N and ice-breaking on Great Lakes; Jul 44–1945 assigned to 1st District—stationed at Woods Hole, MA, and used for A/N duty; 1 Jan 45 assisted the cutter *Nemesis*, following her collision with the SS *Felipe de Neve*.

Iris

1944–45 assigned to 8th District—stationed at Galveston, TX, and used for general A/N duty.

Mallow

1944–45 assigned to 12th District—stationed at San Francisco, CA, and used for general A/N duty.

Mariposa

1944–45 assigned to 3rd District—stationed at Staten Island, NY, and used for general A/N duty.

Redbud

1944–45 assigned to 7th District—stationed at Miami, FL, and used for general A/N duty.

Sagebrush

Mar–Apr 44 general A/N and ice-breaking on Great Lakes; May 44–1945 assigned to the 7th District—stationed at San Juan, PR, and used for general A/N duty.

Salvia

Mar–Apr 44 general A/N and ice-breaking on Great Lakes; May 44–1945 assigned to 5th District—stationed at Portsmouth, VA, and used for general A/N duty.

Sassafras

1944–45 general A/N duty in Western Pacific.

Sedge

1944–45 served in Pacific theater—stationed at Guam, Okinawa, and Shanghai.

Spar

1944–45 assigned to 1st District—stationed at Woods Hole, MA, and used for general A/N duty.

Sundew

1944–45 assigned to 9th District—stationed at Manitowoc, WI, and Milwaukee, WI, and used for general A/N duty.

Sweetbrier

1944 assigned to 12th District for general A/N duty; 1944–45 served in South Pacific; 2 Apr 45 freed grounded LST 846; May 45 under numerous air attacks

at Ie Shima, Ryukyu Islands; Jun 45 refloated YP 41 at Buckner Bay, Okinawa; mid–45 salvaged screw and shaft of the USS *Pennsylvania* from Buckner Bay.

Woodrush

1944–45 assigned to 9th District—stationed at Duluth, MN, and used for general A/N duty.

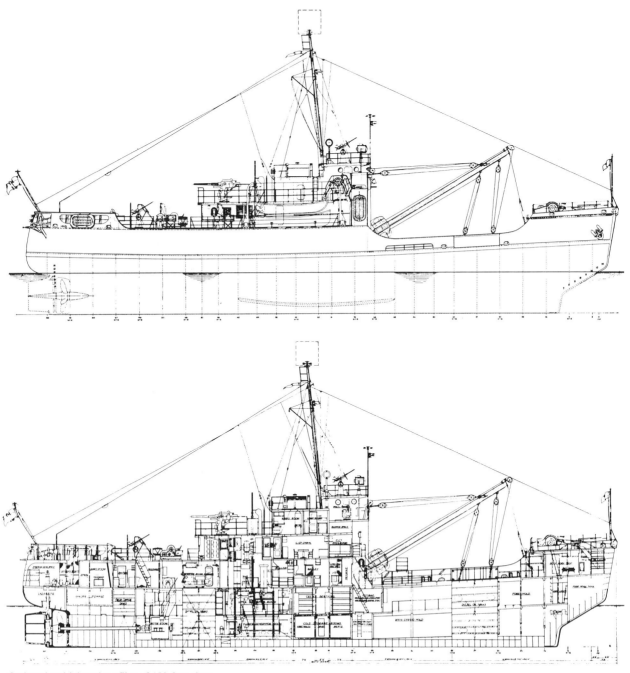

Outboard and inboard profiles of 180-foot class.

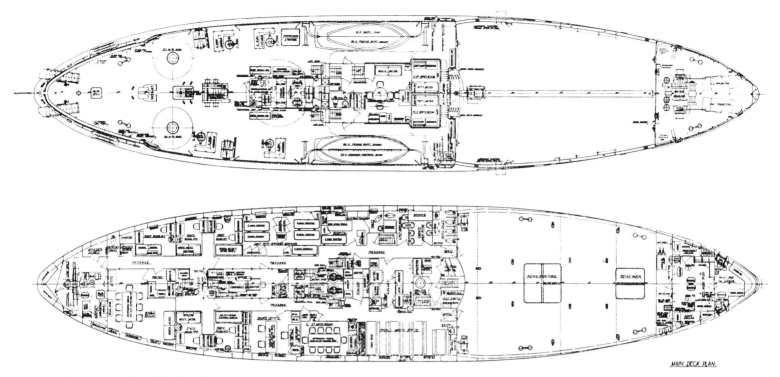

Outboard and inboard profiles of 180-foot class.

The *Basswood*, 12 May 44, in the Straits of Mackinac. The 180s proved to be very good, light icebreakers. If a 180 commissioned during the winter months, she would usually break ice on the Lakes until she could work her way to salt water. (Courtesy of the National Archives.)

The *Sundew*, 8 Jan 45, on Lake Michigan. The 180-foot class was more versatile than previous tender designs. These cutters could break ice and perform search-and-rescue missions, which cutters of previous tender classes could not do.

180-FOOT TENDERS, *MESQUITE* CLASS (180[B] CLASS)

Name	Visual Call Sign	Builder	Keel Laid	Launched	Commissioned	Disposition
Buttonwood	WAGL 306 (bn CG-139)	Marine Iron & Shipbuilding Corp., Duluth, MN	5 Oct 42	30 Nov 42	24 Sep 43	Active
Ironwood	WAGL 297 (bn CG-104)	Coast Guard Yard, Curtis Bay, MD	2 Nov 42	16 Mar 43	4 Aug 43	Active
Mesquite	WAGL 305 (bn CG-138)	Marine Iron & Shipbuilding Corp., Duluth, MN	20 Aug 42	14 Nov 42	27 Aug 43	Active
Papaw	WAGL 308 (bn CG-141)	Marine Iron & Shipbuilding Corp., Duluth, MN	16 Nov 42	19 Feb 43	12 Oct 43	Active
Planetree	WAGL 307 (bn CG-140)	Marine Iron & Shipbuilding Corp., Duluth, MN	4 Dec 42	20 Mar 43	4 Nov 43	Active
Sweetgum	WAGL 309 (bn CG-142)	Marine Iron & Shipbuilding Corp., Duluth, MN	21 Feb 43	15 Apr 43	20 Nov 43	Active

Cost
  See Appropriations remarks
Hull
  Displacement (tons)   935 fl (1945)
  Length   180' oa
  Beam   37' mb
  Draft   12' max (1945)
  Tons per Immersed   10.4
    Inch
Machinery
  Main Engines   1 electric motor connected to 2 Westinghouse generators
      driven by 2 Cooper-Bessemer diesels
  SHP   1,200
  Propellers   Single
Performance
  Max Sustained   13.0 kts, 8,000 mi radius (1945)

Cruising   12.0 kts, 12,000 mi radius (1945)
Economic   8.3 kts, 17,000 mi radius (1945)
Logistics
  Diesel Fuel   28,660 gal
  Complement   6 officers, 74 men (1945)
Deck Gear
  Boom Capacity   20 tons
  Hoist Power   Electricity
Electronics (1945)
  Detection Radar   *Ironwood*: SLa; *Buttonwood*, *Papaw*: SL; all others: SL-1
  Sonar   *Planetree*: QBE-3; *Sweetgum*: QBE-3A; all others: WEA-1
Armament (1945)
  1 3"/50 (single); 4 20mm/80 (single); 2 dc tracks; 2 Mousetraps—not mounted on the *Papaw*, *Planetree*; 4 Y-guns—only 2 on the *Planetree*

Design

The preliminary design for the second set of 180-foot coastwise tenders was prepared by the Coast Guard, and the final design was prepared by A. M. Deering of Chicago, IL. *See* 180-foot tenders, *Cactus* class (180 [A] class) for additional details.

Appropriations

	Appropriations	Contract	Cost (hull & machinery)
Buttonwood	17X0908	7 Oct 42	$ 880,018
Ironwood	17-20X1223	21 Feb 42	1,388,227
Mesquite	17X0908	7 Oct 42	894,798
Papaw	17X0908	7 Oct 42	870,836
Planetree	17X0908	7 Oct 42	872,876
Sweetgum	17X0908	7 Oct 42	871,619

Buttonwood

1943 assigned to 11th District—stationed at Los Angeles, CA; 1944–45 assigned to SERVPAC and served in South Pacific—established buoyage at Tulagi Harbor; mid-44 serviced Australian aids—assisted the SS *Minjak Tanah*, which had grounded on Great Barrier Reef; Nov 44 at Leyte Gulf landing, D day + 35; 25 Dec 44 assisted in fighting fire on board the freighter *Sommeisdijk*, which had been hit by an aerial torpedo.

Ironwood

1944–45 assigned to SERVPAC (3rd Fleet) and served in South Pacific, servicing mooring buoys and torpedo nets; Mar 44 assisted the stranded SS *John Lind;* Jan 45 salvaged a Japanese midget submarine off Cape Esperance; Aug 45–Jul 46 general A/N duties in the Philippines.

Mesquite

Sep–Dec 43 general A/N duty in 5th District; 1944–45 assigned to SERVPAC (7th Fleet) and served in the Pacific; Jul–Aug 45 general A/N duty in the Philippines.

Papaw

1944–45 assigned to CINCPAC and served in the South Pacific; Aug–Oct 44 removed wrecks in Saipan area; Oct 44 caught in a typhoon and damaged, limped into Ulithi Islands; 24 Dec 44 damaged by an explosion in Schonian Harbor—possibly a floating mine; 21 May 45 salvaged Japanese aircraft at Iwo Jima.

Planetree

Mar–Apr 44 general A/N and ice-breaking on Great Lakes; 1944–45 assigned to 13th District—stationed at Seattle, WA, and aided in construction of LORAN stations on Baker, Gardner, and Atafu Islands.

Sweetgum

Mar–Apr 44 general A/N and ice-breaking on Great Lakes; 1944–45 assigned to 7th District—stationed at Miami, FL.

The *Papaw*, 1 Apr 44. Fire monitors are mounted on the forecastle and on an elevated position forward of the mast.

180-FOOT TENDERS, *CACTUS* CLASS (180[A] CLASS)

Name	Visual Call Sign	Builder	Keel Laid	Launched	Commissioned	Disposition
Balsam	WAGL 62 (bn CG-88)	Zenith Dredge Co., Duluth, MN	25 Oct 41	15 Apr 42	14 Oct 42	*Decomm* 6 Mar 75
Cactus	WAGL 270 (bn CG-76)	Marine Iron & Shipbuilding Corp., Duluth, MN	31 Mar 41	25 Nov 41	1 Sep 42	*Decomm* 22 Nov 71; *sold* 9 Oct 73
Citrus	WAGL 300 (bn CG-130)	Marine Iron & Shipbuilding Corp., Duluth, MN	29 Apr 42	15 Aug 42	30 May 43	Active
Clover	WAGL 292 (bn CG-93)	Marine Iron & Shipbuilding Corp., Duluth, MN	3 Dec 41	25 Apr 42	8 Nov 42	Active
Conifer	WAGL 301 (bn CG-131)	Marine Iron & Shipbuilding Corp., Duluth, MN	6 Jul 42	3 Nov 42	1 Jul 43	Active
Cowslip	WAGL 277 (bn CG-91)	Marine Iron & Shipbuilding Corp., Duluth, MN	16 Sep 41	11 Apr 42	17 Oct 42; *recomm* 9 Nov 81	*Decomm* and *sold* 23 Mar 73; *repurchased* 19 Jan 81; active
Evergreen	WAGL 295 (bn CG-102)	Marine Iron & Shipbuilding Corp., Duluth, MN	15 Apr 42	3 Jul 42	30 Apr 43	Active (WAGO in 1962)
Gentian	WAGL 290 (bn CG-90)	Zenith Dredge Co., Duluth, MN	3 Oct 41	23 May 42	3 Nov 42	*Decomm* 19 Mar 76
Laurel	WAGL 291 (bn CG-92)	Zenith Dredge Co., Duluth, MN	17 Apr 42	4 Aug 42	24 Nov 42	Active
Madrona	WAGL 302 (bn CG-132)	Zenith Dredge Co., Duluth, MN	6 Jul 42	11 Nov 42	30 May 43	Active
Sorrel	WAGL 296 (bn CG-103)	Zenith Dredge Co., Duluth, MN	26 May 42	28 Sep 42	15 Apr 43	*Decomm* 31 Oct 75
Tupelo	WAGL 303 (bn CG-133)	Zenith Dredge Co., Duluth, MN	15 Aug 42	28 Nov 42	30 Aug 43	*Decomm* 30 Sep 75
Woodbine	WAGL 289 (bn CG-89)	Zenith Dredge Co., Duluth, MN	2 Feb 42	3 Jul 42	17 Nov 42	*Decomm* 15 Feb 72; *donated* 19 Jun 72

Cost
  See Appropriations remarks

Hull
  Displacement (tons)   935 fl (1945)
  Length   180' oa
  Beam   37' mb
  Draft   12' max (1945)
  Tons per Immersed   10.4
    Inch

Machinery
  Main Engines   1 electric motor connected to 2 Westinghouse generators driven by 2 Cooper-Bessemer-type GND-8, 8-cyl, 4-cycle, diesels
  SHP   1,000
  Propellers   Single

Performance
  Max Sustained   13.0 kts, 8,000 mi radius (1945)
  Cruising   12.0 kts, 12,000 mi radius (1945)
  Economic   8.3 kts, 17,000 mi radius (1945)

Logistics
  Diesel Fuel   30,000 gal
  Complement   6 officers, 74 men (1945)

Deck Gear
  Boom Capacity   20 tons
  Hoist Power   Electricity

Electronics
  Detection Radar
    1943   Bk
    1945   *Balsam, Cactus, Woodbine:* SL-1; *Citrus, Clover, Conifer, Gentian, Tupelo:* SL; all others: SLa
  Sonar   All units: WEA-2 (1945)

Armament (1945)
  1 3'/50 (single); 2 20mm/80 (single)—except 4 on the *Citrus* and *Clover;* 2 dc tracks; 2 Mousetraps; 4 Y-guns

Design
  The preliminary design of the 180-foot coastwise tenders was initiated by the USLHS prior to its amalgamation into the Coast Guard. The final design was executed by Marine Iron & Shipbuilding Corp., Duluth, MN. This design was intended to replace all large or Class "A" tenders. For the first time it added search-and-rescue features to the features designed for tending buoys or servicing lighthouses. Following the amalgamation of the USLHS into the Coast Guard, ice-breaking features were added to the design. The final design produced a single-screw ship with considerable slack bilges and a cutaway forefoot. In addition, the deckhouse aft of the buoy deck was extended to the ship's side, increasing interior space. The search-and-rescue requirement caused a reduction in the beam-to-length ratio, and also gave the ship finer lines at the bow and stern.

Appropriations

	Appropriations	Contract	Cost (hull & machinery)
Balsam	17X0908	12 Jun 41	$916,109
Cactus	17X0908	20 Jan 41	782,381
Citrus	17X0908	23 Feb 42	853,987
Clover	17X0908	28 Oct 41	907,240

	Appropriations	Contract	Cost (hull & machinery)
Conifer	17X0908	23 Feb 42	854,003
Cowslip	17X0908	5 Jul 41	918,873
Evergreen	17-20X1223	2 Feb 42	871,946
Gentian	17X0908	5 Jul 41	911,968
Laurel	17X0908	28 Oct 41	902,656
Madrona	17X0908	23 Feb 42	949,144
Sorrel	17-20X1223	2 Feb 42	952,103
Tupelo	17X0908	23 Feb 42	948,887
Woodbine	17X0908	NA	906,698

Balsam

1942–45 assigned to 12th District and SERVPAC; general A/N duty in South Pacific—aided in construction and servicing of Pacific LORAN stations; logged 50 equator crossings in 19 months; Jun–Jul 45 general A/N duty in Okinawa area; 21 Jul 45 assisted in fighting fires on board the USS *Rawlins,* which had been struck by a kamikaze.

Cactus

1942–45 assigned to 1st District—stationed at Boston, MA; 12 Jun 43 collided with the *Manasquan*—received considerable damage.

Citrus

Apr–May 43 assigned to 9th District—stationed at Detroit, MI, and used for general A/N and ice-breaking on Great Lakes; late 1943 assisted in constructing LORAN station in Greenland; 1944–45 assigned to 17th District—stationed at Ketchikan, AK; assisted in constructing LORAN chain and used for general A/N duty in Alaskan waters; Feb 44 rescued 9 men from a sinking tug; 7 Feb 44 assisted in refloating the *Mary D;* Oct 44 refloated the ATS *Brunswick,* aground in Wrangell Narrows.

Clover

Jan–Feb 43 used to break ice at Cleveland Ledge, Hog Island Channel; early

1943 assigned to 13th District and used for escort work due to shortage of that type; Apr–Sep 43 employed in construction of Bering Sea LORAN chain at St. Paul Island, Unimak Island, St. Matthew Island, and Cape Sarichef; 1944–45 assigned to ALASKASEAFRON and used for general A/N duty; 20 Dec 43 towed damaged PC 780; Jul 45 assisted distressed ATS TP-127.

Conifer

1943 assigned to 13th District—stationed at Astoria, OR; 1943–45 assigned to CINCLANT—stationed at Boston, MA, and employed extensively on weather stations in the Atlantic.

Cowslip

1942–45 assigned to 1st District—stationed at Boston, MA; Jan–Feb 43 used to break ice in Cape Cod Canal; Aug 44 and Jul 45 serviced buoys and antisubmarine nets at Argentia, Newfoundland.

Evergreen

Apr–May 43 general A/N duty and ice-breaking on Great Lakes; mid-43 assigned to 6th District—stationed at Charleston, SC, and used for general A/N; mid-43–45 assigned to 1st District—stationed at Boston, MA; Aug 43–Jul 44 deployed on weather stations in Atlantic; Jul–Oct 44 used for escort duties in Greenland waters; Sep 43 towed the damaged cutter *Northland* to Narsarssuak, Greenland; late 1943–45 used for ice-breaking in Greenland waters.

Gentian

1942–43 assigned to 3rd District—stationed at New York, NY; 1943–45 assigned to 4th District—stationed at Cape May, NJ; May 44 surveyed wrecks in coastal waters of 4th and 5th Districts.

Laurel

1943 assigned to 4th District—stationed at Philadelphia, PA; 1943–45 assigned to CINCLANT (DESLANT)—stationed at Boston, MA, and served as icebreaker and escort in Greenland waters, replacing the *Cactus,* which

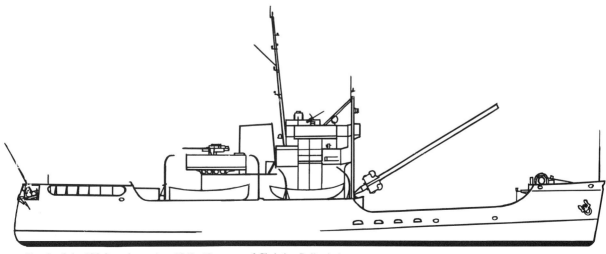

Sketch of the 180-foot class, circa 1943. (Courtesy of Christian Beilstein.)

had been damaged in a collision with the *Manasquan;* Nov 43, and again in Jan 44, damaged by ice; Oct 44 rescued 83 survivors from the SS *Iris;* Mar 45 served on weather station in the Atlantic.

Madrona

Apr 43 general A/N duty and ice-breaking on Great Lakes; mid-1943–45 assigned to 7th District—stationed at Miami, FL, for general A/N duty.

Sorrel

Early 1943 general A/N duty and ice-breaking on Great Lakes; mid-1943 assigned to 8th District—stationed at Galveston, TX; late 1943–45 assigned to CINCLANT—stationed at Boston, MA, and served on weather stations in Atlantic; 1944–45 served in Greenland waters and used for ice-breaking and patrol.

Tupelo

Mid-1943 assigned to 1st District—stationed at Boston, MA; Apr 44 assisted the distressed tug *Atengo* off Salina Cruz, Mexico; 1944–45 assigned to CINC-PAC and served in South Pacific; 13 Jul 44 fought fire on barge at Eniwetok; Oct 44 assisted the SS *Mandillo* at Guam; Nov 44–Aug 45 general A/N duty at Guam.

Woodbine

Dec 42–early 44 assigned to 5th District—stationed at Norfolk, VA; 1944–45 assigned to CINCPAC and served in South Pacific; Aug 44 aided in salvage of a PBM on Saipan; Sep–Oct 44 helped lay a gasoline pipe line to serve B-29s in Tanapag Harbor; 6 Oct 44 assisted in rescue of crew from barge; 23 Jan 45 was in a convoy that experienced the devastating typhoon of 1945 off Japan.

The *Clover,* 2 Feb 43. ASW weapons and 3"/50s made these buoy tenders creditable opponents for submarines. (Courtesy of the National Archives.)

The *Cowslip* in heavy weather. Armament has been removed. The versatile 180s were used to break ice, to tend aids to navigation, to serve on weather station, and to escort convoys.

73-FOOT TENDER

Name	Visual Call Sign	Builder	Launched	Commissioned	Disposition
Oleander	WAGL 264 (bn CG-80)	Jeffersonville Boat & Machine Co., Jeffersonville, IN	24 May 41	20 Sep 41	*Decomm* 31 Jul 77

Cost
  $65,922
Hull
  Displacement (tons)   80 fl (1940)
  Length   73′ oa
  Beam   18′ max
  Draft   5′ max (1940)

Machinery
  Main Engines   2 Gray Marine diesels
  BHP   300
  Propellers   Twin
Performance
  Max Speed   9.0 kts (1940)
  Cruising   7.5 kts, 1,160 mi radius (1945)

Logistics
 Diesel Fuel   1,300 gal
 Complement   0 officers, 9 men (1945)
Deck Gear
 Boom Capacity   3 tons
 Hoist Power   Electricity
Electronics
 None
Armament
 None
Design
 Designed to serve A/N on the Mississippi River and to render aid during floods.

The *Oleander,* Sep 41.

Oleander

1941–45 assigned to 9th District—stationed at Peoria, IL, and used for A/N for 241 miles on Illinois River, Chicago to Mile 80.

114-FOOT TENDERS

Name	Visual Call Sign	Builder	Keel Laid	Launched	Commissioned	Disposition
Dogwood	WAGL 259 (bn CG-77)	Dubuque Boat & Boiler Works, Dubuque, IA	Jul 40 (contracted)	16 Jun 41	17 Sep 41	Active
Forsythia	WAGL 63 (bn CG-94)	Avondale Marine Ways, Westwego, LA	24 Nov 41	15 Apr 42	15 Feb 43	*Decomm* 12 Aug 77
Sycamore	WAGL 268 (bn CG-78)	Dubuque Boat & Boiler Works, Dubuque, IA	Jul 40 (contracted)	16 Jun 41	9 Sep 41	*Decomm* 30 Jun 77

Cost
 $159,000 (*Dogwood* and *Sycamore*); $167,450 (*Forsythia*)
Hull
 Displacement (tons) 230 fl (1940)
 Length   113'9" oa
 Beam   26' max
 Draft   5' max (1940)
Machinery
 Main Engines   *Dogwood* and *Sycamore:* 2 Fairbanks Morse diesels; *Forsythia:* 2 Superior diesels
 BHP   *Dogwood* and *Sycamore:* 400; *Forsythia:* 360
 Propellers   Twin
Performance
 Max Speed   10.0 kts (1940)
 Max Sustained   8.0 kts, 1,900 mi radius (1945)
 Cruising   7.5 kts, 2,100 mi radius (1945)
Logistics
 Diesel Fuel   5,130 gal
 Complement   1 officer, 23 men (1945)
Deck Gear
 Boom Capacity   3 tons
 Hoist Power   Electricity
Electronics
 None

Armament
 None
Design
 This class was designed to replace the aging sternwheeler steamers such as the *Cottonwood* and *Wakerobin* used on the Mississippi River. The new class was much more versatile and much less expensive to maintain.

Dogwood

1941–45 assigned to 9th District—stationed at Paducah, KY (1941–44), Memphis, TN (1944–Mar 45), and Vicksburg, MS (Mar 45 to close of WW II)—and used for A/N for 400 miles on lower Mississippi River from Cairo, IL, to Mile 400; Mar–Apr 45 evacuated 300–400 head of cattle from danger of high water below Angola, LA.

Forsythia

1943–45 assigned to 9th District—stationed at Sewickley, PA, and used for A/N duty for 426 miles on the Allegheny, Monongahila, and Ohio rivers to Dam 22.

Sycamore

1941–45 assigned to 9th District—stationed at La Crosse, WI (1941–44), and Dubuque, IA, and used for A/N duty on the Mississippi River from Minneapolis, MN, to Dubuque, IA.

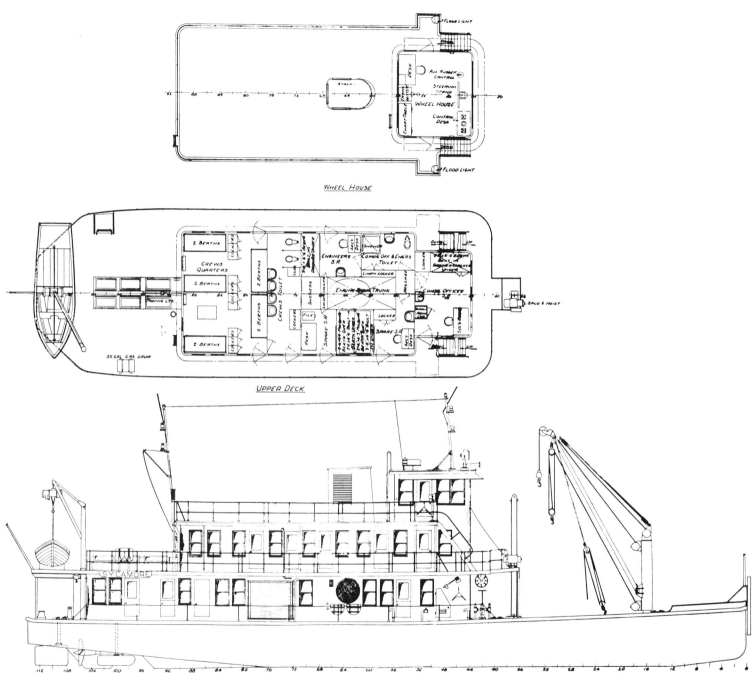

Outboard profile and arrangement of upper deck and wheelhouse of 114-foot *Sycamore*-class Mississippi River tender.

The *Forsythia*, 16 Feb 43. Her class was built to replace the sternwheel steamer, which was very expensive to maintain.

EMERGENCY ACQUISITION

Name	Visual Call Sign	Builder	Launched	Commissioned	Disposition
Azalea (ex-*Minneapolis*)	WAGL 262	Grafton, IL	1915	12 Nov 40 (CG)	*Decomm* 6 May 46; *sold* 14 Nov 46

Cost
  NA
Hull
  Displacement (tons)   352 fl (1945)   Length   149′9″ oa
  Beam   34′4″ max   Draft   4′6″ max (1945)
Machinery
  Main Engines   2 tandem compound steam
  Main Boilers   1 Foster-Wheeler watertube
  SHP   350
  Propellers   Stern paddlewheel
Performance
  Max Speed   9.0 kts (1945)
  Max Sustained   8.0 kts, 630 mi radius (1945)
  Cruising   7.0 kts, 736 mi radius (1945)
Logistics
  Fuel Oil (95%)   15,250 gal
  Complement   2 officers, 14 men (1940, merchant service); 1 officer, 25 men (1945)
Electronics
  None
Armament
  None
Design
  Built as a towboat and acquired from the U.S. Army.

Azalea

1941–45 assigned to 9th District—stationed at St. Louis, MO, and used for A/N duty from Cairo, IL, to Dam 26, and on the Mississippi River from Keokuk, IA, to Alton, IL (161 miles); 1 Feb 42 name changed from the *Minneapolis* to the *Azalea;* Mar–Apr 45 evacuated cattle from Grand Tower, IL, because of high water.

The tender *Azalea* in 1943. She was a typical Mississippi sternwheel steamer. A number of this type were acquired by the CG from the Army Corps of Engineers.

177-FOOT TENDER

Name	Visual Call Sign	Builder	Launched	Commissioned	Disposition
Juniper	WAGL 224	John H. Mathis Co., Camden, NJ	18 May 40	1 Oct 40	*Decomm* 15 Jul 75; *sold* Dec 75

Cost
  NA

Hull
  Displacement (tons)   790 fl (1945)
  Length   177' oa
  Beam   32' mb
  Draft   8'7" max (1945)

Machinery
  Main Engines   2 electric motors connected to 2 generators driven by 2 diesels
  SHP   900
  Propellers   Twin

Performance
  Max Speed   12.5 kts (1945)
  Cruising   11.0 kts, 7,000 mi radius (1945)

Logistics
  Diesel Fuel   18,000 gal
  Complement   1 officer, 3 warrants, 34 men (1945)

Deck Gear
  Boom Capacity   20 tons
  Hoist Power   Electricity

Electronics (1945)
  Detection Radar   SO-8
  Sonar   WEA-2

Armament (1945)
  1 3"/50 (single); 2 20mm/80 (single); 2 dc tracks

Design
  The *Juniper* was the last tender begun for the USLHS. She was under construction when that service was amalgamated into the CG. The *Juniper* was the prototype for the 180-foot tenders and was the first all-welded steel and diesel-electric-propelled coastwise tender. A distinguishing feature was the turtle-back forecastle.

Juniper

1941–45 assigned to 7th District—stationed at Key West, FL, and used for A/N duty.

The *Juniper*, 22 Jun 62, at St Petersburg, FL. Prior to the construction of this tender, all tenders had been designed to service a specific location. This accounts for the large number of small classes. The *Juniper* was the first attempt to design an all-purpose, oceangoing tender. She is the prototype for the 180s, even though there are marked differences between their designs. The *Juniper* had a much shallower draft than the 180s had, and she was twin-, not single-, screwed.

72-FOOT TENDER

Name	Visual Call Sign	Builder	Commissioned	Disposition
Birch	WAGL 256	General Ship & Engine Works, Boston, MA	1939	*Decomm* 24 Feb 63; *sold* 30 Jul 64

Cost
  $74,000
Hull
  Displacement (tons)   137 fl (1945)
  Length   72′4″ oa
  Beam   18′ max
  Draft   3′8″ max (1939); 4′1″ max (1945)
Machinery
  Main Engines   2 Winton diesels
  BHP   300
  Propellers   Twin
Performance
  Max Speed   9.0 kts (1939)
  Cruising   8.0 kts, 1,000 mi radius (1945)
Logistics
  Diesel Fuel   1,300 gal

Complement   0 officers, 9 men (1945)
Deck Gear
  Boom Capacity   2 tons
  Hoist Power   Electricity
Electronics
  None
Armament
  None
Design
  Designed as a bay and sound tender.

Birch

1941–45 assigned to 7th District—stationed at St. Petersburg, FL, and used for A/N duty.

152-FOOT TENDER

Name	Visual Call Sign	Builder	Commissioned	Disposition
Cottonwood (ex-*Le Clair*)	WAGL 209	Grafton, IL	1915 (War Dept); 1939 (CG)	*Decomm* 25 May 46; *sold* 1 May 47

Cost
  Original cost $44,238; acquisition $7,500; conversion $2,500
Hull
  Displacement (tons)   243 fl (1915); 270 fl (1945)
  Length   151′ oa
  Beam   34′8″ mb
  Draft   4′5″ max (1915); 5′ max (1945)
Machinery
  Main Engines   2 tandem compound steam
  Main Boilers   1 Foster-Wheeler Express
  SHP   320
  Propellers   Stern paddlewheel
Performance
  Max Speed   8.0 kts (1915)
  Max Sustained   7.0 kts, 630 mi radius (1945)
  Cruising   6.0 kts, 750 mi radius (1945)
Logistics
  Coal (95%)   28 tons
  Complement   1 officer, 22 men (1915); 2 officers, 1 warrant, 33 men (1945)
Electronics
  None
Armament
  None

Design
  A stern paddlewheel steamer constructed of steel.

Cottonwood

17 May 38 acquired from War Dept; 1941–45 assigned to 9th District—stationed at St. Louis, MO, and Chattanooga, TN, and used for A/N for 650 miles on Tennessee River above the Kentucky Dam.

The tender *Cottonwood*, 13 Feb 45.

122-FOOT TENDER

Name	Visual Call Sign	Builder	Keel Laid	Launched	Commissioned	Disposition
Maple	WAGL 234	Marine Iron & Shipbuilding Co., Duluth, MN	15 Apr 38 (contracted)	29 Apr 39	Jun 39	*Decomm* 1 Jun 73; *trans* to USN 8 Aug 73

Cost
    $190,000

Hull
    Displacement (tons)   342 fl (1938 and 1945)
    Length   122'3" oa
    Beam   27' max
    Draft   7' max (1938); 7'6" max (1945)

Machinery
    Main Engines   2 Superior diesels
    BHP   430
    Propellers   Twin

Performance
    Max Speed   10.0 kts (1938)
    Max Sustained   8.0 kts, 2,900 mi radius (1945)
    Cruising   6.0 kts, 3,500 mi radius (1945)

Logistics
    Diesel Fuel   4,600 gal

Complement   1 officer, 27 men (1945)

Deck Gear
    Boom Capacity   10 tons
    Hoist Power   Electricity

Electronics (1945)
    Detection Radar   SO-1

Armament
    None

Design
    Designed as a bay and sound tender.

Maple

1941–45 assigned to the 9th District—stationed at Ogdensburg, NY, and used for general A/N on Lake Ontario and Lake Erie.

The *Maple*, 29 Apr 39, just prior to launching. Note the rounded forecastle, which prevented buoys from getting hung up on the deck.

122-FOOT TENDERS

Name	Visual Call Sign	Builder	Keel Laid	Launched	Commissioned	Disposition
Narcissus	WAGL 238	John H. Mathis Co., Camden, NJ	15 Apr 38 (contracted)	4 Feb 39	1939	*Trans* to Guyana 5 May 71
Zinnia	WAGL 255	John H. Mathis Co., Camden, NJ	15 Apr 38 (contracted)	4 Feb 39	1939	*Decomm* 14 Jan 72; *trans* to USAF 1 Mar 72

Cost
$220,023 each

Hull
Displacement (tons)   355 fl (1939)
Length   122'2" oa
Beam   27' max
Draft   7' max (1939); 7'6" max (1945)

Machinery
Main Engines   2 Superior diesel
BHP   430
Propellers   Twin

Performance
Max Speed   9.0 kts (1939)
Max Sustained   8.0 kts, 3,000 mi radius (1945)
Economic   6.0 kts, 3,500 mi radius (1945)

Logistics
Diesel Fuel   4,800 gal
Complement   3 officers, 40 men (1945)

Deck Gear
Boom Capacity   10 tons
Hoist Power   Electricity

Electronics (1945)
Detection Radar   SO-8 (*Narcissus* only)

Armament
None

Design
First tenders to be extensively welded; bay and sound design.

Narcissus

1941–45 assigned to 5th District—stationed at Portsmouth, VA, and used for A/N on Delaware Bay and Delaware River; repaired and extended antisubmarine nets at Cape Lookout, NC.

Zinnia

1941–45 assigned to 4th District—stationed at Edgemoor, DE, and used for A/N duty.

The *Narcissus (foreground)* and the *Zinnia* on the building ways, 1938. The *Zinnia*, like many other busy tenders, serviced nets during WW II.

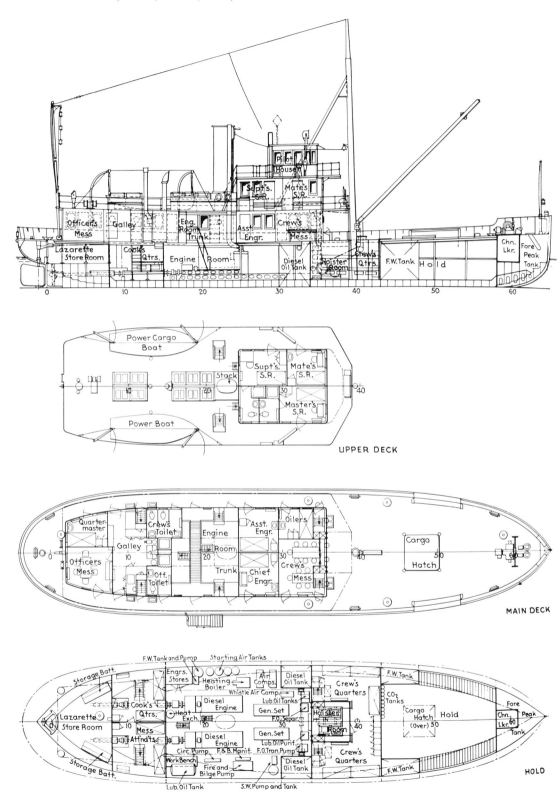

Inboard profile, deck and hold plans of 122-foot tenders. (Courtesy of *Marine Engineering/Log;* copied from *Marine Engineering and Shipping Age* [April, 1940]: 52.)

104-FOOT TENDERS

Name	Visual Call Sign	Builder	Keel Laid	Commissioned	Disposition
Goldenrod	WAGL 213	Dubuque Boat & Boiler Works, Dubuque, IA	21 Jun 37 (contracted)	2 Jun 38	*Decomm* 26 May 73; *trans* to NSF 26 Sep 73
Poplar	WAGL 241	Dubuque Boat & Boiler Works, Dubuque, IA	NA	1939	*Decomm* 17 Jun 73; *trans* to NSF 26 Sep 73

Cost
$115,375 *(Goldenrod)*; $123,200 *(Poplar)*

Hull
Displacement (tons)	170 fl (1939); 196 fl (1945)
Length	103'6" oa
Beam	24' max
Draft	3'6" max (1939); 4'6" max (1945)

Machinery
Main Engines	2 Fairbanks Morse diesels
BHP	400
Propellers	Twin

Performance
Max Speed	9.0 kts (1945)
Max Sustained	8.0 kts, 1,000 mi radius (1945)

Logistics
Diesel Fuel	4,300 gal
Complement	1 officer, 14 men (1945)

Deck Gear
Boom Capacity	2.5 tons

Hoist Power   Electricity

Electronics
  None

Armament
  None

Design
  A river tender, with propellers mounted in tunnels for operation in shallow waters.

Goldenrod

1941–45 assigned to 9th District—stationed at Kansas City, MO, and used for A/N for 446 miles of upper Missouri River, Sioux City, IA, to Boonville, MO; Jun 43 evacuated flood victims from Missouri and Illinois.

Poplar

1941–45 assigned to 9th District—stationed at St. Louis, MO, and used for A/N duty for 276 miles of lower Missouri River (to Boonville, MO), also north on Illinois River to Mile 80.

The *Poplar* on the Mississippi River shortly after WW II. Her class was the first to have tunnel-stern propellers. This design served as the prototype for the 114-foot class.

72-FOOT TENDER

Name	Visual Call Sign	Builder	Commissioned	Disposition
Elm	WAGL 260	Defoe Boat & Motor Works, Bay City, MI	1 Apr 38	*Decomm* 30 Jul 69; *donated* 23 Oct 70

Cost
$77,177

Hull
Displacement (tons)   75 fl (1937); 77 fl (1945)
Length   72'4" oa
Beam   17'6" max
Draft   5' max (1937 and 1945)

Machinery
Main Engines   2 Winton diesels
BHP   330
Propellers   Twin

Performance
Max Speed   9.0 kts (1937)
Cruising   8.0 kts, 900 mi radius (1945)

Logistics
Diesel Fuel   1,300 gal

Complement   0 officers, 9 men (1945)

Deck Gear
Boom Capacity   3.0 tons
Hoist Power   Electricity

Electronics
None

Armament
None

Design
Designed as a bay and sound tender.

Elm

1941–45 assigned to 4th District—stationed at Atlantic City, NJ, and used for A/N duty.

175-FOOT TENDERS

Name	Visual Call Sign	Builder	Keel Laid	Launched	Commissioned	Disposition
Fir	WAGL 212	Moore Dry Dock Co., Oakland, CA	16 Aug 38	NA	1 Oct 40	Active
Hollyhock	WAGL 220	Defoe Boat & Motor Works, Bay City, MI	13 Apr 36	24 Mar 37	7 Aug 37	*Decomm* 31 Mar 82
Walnut	WAGL 252	Moore Dry Dock Co., Oakland, CA	NA	NA	27 Jun 39	Active

Cost
$389,746 (*Fir, Walnut*); $347,800 (*Hollyhock*)

Hull
Displacement (tons)   825 at mean draft (1936); 1,000 fl (1945)
Length   174'10" oa
Beam   32' mb
Draft   10'7" mean (1936); 14'6" max (1945)

Machinery
Main Engines   2 triple-expansion steam, horizontal
Main Boilers   2 Babcock & Wilcox watertube
SHP   1,000
Propellers   Twin

Performance
Max Speed   10.7 kts (*Walnut*—1945)
                                     12.0 kts (others—1945)
Economic   10.0 kts, 2,500 mi radius (*Walnut*—1945)
                                     11.0 kts, 2,300 mi radius (*Hollyhock*—1945)
                                     11.5 kts, 2,000 mi radius (*Fir*—1945)

Logistics
Fuel Oil (95%)   30,400 (*Fir*); 32,000 (*Hollyhock*); 38,500 (*Walnut*)
Complement   4 officers, 1 warrant, 69 men (1945)

Deck Gear
Boom Capacity   20 tons
Hoist Power   Hydraulic

Electronics
Detection Radar   SO-1 (1945)
Sonar   *Fir, Walnut:* WEA-2; *Hollyhock:* none

Armament (1945)
Fir: 1 6-pdr; 2 20mm/80 (single); 2 dc tracks
Hollyhock: none
Walnut: 2 3"/50 (single); 4 20mm/80 (single); 2 dc tracks

Design
Designed as coastwise tenders.

Fir

1941–45 assigned to 13th District—stationed at Seattle, WA, and used for A/N duty.

Hollyhock

1941–45 assigned to 9th District—stationed at Milwaukee, WI, and used for A/N duty on Lake Michigan.

Walnut

1941–45 assigned to 14th District—stationed at Honolulu, HI, and used for A/N duty.

The *Walnut*, 25 Nov 41. Tenders specifically built to service buoys first appeared in operation in the middle of the nineteenth century. As the number of lightships and remote lighthouses rose toward the end of the century, tenders grew in size, being fitted with large tanks for fresh water and increased cargo-carrying capacity. Ice-breaking capability and open-ocean qualities for search-and-rescue operations were not designed into a tender class until the 180s were built during WW II. (Courtesy of the National Archives.)

91-FOOT TENDER

Name	Visual Call Sign	Builder	Launched	Commissioned	Disposition
Jasmine	WAGL 261	The Dravo Constructing Co., Neville Island, Pittsburgh, PA	26 Mar 35	May 35	*Decomm* 18 Jan 65; *sold* 19 May 66
Bluebonnet	WAGL 257	Dubuque Boat & Boiler Works, Dubuque, IA	NA	4 Nov 39	*Decomm* 18 Jan 65; *sold* 19 May 66

Cost
  $132,500 each
Hull
  Displacement (tons)   184 fl (1935 and 1945)
  Length   91′4″ oa; 82′ bp
  Beam   23′ max
  Draft   5′3″ (1935); 6′ max (1945)
Machinery
  Main Engines   2 Cooper-Bessemer, 6-cyl, 4-cycle diesels
  BHP   440
  Propellers   Twin
Performance
  Max Speed   9.0 kts (1945)
  Cruising   8.0 kts, 570 mi radius (1945)
  Economic   7.0 kts, 630 mi radius (1945)
Logistics
  Diesel Fuel   3.75 tons

Complement   0 officers, 11 men (1945)
Electronics
  None
Armament
  None
Design
  Designed as a bay and sound tender.

Bluebonnet

1941–45 assigned to 8th District—stationed at Galveston, TX, and used for A/N duty on the intracoastal waterway, west of New Orleans, LA, and west through Galveston, TX.

Jasmine

1941–45 assigned to 8th District—stationed at New Orleans, LA, and used for A/N duty.

The *Jasmine* on the day of her launching, 26 Mar 35.

81-FOOT TENDER

Name	Visual Call Sign	Builder	Launched	Commissioned	Disposition
Rhododendron	WAGL 267	Commercial Iron Works, Portland, OR	16 Mar 35	12 Apr 35	*Decomm* 20 Aug 58; donated to state of WA 20 Apr 59

Cost
  $75,000
Hull
  Displacement (tons)   140 fl (1935 and 1945)
  Length   81′ oa
  Beam   20′ max
  Draft   6′ max (1935 and 1945)
Machinery
  Main Engines   2 Imperial diesels
  BHP   240
  Propellers   Twin
Performance
  Max Speed   9.0 kts (1935)
Logistics
  Fuel Oil (95%)   NA

Complement   0 officers, 10 men (1945)
Deck Gear
  Boom Capacity   1.5 tons
  Hoist Power   Electricity
Electronics
  None
Armament
  None
Design
  Designed as a bay and sound tender.

Rhododendron

1941–45 assigned to 13th District—stationed at Vancouver, WA, and used for A/N duty; 25 Nov 66 sank off Alaska (as the SS *Kandu*).

The *Rhododendron*, 16 Mar 35, shortly after launching.

124-FOOT TENDER

Name	Visual Call Sign	Builder	Keel Laid	Commissioned	Disposition
Tamarack	WAGL 248	Manitowoc Shipbuilding Corp., Manitowoc, WI	11 Dec 33 (contracted)	1934	*Decomm* 27 Oct 70; *sold* 2 Aug 71

Cost
$233,917

Hull
  Displacement (tons)   400 fl (1934 and 1945)
  Length   124′4″ oa
  Beam   30′3″ mb
  Draft   8′ max (1934)

Machinery
  Main Engines   1 Winton diesel
  BHP   450
  Propellers   Single

Performance
  Max Speed   9.8 kts, (1945)
  Max Sustained   8.9 kts, 7,000 mi radius (1945)
  Cruising   8.0 kts, 8,000 mi radius (1945)

Logistics
  Diesel Fuel   14,000 gal

Complement   2 officers, 30 men (1945)

Deck Gear
  Boom Capacity   10 tons
  Hoist Power   Electricity

Electronics (1945)
  Detection Radar   SO-1

Armament
  None

Design
  Designed as a bay and sound tender.

Tamarack

1941–45 assigned to 9th District—stationed at Manitowoc, WI, and used for A/N on St. Mary's River and as a submarine tender.

The *Tamarack*, 1 Sep 39, prior to the merger of the Lighthouse Service (USLHS) and the CG.

175-FOOT TENDER

Name	Visual Call Sign	Builder	Keel Laid	Launched	Commissioned	Disposition
Hemlock	WAGL 217	Berg Shipbuilding Co., Seattle, WA	12 Jan 33 (contracted)	23 Jan 34	1934	*Decomm* 17 Jun 58; *sold* 2 Aug 61

Cost
  $228,480
Hull
  Displacement (tons)   1,000 fl (1945)
  Length   174'6" oa
  Beam   32' mb
  Draft   13'3" max (1945)
Machinery
  Main Engines   2 triple-expansion steam
  Main Boilers   2 Foster-Wheeler watertube
  SHP   1,000
  Propellers   Twin
Performance
  Max Speed   12.3 kts (1945)
  Max Sustained   12.0 kts, 2,000 mi radius (1945)
  Economic   10.0 kts, 2,400 mi radius (1945)
Logistics
  Fuel Oil (95%)   29,000 gal
  Complement   4 officers, 1 warrant, 69 men (1945)
Electronics (1945)
  Detection Radar   SO-8
Armament (1945)
  2 3"/23 (single); 4 20mm/80 (single); 2 dc tracks
Design
  The *Hemlock* was designed for operating in Alaskan waters. She was given a double bottom and a larger fuel and water capacity than are normally found on a coastwise tender.

Hemlock

1941–45 assigned to 13th and 17th Districts—stationed at Ketchikan, AK, and used for A/N duty; Jan 42 helped to refloat the ATS *David W. Branch;* Dec 42 towed the damaged ATS *Texado;* Oct 43 helped salvage the SS *Prince Rupert;* Jan 44 helped salvage the SS *William L. Thompson;* Sep 44 refloated the SS *F.W.S. Brandt.*

The *Hemlock*, prior to 1 Sep 39. The lighthouse emblem on her bow was fitted on all tenders built for the USLHS.

175-FOOT TENDER

Name	Visual Call Sign	Builder	Keel Laid	Launched	Commissioned	Disposition
Arbutus	WAGL 203	Pusey & Jones Co., Wilmington, DE	21 Jul 32 (contracted)	25 Mar 33	1933	*Decomm* 27 Mar 67; *sold* 24 Mar 69

Cost
$239,800

Hull
Displacement (tons) 997 (1945)
Length 174'7" oa
Beam 33' mb
Draft 14' max (1945)

Machinery
Main Engines 2 triple-expansion steam
Main Boilers 2 Foster-Wheeler watertube
SHP 1,000
Propellers Twin

Performance
Max Speed 11.3 kts (1945)
Max Sustained 11.0 kts, 1,950 mi radius (1945)

Logistics
Fuel Oil (95%) 29,800 gal

Complement 1 officer, 3 warrants, 37 men (1945)

Deck Gear
Boom Capacity 20 tons
Hoist Power Steam

Electronics
Detection Radar BK (1943); SO-1 (1945)
Sonar WEA-2a (1945)

Armament (1945)
1 3"/23 (single); 2 20mm/80 (single)

Design
Designed as a coastwise tender.

Arbutus

1941–45 assigned to 1st District—stationed at Woods Hole, MA, and used for A/N duty; Feb 43 used to tend submarine nets at Newport, RI.

The *Arbutus,* 25 Mar 33, just prior to launching. Note the wooden strakes attached to protect the part of her hull below the waterline from buoys that were being serviced.

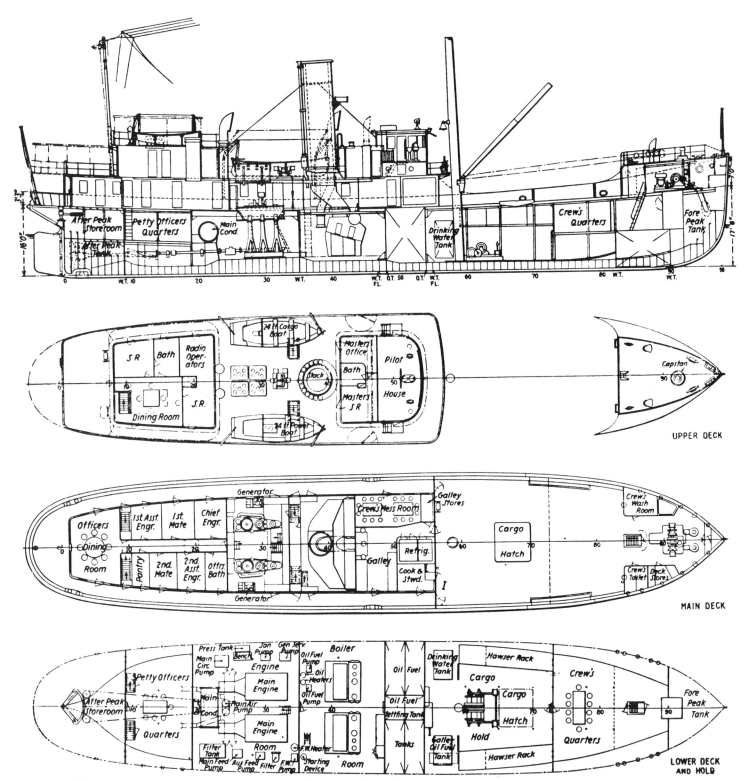

Inboard profile and deck plans of the lighthouse tender *Arbutus*. (Courtesy of *Marine Engineering/Log;* copied from *Marine Engineering and Shipping Age* [June, 1934]: 244.)

131-FOOT TENDER

Name	Visual Call Sign	Builder	Keel Laid	Launched	Commissioned	Disposition
Hickory	WAGL 219	Bath Iron Works, Inc., Bath, ME	13 Apr 32 (contracted)	9 Feb 33	Mar 33	*Decomm* 10 Jan 67; *sold* 28 Apr 69

Cost
$152,480

Hull
Displacement (tons)   400 fl (1933); 497 fl (1945)
Length   131'4" oa
Beam   24'6" mb
Draft   10' max (1933); 10'1" max (1945)

Machinery
Main Engines   1 triple-expansion steam
Main Boilers   1 Babcock & Wilcox watertube
SHP   500
Propellers   Single

Performance
Max Speed   10.0 kts (1933)
Max Sustained   9.4 kts, 1,700 mi radius (1945)

Logistics
Fuel Oil (95%)   16,690 gal
Complement   2 officers, 39 men (1945)

Deck Gear
Boom Capacity   10 tons
Hoist Power   Steam

Electronics (1945)
Detection Radar   SO-8

Armament (1942)
20mm/80; 2 dc tracks

Design
Designed as a coastwise tender.

Hickory

1941–45 assigned to 3rd District—stationed at St. George, Staten Island, NY, and used for A/N in New York Bay and Long Island Sound.

The *Hickory*, 1942. Mounted fore and aft are 20mms, and short depth-charge tracks are on the stern. (Courtesy of A. D. Baker III.)

81-FOOT TENDER

Name	Visual Call Sign	Builder	Keel Laid	Commissioned	Disposition
Dahlia	WAGL 288	Great Lakes Engineering Works, River Rouge, MI	25 Feb 33 (contracted)	Aug 33	*Decomm* 9 Oct 64; *sold* 20 May 65

Cost
$66,566

Hull
　Displacement (tons)　160 fl (1933 and 1945)
　Length　81'2" oa
　Beam　20' mb; 21' max
　Draft　9' max (1933)

Machinery
　Main Engines　1 Winton diesel
　BHP　235
　Propellers　Single

Performance
　Max Speed　10.0 kts (1933); 8.2 kts (1945)
　Cruising　7.1 kts, 1,027 mi radius (1945)

Logistics
　Fuel Oil (95%)　1,425 gal
　Complement　0 officers, 10 men (1945)

Deck Gear
　Boom Capacity　5.0 tons
　Hoist Power　Electricity

Electronics
　None

Armament
　None

Design
　Designed as a bay and sound tender.

Dahlia

1941–45 assigned to 9th District—stationed at Detroit, MI, and used for A/N on Detroit River and St. Clair River.

The *Dahlia*, 23 Oct 35, undergoing inclination tests.

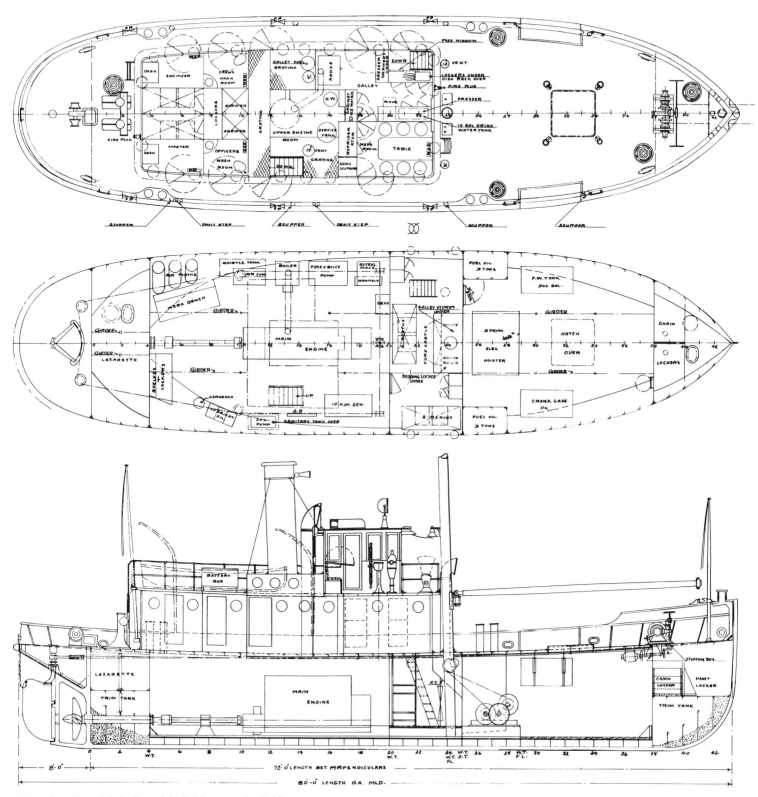

Inboard profile and deck plans of the lighthouse tender *Dahlia*.

93-FOOT TENDER

Name	Visual Call Sign	Builder	Keel Laid	Launched	Commissioned	Disposition
Myrtle	WAGL 263	Dubuque Boat & Boiler Works, Dubuque, IA	15 Feb 32 (contracted)	30 Sep 32	1932	*Decomm* 8 Feb 63; *sold* 19 May 64

Cost
  $95,000
Hull
  Displacement (tons)   186 fl (1932)
  Length   92′8″ oa
  Beam   23′ mb
  Draft   5′ max (1932); 6′ max (1945)
Machinery
  Main Engines   2 Cummins diesels
  BHP   220
  Propellers   Twin
Performance
  Max Speed   8.0 kts, (1932); 6.0 kts (1945)
  Cruising   5.0 kts, 980 mi radius (1945)
Logistics
  Diesel Fuel   800 gal

Complement   0 officers, 11 men (1945)
Deck Gear
  Boom Capacity   3 tons
  Hoist Power   Gasoline
Electronics
  None
Armament
  None
Design
  Designed as a bay and sound tender.

Myrtle

1941–45 assigned to 8th District—stationed at Galveston, TX, and used for A/N in the inland waters and in the Gulf of Mexico.

The *Myrtle*, 18 Jul 50, off Galveston, TX. Her configuration was different from that of the other tenders: her removable pile driver was mounted on the beam of the tender instead of on the bow.

86-FOOT TENDER

Name	Visual Call Sign	Builder	Keel Laid	Commissioned	Disposition
Cherry	WAGL 258	Leathem D. Smith Dock Co., Sturgeon Bay, WI	2 Jan 31 (contracted)	19 May 32	*Decomm* 1 Dec 64; *sold* 20 May 65

Cost
  $109,017
Hull
  Displacement (tons)   202 at mean draft (1932); 254 fl (1945)
  Length   86′3″ oa
  Beam   22′ mb
  Draft   7′9″ mean (1932); 9′6″ max (1945)
Machinery
  Main Engines   1 Winton diesel
  BHP   300
  Propellers   Single
Performance
  Max Speed   9.0 kts (1945)
  Cruising   8.0 kts, 1,600 mi radius (1945)
Logistics
  Diesel Fuel   3,000 gal

Complement   2 officers, 6 men (1932); 0 officers, 10 men (1945)
Deck Gear
  Boom Capacity   7.5 tons
  Hoist Power   Electricity
Electronics
  None
Armament
  None
Design
  Designed as a bay and sound tender, constructed of steel.

Cherry

1941–45 assigned to 9th District—stationed at Buffalo, NY, and used for A/N duty on Lake Erie and the Niagara River.

The *Cherry*, prior to 1 Sep 39.

121-FOOT TENDER

Name	Visual Call Sign	Builder	Keel Laid	Launched	Commissioned	Disposition
Columbine	WAGL 208	Moore Dry Dock Co., Oakland, CA	19 Jan 31 (contracted)	23 Jul 31	21 Oct 31	*Decomm* 8 Oct 65; *sold* 29 Jun 67
Linden	WAGL 228	Merrill Stevens Shipbuilding & Dry Dock Co., Jacksonville, FL	26 Sep 30	7 Mar 31	22 Jul 31	*Decomm* 29 May 69; *sold* 22 May 70
Wistaria	WAGL 254	United Dry Docks, Inc., New York, NY	21 Jul 32 (contracted)	3 Feb 33	Mar 33	*Decomm* 7 Oct 66; *sold* 6 Dec 68

Cost
$179,434 *(Columbine)*; $169,110 *(Linden)*; $129,800 *(Wistaria)*

Hull
Displacement (tons)	323 at mean draft (1935); 400 max (1945)
Length	121'4" oa
Beam	25' mb
Draft	6'9" mean (1935); 8' max (1945)

Machinery
Main Engines   1 electric motor driven by 2 General Electric generators driven by 2 Winton diesels
SHP   240
Propellers   Single, 4 blade

Performance
Max Speed   9.0 kts (1931)
Max Sustained   8.8 kts, 1,200 mi radius (1945)
Cruising   8.0 kts, 1,600 mi radius (1945)

Logistics
Diesel Fuel   3,400 gal
Complement   4 officers, 12 men (1935); 2 officers, 26 men (1945)

Deck Gear
Boom Capacity   10 tons; 8 tons *(Linden* only)
Hoist Power   Electricity; air *(Linden* only)

Electronics
None

Armament
None

Design
This class was designed as a bay and sound tender and was constructed of steel with a large open deck and hold space forward. The *Linden* was the first U.S. tender powered by diesel electric drive.

Columbine

1941–45 assigned to 12th District—stationed at San Francisco, CA, and used for A/N duty in San Francisco Bay.

Linden

1941–45 assigned to 5th District—stationed at Washington, NC, and used for A/N duty.

Wistaria

1941–45 assigned to 5th District—stationed at Baltimore, MD, and used for A/N duty in Delaware Bay and Delaware River.

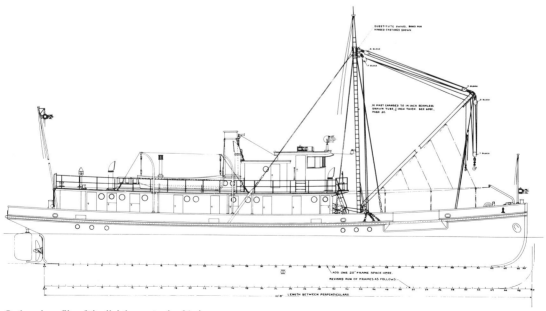

Outboard profile of the lighthouse tender *Linden*.

The *Wistaria* during WW II. She was in the first class of tenders built with diesel-electric drive.

173-FOOT TENDERS

Name	Visual Call Sign	Builder	Keel Laid	Launched	Commissioned	Disposition
Lilac	WAGL 227	Pusey & Jones Co., Wilmington, DE	16 Aug 32 (contracted)	26 May 33	1933	*Decomm* 3 Feb 72; donated 6 Jun 72
Mistletoe	WAGL 237	Pusey & Jones Co., Wilmington, DE	NA	NA	15 Sep 39	*Decomm* 15 Aug 68; *sold* 14 Aug 69
Violet	WAGL 250	Manitowoc Shipbuilding Corp., Manitowoc, WI	6 Sep 29 (contracted)	21 Aug 30	1930	*Decomm* 2 Jan 62; *sold* 8 Mar 63

Cost
$334,900 *(Lilac)*; $378,800 *(Mistletoe)*; $337,745 *(Violet)*

Hull
Displacement (tons)   799 fl (1945)
Length   173'4" oa
Beam   32' mb
Draft   11' max (1945)

Machinery
Main Engines   2 triple-expansion steam
Main Boilers   2 Babcock & Wilcox watertube
SHP   1,000
Propellers   Twin

Performance
Max Speed   11.5 kts (1945)
Max Sustained   11.0 kts, 1,700 mi radius (1945)
Economic   7.0 kts, 1,800 mi radius (1945)

Logistics
Fuel Oil (95%)   29,000 gal
Complement   1 officer, 3 warrants, 37 men (1945)

Deck Gear
Boom Capacity   20 tons
Hoist Power   Steam

Electronics (1945)
Detection Radar   *Mistletoe:* SO-8; others: SO-1
Sonar   WEA-2

Armament (1945)
    1 3"/50 (single); 2 20mm/80 (single); 2 dc tracks
Design
    Designed as a coastwise tender.

Lilac

1941–45 assigned to the 5th District—stationed at Edgemoor, DE, and used for A/N duty in Delaware River.

Mistletoe

1941–45 assigned to 5th District—stationed at Portsmouth, VA, and used for A/N duty in Norfolk, VA.

Violet

1941–45 assigned to 5th District—stationed at Baltimore, MD, and used for A/N duty in Chesapeake Bay.

The *Mistletoe*, 17 Jul 43. A 3"/50 is on the forecastle, and two 20mms are on the deckhouse aft. Radar has not yet been fitted. (Courtesy of A. D. Baker III.)

EMERGENCY ACQUISITION

Name	Visual Call Sign	Builder	Commissioned	Disposition
Alder	WAGL 216	NA	1917 (commercial service); 1930 (CG)	*Decomm* 11 Dec 47; *sold* 14 Jun 48

Cost
  NA
Hull
  Displacement (tons)   80 fl (1917 and 1945)
  Length   72' oa
  Beam   16' mb
  Draft   7'6" max (1912)
Machinery
  Main Engines   1 Atlas Imperial diesel
  BHP   110
  Propellers   Single
Performance
  Max Speed   8.0 kts (1930)
  Cruising   8.0 kts, 875 mi radius (1930)

Logistics
  Complement   0 officers, 13 men (1942); 0 officers, 9 men (1945)
Electronics
  None
Armament (1945)
  1 dc track
Design
  Constructed of wood for commercial service; purchased by U.S. Lighthouse Service in Mar 1924. She exploded and sank in Jun 1929, but was raised and rebuilt the following year.

Alder

1941–45 assigned to 13th and 17th Districts—stationed at Ketchikan, AK, and used for A/N duty; 27 Dec 42 damaged while towing the SS *Tongass*.

80-FOOT TENDER

Name	Visual Call Sign	Builder	Launched	Commissioned	Disposition
Althea	WAGL 223	New London Ship & Engine Co., Groton, CT	24 Feb 30	30 Apr 30	*Decomm* 10 Nov 62; *sold* 26 Nov 63
Poinciana	WAGL 266	Electric Boat Co., Groton, CT	7 Jun 30	8 Jul 30	*Decomm* 17 Aug 62; *sold* 26 Nov 63

Cost
  $70,608 *(Althea)*; $82,743 *(Poinciana)*
Hull
  Displacement (tons)   108 at mean draft (1930); 120 max (1945)
  Length   80'9" oa
  Beam   19' mb
  Draft   3'8" mean draft (1930)
Machinery
  Main Engines   2 Cummins 4-cyl, 4-cycle diesels
  BHP   220
  Propellers   Twin, 4 blade
Performance
  Max Speed   7.0 kts (1930)
  Cruising   6.0 kts, 875 mi radius (1945)
Logistics
  Diesel Fuel   1,000 gal
  Complement   2 officers, 6 men (1930); 0 officers, 9 men (1945)
Deck Gear
  Boom Capacity   1.5 tons
  Hoist Power   Electricity
Electronics
  None
Armament
  None

Design
  Small light-draft bay and sound tenders for service in inland waters of the South Atlantic coast. Constructed of steel.

Althea

1941–45 assigned to 7th District—stationed at Fort Pierce, FL, and used for A/N duty.

Poinciana

1941–45 assigned to 7th District—stationed at Ft. Lauderdale, FL, and Miami, FL, and used for A/N duty.

The *Althea*, prior to 1 Sep 39.

103-FOOT TENDER

Name	Visual Call Sign	Builder	Keel Laid	Commissioned	Disposition
Beech	WAGL 205	Southern Shipyard Corp., Newport News, VA	16 Aug 26 (contracted)	Jan 28	*Decomm* 23 Jan 63; *sold* 28 Aug 64

Cost
  $133,306

Hull
Displacement (tons)	255 fl (1929)
Length	103′ oa
Beam	23′ max; 22′8″ mb
Draft	7′ max (1929); 9′ max (1945)

Machinery
Main Engines	1 Cooper-Bessemer diesel
BHP	300
Propellers	Single

Performance
Max Speed	8.0 kts (1929)
Max Sustained	7.0 kts, 1,750 mi radius (1945)
Cruising	6.0 kts, 2,000 mi radius (1945)

Logistics
Diesel Fuel	3,150 gal
Complement	1 officer, 21 men (1945)

Deck Gear
Boom Capacity	10 tons
Hoist Power	Electricity

Electronics
  None

Armament
  None

Design
  A bay and sound tender, the *Beech* was originally fitted with a steam plant, which was removed in 1940.

Beech

1941–45 assigned to 3rd District—stationed at St. George, Staten Island, NY, and used for A/N duty.

The *Beech*, probably in 1928, shortly after completing.

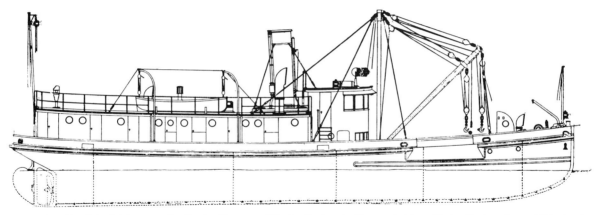

Outboard profile of the lighthouse tender *Beech*. (Courtesy of *Marine Engineering/Log;* copied from *Marine Engineering and Shipping Age* [September, 1926]: 509.)

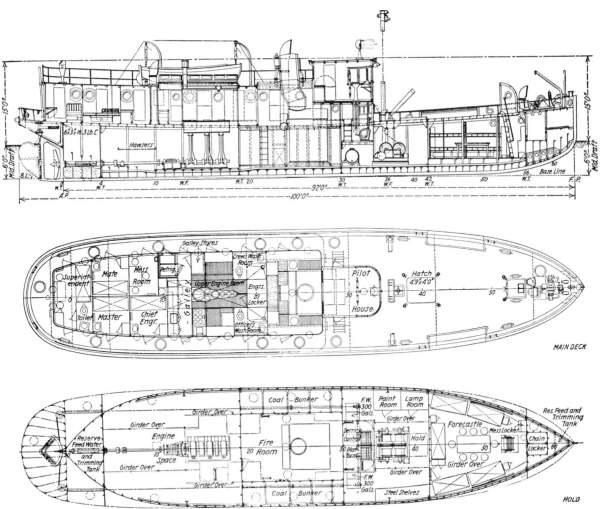

Inboard profile and deck plans of the lighthouse tender *Beech*. (Courtesy of *Marine Engineering/Log;* copied from *Marine Engineering and Shipping Age* [September, 1926]: 511.)

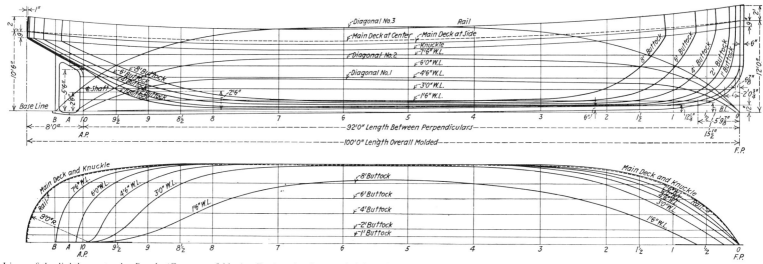

Lines of the lighthouse tender *Beech*. (Courtesy of *Marine Engineering/Log;* copied from *Marine Engineering and Shipping Age* [September, 1926]: 508.)

200-FOOT TENDER

Name	Visual Call Sign	Builder	Keel Laid	Commissioned	Disposition
Willow	WAGL 253	Dubuque Boat & Boiler Works, Dubuque, IA	3 Jul 24 (contracted)	4 Oct 27	*Decomm* and *trans* to Army Corps of Engineers 1 Mar 45

Cost
  $348,732

Hull
  Displacement (tons)   1,070 fl (1927)
  Length   200′ oa
  Beam   65′ max (over guards)
  Draft   6′6″ max (1927)

Machinery
  Main Engines   2 noncondensing steam
  Main Boilers   6 western river type, 225 psi
  SHP   800
  Propellers   Paddlewheel

Performance
  Max Speed   7.5 kts (1945)
  Max Sustained   5.0 kts, 1,000 mi radius (1945)
  Economic   4.0 kts, 1,300 mi radius (1945)

Logistics
  Fuel Oil (95%)   46,400 gal
  Complement   2 officers, 20 men (1942)

Electronics
  None

Armament
  None

Design
  The *Willow* was designed for service on the Mississippi River. Two main features of the *Willow*'s design were the complete plating of the underside of the guards, and the longitudinal stiffness of the hull obtained by using a system of guiders instead of hog braces.

Willow

1941–45 assigned to 9th District—stationed at Memphis, TN, and used for A/N duty; 15 Dec 44 collided with LST 841—both ships received considerable damage.

The *Willow* flying the USLHS pennant, indicating that the photograph was taken prior to 1 Sep 39.

182-FOOT TENDER

Name	Visual Call Sign	Builder	Keel Laid	Commissioned	Disposition
Wakerobin	WAGL 251	The Dravo Constructing Co., Neville Island, Pittsburg, PA	9 Oct 25 (contracted)	15 Apr 27	*Trans* to Army Corps of Engineers 20 Apr 55

Cost
$187,500

Hull
Displacement (tons) 622 fl (1927); 575 light (1927)
Length 182′ oa
Beam 43′ mb
Draft 4′2″ (1927)

Machinery
Main Engines 2 horizontal steam
Main Boilers 2 Babcock & Wilcox sectional header, 200 psi
SHP 550
Propellers Stern paddlewheel, 11′4″ diameter

Performance
Max Sustained 9.0 kts, 1,470 mi radius (1947)
Economic 5.0 kts, 1,690 mi radius (1947)

Logistics
Fuel Coal
Complement 1 officer, 1 warrant, 34 men (1947)

Electronics
None

Armament
None

Design
Designed as a stern-wheel river steamer built of steel and wood.

Wakerobin

1941–45 assigned to 9th District—stationed at Keokuk, IA, and Vicksburg, MS; from Vicksburg used for A/N duty on 438 miles of lower Mississippi River, from Mile 400 to Baton Rouge, LA.

The *Wakerobin* in 1945.

99-FOOT TENDER

Name	Visual Call Sign	Builder	Commissioned	Disposition
Pine (ex-*Petrel*)	WAGL 162	Defoe Boat & Motor Works, Bay City, MI	16 Jul 26 (CG); 1 Nov 41 (USN); 1 Jan 46 (CG)	*Decomm* 25 Aug 47; *sold* 15 Jul 48

Cost
$78,692

Hull
Displacement (tons)   210 fl (1926 and 1945)
Length   99'8" oa
Beam   23' mb
Draft   4'6" mean (1926); 7'8" max (1945)

Machinery
Main Engines   2 Gray Marine diesels
BHP   300
Propellers   Twin

Performance
Max Sustained   8.5 kts, 1,953 mi radius (1926)
Cruising   6.5 kts, 3,000 mi radius (1945)

Logistics
Diesel Fuel   5,078 gal
Complement   0 officers, 15 men (1926); 0 officers, 11 men (1945)

Electronics (1943)
Detection Radar   BK

Armament
None

Design
Designed as a bay and sound tender.

Pine

1 Jul 40 name changed from the *Petrel* to the *Pine;* 1 Nov 41 transferred to USN; 1941–45 assigned to 1st District—stationed at Portland, ME, and used for A/N duty.

The tender *Pine* during WW II.

99-FOOT TENDER

Name	Visual Call Sign	Builder	Commissioned	Disposition
Phlox (ex-*Nansemond*)	WAGL 161	Defoe Boat & Motor Works, Bay City, MI	1 Jun 26	*Decomm* 26 Aug 47; *sold* 20 Jan 49

Cost
$80,000

Hull
Displacement (tons)   210 fl (1925 and 1945)
Length   99'8" oa
Beam   23' mb
Draft   8' max (1925 and 1945)

Machinery
Main Engines   2 Gray Marine diesels
BHP   330
Propellers   Twin

Performance
Max Sustained   10.0 kts, 2,492 mi radius (1925)
Economic   6.5 kts, 3,000 mi radius (1945)

Logistics
Diesel (95%)   5,980 gal
Complement   0 officers, 15 men (1925); 0 officers, 11 men (1945)

Electronics
None

Armament
1925   1 3"/23
1945   None

Design
Designed as a bay and sound tender; name changed from the *Nansemond* to the *Phlox* on 1 Sep 41.

Phlox

1941–43 assigned to 9th District—stationed at Alpena, MI, and used for A/N duty; 1943–45 assigned to 1st District—stationed at Woods Hole, MA.

The tender *Phlox*, 24 Mar 45. Note the protection on the ship's side to prevent damage from buoys that were being serviced.

99-FOOT TENDER

Name	Visual Call Sign	Builder	Keel Laid	Launched	Commissioned	Disposition
Forward	WAGL 160	Defoe Boat & Motor Works, Bay City, MI	16 Jan 25 (contract awarded)	7 Nov 25	14 Nov 25	*Decomm* 18 Aug 47; *sold* 9 Sep 47

Cost
  $80,000

Hull
  Displacement (tons)   210 fl (1925 and 1945)
  Length   99'8" oa
  Beam   23' mb
  Draft   8' max (1925 and 1945)

Machinery
  Main Engines   2 Gray Marine diesels
  BHP   330
  Propellers   Twin

Performance
  Max Speed   9.0 kts (1925)
  Max Sustained   9.0 kts, 2,492 mi radius (1925)
  Cruising   8.0 kts, 4,000 mi radius (1925)

Logistics
  Fuel Oil (95%)   4,500 gal

Complement   2 warrants, 15 men (1925); 0 officers, 11 men (1945)

Electronics
  None

Armament
  1925   1 3"/23
  1945   1 3"/23; 1 20mm/80; 2 dc tracks

Design
  Designed as a bay and sound tender.

Forward

1941–44 assigned to 7th District—stationed at Miami, FL, and used for A/N duty; 19 Feb 42 assisted in rescue of 18 survivors from the tanker *Pan Massachusetts*; 1944–45 assigned to CG Headquarters—stationed at Curtis Bay, MD, and used for transporting freight.

164-FOOT CLASS

Name	Visual Call Sign	Builder	Keel Laid	Commissioned	Disposition
Greenbrier	WAGL 214	Charles Ward Engineering Works, Charleston, WV	19 Sep 22	20 Jun 24	*Decomm* 19 Sep 47; *sold* 19 Apr 48

Cost
  $128,000
Hull
  Displacement (tons)   440 fl (1924 and 1945)
  Length   164′6″ oa
  Beam   32′6″ mb
  Draft   4′ max (1924); 5′6″ max (1945)
Machinery
  Main Engines   Noncondensing steam
  Main Boilers   3 fire tube
  SHP   500
  Propellers   Stern paddlewheel
Performance
  Max Speed   10.0 kts (1945)
  Max Sustained   9.0 kts, 600 mi radius (1945)
  Cruising   8.0 kts, 790 mi radius (1924)
  Economic   7.0 kts, 800 mi radius (1945)
Logistics
  Coal   100 tons
  Complement   1 officer, 25 men (1924); 1 officer, 26 men (1945)
Electronics
  None
Armament
  None
Design
  With a steel hull and a composite superstructure, the *Greenbrier* was a typical stern-

wheel river steamer. About 95% of her space was allotted to hotel features, and about 5% to buoy-tending features.

Greenbrier

1941–45 assigned to the 9th District—stationed at Cincinnati, OH, and used for A/N duty for 443 miles on the Kanawha River and Ohio River, Dam 22 to Dam 44.

The *Greenbrier* at work, sometime after 1 Sep 39. She was one of the first inland buoy tenders built for the USLHS. The *Greenbrier* was a typical river steamer: about 95% of her space was allocated to hotel and 5% to buoy tending.

EMERGENCY ACQUISITION (172-FOOT TENDERS)

Name	Visual Call Sign	Builder	Commissioned	Disposition
Ilex (ex-*General Edmund Kirby*)	WAGL 222	Fabricated Shipbuilding Corp., and Coddington Engineering Co., Milwaukee, WI	1919 (USA); 1924 (USLHS)	*Decomm* 17 Apr 47; *sold* 14 Oct 47
Lotus (ex-*Colonel Albert Todd*)	WAGL 229	Milwaukee, WI	1920 (USA); 1924 (USLHS)	*Decomm* 5 Nov 46; *sold* 11 Jun 47
Lupine (ex-*General W. P. Randolph*)	WAGL 230	Fabricated Shipbuilding Corp., and Coddington Engineering Co., Milwaukee, WI	1918 (USA); 14 Apr 27 (USLHS)	*Decomm* 7 Jan 47; *sold* 28 Nov 47
Speedwell (ex-*Colonel John V. White*)	WAGL 245	Milwaukee, WI	1920 (USA); 23 Apr 23 (USLHS)	*Decomm* 19 Jun 47; *sold* 30 Dec 47
Spruce (ex-*Colonel Garland N. Whistler*)	WAGL 246	New Orleans, LA	1920 (USA); 22 Dec 23 (USLHS)	*Trans* to Coast & Geodetic Survey 17 May 50
Acacia (ex-*General John F. Story*)	WAGL 200	Fabricated Shipbuilding Corp., and Coddington Engineering Co., Milwaukee, WI	1920 (USA); 14 Apr 27 (USLHS)	Sunk by enemy, 16°17′N, 63°44′W, 15 Mar 42

Cost
$540,000 each; alterations $41,022 to $110,963

Hull
Displacement (tons)	1,130 fl (1942 and 1945)
Length	172' oa
Beam	32' mb
Draft	11'6" max (1942)

Machinery
Main Engines	2 Allis Chalmers compound, inverted, reciprocating steam
Main Boilers	2 Page & Burton watertube
SHP	1,000
Propellers	Twin

Performance
Max Sustained	11.0 kts, 1,692 mi radius (1942)
Cruising	10.0 kts, 1,800 mi radius (1945)
Economic	8.0 kts, 2,000 mi radius (1945)

Logistics
Fuel Oil (95%)	33,600 gal
Complement	3 officers, 41 men (1942); 3 officers, 1 warrant, 55 men (1945)

Deck Gear
Boom Capacity	20 tons

Electronics
Detection Radar	
1943	*Ilex, Lotus:* BK
1945	*Lotus:* SO-8; all others: SO-1
Sonar (1945)	*Ilex, Lotus:* WEA-2; *Speedwell, Spruce:* WEA-2a

Armament (1945)
Lotus, Speedwell, Spruce: 1 3"/50, 2 20mm/80 (single), 2 dc tracks; *Lupine:* 1 3"/50, 2 20mm/80 (single); *Ilex:* 2 20mm/80

Design
Formerly mine planters, these vessels underwent extensive alterations to convert to tenders. The forecastle head was shortened and rounded; a steel main deck was added forward; new windows were installed in the pilothouse; and a new refrigerating plant was added. These units were six of the nine mine planters that were transferred to the USLHS in 1922.

Acacia

1941–42 assigned to the 10th District—stationed at San Juan, PR, and used for A/N duty; 15 Mar 42 shelled and machine-gunned by U-161—sunk without loss of life.

Ilex

1941–45 assigned to the 1st District—stationed at South Portland, ME, and used for A/N duty and to service submarine nets; 5 Mar 43 rescued 35 from the grounded freighter *Hartwelson.*

Lotus

1941–43 assigned to 1st District—stationed at Chelsea, MA, and used for A/N duty; Jul 41 laid buoys and antisubmarine nets at Argentia, Newfoundland; 1943–44 assigned to the 10th District—stationed at San Juan, PR; 1944–45 assigned to the 5th District—stationed at Norfolk, VA.

Lupine

1941–43 assigned to the 12th District—stationed at San Francisco, CA, and used for A/N duty; 1943–45 assigned to the 11th District—stationed at San Pedro, CA.

Speedwell

1941–45 assigned to the 5th District—stationed at Portsmouth, VA, and used for A/N duty.

Spruce

1941–45 assigned to the 10th District—stationed at San Juan, PR, and used for A/N duty.

The *Lupine* off the California coast, 1 Jul 43. The USLHS acquired six of these former mine planters from the Army following WW I. Their hull form was left unchanged. A turtleback forecastle was installed, and the anchor was mounted high to prevent the ship from being hung up on a buoy it was servicing.

157-FOOT TUG

Name	Visual Call Sign	Builder	Launched	Commissioned	Disposition
Kickapoo (ex-*Baldridge*)	WAGL 56	Bethlehem Steel, Elizabeth Port, NJ	1919	1919 (USSB); 21 Jan 22 (CG)	*Decomm* 24 Aug 45; *sold* 7 Jul 47

Cost
  NA
Hull
  Displacement (tons)   840 fl (1922); 848 fl (1945)
  Length   157'4" oa
  Beam   35' mb
  Draft   12' max (1922); 14'6" max (1945)
Machinery
  Main Engines   1 triple expansion steam
  Main Boilers   2 Scotch
  SHP   1,000
  Propellers   Single
Performance
  Max Speed   11.5 kts (1922 and 1945)
  Max Sustained   11.5 kts, 2,386 mi radius (1922)
  Cruising   7.8 kts, 3,170 mi radius (1922)
Logistics
  Coal   160 tons
  Complement   3 officers, 35 men (1922); 1 officer, 3 warrants, 36 men (1945)
Electronics
  Detection Radar   None (1941); SO-8 (1945)
Armament
  1922   2 1-pdrs.
  1945   None
Design
  This tug was transferred from the Shipping Board Emergency Fleet Corps on 31 Oct 21 under Executive Order No. 3564. Her name was changed from the *Baldridge* to the *Kickapoo* on 9 Nov 21. She was classified as a buoy tender during WW II.

Kickapoo

1941–45 assigned to 1st District—stationed at Buzzards Bay, MA (41–Oct 44), and Rockland, ME (Oct 44–45); used for ice-breaking and general A/N duty.

On 2 Jan 25, the *Kickapoo* rescued all passengers and crew, a total of 227 men, from the steamer *Mohawk* off Brandywine Shoals, DE.

75-FOOT TENDER

Name	Visual Call Sign	Builder	Keel Laid	Launched	Commissioned	Disposition
Aster	WAGL 269	M.M. Flechas, Pascagoula, MS	27 Apr 21 (contracted)	16 Dec 21	17 Jan 22	*Decomm* 24 Jan 46

Cost
  $19,909
Hull
  Displacement (tons)   109 fl (1921 and 1945)
  Length   75'10" oa
  Beam   21'8" max
  Draft   5'7" max (1921 and 1945)
Machinery
  Main Engines   2 Fairbanks Morse diesels
  BHP   90
  Propellers   Twin, 3 blades

Performance
  Max Speed   7.8 kts (1921)
Logistics
  Diesel Fuel   496 gal
  Complement   2 officers, 8 men (1922); 0 officers, 9 men (1945)
Electronics
  None
Armament
  None

Design

Constructed entirely of wood, the *Aster* had provisions for a pile driver attached to her side. Initially, she had 2 Standard Motor Co. gasoline engines.

160-FOOT TENDERS

Name	Visual Call Sign	Builder	Keel Laid	Launched	Commissioned	Disposition
Hawthorn	WAGL 215	Consolidated Shipbuilding Corp., Morris Heights, NY	14 Jan 20	18 Jun 21	28 Dec 21	*Decomm* 24 Jul 64; *sold* 29 Nov 65
Oak	WAGL 239	Consolidated Shipbuilding Corp., Morris Heights, NY	14 Jan 20	28 Jun 21	31 Dec 21	*Decomm* 6 Nov 64; *trans* to Smithsonian 3 Mar 67

Cost

$357,250 each

Hull

Displacement   875 mean draft (1921); 950 max (1945)

Length   160' oa

Beam   30' mb

Draft   9'6" mean (1921); 10'6" max (1945)

Machinery

Main Engines   1 triple-expansion steam

Main Boilers   1 Scotch, 200 psi

SHP   700

Propellers   Single

Performance

Max Speed   8.0 kts (1921)

9.0 kts (1945)

Cruising   8.0 kts, 1,750 mi radius (1945)

Logistics

Fuel Oil (95%)   21,300 gal

Complement   4 officers, 23 men (1922)

Deck Gear

Boom Capacity   20 tons

Hoist Power   Steam

Electronics

Detection Radar   BK (1943); SO-8 (1945)

Armament (1945)

Oak: 1 3"/23, 1 20mm/80; *Hawthorn:* none

Design

Bay and sound tenders of steel construction; these vessels had an extra large buoy deck and a clear passage around the main deckhouse.

Aster

1941–45 assigned to the 8th District—stationed at Mobile, AL, and used for A/N duty in the Gulf of Mexico.

Hawthorn

1941–45 assigned to the 3rd District—stationed at New London, CT, and used for A/N duty.

Oak

1941–45 assigned to the 3rd District—stationed at St. George, Staten Island, NY, and used for A/N duty.

The *Oak*, prior to WW II. Her steam plant was placed on exhibit at the Smithsonian Institution in 1978.

EMERGENCY ACQUISITION (108-FOOT TENDER)

Name	Visual Call Sign	Builder	Launched	Commissioned	Disposition
Shrub (ex-*S. P. Mansfield*)	WAGL 244	William G. Abbott Shipbuilding Co., Milford, DE	1912	20 Jun 17 (USN); 31 Jul 20 (USLHS)	*Decomm* 1 Jul 47; *sold* 29 Dec 47

Cost
  $42,000

Hull
  Displacement (tons)   436 fl (1945)   Beam   29' mb
  Length   107' oa   Draft   6'9" max (1945)

Machinery
  Main Engines   1 compound reciprocating steam
  Main Boilers   1 watertube, 150 psi
  SHP   278
  Propellers   Single

Performance
  Max Speed   9.0 kts (1945)
  Max Sustained   8.0 kts, 750 mi radius (1945)

Logistics
  Coal   42 tons
  Complement   2 officers, 13 men (1919); 2 officers, 27 men (1945)

Electronics (1943)
  Detection Radar BK

Armament
  None

Design
  The *Shrub* was constructed of wood as a freight steamer.

Shrub

1941–45 assigned to the 1st District—stationed at Bristol, RI, and used for A/N duty.

The *Shrub*, 1925. The first buoy tender acquired was the *Rush*, a former revenue cutter transferred to the USLHS in 1850. The first steam buoy tender was the *Shubrick*, built at the Philadelphia Navy Yard in 1857.

201-FOOT TENDER

Name	Visual Call Sign	Builder	Keel Laid	Launched	Commissioned	Disposition
Cedar	WAGL 207	Craig Shipbuilding Co., Long Beach, CA	4 May 15 (contracted)	27 Dec 16	30 Jun 17	*Decomm* 29 Jun 50; *sold* 27 Jun 55

Cost
  $248,189

Hull
  Displacement (tons)   1,800 at mean draft (1917); 1,750 fl (1945)
  Length   200'8" oa; 188' bp
  Beam   36'6" max
  Draft   13' mean (1917); 17'6" max (1945)

Machinery
  Main Engines   California Shipbuilding triple-expansion reciprocating, 3-cyl steam
  Main Boilers   2 Scotch Marine, 190 psi
  SHP   1,250
  Propellers   Single

Performance
  Max Speed   12.0 kts
  Max Sustained   12.0 kts, 4,848 mi radius (1942)
  Economic   8.0 kts, 5,000 mi radius (1945)

Logistics
  Fuel Oil (95%) 110,403 gal
  Complement   7 officers, 22 men (1917); 3 officers, 41 men (1942); 4 officers, 1 warrant, 75 men (1945)

Electronics
  Detection Radar None (1943); SO-8 (1945)
  Sonar   WEA-2 (1945)

Armament
  1943   1 dc track
  1945   2 20mm/80 (single); 2 dc tracks

Design

The *Cedar* was designed to operate in Alaskan waters. Her hull was steel, her superstructure was wood, and she had a double bottom. The *Cedar* was the largest tender built for the USLHS.

Cedar

1941–45 assigned to the 13th and 17th Districts—stationed at Ketchikan, AK, and used for A/N duty; 1942–43 operated in Aleutian Islands in support of naval operations; 11 Sep 44 assisted in refloating the freighter *Kolosnik*.

The *Cedar*, 13 May 44, at Seattle, WA. Until WW I, the USLHS divided its tenders into four groups based on length. By WW II, the tenders had been divided into four groups based on mission. These were coastwise tenders, bay and sound tenders, river tenders, and buoy boats. (Courtesy of the U.S. Navy.)

90-FOOT TENDER

Name	Visual Call Sign	Builder	Keel Laid	Launched	Commissioned	Disposition
Palmetto	WAGL 265	Merrill-Stevens Dry Dock & Repair Co., Jacksonville, FL	3 Sep 15 (contracted)	30 Jun 16	19 Mar 17	*Decomm* 23 May 58; *sold* 13 Apr 59

Cost
$28,975

Hull

Displacement (tons)	170 fl (1916 and 1945)
Length	90' oa
Beam	22' mb
Draft	4' mean (1916); 7'6" max (1945)

Machinery

Main Engines	2 Superior diesel
BHP	350
Propellers	Twin

Performance

Max Speed	7.5 kts (1945)
Max Sustained	7.5 kts, 915 mi radius (1916)
Cruising	7.0 kts, 1,000 mi radius (1945)

Logistics

Diesel	1,368 gal
Complement	3 officers, 8 men (1917); 0 officers, 11 men (1945)

Electronics
None

Armament
None

Design

Constructed for shoal-water service in the Jacksonville, FL, area. She had a steel hull, wood deck and superstructure; her original machinery was two 4-cylinder internal-combustion engines.

Palmetto

1941–45 assigned to the 6th District—stationed at Charleston, SC, and used for A/N duty.

The *Palmetto*, 22 Feb 49, with pile driver erected forward. She had a plumb stern. Initially, she had a gasoline engine and a gasoline-powered hoist.

138-FOOT TENDER

Name	Visual Call Sign	Builder	Keel Laid	Launched	Commissioned	Disposition
Rose	WAGL 242	Anderson Steamboat Co., Seattle, WA	6 Nov 14 (contracted)	19 Feb 16	8 Aug 16	*Decomm* 15 Oct 47; *sold* 14 Jun 48

Cost
  $92,135

Hull
  Displacement (tons)   567 at mean draft (1917); 692 fl (1945)
  Length   127'9" oa (1916); 137'9" oa (1936); *see* Design
  Beam   24'6" max
  Draft   9'4" mean (1917); 10' max (1945)

Machinery
  Main Engines   2 triple-expansion, inverted, direct-acting steam
  Main Boilers   2 Almy watertube
  SHP   330
  Propellers   Twin, 4 blade

Performance
  Max Speed   10.3 kts (1945)
  Max Sustained   10.0 kts, 1,260 mi radius (1916)
                         10.0 kts, 700 mi radius (1945)

  Economic   8.0 kts, 1,000 mi radius (1945)

Logistics
  Fuel Oil (95%)   13,247 gal
  Complement   4 officers, 16 men (1917); 3 officers, 32 men (1945)

Electronics (1945)
  Detection Radar   SO-1

Armament (1945)
  2 20mm/80 (single)

Design
  A coastwise tender constructed of steel; in 1936 she was lengthened by 10 feet. A section was added just forward of the main deckhouse.

Rose

1941–45 assigned to the 13th District—stationed at Astoria, OR, and used for A/N duty.

The *Rose*, 17 Aug 36. A 10-foot section has just been added forward of the main deckhouse.

110-FOOT TENDER

Name	Visual Call Sign	Builder	Keel Laid	Commissioned	Disposition
Camellia	WAGL 206	Racine Boat Manufacturing Co., Muskegon, MI	18 Oct 09	13 Jul 11	*Decomm* 18 Aug 47; *sold* 29 Dec 47

Cost
  $57,412

Hull
  Displacement (tons)   377 fl (1911 and 1945)
  Tonnage   183 gross
  Length   110′ oa
  Beam   24′ max
  Draft   7′7″ max (1911); 8′ max (1945)

Machinery
  Main Engines   2 Atlas Imperial diesels
  BHP   220
  Propellers   Twin

Performance
  Max Speed   9.0 kts (1911)
       8.3 kts (1945)
  Max Sustained   9.0 kts, 1,732 mi radius (1911)
       8.0 kts, 1,920 mi radius (1945)

Cruising   7.0 kts, 2,100 mi radius (1945)

Logistics
  Diesel Fuel   6,165 gal
  Complement   4 officers, 12 men (1911); 0 officers, 23 men (1945)

Deck Gear
  Boom Capacity   5 tons

Electronics
  None

Armament
  None

Design
  Built for the shoal waters of the Gulf of Mexico; steel hull and wooden superstructure.

Camellia

1941–45 assigned to 8th District—stationed at New Orleans, LA, and used for A/N duty.

190-FOOT TENDERS (*MANZANITA* CLASS, "8 TENDER" CLASS)

Name	Visual Call Sign	Builder	Commissioned	Disposition
Anemone	WAGL 202	New York Shipbuilding Co., Camden, NJ	1908	*Decomm* and *trans* to Philippines 1 Jul 47
Cypress	WAGL 211	New York Shipbuilding Co., Camden, NJ	1908	*Decomm* 20 Aug 46; *sold* 18 Mar 47
Hibiscus	WAGL 218	New York Shipbuilding Co., Camden, NJ	1908	*Decomm* 3 Sep 46; *sold* 26 Jun 47
Kukui	WAGL 225	New York Shipbuilding Co., Camden, NJ	1908	*Decomm* 1 Feb 46; *sold* 8 Apr 47
Manzanita	WAGL 233	New York Shipbuilding Co., Camden, NJ	1908	*Decomm* 29 Nov 46; *sold* 30 Apr 47
Orchid	WAGL 240	New York Shipbuilding Co., Camden, NJ	1908	*Decomm* and *trans* to Philippines 1 Dec 45
Sequoia	WAGL 243	New York Shipbuilding Co., Camden, NJ	1908	*Decomm* and *trans* to Philippines 1 Jul 47
Tulip	WAGL 249	New York Shipbuilding Co., Camden, NJ	1908	*Decomm* 1 Dec 45; *trans* to Philippines 5 Jul 47

Cost
$191,633 each

Hull

Displacement (tons)	1,057 fl (1908 and 1945)
Length	190′ oa
Beam	30′ mb
Draft	13′ max (1908); 14′ max (1945)

Machinery

Main Engines	2 triple-expansion steam
Main Boilers	2 (various types)
SHP	1,000
Propellers	Twin

Performance

Max Speed	12.0 kts (1908)
	13.5 kts (1945)
Max Sustained	12.0 kts, 1,992 mi radius (1908)
Cruising	10.0 kts, 2,550 mi radius (1945)

Logistics

Fuel Oil (95%)	33,297 gal
Complement	3 officers, 39 men (1908); 3 officers, 41 men (1945)

Electronics (1945)

Detection Radar	*Hibiscus, Orchid, Sequoia:* SO-1; *Tulip:* SO-8; others: none
Sonar	All, except *Anemone, Cypress:* WEA-2

Armament (1945)

	3"/50	3"/23	20mm/80	dc tracks	dc projectors
Anemone		1	2	2	
Cypress		1	2	2	
Hibiscus	1		3		2
Kukui			5	2	
Manzanita			2		
Orchid		1	2	2	
Sequoia	1		2	1	
Tulip		1	2	2	

Design

The *Manzanita* class, designed by the Navy Department, incorporated numerous innovations as compared with previous designs. Constructed of steel and completed as coal burners, the tenders of this class were the first of their kind constructed. They were built with vertical sides, which provided a flat surface on which buoy pads could be attached. Also, the vertical flat sides reduced the tendency of a buoy to slide beneath the hull when the tender was maneuvering alongside. The deck edge on the forecastle was rounded in order to prevent the buoy cage or lantern from catching. Steel replaced wood for the booms, and wire rope replaced manila. The boom was somewhat longer than what might be expected to permit a special rigging for the transfer of supplies to lighthouses on inaccessible rocks and cliffs. Water capacity was significantly increased, with separate tanks for lighthouse replenishment. These ships had fine lines as opposed to their predecessors, making them faster and more maneuverable. They heeled sharply, however, when lifting buoys.

Anemone

1941–45 assigned to the 1st District—stationed at Woods Hole, MA, and used for A/N duty and to service antisubmarine nets.

Cypress

1941–45 assigned to the 6th District—stationed at Charleston, SC, and used for A/N duty.

Hibiscus

1941–45 assigned to the 1st District—stationed at South Portland, ME, and used for A/N duty; 28 May 42 badly burned and beached; 16 Oct 42 returned to service; 1944–45 serviced buoys and antisubmarine nets at Argentia, Newfoundland.

Kukui

1941–45 assigned to the 14th District—stationed at Honolulu, HI, and used for A/N duty.

Manzanita

1941–45 assigned to the 13th District—stationed at Astoria, OR, and used for A/N duty; Oct 43 laid antisubmarine cables off Prince Rupert, BC, Canada, and Dutch Harbor, AK.

Orchid

1941–45 assigned to the 5th District—stationed at Portsmouth, VA, and used for A/N duty.

Sequoia

1941–45 assigned to the 12th District—stationed at San Francisco, CA, and used for A/N duty.

Tulip

1941–45 assigned to the 3rd District—stationed at St. George, Staten Island, NY, and used for A/N duty.

The *Orchid*, 20 Jan 43, at Norfolk Navy Yard, Portsmouth, VA. She is not yet fitted with radar.

174-FOOT TENDER

Name	Visual Call Sign	Builder	Keel Laid	Launched	Commissioned	Disposition
Sunflower	WAGL 247	Wilmington, DE	14 Sep 05 (contracted)	4 Aug 06	23 Mar 07	*Decomm* 10 Jan 46; *sold* 19 Feb 47

Cost
  $124,958
Hull
  Displacement (tons)   1,246 fl (1907)
  Length   174' oa
  Beam   32' mb
  Draft   12'2" (1907); 13'3" (1945)
Machinery
  Main Engines   2 triple-expansion steam
  Main Boilers   2 Babcock & Wilcox watertube
  SHP   900
  Propellers   Twin
Performance
  Max Speed   12.0 kts (1945)
  Max Sustained   11.9 kts, 2,023 mi radius (1907)
    11.0 kts, 1,500 mi radius (1945)
  Economic   7.0 kts, 2,000 mi radius (1945)
Logistics
  Fuel Oil (95%)   35,000 gal
  Complement   2 officers, 30 men (1907); 1 officer, 3 warrants, 37 men (1945)
Electronics
  Detection Radar   None
  Sonar   WEA-2a (1945)
Armament (1945)
  1 20mm/80; 2 dc tracks
Design
  The *Sunflower* was the first tender to use wire rope in place of manila. She was converted from coal to oil in 1931.

Sunflower

1941–45 assigned to the 8th District—stationed at Galveston, TX, and used for A/N duty.

The *Sunflower*, 29 Jun 43. She is flying the CG ensign from her foremast. The gun position at the forecastle is for a 20mm/80.

126-FOOT TENDER

Name	Visual Call Sign	Builder	Commissioned	Disposition
Aspen	WAGL 204	Craig Shipbuilding Co., Toledo, OH	8 May 06	*Decomm* 25 Jan 47; *sold* 26 Jan 48

Cost
$70,573

Hull
Displacement (tons)   415 fl (1906); 465 fl (1945)
Length   125'9" oa
Beam   25' max
Draft   8'3" max (1906); 9'6" max (1945)

Machinery
Main Engines   1 compound reciprocating steam
Main Boilers   1 Scotch
SHP   424
Propellers   Single

Performance
Max Speed   10.5 kts (1906)
Max Sustained   9.5 kts, 740 mi radius (1945)

Logistics
Coal (95%)   40 tons
Complement   1 officer, 16 men (1906); 2 officers, 23 men (1942)

Electronics
None

Armament
None

Design
Designed as a bay and sound tender.

Aspen

1941–45 assigned to the 9th District—stationed at Sault Ste. Marie, MI, and used for A/N duty on the Great Lakes.

173-FOOT TENDERS

Name	Visual Call Sign	Builder	Commissioned	Disposition
Magnolia	WAGL 231	Baltimore, MD	5 May 04	Rammed & sunk 25 Aug 45
Ivy	[WAGL]	NA	9 May 04	*Decomm* 6 Nov 40; *sold* 25 Apr 41

Cost
$124,874 *(Magnolia)*; $123,800 *(Ivy)*

Hull
Displacement (tons)   880 fl (1904); 916 fl (1945)
Length   173' oa
Beam   30'6" mb
Draft   9'6" max (1904)

Machinery
Main Engines   2 compound reciprocating steam
Main Boilers   2 Page & Burton watertube
SHP   700
Propellers   Twin

Performance
Max Sustained   11.5 kts, 1,483 mi radius (1904)
Cruising   10.5 kts, 1,400 mi radius (1945)

Logistics
Fuel Oil (95%)   28,441 gal
Complement   3 officers, 29 men (1904); 1 officer, 3 warrants, 37 men (1945)

Electronics (1945)
Detection Radar   SO-8
Sonar   WEA-2a *(Magnolia)*

Armament (1945)
1 3"/50; 2 20mm/80 (single); 2 dc tracks

Design
Designed as a bay and sound tender.

Magnolia

1941–45 assigned to the 8th District—stationed at Mobile, AL, and used for A/N duty; 25 Aug 45 rammed and sunk by the SS *Marguerite le Hand* in the Gulf of Mexico off Mobile Bay—1 life lost and 49 survivors.

Ivy

Decommissioned before WW II.

The remains of the *Magnolia*, sunk 25 Aug 45.

The *Ivy* while in the USLHS. The pilothouse was designed to provide maximum visibility for the ship handler. Most tenders were fitted with a superintendent's quarters aft. This was always ready for his visit.

165-FOOT TENDER

Name	Visual Call Sign	Builder	Commissioned	Disposition
Crocus	WAGL 210	Shooters Is., NY	26 Jul 05	*Decomm* 13 Jul 46

Cost
  $119,713

Hull
Displacement (tons)	910 fl (1904 and 1945)
Length	164'7" oa; 154'6" bp
Beam	29' mb
Draft	12'3" max (1904); 13' max (1945)

Machinery
Main Engines	2 compound reciprocating steam
Main Boilers	2 Scotch
SHP	700
Propellers	Twin

Performance
Max Speed	9.0 kts (1904)
Max Sustained	9.0 kts, 1,062 mi radius (1904)
	10.0 kts, 1,050 mi radius (1945)
Cruising	9.0 kts, 1,275 mi radius (1945)

Logistics
Coal (95%)	95 tons
Complement	3 officers, 28 men (1904); 1 officer, 3 warrants, 35 men (1945)

Electronics
  None

Armament
  None

Design
  Composite construction with a steel hull.

Crocus

1941–45 assigned to 9th District—stationed at Toledo, OH, and used for A/N duty.

The *Crocus*, sometime early in her career. Tenders that served in inland waters retained their peacetime paint scheme throughout the war.

179-FOOT TENDER

Name	Visual Call Sign	Builder	Keel Laid	Commissioned	Disposition
Heather	[WAGL]	Seattle, WA	Feb 01 (contracted)	10 Jun 03	*Decomm* and *trans* to War Dept. 6 Sep 40

Cost
$211,817

Hull
Displacement (tons)   730 fl (1903); 631 light (1926); 831 fl (1926)
Length   178'6" oa; 165' bp
Beam   28'6" mb
Draft   15' max (1926)

Machinery
Main Engines   1 diesel
BHP   685
Propellers   Single

Logistics
Complement   7 officers, 20 men (1926)

Electronics
None

Armament
None

Design
Composite construction; originally engineered with compound steam, coal fueled.

Heather

3 Sep 40 on loan to the War Department; 6 Sep 40 transferred to the War Department.

169-FOOT CUTTER

Name	Visual Call Sign	Builder	Keel Laid	Commissioned	Disposition
Larkspur	WAGL 226	Port Richmond, NY	1 Apr 01 (contracted)	24 Feb 03	*Decomm* 10 Jan 46; *sold* 19 Feb 46

Cost
$123,259

Hull
Displacement (tons)   703 fl (1903); 888 fl (1945)
Length   169'2" oa; 162' bp
Beam   30' mb
Draft   11' max (1903); 12' max (1945)

Machinery
Main Engines   2 compound express steam
Main Boilers   2 watertube express
SHP   700
Propellers   Twin

Performance
Max Sustained   10.0 kts, 1,190 mi radius (1903)
   9.0 kts, 1,640 mi radius (1945)
Cruising   8.0 kts, 1,830 mi radius (1945)

Logistics
Fuel Oil (95%)   30,000 gal
Complement   2 officers, 27 men (1903); 1 officer, 3 warrants, 37 men (1945)

Electronics
Detection Radar   None
Sonar   WEA-2a (1945)

Armament (1945)
2 20mm/80 (single)

Design
Composite construction with a steel hull; initially fueled with coal.

Larkspur

1941–45 assigned to the 8th District—stationed at Mobile, AL, and used for A/N duty.

The *Larkspur*, 29 Jun 43. Tender is armed with a 20mm on the forecastle, a 20mm on the aft deckhouse, and a short depth-charge track on the stern. As completed, the *Larkspur* had two masts and was fitted with sails for auxiliary power. Most large tenders built before WW I were provided with sails.

161-FOOT TENDER

Name	Visual Call Sign	Builder	Keel Laid	Launched	Commissioned	Disposition
Hyacinth	WAGL 221	Port Huron, MI	18 Oct 01	26 Jul 02	26 Jun 03	*Decomm* 15 Nov 45; *sold* 19 Oct 46

Cost
  $115,000

Hull
  Displacement (tons)   950 fl (1903); 885 fl (1945)
  Length   160′6″ oa; 150′8″ bp
  Beam   28′ mb
  Draft   12′ max (1903); 12′6″ max (1945)

Machinery
  Main Engines   1 compound express steam
  Main Boilers   2 Scotch
  SHP   768
  Propellers   Single

Performance
  Max Speed   11.5 kts (1945)
  Max Sustained   11.0 kts, 1,012 mi radius (1903)

Cruising   10.0 kts, 2,000 mi radius (1945)

Logistics
  Fuel Oil (95%)   27,000 gal
  Complement   2 officers, 24 men (1903); 1 officer, 3 warrants, 35 men (1945)

Electronics (1945)
  Detection Radar   SO-1

Armament
  None

Design
  Composite construction with a steel hull.

Hyacinth

1941–45 assigned to the 9th District—stationed at Milwaukee, WI, and used for A/N duty.

The *Hyacinth*. This tender served on the Great Lakes throughout the war. Pre–WW II tenders were surprisingly fine forward, full at midships, and fine aft.

164-FOOT TENDER

Name	Visual Call Sign	Builder	Commissioned	Disposition
Hydrangea (ex-*Mayflower*)	WAGL 236	Bath, ME	Nov 97	*Decomm* and *trans* to Maritime Commission 8 Oct 45

Cost
  $74,872

Hull
  Displacement (tons)   650 fl (1897); 821 fl (1945)
  Length   164′ oa   Beam   30′ mb
  Draft   8′1″ max (1897); 9′ max (1945)

Machinery
  Main Engines   2 Steeple compound reciprocating steam
  Main Boilers   2 Almy watertube
  SHP   325
  Propellers   Twin

Performance
  Max Speed   9.5 kts (1945)
  Max Sustained   10.0 kts, 1,330 mi radius (1897)
  Cruising   8.5 kts, 1,000 mi radius (1945)
  Economic   7.5 kts, 1,100 mi radius (1945)

Logistics
  Coal (95%)   120 tons
  Complement   3 officers, 40 men (1897); 1 officer, 3 warrants, 36 men (1945)

Electronics
  None

Armament (1945)
  2 20mm/80 (single); 2 dc tracks

Design
  Designed as a bay and sound tender; she had a steel hull.

Hydrangea

1941–45 assigned to 5th District—stationed at Norfolk, VA, and used for A/N duty; established antisubmarine nets at Cape Lookout, NC; 15 Aug 43 name changed from the *Mayflower* to the *Hydrangea*.

The *Hydrangea* as the *Mayflower* prior to service in the CG. From stem to stern, buoy tenders were protected by rubbing strakes at the waterline and the main-deck levels. These strakes were wooden with angle-iron edges.

164-FOOT TENDER

Name	Visual Call Sign	Builder	Commissioned	Disposition
Mangrove	WAGL 232	Crescent Shipyard, Elizabeth, NJ	1 Dec 97	*Decomm* 22 Aug 46; *sold* 6 Mar 47

Cost
  $74,998
Hull
  Displacement (tons)   821 fl (1897 and 1945)
  Tonnage   606 gross (1897)
  Length   164' oa; 155' bp
  Beam   30' mb
  Draft   8'6" max (1897 and 1945)
Machinery
  Main Engines   2 compound reciprocating steam
  Main Boilers   2 Page & Burton watertube
  SHP   550
  Propellers   Twin
Performance
  Max Speed   10.5 kts (1945)
  Max Sustained   10.0 kts, 821 mi radius (1897)

Logistics
  Coal (95%)   90 tons
  Complement   2 officers, 29 men (1897); 1 officer, 3 warrants, 36 men (1945)
Electronics (1945)
  Detection Radar   SO-1
Armament
  2 20mm/80 (single)
Design
  Composite construction with a steel hull; sister-ship *Mayflower* had been discarded before WW II.

Mangrove

1941–45 assigned to the 6th District—stationed at Charleston, SC, and used for A/N duty; 8 Jul 43 grounded without serious damage.

166-FOOT TENDER

Name	Visual Call Sign	Builder	Keel Laid	Launched	Commissioned	Disposition
Amaranth	WAGL 201	Cleveland, OH	21 May 91 (contracted)	18 Dec 91	14 Apr 92	*Decomm* 29 Sep 45; *sold* 19 Oct 46

Cost
  $74,994
Hull
  Displacement (tons)   1,125 fl (1942)
  Length   166' oa
  Beam   28' max
  Draft   13' max (1942)
Machinery
  Main Engines   1 compound reciprocating steam
  Main Boilers   2 Scotch
  SHP   672
  Propellers   Single
Performance
  Max Speed   11.4 kts (1942)
  Max Sustained   11.0 kts, 1,330 mi radius (1942)

Logistics
  Coal (95%)   110 tons
  Complement   1 officer, 3 warrants, 35 men (1942)
Electronics
  None
Armament
  None
Design
  Designed as a bay and sound tender.

Amaranth

1941–45 assigned to the 9th District—stationed at Duluth, MN, and used for A/N duty.

160-FOOT TENDER

Name	Visual Call Sign	Builder	Keel Laid	Commissioned	Disposition
Marigold	WAGL 235	Wyndotte, MI	4 Mar 90 (contracted)	4 Oct 90	*Decomm* 3 Oct 45; *sold* 19 Oct 46

Cost
  $84,871
Hull
  Displacement (tons)   587 fl (1890); 550 fl (1945)
  Length   159'6" oa; 150' bp
  Beam   27' mb
  Draft   8'6" max (1890); 13' max (1945)
Machinery
  Main Engines   1 triple-expansion steam
  Main Boilers   2 Scotch
  SHP   600
  Propellers   Single
Performance
  Max Speed   11.0 kts (1945)
  Max Sustained   10.0 kts, 815 mi radius (1890)
                         10.0 kts, 800 mi radius (1945)
Logistics
  Coal (95%)   65 tons
  Complement   2 officers, 24 crew (1890); 1 officer, 3 warrants, 35 men
                           (1945)
Electronics
  Probably none
Armament
  None
Design
  Composite construction with an iron hull.

Marigold

1941–45 assigned to the 9th District—stationed at Detroit, MI, and used for
A/N duty.

The *Marigold*, 24 Jun 41. The USLHS was incorporated into the CG on 1 Sep 39.
Tending aids to navigation became a federal responsibility on 7 Aug 1789, when the
lighthouses were transferred from the various states to the new federal government.
The *Marigold*, now a CG tender, no longer carries the USLHS emblem on her bow.
(Courtesy of the University of Detroit.)

WARC—CABLE-LAYING SHIPS

166-FOOT CABLE LAYER

Name	Visual Call Sign	Builder	Commissioned	Disposition
Pequot (ex-*General Samuel M. Mills*)	WARC 58	American Brown Boveri Electric Corp., Camden, NJ	1 May 22 (1st CG tour); 1 Jan 46 (2nd CG tour)	*Trans* to USN 1 Nov 41; *decomm* 8 Dec 46; *sold* 5 Sep 47

Cost
  $300,000
Hull
  Displacement (tons)   960 (1938); 1,106 (1945)
  Length   165'9" oa
  Beam   32' mb
  Draft   11'4" (1938); 12'3" (1945)
Machinery
  Main Engines   2 compound expansion steam, 2-cyl
  Main Boilers   2 Foster-Wheeler
  SHP   900
  Propellers   Twin
Performance
  Max   12.0 kts (1938)
  Max Sustained   11.0 kts, 1,000 mi radius (1945)
  Cruising   10.0 kts, 1,250 mi radius (1945)
  Economic   7.8 kts, 1,670 mi radius (1938)

Logistics
  Coal   125 tons
  Complement   5 officers, 48 men (1938); 4 officers, 2 warrants, 63 men
                           (1945)
Electronics (1945)
  Detection Radar   SO-1
Armament
  1938   None
  1945   2 20mm/80 (single)
Design
  Constructed as a cable-laying and repair ship.

Pequot

1941–45 assigned to CG Headquarters—stationed at Boston, MA, and used
to lay cables to remote stations.

The *Pequot* was the only cable layer in the CG during this era. She was used to lay communications and power cables to isolated stations.

WAL—LIGHTSHIPS

115-FOOT LIGHTSHIP

Name	Builder	Launched	Commissioned	Disposition
LS 118 (f-LS 539)	Rice Brothers Corp., East Boothbay, ME	4 Jun 38	11 Sep 38	*Decomm* 7 Nov 72; donated to Lewes, DE, Historical Soc. 9 Aug 73

Cost
$223,900

Hull
Displacement (tons)   412 fl (1946)
Length   114'9" oa
Beam   26' mb
Draft   11'1" max (1946)

Machinery
Main Engines   1 Cooper-Bessemer EN 8 diesel
BHP   400
Propellers   Single

Performance
Max Speed   8.0 kts, 3,760 mi radius (1946)

Logistics
Diesel (95%)   12,500 gal

Complement   0 officers, 11 men (1946)

Electronics
Detection Radar   BK (1943); SO-1 (1945)
Sonar   None

Armament
None

Design
Constructed for the Cornfield Point Station.

LS 118

Pre–WW II served as Cornfield Point LS; 1942–45 assigned to 3rd District—stationed at New London, CT, and used as Cornfield Point LS.

LS 118, 4 Jun 38, launching. She already bears her station name. Lightships had numbers, stations had names. A lightship frequently served on a station for a decade or more. However, most lightships did serve on three or four different stations during their long careers. The station name painted on the hull would be changed as the lightship moved from one station to another.

149-FOOT LIGHTSHIPS

Name	Builder	Commissioned	Disposition
LS 112 (f-LS 534)	Pusey & Jones Co., Wilmington, DE	1936	*Decomm* and *trans* to Dept of Labor, NY 28 May 75

Cost
  $300,956
Hull
  Displacement (tons)   1,050 fl (1946)
  Length   148'10" oa
  Beam   31' mb
  Draft   16'3" max (1946)
Machinery
  Main Engines   Compound reciprocating steam
  Main Boilers   2 Babcock & Wilcox
  SHP   600
  Propellers   Single
Performance
  Max Speed   12.0 kts, 2,000 mi radius (1946)
Logistics
  Fuel Oil (95%)   37,300 gal

Complement   1 officer, 18 men (1946)
Electronics
  Detection Radar   BK (1943); SO-1 (1945)
Armament (1945)
  1 3"/50
Design
  Built specifically for the Nantucket station following the sinking of LS 117 by the *Olympic*. The hull was divided into watertight compartments; six different exits were provided to the upper deck, and other safety design features were incorporated.

LS 112

Pre–WW II served as Nantucket Shoals LS; 1942–45 assigned to 1st District—stationed at Woods Hole, MA, and used as an examination ship; 1 Sep 43 rammed by a barge being towed by the tug *Sequin*—moderate damage.

The hull of LS 112 had greater subdivision than any previous lightship. Designed for the Nantucket Shoals station, where lightships were frequently hit by passing traffic, LS 112 was constructed to replace LS 117, which had been run down by the liner *Olympic* in dense fog on 15 May 34. The White Star Line, owners of the *Olympic*, paid for the construction of the new lightship.

133-FOOT LIGHTSHIPS

Name	Builder	Keel Laid	Commissioned	Disposition
LS 100 (f-LS 523)	Albina Marine Iron Works, Portland, OR	28 Mar 28 (contracted)	10 Feb 30	*Decomm* 12 May 71; *trans* to USN 6 Aug 71
LS 113 (f-LS 535)	Albina Marine Iron Works, Portland, OR	28 Mar 28 (contracted)	15 Jun 30	*Decomm* 1 Oct 68; donated 7 Jun 69
LS 114 (f-LS 536)	Albina Marine Iron Works, Portland, OR	28 Mar 28 (contracted)	1930	*Decomm* 5 Nov 71
LS 115 (f-LS 537)	Charleston Dry Dock & Machine Co., Charleston, SC	4 Oct 28 (contracted)	14 Jul 30 (completed)	*Decomm* 4 Nov 65; donated 5 Sep 67
LS 116 (f-LS 538)	Charleston Dry Dock & Machine Co., Charleston, SC	4 Oct 28 (contracted)	14 Aug 30	*Decomm* 5 Jan 71; *trans* to NPS 25 Aug 71
LS 117	Charleston Dry Dock & Machine Co., Charleston, SC	4 Oct 28 (contracted)	1930	*Sank* 15 May 34

Cost
$744,833 (LS 100, 113, 114); $741,090 (LS 115, 116, 117)

Hull
Displacement (tons)	630 at mean draft (1930)
Length	133′3″ oa; 108′9″ wl
Beam	30′ mb
Draft	13′ mean draft (1930)

Machinery
Main Engines	1 General Electric motor driven by 4 generators driven by 4 Winton diesels
SHP	350
Propellers	Single

Performance
Max Speed	7.5 kts, 5,000 mi radius (1946)

Logistics
Diesel Oil (95%)	21,000 gal
Complement	LS 113, 100: 6 officers, 42 men (1946); all others: 6 officers, 11 men (1930); 1 officer, 14 men (1946)

Electronics (1945)
Detection Radar	SO-8 (LS 113); SO-1 (others)
Sonar	QBE (LS 100); others none

Armament (1945)
LS 116: 2 20mm/80; LS 114: 1 6-pdr, 1 1-pdr; LS 113: 1 4″/50; LS 100, 115: none

Design
Constructed of steel; mounted a 375mm lens lantern. Also fitted with fog-signal apparatus.

LS 100

Pre–WW II served as Blunts Reef LS; 1942–45 assigned to WESTSEA-FRON—stationed at Eureka, CA, and served as examination ship.

LS 113

Pre–WW II served as Swiftsure Banks LS; 1942–45 assigned to NOWEST-SEAFRON and ALASKASEAFRON—stationed at Ketchikan, AK, and served as examination ship.

LS 114

Pre–WW II served as Fire Island LS; 1942–45 assigned to 3rd District—stationed at Bay Shore, NY, and used as examination ship.

LS 115

Pre–WW II served in NC as Frying Pan Shoals LS; 1942–44 assigned to 15th District—stationed at Cristobal, Canal Zone, and used as examination ship; 1944–45 assigned to 6th District—stationed at Charleston, SC, and used as examination ship.

LS 116

Pre–WW II served as Chesapeake Bay LS; 1941–45 assigned to 1st District—stationed at Sandwich, MA, and used as examination ship.

LS 117

Pre–WW II served as Nantucket Shoals LS; 15 May 34 was rammed and cut in two by the ocean liner *Olympic* in dense fog—7 of 11 lives lost.

LS 115, 26 Dec 29, fitting out. The first American lightship was used on the Chesapeake Bay in 1820. Lightships reached their heyday between WW I and WW II. Following WW II, technology overtook these once-common sentinels. They were replaced by Texas tower structures and large navigation buoys.

LS 107, 23 Jul 43. Lightships used for guard duty were painted gray and armed—often with a 3″/23 or 3″/50 and two 20mm/80s. All ships entering port were required to identify themselves to the guard ship. Lightships were well suited to this duty: they could maintain their stations for long periods under almost all weather conditions.

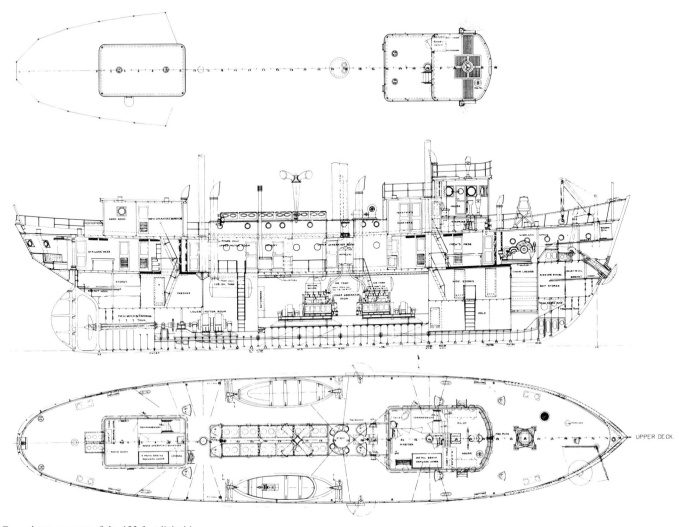

General arrangement of the 133-foot lightship.

132-FOOT LIGHTSHIPS

Name	Builder	Keel Laid	Launched	Completed	Disposition
LS 106 (f-LS 528)	Bath Iron Works, Bath, ME	8 Jul 21 (contracted)	NA	14 Jun 23	*Decomm* 17 Oct 67; *trans* to Surinam 4 Jun 68
LS 107 (f-LS 529)	Bath Iron Works, Bath, ME	8 Jul 21 (contracted)	NA	22 Feb 24 (delivered)	*Decomm* 15 Apr 68; *trans* to Hampton, VA, as museum 21 Nov 68
LS 108 (f-LS 530)	Bath Iron Works, Bath, ME	8 Jul 21 (contracted)	NA	17 Sep 23 (delivered)	*Decomm* 31 Aug 70; donated 29 Dec 71
LS 109 (f-LS 531)	Bath Iron Works, Bath, ME	8 Jul 21 (contracted)	16 Aug 23	10 Nov 23 (delivered)	*Decomm* 8 Dec 66; *trans* to AID 20 Feb 67
LS 110 (f-LS 532)	Bath Iron Works, Bath, ME	8 Jul 21 (contracted)	NA	22 Jan 24 (delivered)	*Decomm* 3 Nov 71; donated 30 Mar 72
LS 111 (f-LS 533)	Bath Iron Works, Bath, ME	14 Jun 24 (contracted)	14 Jun 24	20 Dec 26 (*see* Design)	*Decomm* and *trans* to USN 11 Jul 69

Cost

$200,000 (LS 106, 107, 108); $160,000 (LS 109, 110); $90,000 (LS 111—*see* Design remarks)

Hull

Displacement (tons)	775 fl (1923)
Length	132'4" oa
Beam	30' mb
Draft	15' max (1946)

Machinery

Main Engines	2 compound steam engines (LS 106–110); diesel (LS 111)
Main Boilers	2 single-end Scotch marine, 120 psi (LS 106–110)
SHP	914 (LS 106–110)
Propellers	Single, 4 bladed

Performance

Max Speed	9.0 kts, 2,700 mi radius (1945)
Max Sustained	8.0 kts, 3,000 mi radius (1945)

Logistics

Fuel Oil (95%)	41,800 gal (LS 106–110)
Diesel (95%)	45,000 gal (LS 111)
Complement	6 officers, 10 men (1923); 1 officer, 14 men (1945)

Electronics
Detection Radar

1943	BK (LS 106, 110)
1945	SO-1 (LS 106–110); SO-8 (LS 111)

Armament (1945)

LS 108: 1 6-pdr.; all others: none

Design

This class was constructed of steel. Standard Oil Company paid for LS 111 to replace a lightship sunk in a collision with one of its barges. LS 111 was launched by Bath Iron Works and outfitted at the government depot at Staten Island, NY. She was identical to her sisters except for her diesel machinery, and she was the first diesel-powered lightship of the USLHS.

LS 106

Pre–WW II served as relief LS; 1942–45 assigned to 1st District—stationed at Woods Hole, MA, and used as examination ship.

LS 107

Pre–WW II served as Winter Quarter LS; 1942–45 assigned to 5th District—stationed at Portsmouth, VA, and served as examination ship.

LS 108

Pre–WW II served as Five Fathom Banks LS; 1942–45 assigned to 4th District—stationed at Edgemoor, DE, and used as examination ship.

LS 109

Pre–WW II served as relief LS; 1942–45 assigned to the 6th District—stationed at Charleston, SC, and served as relief LS.

LS 110

Pre–WW II served as Pollock Rip LS; 1942–44 assigned to 1st District—stationed at Woods Hole, MA, and served as examination ship; 1944–45 assigned to 1st District—stationed at Woods Hole, MA, and served as Pollock Rip LS.

LS 111

Pre–WW II served as Ambrose Channel LS; 1942–45 assigned to 3rd District—stationed at Fort Hancock, NJ, and served as Ambrose Channel LS.

146-FOOT LIGHTSHIP

Name	Builder	Keel Laid	Launched	Completed	Disposition
LS 105 (f-LS 527)	Consolidated Shipbuilding Corp., Morris Heights, NY	31 Dec 19 (contracted)	22 Nov 21	8 Apr 22	Rammed & sunk 20 Jul 44

Cost

$437,404

Hull

Displacement (tons)	825 fl (1922)
Length	146'3" oa; 121'6" bp
Beam	30' mb
Draft	12'7" mean (1922)

Machinery

Main Engines	Fore and aft compound steam
Main Boilers	2 single-end tubular Scotch marine
SHP	475
Propellers	Single

Performance

Max Speed	NA

Logistics

Fuel Oil (95%)	NA
Complement	6 officers, 10 men (1922)

Electronics
None

Armament
None

Design

Constructed entirely of steel, LS 105 was built to replace LS 71, which was sunk by gunfire from a German U-boat on 6 Aug 17 on Diamond Shoals, NC.

LS 105

Pre–WW II served as Diamond Shoals LS; 1942–44 assigned to 5th District—stationed at Portsmouth, VA, and served as an examination ship; 20 Jul 44 was rammed and sunk.

LS 105, prior to WW II. She was rammed and sunk on 20 Jul 44. LS 105 had been built to replace LS 71, which had been sunk by a German U-boat in WW I.

96-FOOT LIGHTSHIP

Name	Builder	Keel Laid	Launched	Completed	Disposition
LS 103 (f-LS 526)	Consolidated Shipbuilding Corp., Morris Heights, NY	5 Jun 18	1 May 20	22 Dec 20	*Decomm* 25 Aug 70; donated to Port Huron, MI 5 Jun 71

Cost
  $161,074

Hull
  Displacement (tons)   310 at mean draft (1921 and 1945)
  Length   96′5″ oa
  Beam   24′ mb
  Draft   9′ mean (1921); 10′ max (1945)

Machinery
  Main Engines   Fore-and-aft 2-cyl compound reciprocating steam
  Main Boilers   2 Scotch (1923); 1 Scotch (1945)
  SHP   175 (1923); 285 (1945)
  Propellers   Single

Performance
  Max Speed   8.0 kts, 950 mi radius (1945)

Logistics
  Fuel Oil (95%)   Coal (1923); 820 gal (1945)
  Complement   4 officers, 5 men (1920); 10 men (1945)

Electronics (1945)
  Detection Radar   SO-1

Armament
  None

Design
  LS 103 was constructed with a steel hull and superstructure. She was the only lightship to be painted black, all others having a red hull. As a "black light station," she was passed to port like a black buoy was.

LS 103

Pre–WW II served as Lake Huron LS; 1942–45 assigned to the 9th District—stationed at Port Huron, MI, and served as Lake Huron LS.

92-FOOT LIGHTSHIP

Name	Builder	Keel Laid	Launched	Completed	Disposition
LS 99 (f-LS 522)	Rice Brothers Corp., East Boothbay, ME	29 Jun 16 (contracted)	7 Nov 19	21 Jul 21	*Decomm* 24 May 56; *sold* 5 Nov 56

Cost
$97,220

Hull
Displacement (tons)   215 at mean draft (1921)
Length   91'8" oa
Beam   22' mb
Draft   10'7" max (1920)

Machinery
Main Engines   1 compound reciprocating steam
Main Boilers   1 heating
SHP   350
Propellers   Single

Performance
Max Speed   NA

Logistics
Fuel Oil (95%)   Coal
Complement   4 officers, 3 men (1921); 0 officers, 13 men (1945)

Electronics
Detection Radar   None (1943); SO-1 (1945)

Armament
1 3"/50, 2 20mm/80 (single)

Design
Constructed for service on the Great Lakes, LS 99 sustained a fire during construction and was delayed.

LS 99

Pre–WW II served as relief LS; 1942–44 assigned to the 7th District—stationed at Port Everglades, FL, and used as examination ship.

LS 99, 29 Mar 43. She is being assisted by a tug on her port side, which clutters her profile in this photograph.

102-FOOT LIGHTSHIPS

Name	Builder	Keel Laid	Launched	Completed	Disposition
LS 101 (f-LS 524)	Pusey & Jones Co., Wilmington, DE	6 Mar 15 (contracted)	12 Jan 16	25 Sep 16	*Decomm* 23 Mar 64; donated 3 Sep 64
LS 102 (f-LS 525)	Pusey & Jones Co., Wilmington, DE	6 Mar 15 (contracted)	27 Nov 15	3 Jan 17	*Decomm* 25 Oct 63; *sold* 2 Mar 65

Cost
$108,507 (LS 101); $110,065 (LS 102)

Hull
Displacement (tons)	360 fl (1945)
Length	101'10" oa
Beam	25' mb
Draft	11'4" mean (1917); 12' max (1945)

Machinery
Main Engines	1 4-cyl, 2-cycle Mietz & Weiss engine
Main Boilers	1 boiler
SHP	200
Propellers	Single

Performance
Max Speed	8.0 kts, 2,200 mi radius (1945)

Logistics
Kerosene (95%)	7,000 gal
Complement	4 officers, 7 men (1917); 0 officers, 12 men (1945)

Electronics (1945)
Detection Radar	SO-1

Armament
None

Design
Constructed of steel.

LS 101

Pre–WW II served as Overfalls LS; 1942–45 assigned to the 4th District—stationed at Lewes, DE, and served as Overfalls LS.

LS 102

Pre–WW II served as Brenton Reef LS; 1942–45 assigned to the 1st District—stationed at Bristol, RI, and served as Brenton Reef LS.

LS 101. Not all lightships were removed from their stations and painted gray during WW II. LS 101 served on the Overfalls throughout the war.

101-FOOT LIGHTSHIPS

Name	Builder	Keel Laid	Launched	Completed	Disposition
LS 96 (f-LS 520)	Racine-Truscott-Shell Lake Boat Co., Muskegon, MI	24 Apr 13 (contracted)	21 Apr 14	24 Apr 15	*Decomm* 18 Jan 55; *sold* 28 Jul 55
LS 98 (f-LS 521)	Racine-Truscott-Shell Lake Boat Co., Muskegon, MI	24 Apr 13 (contracted)	9 Jun 14	12 Jun 15	*Decomm* 18 Jan 55; *sold* 28 Jul 55

Cost
$71,292 (LS 96); $87,025 (LS 98)

Hull
Displacement (tons)	260 fl (1914)
Length	101' oa
Beam	23'6" mb
Draft	10'9" max (1914); 11'6" max (1945)

Machinery
Main Engines	Internal combustion
Main Boilers	?
BHP	170
Propellers	Single

Performance
Max Speed	5.0 kts, 1,400 mi radius (1945)

Logistics
Kerosene (95%)	4,570 gal (LS 96); 3,500 gal (LS 98)
Complement	3 officers, 4 men (1914); 0 officers, 12 men (1945)

Electronics (1945)
Detection Radar	SO-1

Armament
  None
Design
  Steel hull

LS 96

Pre–WW II served as Cross Rip LS; 1942–45 assigned to the 1st District—stationed at Woods Hole, MA, and served as Cross Rip LS.

LS 98

Pre–WW II served on Handkerchief LS; 1942–45 assigned to the 1st District—stationed at Woods Hole, MA, and served as Handkerchief LS.

LS 96, Jun 37. This lightship remained on station throughout WW II.

108-FOOT LIGHTSHIP

Name	Builder	Keel Laid	Completed	Disposition
LS 95 (f-LS 519)	Muskegon, MI	14 Jun 10	30 Nov 12	*Decomm* 15 Jan 65; donated 21 May 66

Cost
  $74,558
Hull
  Displacement (tons)   345 fl (1912); 368 fl (1945)
  Length   108′5″ oa
  Beam   23′ mb
  Draft   10′8″ max (1912); 11′6″ max (1945)
Machinery
  Main Engines   1 Atlas Imperial diesel
  BHP   375
  Propellers   Single
Performance
  Max Speed   7.0 kts, 2,700 mi radius (1945)
Logistics
  Diesel (95%)   10,000 gal
  Complement   4 officers, 5 men (1912); 0 officers, 12 men (1945)
Electronics (1945)
  Detection Radar   SO-1
Armament
  None
Design
  With a steel hull and wooden deckhouses, she sank 4 days before delivery and had to be rebuilt. On 4 Jul 12, LS 95 was delivered unfinished, and was completed at the government depot at Staten Island, NY, on 27 Sep 12. First date on station was 30 Nov 12.

LS 95

Pre–WW II served as relief LS; 1942–45 assigned to 4th District—stationed at Edgemoor, DE, and served as relief LS.

LS 95, serving on Diamond Shoals light station before WW I. LS 95 served as a relief ship for the 4th District throughout WW II.

136-FOOT LIGHTSHIP

Name	Builder	Keel Laid	Completed	Disposition
LS 94 (f-LS 518)	Racine Boat Manufacturing Co., Muskegon, MI	28 May 09	13 Jun 11	*Decomm* 15 Dec 54; *sold* 16 Nov 55

Cost
$104,604

Hull
Displacement (tons)   660 fl (1911)
Length   135′6″ oa
Beam   29′ mb
Draft   12′9″ max (1911 and 1945)

Machinery
Main Engines   1 Atlas Imperial diesel
BHP   375
Propellers   Single

Performance
Max Speed   8.5 kts, 5,300 mi radius (1945)

Logistics
Diesel (95%)   17,950 gal
Complement   5 officers, 10 men (1911); 1 officer, 13 men (1945)

Electronics (1945)
Detection Radar   SO-1

Armament
None

Design
Hull is constructed of steel, deckhouses of wood.

LS 94

Pre–WW II served as Savannah LS; 1942–45 assigned to the 6th District—stationed at Charleston, SC, and served as Savannah LS.

135-FOOT LIGHTSHIPS

Name	Builder	Completed	Disposition
LS 84 (f-LS 509)	New York Shipbuilding Co., Camden, NJ	1907	*Decomm* 26 Oct 65; donated for museum 7 Aug 68
LS 85 (f-LS 510)	New York Shipbuilding Co., Camden, NJ	1907	*Decomm* 15 Nov 62; *sold* 17 Oct 63
LS 86 (f-LS 511)	New York Shipbuilding Co., Camden, NJ	1907	*Decomm* 28 Feb 59; *sold* 30 Dec 59
LS 87 (f-LS 512)	New York Shipbuilding Co., Camden, NJ	1907	*Decomm* 4 Mar 66; donated for museum 4 Aug 68
LS 88 (f-LS 513)	New York Shipbuilding Co., Camden, NJ	1908	*Decomm* 23 Nov 60; *sold* 25 Jul 62
LS 90 (f-LS 514)	Fore River Shipbuilding Co., Quincy, MA	1908	*Decomm* 30 Sep 52; *sold* 21 Jul 55
LS 91 (f-LS 515)	Fore River Shipbuilding Co., Quincy, MA	1908	*Decomm* 30 Nov 61; *sold* 11 Mar 63
LS 92 (f-LS 516)	Fore River Shipbuilding Co., Quincy, MA	1908	*Decomm* 28 Jun 51; *sold* 7 Dec 54
LS 93 (f-LS 517)	Fore River Shipbuilding Co., Quincy, MA	1908	*Decomm* 9 Apr 51; *sold* 2 Nov 55

Cost
$99,000 (84–88); $107,213 (90–93)

Hull
Displacement (tons)   563 fl (1907); 683 fl (1945)
Length   135′5″ oa
Beam   29′ max
Draft   12′6″ max (1907); 13′6″ max (1945)

Machinery
Main Engines   Compound reciprocating steam (LS 85, 86, 90–93); 1 Atlas Imperial diesel (LS 84); 1 Winton diesel (LS 87); diesel-electric (LS 88)
Main Boilers   2 Almy watertube (LS 85, 86, 90–93)
SHP   350 (LS 85, 86, 88); 380 (LS 90–93)
BHP   375 (LS 84); 300 (LS 87)

Performance
Max Speed (1945)
8.0 kts, 6,140 mi radius (LS 84)
9.0 kts,   800 mi radius (LS 85, 86, 90, 92)
9.0 kts, 5,400 mi radius (LS 87)
9.0 kts, 10,000 mi radius (LS 88)
10.0 kts, 3,600 mi radius (LS 91)
9.0 kts, 2,500 mi radius (LS 93)

Logistics
Fuel Oil (95%)   15,000 gal (LS 90, 91); 19,870 gal (LS 93)
Diesel (95%)   18,300 gal (LS 84, 87); 24,000 gal (LS 88)
Coal (95%)   110 tons (LS 85, 86); 95 tons (LS 92)
Complement   5 officers, 9 men (1904); 13 men (LS 84–87, 90, 92, 93), 4 officers, 40 men (LS 88, 91) (1945)

Electronics
Detection Radar   BK (LS 85–86) (1943), SO-1 (LS 84–88, 91–92), SO-9 (LS 90), none (LS 93) (1945)

Armament (1945)
None (LS 84, 86, 92, 93), 1 6-pdr (LS 85); 1 6-pdr, 1 1-pdr (LS 87); 1 3″/23 (LS 88); 1 3″/50 (LS 90); 1 3″/50, 2 20mm (LS 91)

Design
Steel hull.

LS 84

Pre–WW II served as St. John's River LS; 1942–45 assigned to the 6th District—stationed at Charleston, SC. and served as St. John's River LS.

LS 85

Pre–WW II served as relief LS; 1942–44 assigned to the 1st District—stationed at Chelsea, MA, and used as examination ship; 1944–45 assigned to the 1st District—stationed at Chelsea, MA, and served as relief LS.

LS 86

Pre–WW II served as Hen and Chickens LS; 1942–45 assigned to 1st District—stationed at Woods Hole, MA, and served as Hen and Chickens LS.

LS 87

Pre–WW II served as Scotland LS; 1942–45 assigned to the 3rd District—stationed at Fort Hancock, NJ, and served as examination ship.

LS 88

Pre–WW II served as Umatilla Reef LS; 1942–45 assigned to NOWESTSEA-FRON—stationed at Seattle, WA, and served as examination ship.

LS 90

Pre–WW II served as Portland LS; 1942–44 assigned to the 7th District—stationed at Key West, FL, and served as examination ship; 1944–45 assigned to the 7th District—stationed at Key West, FL, and used as Portland LS.

LS 91

Pre–WW II served as Relief LS; 1942–43 assigned to CG Headquarters—stationed at Curtis Bay, MD, and used for training; 1943–45 assigned to the 7th District—stationed at Key West, FL, and used as examination ship.

LS 92

Pre–WW II served as relief LS; 1942–45 assigned to the 13th District—stationed at Seattle, WA, and served as relief LS.

LS 93

Pre–WW II served as the Columbia River LS; 1942–45 assigned to the 13th District—stationed at Astoria, OR, and served as Columbia River LS.

LS 91, 28 Jul 43. She is armed with two 20mms on the wings of the bridge and a 3″/50 on the poop deck. LS 91 has not yet been fitted with radar.

129-FOOT LIGHTSHIPS

Name	Builder	Completed	Disposition
LS 76 (f-LS 504)	Burles Drydock Co., Port Richmond, NY	26 May 04	*Decomm* 16 Sep 60; *sold* 9 Oct 61
LS 77	NA	1906	*Sold* Apr 40
LS 78 (f-LS 505)	New York Shipbuilding Co., Camden, NJ	1904	*Sank* 24 Jun 60
LS 79 (f-LS 506)	New York Shipbuilding Co., Camden, NJ	1904	*Decomm* 3 Mar 67; donated 13 Oct 67
LS 80	NA	1904	*Sold* 13 Dec 34
LS 81 (f-LS 507)	Camden, NJ	1904	*Decomm* 4 Apr 51; *sold* 21 Jul 55
LS 82	Muskegon, MI	12 Jul 12	
LS 83 (f-LS 508)	Camden, NJ	1904	*Decomm* 18 Jul 60; donated 1 Oct 63

Cost
$13,950 (LS 77); $89,000 (LS 78–79); $85,000 (LS 80); $49,594 (LS 82)

Hull

Displacement (tons)	578 fl (1904); 668 fl (1945)
Tonnage	465 gross (1904); 188 net (1904)
Length	129'6" oa
Beam	28'8" max
Draft	12'6" max (1904 and 1945)

Machinery

Main Engines	1 compound reciprocating steam (LS 76, 83); 1 Winton diesel (LS 78); 1 Cooper-Bessemer diesel (LS 79); 1 Atlas Imperial diesel (LS 81)
Main Boilers	2 Foster-Wheeler watertube (LS 76); 2 Babcock & Wilcox (LS 83)
SHP	380 (LS 76); 350 (LS 83)
BHP	300 (LS 78, 79); 375 (LS 81)
Propellers	Single

Performance

Max Speed (1945)	10.0 kts, 1,800 mi radius (LS 76)
	8.9 kts, 5,150 mi radius (LS 78)
	5.0 kts, 4,500 mi radius (LS 79)
	9.0 kts, 1,750 mi radius (LS 83)

Logistics

Fuel Oil (95%)	17,430 gal (LS 76, 83)
Diesel (95%)	15,000 gal (LS 78, 79); 26,000 gal (LS 81)
Complement	3 officers, 5 men (1904); 12 men (LS 76, 78, 79, 81) (1945); 6 officers, 42 men (LS 83) (1945)

Electronics (1945)

Detection Radar	All units: SO-1
Sonar	LS 83 only: QBE

Armament (1945)
LS 81: 1 3"/50; LS 76, 78, 79, 83: none

Design
Steel hull.

LS 76

Pre–WW II served as relief LS; 1942–45 assigned to CG Headquarters—stationed at Alameda, CA, and used for training.

LS 77

Pre–WW II served as Pestigo Reef LS in the Great Lakes; Apr 40, sold.

LS 78

Pre–WW II served as relief LS; 1942–45 assigned to 1st and 3rd Districts—stationed at Staten Island, NY, and used for examination ship; 24 Jun 60 sank in a collision with the SS *Green Bay*.

LS 79

Pre–WW II served as Barnegat LS; 1942–45 assigned to the 4th District—stationed at Edgemoor, DE, and used as examination ship.

LS 80

Pre–WW II served as Cape Charles LS.

LS 81

Pre–WW II served as Boston LS; 1942–45 assigned to the 5th District—stationed at Norfolk, VA, and served as examination ship.

LS 82

Pre–WW II served as relief LS.

LS 83

Pre–WW II served as San Francisco LS; 1942–45 assigned to the 12th District—stationed at San Francisco, CA, and used as examination ship.

LS 83, 19 Aug 42. Stern-wheeler *Delta Queen* lies in the background; she served in the CG from 15 Dec 41 until 31 Aug 42.

123-FOOT LIGHTSHIP

Name	Builder	Keel Laid	Completed	Disposition
LS 73 (f-LS 503)	Baltimore, MD	29 Dec 99 (contracted)	1901	Lost in hurricane 14 Sep 44

Cost
  $99,000

Hull
  Displacement (tons)   693 fl (1901)
  Tonnage   538 gross (1901)
  Length   123′9″ oa
  Beam   28′6″ mb
  Draft   14′ max (1901)

Machinery
  Main Engines   Reciprocating steam
  IHP   400

Performance
  Max Speed   NA

Logistics
  Complement   5 officers, 9 men (1901)

Electronics
  None

Armament
  None

Design
  Steel hull.

LS 73

Pre–WW II served as Vineyard Sound LS; 1942–45 assigned to the 1st District—stationed at Woods Hole, MA, and served as Vineyard Sound LS; 14 Sep 44 lost in a hurricane with all hands.

119-FOOT LIGHTSHIPS

Name	Builder	Completed	Disposition
LS 53 (f-LS 501)	West Bay City, MI	1892	*Decomm* 15 Jun 51; *sold* 19 Jul 55
LS 54 (f-LS 502)	West Bay City, MI	1892	*Decomm* 23 Jul 46; *sold* 15 Sep 47

Cost
$61,538 (LS 53); $62,030 (LS 54)

Hull
Displacement (tons)   487 fl (1892); 475 fl (1945)
Tonnage   310 gross
Length   118'10" oa
Beam   26'6" mb
Draft   12'6" max (1892); 11' max (1945)

Machinery
Main Engines   F. W. Wheeler & Co., compound condensing
Main Boilers   2 Wicks Brothers tubular cylindrical, 50 psi
SHP   170
Propellers   Single

Performance
Max   6.0 kts, 2,000 mi radius (LS 53) (1945)
Max Sustained   5.0 kts,   800 mi radius (LS 54) (1945)

Logistics
Kerosene   8,300 gal
Complement   2 officers, 5 men (1911); 0 officers, 10 men (1945)

Electronics (1945)
Detection Radar   SO-1

Design
Designed by W. Sylven: LS 53 had an iron hull, LS 54 had a steel hull.

LS 53

Pre–WW II served as Stone Horse Shoal LS; 1942–45 assigned to the 1st District—stationed at Woods Hole, MA, and served as Stone Horse Shoal LS.

LS 54

Pre–WW II served as relief LS; 1942–45 assigned to the 1st District—stationed at Woods Hole, MA, and served as relief LS.

LS 53 prior to WW II. At this point in her career, LS 53 was serving as a relief lightship. Relief lightships substituted for primary lightships when they were off station. The primary lightship had the name of the station painted on the hull. A district with numerous lightship stations, such as the 1st District, might have as many as six relief lightships with the word *Relief* painted on their hulls. This practice makes the identification of specific relief lightships difficult.

PATROL TYPES (WYP, WPY, WPYc, WPR)

Almost without exception, all of these craft were emergency acquisitions. The WYP—district patrol vessel—led the most active career of the different types. The WYP may be divided into three categories: East Coast trawlers and whalers; East Coast menhaden-type fishing craft; and West Coast whalers. The East Coast trawlers and whalers operated out of Boston for the most part and were active in Greenland waters. They bore Eskimo names for animals, such as the *Aklak* and the *Nogak*, and were camouflaged in blue and white paint. The whalers were particularly sought after by the Coast Guard because of their ice-going capabilities. The Menhaden types were stationed in the mid-Atlantic states. In most cases, their original names were retained in whole or part and preceded by the capital initials EM, which stood for emergency manning. Most Coast Guard records have these initials as part of the boat's official name. The West Coast whalers were stationed both in California and Alaska. Their careers were not as active as those of their East Coast counterparts.

The WPYc, coastal yachts, were almost all sail vessels. In general, a sail vessel between 100 and 200 feet was considered a WPYc. Those less than 100 feet were considered small craft and given CG numbers; those 200 feet or more were gunboats, or WPG.

WYP—DISTRICT PATROL VESSELS

EMERGENCY ACQUISITION

Name	Visual Call Sign	Builder	Commissioned	Disposition
Bellefonte (ex-*Albatross* III, ex-*Harvard*)	WYP 373	Bath Iron Works Inc., Bath, ME	1926 (commercial); 6 Apr 44 (CG)	*Decomm* 16 Apr 44; *ret* to Fish & Wildlife Service, Dept I 22 Aug 44

Cost
  Acquisition Dept of Interior; conversion $616,534
Hull
  Displacement (tons)   644 fl (1944)
  Tonnage   341 gross (1944)
  Length   178'9" oa; 157'9" bp
  Beam   24' max
  Draft   14'10" max (1944)
Machinery
  Main Engines   1 diesel
  BHP   800
  Propellers   Single
Performance
  Max Speed   14.0 kts (1943)
Logistics
  Fuel Oil (95%)   20,382 gal

Complement   7 officers, 6 warrants, 57 men (1944)
Electronics
  Probably none
Armament (1944)
  1 3"/50 (single); 2 20mm/80 (single); 2 dc projectors; 2 dc tracks; 2 Mousetraps

Design
  The *Bellefonte* was acquired from the Fish & Wildlife Service, Dept. I. Her Mariform bow was especially constructed for ice-breaking, but her lack of stability prevented her from serving as planned. Because the submarine threat soon lifted, the *Bellefonte* saw but short service.

Bellefonte

1944 assigned to 3rd District—stationed in New York, NY, and spent most of her career under conversion.

The *Bellefonte*, 27 Mar 44. Note that she is not fitted with radar. This ship was to have been assigned to CINCLANT for operation in Greenland waters, but her lack of stability precluded this.

EMERGENCY ACQUISITION

Name	Visual Call Sign	Builder	Commissioned	Disposition
EM *Wilcox* (ex-*Rowland H. Wilcox*)	WYP 333	R. Palmer & Sons, Noank, CT	1911 (commercial); 8 Sep 43 (CG)	*Sank* 30 Sep 43

Cost
  Acquisition chartered for $500/month; conversion $122,400

Hull
  Displacement (tons) 435 fl (1943)
  Tonnage 247 gross (1941); 119 net (1941)
  Length 132' oa
  Beam 22'3" max
  Draft 10'7" max (1943)

Machinery
  Main Engines 1 diesel
  BHP 500
  Propellers Single

Performance
  Max Speed NA

Logistics
  Fuel Oil (95%) NA
  Complement 32 men (commercial); 38 men (1941)

Electronics
  Probably none

Armament
  1 20mm/80; dc tracks

Design
  A former Menhaden fishing craft that was under charter.

EM *Wilcox*

1943 assigned to CARIBSEAFRON—stationed at San Juan, PR; 30 Sep 43 foundered and sank during a storm 94 mi due east of Nags Head, NC—37 survivors, 1 man lost.

EMERGENCY ACQUISITION

Name	Visual Call Sign	Builder	Commissioned	Disposition
EM *Stephen McKeever* (ex-*Stephen W. McKeever, Jr.*)	WYP 363	R. Palmer & Sons, Noank, CT	1911 (commercial); 19 Jul 43 (CG)	*Decomm* 3 Dec 43; *ret* to owner 29 Dec 43

Cost
    Acquisition chartered for $500/month; conversion $105,516

Hull
Displacement (tons)	390 fl (1943)
Tonnage	223 gross (1941); 104 net (1941)
Length	128' oa
Beam	22'2" max
Draft	10' max (1941)

Machinery
Main Engines	1 diesel
BHP	300
Propellers	Single

Performance
Max Speed	NA

Logistics
Complement	20 men (commercial)

Electronics
    Probably none

Armament
    NA

Design
    A former fishing craft that was under charter.

EM *Stephen McKeever*

1943 assigned to EASTSEAFRON—stationed at Little Creek, VA, and used for patrol duty.

EMERGENCY ACQUISITION

Name	Visual Call Sign	Builder	Commissioned	Disposition
EM *Warren Edwards* (ex- *E. Warren Edwards*)	WYP 354	William G. Abbott Shipbuilding Co., Milford, DE	1918 (commercial); 5 Jul 43 (CG)	*Decomm* 1 Oct 43; *ret* to owner 1 Nov 43

Cost
    Acquisition chartered for $500/month; conversion $114,044

Hull
Displacement (tons)	380 fl (1942)
Tonnage	231 gross (1941); 30 net (1941)
Length	152'2" oa
Beam	21' max
Draft	10'2" max (1943)

Machinery
Main Engines	1 diesel
BHP	150
Propellers	Single

Performance
Max Speed	NA

Logistics
Complement	4 men (commercial)

Electronics
    Probably none

Armament
    NA

Design
    A former fishing craft that was under charter.

EM *Warren Edwards*

1943 assigned to CARIBSEAFRON—stationed at Norfolk, VA, and San Juan, PR, and used for patrol duty.

EMERGENCY ACQUISITION

Name	Visual Call Sign	Builder	Commissioned	Disposition
EM *Dow* (ex-*Annie Dow*)	WYP 353	Humphreys Marine Railway, Inc., Weems, VA	1924 (commercial); 24 Jun 43 (CG)	Abandoned at sea 14 Oct 43; *sold* 20 Aug 48

Cost
  Acquisition chartered for $500/month; conversion $105,872
Hull
  Displacement (tons)   435 fl (1943)
  Tonnage   241 gross (1941); 59 net (1941)
  Length   134'3" oa
  Beam   21'7" max
  Draft   10'8" (1943)
Machinery
  Main Engines   1 diesel
  BHP   400
  Propellers   Single
Performance
  Max Speed   10.0 kts (1943)

Max Sustained   10.0 kts, 2,000 mi radius (1943)
Logistics
  Complement   30 men (commercial)
Electronics
  Probably none
Armament
  NA
Design
  A former fishing craft which was under charter.

EM *Dow*

1943 assigned to CARIBSEAFRON—stationed at San Juan, PR; 14 Oct 43 abandoned in a gale off Mayagüez, PR—crew rescued by the cutter *Marion*.

EMERGENCY ACQUISITION

Name	Visual Call Sign	Builder	Commissioned	Disposition
EM *Edwards* (ex-*Wilbert A. Edwards*)	WYP 357	M. M. Davis & Son, Solomons, MD	1912 (commercial); 24 Jun 43 (CG)	*Decomm* 15 Mar 44; *ret* to owner 24 Mar 44

Cost
  Acquisition chartered for $500/month; conversion $108,142
Hull
  Displacement (tons)   550 fl (1942)
  Tonnage   343 gross (1941); 94 net (1941)
  Length   143'4" oa
  Beam   24' max
  Draft   11'6" max (1941)
Machinery
  Main Engines   1 diesel
  BHP   600
  Propellers   Single
Performance
  Max Speed   NA

Logistics
  Complement   29 men (commercial)
Electronics
  Probably none
Armament
  NA
Design
  A former fishing craft, she was fitted with a steam plant prior to CG service. During CG service, she was chartered.

EM *Edwards*

1943–44 assigned to CARIBSEAFRON—stationed at San Juan, PR, and used for patrol duty.

EMERGENCY ACQUISITION

Name	Visual Call Sign	Builder	Commissioned	Disposition
EM *Messick* (ex-*W. L. Messick*)	WYP 358.	Smith & McCoy Co., Norfolk, VA	1911 (commercial); 24 Jun 43 (CG)	*Decomm* 2 Mar 44; *ret* to owner 13 Mar 44

Cost
  Acquisition chartered for $500/month; conversion $106,900
Hull
  Displacement (tons)   534 fl (1943)
  Tonnage   326 gross (1941); 75 net (1941)
  Length   131'8" oa
  Beam   23'5" mb
  Draft   12'5" max (1943)

Machinery
  Main Engines   1 diesel
  BHP   600
  Propellers   Single
Performance
  Max Speed   NA

Logistics
  Complement   30 men (commercial)
Electronics
  Probably none
Armament
  NA

Design
  A former fishing craft that was under charter.

EM *Messick*

1943–44 assigned to CARIBSEAFRON—stationed at San Juan, PR, and used for patrol duty.

EMERGENCY ACQUISITION

Name	Visual Call Sign	Builder	Commissioned	Disposition
EM *Joe* (ex-*Little Joe*)	WYP 356	Humphreys Marine Railway, Inc., Weems, VA	1922 (commercial); 9 Jun 43 (CG)	*Decomm* 22 Feb 44; *ret* to owner 6 Mar 44

Cost
  Acquisition chartered for $500/month; conversion $110,874
Hull
  Displacement (tons)   440 fl (1943)
  Tonnage   250 gross (1941); 75 net (1941)
  Length   134'3" oa
  Beam   21'7" mb
  Draft   10'9" max (1943)
Machinery
  Main Engines   1 diesel
  BHP   500
  Propellers   Single
Performance
  Max Speed   NA

Logistics
  Complement   30 men (commercial)
Electronics
  Probably none
Armament
  NA
Design
  A former fishing craft that was under charter.

EM *Joe*

1943–44 assigned to CARIBSEAFRON—stationed at San Juan, PR, and used for patrol duty.

EMERGENCY ACQUISITION

Name	Visual Call Sign	Builder	Commissioned	Disposition
EM *Pelican* (ex-*Pelican*)	WYP 329	Portland Shipbuilding Co., South Portland, ME	1919 (Commercial); 4 Jun 43(CG)	*Decomm* 6 Aug 43; to WSA 14 Mar 46

Cost
  Acquisition chartered for $560/month; conversion $135,360
Hull
  Displacement (tons)   690 fl (1943)
  Tonnage   384 gross (1941); 46 net (1941)
  Length   150'4" oa
  Beam   25' max
  Draft   13'3" max (1943)
Machinery
  Main Engines   Steam
  SHP   700
  Propellers   Single
Performance   Max Speed   NA

Logistics
  Complement   32 men (commercial)
Electronics   Armament
  Probably none   NA
Design
  A former Menhaden fishing craft that was under charter.

EM *Pelican*

1943 assigned to EASTSEAFRON—stationed at Little Creek, VA, and used for patrol duty.

EMERGENCY ACQUISITION

Name	Visual Call Sign	Builder	Commissioned	Disposition
Globe (ex-*Globe IX*)	WYP 381	Moss Vaerft & Dokk, Moss, Norway	1937 (commercial); 5 Apr 43 (CG)	*Decomm* 7 Jul 43; *ret* to WSA 9 Jul 43

Cost
  Acquisition WSA loan; conversion $13,750
Hull
  Displacement (tons)   600 fl (1943)
  Length   130'1" oa
  Beam   25'2" max
  Draft   13'3" (1942)
Machinery
  Main Engines   Steam
Performance
  Max Speed   NA
Logistics
  Complement   NA

Electronics
  Probably none
Armament
  NA

Design
  A former whaler.

Globe

1943 assigned to WESTSEAFRON—stationed at San Diego, CA, and used for patrol duty.

EMERGENCY ACQUISITION

Name	Visual Call Sign	Builder	Commissioned	Disposition
Ottern	WYP 379	Smiths Dock Co., South Bork Mdf., Norway	1937 (commercial); 5 Apr 43 (CG)	*Decomm* and *ret* to owner 7 Jul 43

Cost
  Acquisition WSA loan; conversion $13,750
Hull
  Displacement (tons)   260 fl (1942)
  Length   138' oa
  Beam   26'4" max
  Draft   14'8" (1942)
Machinery
  Main Engines   Steam
  SHP   1,216
  Propellers   Single
Performance
  Max Speed   NA

Logistics
  Complement   NA
Electronics
  Probably none
Armament
  NA
Design
  A former whaler.

Ottern

1943 assigned to WESTSEAFRON—stationed at Monterey, CA, and used for patrol duty.

EMERGENCY ACQUISITION

Name	Visual Call Sign	Builder	Commissioned	Disposition
EM *Seabird* (ex-*Sea Bird*)	WYP 330	Portland Shipbuilding Co., South Portland, ME	1919 (commercial); 1 Apr 43 (CG)	*Decomm* 22 Nov 43; *ret* to owner 19 Jul 44

Cost
  Acquisition chartered for $850/month; conversion $135,360
Hull
  Displacement (tons)   690 fl (1943)
  Tonnage   386 gross (1941); 48 net (1941)
  Length   163' oa; 150'4" bp
  Beam   25' max
  Draft   13'3" max (1943)
Machinery
  Main Engines   Steam
  SHP   700
  Propellers   Single

Performance
  Max Speed   7.0 kts (1943)
  Max Sustained   7.0 kts, 1,200 mi radius (1943)
Logistics
  Complement   NA
Electronics   Armament
  Probably none   NA
Design
  A former Menhaden-type fishing craft.

EM *Seabird*

1943 assigned to EASTSEAFRON—stationed at Little Creek, VA, and used for patrol duty.

EMERGENCY ACQUISITION

Name	Visual Call Sign	Builder	Commissioned	Disposition
EM *Euphane* (ex-*Helen Euphane*)	WYP 360	E. James Tull, Pocomoke City, MD	1902 (commercial); 23 Mar 43 (CG)	*Decomm* 22 Nov 43; *ret* to owner 29 Dec 44

Cost
  Acquisition chartered for $500/month; conversion $100,500

Hull
  Displacement (tons)   293 fl (1943)
  Length   124′ oa
  Beam   20′4″ max
  Draft   9′3″ max (1943)

Machinery
  Main Engines   1 diesel
  BHP   380
  Propellers   Single

Performance
  Max Speed   NA

Logistics
  Complement   NA

Electronics
  Probably none

Armament
  NA

Design
  A former fishing craft.

EM *Euphane*

1943 assigned to EASTSEAFRON—stationed at Cape May, NJ, and used for patrol duty.

EMERGENCY ACQUISITION

Name	Visual Call Sign	Builder	Commissioned	Disposition
Caddo (ex-*Tanginak*; ex-*Tyee Junior*)	WYP 174	Moran Co., Seattle, WA	1907 (commercial); 9 Mar 43 (CG)	*Decomm* 16 Mar 44

Cost
  Chartered for $35,000

Hull
  Displacement (tons)   372 fl (1942)
  Tonnage   151 gross (1941); 71 net (1941)
  Length   103′ oa; 97′9″ bp
  Beam   17′7″ max
  Draft   11′8″ max (1942)

Machinery
  Main Engines   Steam
  SHP   350
  Propellers   Single

Performance
  Max Speed   NA

Logistics
  Complement   10 (commercial)

Electronics
  None

Armament (1943)
  1 20mm/80, 2 short dc tracks

Design
  A former whaler.

Caddo

1943–44 assigned to the 13th District—stationed at Ketchikan, AK, and used for patrol duty.

The *Caddo*, 10 Mar 43, in Puget Sound. This former whaler was used for patrol duty in Alaskan waters. Craft like her were well suited to patrol and ASW duty in northern areas: they had ice stiffening and were staunchly built (the hull had a number of scantlings that exceeded the number various classification societies required).

EMERGENCY ACQUISITION

Name	Visual Call Sign	Builder	Commissioned	Disposition
EM *Vernon McNeal* (ex-*A. Vernon McNeal*; ex-*Charles J. Colonna*; ex-*Steamer*)	WYP 318	Charles J. Colonna Shipyard, Berkley, VA	1904 (commercial); 9 Mar 43 (CG)	*Decomm* 22 Feb 44; *ret* to owner 13 Mar 44

Cost
  Acquisition chartered for $750/month; conversion $122,400

Hull
  Displacement (tons) 400 fl (1942)
  Length 136′ oa; 123′5″ bp
  Beam 22′ max
  Draft 10′5″ (1942)

Machinery
  Main Engines 1 Fairbanks Morse diesel
  BHP 450
  Propellers Single

Performance
  Max Speed NA

Logistics
  Complement NA

Electronics
  Probably none

Armament
  NA

Design
  A former fishing craft.

EM *Vernon McNeal*

1943–44 assigned to CARIBSEAFRON—stationed at San Juan, PR, and used for patrol duty.

EMERGENCY ACQUISITION

Name	Visual Call Sign	Builder	Commissioned	Disposition
Kodiak	WYP 173	J. F. Duthie & Co., Seattle, WA	1912 (commercial); 9 Mar 43 (CG)	*Decomm* 16 Mar 44; *ret* to WSA 20 Apr 43

Cost
  Acquisition WSA loan; conversion $24,000

Hull
  Displacement (tons) 173 fl (1943)
  Tonnage 148 gross (1941); 101 net (1941)
  Length 106′10″ oa
  Beam 19′2″ max
  Draft 12′4″ max (1943)

Machinery
  Main Engines Triple expansion
  SHP 375
  Propellers Single

Performance
  Max Speed 9.5 kts (1943)
  Max Sustained 9.5 kts, 2,900 mi radius (1943)

Logistics
  Complement 10 (commercial)

Electronics Probably none

Armament (1943)
  1 20mm/80, 2 short dc tracks

Design
  A former steel-hulled whaler.

Kodiak

1943–44 assigned to the 13th District—stationed at Ketchikan, AK, and used for patrol duty.

The *Kodiak*, 10 Mar 43, flying the CG ensign from the top of her mast. She is armed with a 20mm/80 (canvas covered) on her bow and two short depth-charge tracks on her stern. The qualities of a whale catcher—speed, quickness, and an excellent turning radius—made this type of vessel a valuable patrol and ASW platform.

EMERGENCY ACQUISITION

Name	Visual Call Sign	Builder	Commissioned	Disposition
EM *Northumber-land;* (ex-*North-umberland*)	WYP 361	Pocomoke City, MD	1897 (commercial); 8 Mar 43 (CG)	*Decomm* 1 Mar 44; *ret* to owner 20 Mar 44

Cost
  Acquisition chartered for $850/month; conversion $135,360
Hull
  Tonnage (tons)   167 gross (1941); 99 net (1941)
  Length   134′2″ oa
  Beam   20′2″ max
  Draft   9′3″ max (1943)
Machinery
  Main Engines   1 diesel
  BHP   450
  Propellers   Single
Performance
  Max Speed   9.5 kts (1943)

Logistics
  Complement   9 men (commercial)
Electronics
  Probably none
Armament (1943)
  1 6-pdr.; 2 20mm/80; 2 short dc tracks
Design
  A former menhaden fishing craft.

EM *Northumberland*

1943–44 assigned to CARIBSEAFRON—stationed at San Juan, PR, and used for patrol duty.

The EM *Northumberland,* a menhaden boat, early 1943. EM stood for emergency manning; most CG records treat the EM as part of the ship's name. A menhaden is a fish of the herring family. A menhaden boat is a single-screw, wooden craft used in the menhaden fisheries from Florida to New Jersey. The vessel is used to carry crew, gear, and catch between the shore factory and the fishing grounds. When at the fishing grounds, the craft serves as a base from which small boats operate. All menhaden-type craft that served in the CG during WW II were stationed in the EASTSEAFRON.

EMERGENCY ACQUISITION

Name	Visual Call Sign	Builder	Commissioned	Disposition
Pol (ex-*Pol VII*)	WYP 382	Nylands Verksted, Oslo, Norway	1936 (commercial); 25 Feb 43 (CG)	*Decomm* and *ret* to owner 7 Jul 43

Cost
 Acquisition WSA loan; conversion $13,750

Hull
 Displacement (tons) 260 fl (1942)
 Length 142′ oa; 138′11″ bp
 Beam 25′9″ max
 Draft 14′8″ (1942)

Machinery
 Main Engines Steam
 SHP 1,216
 Propellers Single

Performance
 Max Speed NA

Logistics
 Complement NA

Electronics
 Probably none

Armament
 NA

Design
 A former whaler.

Pol

1943 assigned to WESTSEAFRON—stationed at Morro Bay, CA, and used for patrol duty.

EMERGENCY ACQUISITION

Name	Visual Call Sign	Builder	Commissioned	Disposition
EM *Covington* (ex-*William T. Covington, Jr.*)	WYP 314	M. M. Davis & Son, Solomons, MD	1923 (commercial); 17 Feb 43 (CG)	*Decomm* 30 Jun 43; *ret* to owner 7 Jul 43

Cost
 Acquisition chartered for $750/month; conversion $116,100

Hull
 Displacement (tons) 440 fl (1943)
 Tonnage 263 gross (1941); 30 net (1941)
 Length 129′11″ oa
 Beam 22′4″ max
 Draft 10′ max (1943)

Machinery
 Main Engines 1 diesel
 BHP 400
 Propellers Single

Performance
 Max Speed 11.0 kts (1943)

Logistics
 Complement 34 men (commercial)

Electronics
 Probably none

Armament
 NA

Design
 A former fishing boat.

EM *Covington*

1943 assigned to CARIBSEAFRON—stationed at San Juan, PR, and used for patrol duty.

EMERGENCY ACQUISITION

Name	Visual Call Sign	Builder	Commissioned	Disposition
EM *Humphreys* (ex-*H.R. Humphreys*)	WYP 325	Humphreys Marine Railway, Weems, VA	1919 (commercial); 26 Jan 43 (CG)	*Decomm* and *ret* to owner 27 Mar 44

Cost
 Acquisition chartered for $500/month; conversion $113,400

Hull
Displacement (tons)	350 fl (1943)
Tonnage	211 gross (1941); 48 net (1941)
Length	126'1" oa
Beam	20'7" max
Draft	9'7" max (1943)

Machinery
Main Engines	1 diesel
BHP	380
Propellers	Single

Performance
Max Speed	9.5 kts (1943)
Max Sustained	9.5 kts, 3,320 mi radius (1943)

Logistics
Complement	37 men (commercial)

Electronics
  Probably none

Armament
  NA

Design
  A former fishing craft.

EM *Humphreys*

1943–44 assigned to CARIBSEAFRON—stationed at San Juan, PR, and used for patrol duty.

EMERGENCY ACQUISITION

Name	Visual Call Sign	Builder	Commissioned	Disposition
EM *Rowe* (ex-*W.R. Rowe*)	WYP 328	E. James Tull, Pocomoke City, MD	1901 (commercial); 25 Jan 43 (CG)	*Decomm* 9 Jun 43; *ret* to owner 5 Jul 43

Cost
  Acquisition chartered for $850/month; conversion $129,600

Hull
Displacement (tons)	380 fl (1943)
Tonnage	218 gross (1941); 97 net (1941)
Length	132'5" oa
Beam	20'9" max
Draft	10'9" max (1943)

Machinery
Main Engines	1 diesel
BHP	540
Propellers	Single

Performance
Max Speed	11.0 kts (1943)

Logistics
Complement	26 men (commercial)

Electronics
  Probably none

Armament (1943)
  Prob 1 6-pdr; 2 20mm/80 AA; 2 short dc tracks

Design
  A former mehanden-type fishing craft.

EM *Rowe*

1943 assigned to CARIBSEAFRON—stationed at San Juan, PR, and used for patrol duty.

The EM *Rowe*, 20 Mar 43. Note the wire guides, one atop the bridge structure and the other between the mast and the stack, for the 20mm guns. The guides prevented the guns from firing into the superstructure. The guns are not in place.

EMERGENCY ACQUISITION

Name	Visual Call Sign	Builder	Commissioned	Disposition
EM *Brusstar* (ex-*William S. Brusstar*)	WYP 312	Baltimore, MD	1902 (commercial); 25 Jan 43 (CG)	*Decomm* and *ret* to owner 16 Jun 43

Cost
   Acquisition chartered for $850/month; conversion $117,000
Hull
   Displacement (tons)   345 fl (1943)
   Tonnage   202 gross (1941); 77 net (1941)
   Length   130'6" oa
   Beam   20'
   Draft   9'6" max (1943)
Machinery
   Main Engines   Steam
   SHP   400
   Propellers   Single
Performance
   Max Speed   11.0 kts (1943)
Logistics
   Complement   6 men (commercial)
Electronics
   Probably none
Armament (1943)
   1 6-pdr; 2 20mm/80; 2 short dc tracks
Design
   A former menhaden-type wood fishing vessel.

EM *Brusstar*

1943 assigned to CARIBSEAFRON—stationed at San Juan, PR, and used for patrol duty.

The EM *Brusstar*, 9 Feb 43. Note the narrow beam of the menhaden design. (Courtesy of the Smithsonian Institution.)

EMERGENCY ACQUISITION

Name	Visual Call Sign	Builder	Commissioned	Disposition
EM *Conant* (ex-*Henry W. Conant*)	WYP 320	William G. Abbott Shipbuilding Co., Milford, DE	1919 (commercial); 25 Jan 43 (CG)	*Decomm* 16 Nov 43; *ret* to owner 1 Dec 43

Cost
   Acquisition chartered for $750/month; conversion $111,600
Hull
   Displacement (tons)   385 fl (1943)

Tonnage   260 gross (1941); 23 net (1941)
Length   124'4" oa
Beam   22'3" max
Draft   10'1" max (1943)

Machinery
    Main Engines   Steam
    SHP   200
    Propellers   Single
Performance
    Max Speed   11.0 kts
    Cruising   9.0 kts, 675 mi radius (1943)
Logistics
    Complement   32 (commercial)

Electronics
    Probably none
Design
    A former menhaden-type fishing craft.

Armament
    NA

EM *Conant*

1943 assigned to EASTSEAFRON—stationed at Cape May, NJ, and used for patrol duty.

EMERGENCY ACQUISITION

Name	Visual Call Sign	Builder	Commissioned	Disposition
Thorfinn	WYP 383	Okers Mek. Vaerks, Oslo, Norway	1929 (commercial); 25 Jan 43 (CG)	*Decomm* 2 Jul 43

Cost
    Acquisition WSA loan; conversion $13,750
Hull
    Displacement (tons)   249 fl (1943)
    Length   116' oa
    Beam   23'9" max
    Draft   13'2" (1942)
Machinery
    Main Engines   Steam
    SHP   1,200
    Propellers   Single
Performance
    Max Speed   NA

Logistics
    Complement   NA
Electronics
    Probably none
Armament
    NA
Design
    A former whaler.

Thorfinn

1943 assigned to WESTSEAFRON—stationed at San Pedro, CA, and used for patrol duty.

EMERGENCY ACQUISITION

Name	Visual Call Sign	Builder	Commissioned	Disposition
Thoris (ex-*Almos*)	WYP 378	Framnaes Mek. Vaerks A/S, Sordefjord, Norway	1939 (commercial); 25 Jan 43 (CG)	*Decomm* and *ret* to owner 7 Jul 43

Cost
    Acquisition WSA loan; conversion $13,750
Hull
    Displacement (tons)   616 fl (1943)   Length   134' oa; 125'5" bp
    Beam   25'6" max   Draft   13'9" (1942)
Machinery
    Main Engines   Steam
    SHP   1,400   Propellers   Single
Performance
    Max Speed   NA

Logistics
    Complement   NA
Electronics
    Probably none
Armament
    NA
Design   A former whaler.

Thoris

1943 assigned to WESTSEAFRON—stationed at San Pedro, CA, and used for patrol duty.

EMERGENCY ACQUISITION

Name	Visual Call Sign	Builder	Commissioned	Disposition
Thorfjell	WYP 384	Koldraes Mek. Vaerks, Tønsberg, Norway	1934 (commercial); 25 Jan 43 (CG)	*Decomm* 2 Jul 43

Cost
    Acquisition WSA loan; conversion $13,750
Hull
    Displacement (tons)   635 fl (1942)
    Length   126'1" oa; 126' bp
    Beam   25'1" max
    Draft   14'2" (1942)
Machinery
    Main Engines   Steam
    SHP   1,200
    Propellers   Single
Performance
    Max Speed   NA

Logistics
    Complement   NA
Electronics
    Probably none
Armament
    NA
Design
    A former whaler.

Thorfjell

1943 assigned to WESTSEAFRON—stationed at San Pedro, CA, and used for patrol duty.

EMERGENCY ACQUISITION

Name	Visual Call Sign	Builder	Commissioned	Disposition
EM *Pocahontas* (ex-*Pocahontas*)	WYP 362	William G. Abbott Shipbuilding Co., Milford, DE	1914 (commercial); 22 Jan 43 (CG)	*Decomm* 13 Nov 43; *ret* to WSA 23 Mar 45

Cost
    NA
Hull
    Displacement (tons)   535 fl (1943)
    Tonnage   286 gross (1941); 147 net (1941)
    Length   139'7" oa
    Beam   24'2" max
    Draft   11'5" max (1943)
Machinery
    Main Engines   Steam
    SHP   500
    Propellers   Single
Performance
    Max Speed   12.0 kts (1943)
    Max Sustained   10.5 kts, 1,260 mi radius (1943)
Logistics
    Complement   29 men (commercial—1941)
Electronics   Armament (1943)
    Probably none   Prob 1 6-pdr; 2 20mm/80; 2 short dc tracks
Design
    A former menhaden-type fishing craft.

EM *Pocahontas*

1943 assigned to EASTSEAFRON—stationed at Little Creek, VA, and used for patrol duty.

The EM *Pocahontas*, a menhaden craft, 2 Feb 43. Supporting struts under the 20mm gun platform distinguish her from many of her near sisters. Menhaden vessels were made of wood; they had a good sheer forward and a low stern to facilitate the handling of fish and small boats. Each vessel was equipped with three open boats, a striker boat stowed over the main hatch aft the mast and two purse boats hung near the stern (not shown above). Note the catwalk, in the superstructure amidships, which allowed access fore and aft during rough weather when the main deck was flooded.

EMERGENCY ACQUISITION

Name	Visual Call Sign	Builder	Commissioned	Disposition
Globe Eight (ex-*Globe VIII*)	WYP 380	Moss Vaerft & Dokk, Moss, Norway	1936 (commercial); 29 Dec 42 (CG)	*Decomm* 3 Jul 43; *ret* to WSA 4 Jul 43

Cost
    Acquisition WSA loan; conversion $13,750

Hull

Displacement (tons)	587 fl (1942)
Length	136' oa; 128'3" bp
Beam	25'3" max
Draft	13'2" (1942)

Machinery

Main Engines	Steam
SHP	1,300
Propellers	Single

Performance

Max Speed	NA

Logistics

Complement	NA

Electronics
    Probably none

Armament
    NA

Design
    A former whaler.

Globe Eight

1942–43 assigned to WESTSEAFRON—stationed at San Francisco, CA, and used for patrol duty.

EMERGENCY ACQUISITION

Name	Visual Call Sign	Builder	Commissioned	Disposition
EM *Margaret* (ex-*Margaret*)	WYP 323	Rappahannock Marine Railway Co., Weems, VA	1912 (commercial); 28 Dec 42 (CG)	*Decomm* 7 Jun 43; *ret* to owner 24 Jun 43

Cost
    Acquisition chartered for $850/month; conversion $115,200

Hull

Displacement (tons)	468 fl (1942)
Tonnage	268 gross (1941); 121 net (1941)
Length	128' oa
Beam	23'3" max
Draft	11'4" max (1942)

Machinery

Main Engines	Steam
SHP	500
Propellers	Single

Performance

Max Speed	11.0 kts (1942)

Logistics

Complement	34 men (commercial)

Electronics
    None

Armament (1943)
    1 6-pdr; 2 20mm/80; dc tracks

Design
    A former menhaden-type fishing vessel.

The EM *Margaret*, 31 Jan 43.

EM *Margaret*

1942–43 assigned to EASTSEAFRON—stationed at Cape May, NJ, and used for patrol duty.

EMERGENCY ACQUISITION

Name	Visual Call Sign	Builder	Commissioned	Disposition
Thorgaut	WYP 377	Framnaes Mek. Vaerks, Sordefjord, Norway	1939 (commercial); 28 Dec 42 (CG)	*Decomm* and *ret* to WSA 3 Jul 43

Cost
  Acquisition WSA loan; conversion $13,750

Hull
Displacement (tons)	675 fl (1942)
Length	135′9″ oa; 128′3″ bp
Beam	25′6″ max
Draft	14′9″ (1942)

Machinery
Main Engines	Steam
SHP	1,363
Propellers	Single

Performance
Max Speed	NA

Logistics
Complement	NA

Electronics
  Probably none

Armament
  NA

Design
  A former whaler.

Thorgaut

1942–43 assigned to WESTSEAFRON—stationed at Eureka, CA, and used for patrol duty.

EMERGENCY ACQUISITION

Name	Visual Call Sign	Builder	Commissioned	Disposition
Belmont (ex-*Thorarinn*)	WYP 341	Akers Mek. Vaerks, Oslo, Norway	1929 (commercial); 14 Dec 42 (CG)	*Decomm* 18 Oct 45; *sold* 20 Nov 46

Cost
  Acquisition WSA loan; conversion $220,285

Hull
Displacement (tons)	588 fl (1942)
Length	115′7″ oa
Beam	23′9″ max
Draft	13′2″ max (1942)

Machinery
Main Engines	Steam
SHP	750
Propellers	Single

Performance
Cruising	12.0 kts, 1,900 mi radius (1942)

Logistics
Complement	NA

Electronics
  Probably none

Armament
  NA

Design
  A former whaler; while in CG service she proved to be a very crowded and wet craft.

Belmont

1942–45 assigned to EASTSEAFRON—stationed at Balboa, CZ, and Miami, FL, and used for patrol duty.

EMERGENCY ACQUISITION

Name	Visual Call Sign	Builder	Commissioned	Disposition
EM *Reed* (ex-*E. Warren Reed*)	WYP 322	Pocomoke City, MD	1899 (commercial); 11 Dec 42 (CG)	*Decomm* 8 Mar 43; *ret* to owner 15 Mar 43

Cost
  Acquisition $15,000; conversion $76,000

Hull
Displacement (tons)	325 fl (1942)
Tonnage	165 gross (1941); 90 net (1941)
Length	122′2″ oa
Beam	19′8″ max
Draft	9′7″ max (1943)

Machinery
Main Engines	1 diesel
BHP	200
Propellers	Single

Performance
Max Speed	11.0 kts (1943)

Logistics
Complement	24 men (commercial)

Electronics
  None

Armament (1943)
  1 6-pdr; 2 20mm/80; 2 short dc tracks

Design
  A former coastal freighter.

ED *Reed*

1942–43 assigned to CARIBSEAFRON—stationed at San Juan, PR, and used for patrol duty.

The EM *Reed*, 22 Jan 43, in Baltimore Harbor. The small crane aft is used to fill depth-charge tracks.

EMERGENCY ACQUISITION

Name	Visual Call Sign	Builder	Commissioned	Disposition
Bronco (ex-*Star* 18)	WYP 340	Akers Mek. Vaerks, Oslo, Norway	1930 (commercial); 7 Dec 42 (CG)	*Decomm* 30 Jun 45; *sold* 20 Nov 46

Cost
  Acquisition WSA loan; conversion $225,839
Hull
  Displacement (tons)   588 fl (1942)
  Tonnage   249 gross
  Length   123'1" oa; 116' bp
  Beam   23'9" max
  Draft   13'2" max (1942)
Machinery
  Main Engines   Reciprocating steam
  Main Boilers   Scotch boilers
  SHP   750
  Propellers   Single
Performance
  Max Speed   10.0 kts (1942)
  Max Sustained   10.0 kts, 3,100 mi radius (1942)

Logistics
  Fuel Oil (95%)   110 tons
  Complement   NA
Electronics
  Detection Radar   SO-1; BN (1944)
  Sonar   WEA-2 (1945)
Armament (1944)
  1 3"/50; 2 dc tracks
Design
  A former whaler; while in CG service proved to be a very crowded and wet ship.

Bronco

1942–45 assigned to the CARIBSEAFRON—stationed at Balboa, CZ, and used for patrol duty.

EMERGENCY ACQUISITION

Name	Visual Call Sign	Builder	Commissioned	Disposition
Bodega (ex-*Thordr*)	WYP 342	Akers Mek. Vaerks, Oslo, Norway	1930 (commercial); 21 Nov 42 (CG)	Abandoned 20 Dec 43

Cost
  Acquisition WSA loan; conversion $283,541
Hull
  Displacement (tons)   588 oa (1942)
  Length   123'1" oa; 115'7" bp
  Beam   23'9" max
  Draft   13'2" (1942)
Machinery
  Main Engines   Steam
  SHP   750
  Propellers   Single
Performance
  Max Speed   NA
Logistics
  Complement   NA
Electronics
  Probably none
Armament
  NA
Design
  The *Bodega* was the former whaler *Thordr;* while in CG service she proved to be a very crowded and wet ship.

Bodega

1942–43 assigned to the PASEAFRON—stationed on East Coast and at Balboa, CZ—operated in the Caribbean; 20 Dec 43 stranded while attempting to rescue crew from the SS *James Withycombe* off the Panama Canal—and abandoned.

The *Thordr,* 30 Sep 42, in Boston Harbor prior to serving in the CG as the *Bodega.* She still flies a Norwegian flag. The *Bodega* was acquired for operation in Greenland waters, but she was assigned to the Caribbean area instead because she proved to be very "wet." During peacetime, a whale catcher such as the *Thordr* mounted a muzzle-loading gun, which fired a harpoon with a 3.5" bore on the bow. Steam pipes were run through the bin where the line was stored to prevent it from freezing into a solid mass.

EMERGENCY ACQUISITION

Name	Visual Call Sign	Builder	Commissioned	Disposition
Alatok (ex-*Hekla*)	WYP 172	Cochrane & Sons, Ltd., Selby, England	1922 (commercial); 22 Aug 42 (CG)	*Decomm* and *ret* to WSA 27 Dec 43; *ret* to owner 13 Mar 44

Cost
  Acquisition $80,000; conversion $92,000
Hull
  Displacement (tons)   775 fl (1942)
  Tonnage   387 gross (1942)
  Length   150'3" oa
  Beam   25' mb
  Draft   13'5" max (1942)
Machinery
  Main Engines   1 triple-expansion steam

  BHP   500
  Propellers   Single
Performance
  Max Speed   9.0 kts (1942)
  Max Sustained   9.0 kts, 4,700 mi radius (1942)
Logistics
  Fuel Oil (95%)   1,100 barrels
  Complement   NA
Electronics
  None

Armament (1943)

  1 3″/50; 2 20mm/80; 2 short dc tracks

Design

  A former steel-hulled trawler.

Alatok

1942–43 assigned to CINCLANT—stationed at Boston, MA, and used on Greenland Patrol.

The *Alatok*, 19 Mar 43. The 3″/50 mounted forward is a better gun than most of those the WYPs received.

EMERGENCY ACQUISITION

Name	Visual Call Sign	Builder	Commissioned	Disposition
Amarok (ex-*Lark*; ex-*Greyhound One*)	WYP 166	Russell Erie Basin Shipyard, Inc., Brooklyn, NY	1938 (commercial); 31 Jul 42 (CG)	*Decomm* 5 Feb 44

Cost

  Acquisition $3,539; conversion $75,000

Hull

Displacement (tons)	450 fl (1942)
Tonnage	237 gross (1941); 123 net (1941)
Length	128′ oa; 119′3″ bp
Beam	24′1″ max
Draft	12′7″ max (1942)

Machinery

Main Engines	1 diesel
BHP	375
Propellers	Single

Performance

Max Speed	10.0 kts (1942)
Max Sustained	10.0 kts, 3,500 mi radius (1942)
Cruising	9.0 kts, 4,600 mi radius (1942)

Logistics

Complement	16 men (commercial)

Electronics

  None

Armament (1943)

  1 3″/23; 2 20mm/80; 2 short dc tracks

Design

  A former trawler.

Amarok

1942–44 assigned to CINCLANT—stationed at Boston, MA, and used for Greenland Patrol.

The *Amarok*, 14 May 43. Note the light machine gun in place just forward of the depth-charge tracks.

EMERGENCY ACQUISITION

Name	Visual Call Sign	Builder	Commissioned	Disposition
Aklak (ex-*Weymouth*)	WYP 168	Bethlehem Steel Co., Fore River, Quincy, MA	1941 (commercial); 16 Jul 42 (CG)	*Decomm* 10 Mar 44; *ret* to owner 5 Apr 44

Cost
  Acquisition WSA loan; conversion $75,000
Hull
  Displacement (tons)   395 fl (1942)
  Tonnage   170 gross (1941)
  Length   116' oa; 110' bp
  Beam   22'5" mb
  Draft   10'6" (1942)
Machinery
  Main Engines   1 Nelseco 6-cyl, 4-cycle diesel
  BHP   375
  Propellers   Single
Performance
  Max Speed   10.0 kts (1942)
  Cruising   10.0 kts, 2,800 mi radius (1942)

Economic   8.9 kts, 5,600 mi radius (1942)
Logistics
  Diesel Fuel (95%)   5,890 gal
  Complement   NA
Electronics
  None
Armament (1943)
  1 6-pdr; 2 20mm/80; 2 short dc tracks
Design
  A former steel-hulled trawler.

Aklak

1942–44 assigned to CINCLANT—stationed at Boston, MA, and used on Greenland Patrol; 12 Aug 42 freed the stranded USA *Armstrong*.

The *Aklak* off Greenland. The man standing atop the bridge is raising an "anchored ball."

EMERGENCY ACQUISITION

Name	Visual Call Sign	Builder	Commissioned	Disposition
Arluk (ex-*Atlantic*)	WYP 167	Bethlehem Steel Corp., Fore River, Quincy, MA	1934 (commercial); 16 Jul 42 (CG)	*Decomm* and *ret* to owner 6 Jul 44

Cost
  Acquisition WSA loan; conversion $75,000
Hull
  Displacement (tons)   370 fl (1942)
  Tonnage   163 gross (1941); 84 net (1941)
  Length   110'3" oa; 102'5" bp
  Beam   22'1" max
  Draft   10'6" max (1942)
Machinery
  Main Engines   1 diesel
  BHP   250
  Propellers   Single
Performance
  Max Speed   9.0 kts (1942)
  Max Sustained   9.0 kts, 3,660 mi radius (1942)
  Cruising   8.0 kts, 4,530 mi radius (1942)
Logistics
  Complement   15 men (commercial)
Electronics
  None
Armament (1943)
  1 6-pdr; 2 20mm/80; 2 short dc tracks
Design
  The *Arluk* is the former trawler *Atlantic*.

Arluk

1942–44 assigned to CINCLANT—stationed at Boston, MA, and used on Greenland Patrol.

The *Arluk* off Greenland. As the U-boat threat abated in 1944, most such former trawlers were released from the CG.

EMERGENCY ACQUISITION

Name	Visual Call Sign	Builder	Commissioned	Disposition
Arvek (ex-*Triton*)	WYP 165	Bethlehem Steel Co., Fore River, Quincy, MA	1936 (commercial); 16 Jul 42 (CG)	*Decomm* 29 Jul 44

Cost
  Acquisition WSA loan; conversion $75,000
Hull
  Displacement (tons)   336 fl (1942)
  Tonnage   172 gross (1941); 84 net (1941)
  Length   110'3" oa; 102'5" bp
  Beam   22'1" max
  Draft   10'6" max (1942)
Machinery
  Main Engines   1 diesel

BHP   350
Propellers   Single
Performance
  Max Speed   9.0 kts (1942)
  Max Sustained   9.0 kts, 2,800 mi radius (1942)
Logistics
  Complement   12 men (commercial)
Electronics
  Detection Radar   None
  Sonar   None

Armament
| 1942 | 1 6-pdr; 2 20mm/80; 2 short dc tracks |
| 1944 | 4 20mm/80; 2 short dc tracks |

Design   A former trawler.

Arvek

1942–44 assigned to CINCLANT—stationed at Boston, MA, and used on Greenland Patrol.

The *Arvek* in moderate seas. She mounts four 80mm/20s—two on the forecastle and two on the bridge wings—plus two short depth-charge tracks on the stern.

EMERGENCY ACQUISITION

Name	Visual Call Sign	Builder	Commissioned	Disposition
Nogak (ex-*St. George*)	WYP 171	Snow Shipyards, Inc., Rockland, ME	1940 (commercial); 7 Jul 42 (CG)	*Decomm* and *ret* to WSA 24 Jul 44

Cost
  Acquisition WSA loan; conversion $75,000

Hull
Displacement (tons)	300 fl (1942)
Tonnage	176 gross (1941); 99 net (1941)
Length	111′ oa; 105′5″ bp
Beam	23′6″ mb
Draft	11′8″ max (1942)

Machinery
Main Engines	1 Fairbanks Morse, 5-cyl diesel
BHP	500
Propellers	Single

Performance
Max Speed	10.0 kts (1942)
Max Sustained	9.5 kts, 1,812 mi radius (1942)
Cruising	9.0 kts, 2,300 mi radius (1942)

Logistics
| Complement | 10 men (commercial) |

Electronics
  None

Armament (1942)
  1 6-pdr; 2 20mm/80; 2 short dc tracks

Design   A former wooden-hulled trawler.

Nogak

1942–44 assigned to CINCLANT—stationed at Boston, MA, and used on Greenland Patrol.

The *Nogak* painted in a Thayer Measure 16 camouflage scheme, which had three colors: the vertical surfaces were light blue and white; the decks and horizontal surfaces were a very dark blue. This scheme was used in areas where U-boats attacked at night or during low visibility. Most cutters operating in Greenland waters were painted like this at one time or another.

EMERGENCY ACQUISITION

Name	Visual Call Sign	Builder	Commissioned	Disposition
Aivik (ex-*Arlington*)	WYP 164	Bath Iron Works, Inc., Bath, ME	1936 (commercial); 24 Jun 42 (CG)	*Decomm* 21 Jul 44; *ret* to owner 11 Sep 44

Cost
  Acquisition WSA loan; conversion $75,000

Hull
  Displacement (tons)   590 fl (1942)
  Tonnage   251 gross (1941); 155 net (1941)
  Length   128'3" oa; 118'2" bp
  Beam   23'5" mb
  Draft   11'6" max (1942)

Machinery
  Main Engines   1 Fairbanks Morse, 5-cyl, 2-cycle diesel
  BHP   525
  Propellers   Single

Performance
  Max Speed   10.5 kts (1942)
  Cruising   10.2 kts, 1,800 mi radius (1942)

Economic   8.5 kts, 2,600 mi radius (1942)

Logistics
  Diesel Fuel (95%)   11,800 gal
  Complement   15 men (commercial)

Electronics
  Detection Radar   Probably none   Sonar   WEA (1942)

Armament (1942)
  2 20mm/80 (single)

Design   A former steel-hulled fishing trawler.

Aivik

1942–44 assigned to CINCLANT—stationed at Boston, MA; used for weather-station duty and Greenland Patrol; 21 May 43 rescued 42 survivors from the SS *Svend Foyne,* which had collided with an iceberg.

EMERGENCY ACQUISITION

Name	Visual Call Sign	Builder	Commissioned	Disposition
Natsek (ex-*Belmont*)	WYP 170	Snow Shipyards, Inc., Rockland, ME	1941 (commercial); 19 Jun 42 (CG)	Lost at sea 17 Dec 42

Cost
  Acquisition $2,122; conversion $150,000
Hull
  Displacement (tons)   450 fl (1942)
  Tonnage   225.5 gross (1942)
  Length   116'9" oa
  Beam   23'6" mb
  Draft   11'8" max (1942)
Machinery
  Main Engines   1 Fairbanks Morse, 5-cyl, 2-cycle diesel
  BHP   575
  Propellers   Single
Performance
  Max Speed   11.0 kts (1942)
  Cruising   9.5 kts, 2,750 mi radius (1942)
Logistics
  Diesel Fuel (95%)   8,400 gal
  Complement   1 officer, 23 men
Electronics
  None
Armament (1942)
  1 6-pdr; 2 20mm/80; 2 short dc tracks
Design
  A former wooden trawler.

Natsek

1942 assigned to CINCLANT—stationed at Boston, MA, and used on Greenland Patrol; 17 Dec 42 last seen off Belle Isle, Newfoundland, in a blinding snowstorm. Lost with all hands, 1 officer, 22 men, and 1 naval enlisted man—believed to have capsized because of icing.

The *Natsek*, 25 Jun 42, in Boston Harbor. She was lost with all hands during a blinding snowstorm. The *Natsek* was last seen off Belle Island on 17 Dec 42. She was believed to be a victim of icing, which occurs when ice forms on the superstructure and increases top weight to the point at which the vessel capsizes.

EMERGENCY ACQUISITION

Name	Visual Call Sign	Builder	Commissioned	Disposition
Atak (ex-*Winchester*)	WYP 163	Bath Iron Works, Inc., Bath, ME	1937 (commercial); 14 Jun 42 (CG)	*Decomm* 15 Jul 44; *trans* to WSA 1 Aug 44

Cost
  Acquisition $7,875; conversion $75,000
Hull
  Displacement (tons)   443 fl (1942)
  Tonnage   243 gross (1941); 145 net (1941)
  Length   128' oa; 118'2" bp
  Beam   23'5" max
  Draft   11'8" max (1942)

Machinery
  Main Engines   1 Fairbanks Morse, 5-cyl, 2-cycle diesel
  BHP   550
  Propellers   Single
Performance
  Max Speed   10.5 kts (1942)
  Max Sustained   10.0 kts, 4,500 mi radius (1942)
  Cruising   9.5 kts, 5,000 mi radius (1942)

Logistics
  Diesel Fuel (95%)   11,800 gal
  Complement   17 men (commercial)
Electronics
  None
Armament (1942)
  1 6-pdr; 2 20mm/80; 2 short dc tracks
Design
  A former trawler.

Atak

1942–44 assigned to CINCLANT—stationed at Boston, MA, and used on Greenland Patrol.

The *Atak*, 21 Jun 42.

EMERGENCY ACQUISITION

Name	Visual Call Sign	Builder	Commissioned	Disposition
Nanok (ex-*North Star*)	WYP 169	Snow Shipyards, Inc., Rockland, ME	1941 (commercial); 7 Jun 42 (CG)	*Decomm* 25 Jul 44; *ret* to owner 14 Sep 44

Cost
  Acquisition WSA loan; conversion $150,000
Hull
  Displacement (tons)   300 fl (1942)
  Tonnage   220 gross (1941); 101 net (1941)
  Length   120' oa; 115' bp
  Beam   23'5" max
  Draft   12' max (1942)
Machinery
  Main Engines   1 Fairbanks Morse, 2-cycle diesel
  BHP   500
  Propellers   Single
Performance
  Max Speed   9.5 kts (1942)

Max Sustained   9.5 kts, 1,775 mi radius (1942)
Logistics
  Fuel Oil (95%)   8,000 gal
  Complement   17 men (commercial)
Electronics
  Probably none
Armament
  NA
Design
  A former freighter.

Nanok

1942–44 assigned to CINCLANT—stationed at Boston, MA; operated off Greenland.

EMERGENCY ACQUISITION

Name	Visual Call Sign	Builder	Commissioned	Disposition
Busko	[WYP]	Hans Graudal, Opsanger, Norway	1926 (commercial); 24 Jan 42 (CG)	?

Cost
  NA
Hull
  Tonnage   159 registered, 142 gross, 61 net (1942)
  Length   105'0" bp
  Beam   22'7" max
  Draft   10'7" (1942)
Machinery   Performance
  NA   NA
Logistics
  NA

Electronics
  Probably none
Armament
  NA
Design
  A former fishing craft.

Busko

1942–? assigned to CINCLANT—stationed at Boston, MA, and used in Greenland waters.

EMERGENCY ACQUISITION

Name	Visual Call Sign	Builder	Commissioned	Disposition
Trinity	[WYP]	NA	? (commercial); 14 Jan 42 (CG)	*Ret* to Navy 2 May 42

Cost
  Acquired from Navy
No characteristics available

Trinity

Acquired from USN; CG service not available.

EMERGENCY ACQUISITION

Name	Visual Call Sign	Builder	Commissioned	Disposition
Holy Cross	[WYP]	Bath Iron Works, Inc., Bath, ME	1928 (commercial); 14 Jan 42 (CG)	*Ret* to Navy 2 May 42

Cost
  Acquired from Navy
Hull
  Displacement (tons)   410 est. (1943)
  Length   123'10" oa; 116' bp
  Beam   23' mb max
  Draft   11'6" max (1943)
Machinery
  Main Engines   Fairbanks Morse diesel
  Propellers   Single
Performance
  Max Speed   10 kts (1943)

Logistics
  Complement   NA
Electronics
  Probably none
Armament (1943)
  1 3"/50; prob 2 20mm/80; 2 short dc tracks
Design
  Designed as a beam trawler.

Holy Cross

Acquired from USN; CG service NA; returned to USN and became the *Kite*.

WPY—YACHTS

EMERGENCY ACQUISITION, *KIL* CLASS

Name	Visual Call Sign	Builder	Commissioned	Disposition
Marita (ex-*Kaspar*; ex-*Kilmacrennan*)	WPY 175	South Bank on Lees, England	1918 (HMS); 30 Jan 43 (CG)	*Decomm* 13 Nov 44; *sold* 3 May 45

Cost
  Acquisition WSA loan; conversion $28,008
Hull
  Displacement (tons)   1,450 fl (1942)
  Tonnage   632 gross (1941); 269 net (1941)
  Length   183' oa; 172'2" bp
  Beam   30' max
  Draft   17' max
Machinery
  Main Engines   Steam
  Main Boilers   1 Scotch
  SHP   700
  Propellers   Single
Performance
  Max Speed   7.0 kts (1943)

Logistics
  Complement   14 men (commercial); 85 men (1942)
Electronics   NA
Armament (1943)
  2 3"/50 (single); 4 20mm/80 (single); 2 dc projectors; 2 dc tracks
Design
  The *Kil*-class patrol gunboats were designed for coastal patrol and ASW during WW I. Eighty-one units were constructed for the Royal Navy. They were recognizable by their "double-ended" appearance.

Marita

1943–44 assigned to the Armed School Section Base, Little Creek, VA, and used for training; 1944 assigned to the 8th District—stationed at Gulfport, MS.

The *Marita*, 26 Apr 43, a KIL-class gunboat designed for patrol and ASW during WW I.

WPYc—COASTAL YACHTS

EMERGENCY ACQUISITION

Name	Visual Call Sign	Builder	Commissioned	Disposition
Amethyst (ex-*Samona II*)	WPYc 3	Craig Shipbuilding Co., Long Beach, CA	1931 (private); 10 Mar 44 (CG)	*Decomm* 27 Feb 46; *trans* to Maritime Commission 11 Sep 46

Cost
  NA

Hull
  Displacement (tons)   525 (1944)
  Length   147' oa
  Beam   23'10" max
  Draft   11" max (1944)

Machinery
  Main Engines   NA

Performance
  Max Speed   14.5 kts (1944)

Logistics
  Complement   46 men (1944)

Electronics
  NA

Armament (1944)
  1 3"

Design
  A former deep-sea trawler.

Amethyst

Acquired from USN; 1944–46 stationed at Mare Island, CA, and used on patrol, plane guard, and weather patrol.

EMERGENCY ACQUISITION

Name	Visual Call Sign	Builder	Commissioned	Disposition
Madalan (ex-*Malaina*; ex-*Illyria*)	WPYc 345	Marco U. Martinolich, Lussinpriccolo, Italy	1928 (private); 1 Apr 43 (CG)	*Decomm* 7 Jul 45; to WSA 16 Oct 45

Cost
 Acquisition $45,000; conversion $44,507
Hull
Tonnage	357 gross (1941); 242 net (1941)
Length	147′6″ oa; 121′ wl
Beam	30′2″ max
Draft	14′9″ max (1943)

Machinery
Main Engines	1 Cooper-Bessemer, 6-cyl diesel
BHP	300
Propellers	Single

Performance
| Max Sustained | 8.0 kts, 4,895 mi radius (1943) |
| Cruising | 7.0 kts, 5,280 mi radius (1943) |

Logistics
| Complement | 35 men (1943) |

Electronics
| Detection Radar | None |

Armament (1943)
 2 20mm/80; 2 dc projectors
Design
 A brigantine yacht designed by Henry J. Gielow, Inc.

Madalan

1943–45 assigned to the 3rd District—stationed at Greenport, NY, and Fort Tilden, NY, and used for training.

The *Madalan*, armed with two 20mm guns and depth-charge projectors. She was used for training throughout WW II.

EMERGENCY ACQUISITION

Name	Visual Call Sign	Builder	Commissioned	Disposition
Nellwood (ex-*Nellwood II*; ex-*Murdona*; ex-*Acania*)	WPYc 337	Pusey & Jones Co., Wilmington, DE	1929 (private); 26 Mar 43 (CG)	*Decomm* 15 Nov 46; *sold* 23 Sep 47

Cost
 Acquisition $91,400; conversion $19,163
Hull
Displacement (tons)	294 fl (1943)
Tonnage	244 gross (1941); 165 net (1941)
Length	126′1″ oa; 115′6″ bp
Beam	21′11″ max
Draft	9′ max (1943)

Machinery
Main Engines	2 Winton Model 133 diesels
BHP	1,000
Propellers	Twin

Performance
| Max Speed | 13.0 kts (1943) |
| Max Sustained | 13.0 kts, 2,830 mi radius (1943) |

Logistics
| Diesel Fuel (95%) | 7,000 gal |
| Complement | 5 officers, 2 warrants, 45 men (1943) |

Electronics | None |

Armament (1943)
 1 6-pdr; 2 20mm/80; 2 Mousetraps; 2 short dc tracks
Design
 A former steel-hulled yacht; designed by John H. Wells, Inc.; 29 Nov 44 converted to a fire boat.

Nellwood

1943–44 assigned to the 13th District; 1944–45 assigned to SERVPAC—stationed at San Diego, CA, and used for training.

The *Nellwood*. Two ASW Mousetrap racks are in a raised position on her forecastle; however, the rockets are not in place. Each launcher held four rockets, and each rocket weighed 80 lbs, 40 lbs of which was a TNT charge. The name Mousetrap was derived from the appearance of the launcher. (Courtesy of the Smithsonian Institution.)

EMERGENCY ACQUISITION

Name	Visual Call Sign	Builder	Commissioned	Disposition
Thalassa	WPYc 348	Ditchburn Boats, Ltd., Orillia, Canada	1930 (private); 5 Feb 43 (CG)	*Decomm* 3 Jul 45; to WSA 26 Jun 46

Cost
  Acquisition $27,500; conversion $52,442
Hull
  Tonnage   138 gross (1941); 96 net (1941)
  Length   100' oa; 92' wl
  Beam   18' mb
  Draft   5'6" (1943)
Machinery
  Main Engines   2 Winton diesels
  BHP   400   Propellers   Twin
Performance
  Max Sustained 10.0 kts, 550 mi radius (1943)
  Cruising   6.0 kts, 770 mi radius (1943)
Electronics   Armament (1943)
  None   2 .50 cal mg; dc tracks
Design
  A wooden yacht designed by the builder.

Thalassa

1943–44 assigned to the 3rd District—stationed at Fort Tilden, NY, and used for training; 1944–45 assigned to the 3rd District—stationed at Fort Hancock, NJ, and used for training.

The *Thalassa* in New York Harbor. The CG ensign flying from the mast has been used by the service since 1799, although many subtle changes have been made in its design over the years.

EMERGENCY ACQUISITION

Name	Visual Call Sign	Builder	Commissioned	Disposition
Gertrude L. Thebaud	WPYc 386	A.D. Story, Essex, MA	1930 (commercial); 24 Dec 42 (CG)	*Decomm* and *ret* to owner 10 Feb 44

Cost
  Acquisition $42,000; conversion $15,812
Hull
  Displacement (tons)   500 fl (1943)
  Tonnage   137 gross (1941); 93 net (1941)
  Length   133′ oa; 115′8″ bp
  Beam   25′2″ max
  Draft   12′2″ max (1941)
Machinery
  Main Engines   1 Sterling, Model GR-8, 8-cyl diesel
  BHP   180
  Propellers   Single
Performance
  Max Speed   9.0 kts (1943)

Cruising   8.5 kts, 2,377 mi radius (1943)
Logistics
  Complement   20 men (commercial)
Electronics
  Probably none
Armament
  NA
Design
  A 2-masted wooden fishing schooner.

Gertrude L. Thebaud

1942–44 assigned to the 1st District—stationed at Gloucester, MA, and used on picket duty.

EMERGENCY ACQUISITION

Name	Visual Call Sign	Builder	Commissioned	Disposition
Boulder (ex-*Elkhorn*)	WPYc 352	Boston, MA	1906 (commercial); 4 Dec 42 (CG)	*Decomm* 15 Jun 43

Cost
  Acquisition $19,000; conversion $14,185
Hull
  Displacement (tons)   127 fl (1942)
  Tonnage   55 gross (1941); 37 net (1941)
  Length   104′6″ oa; 96′5″ wl
  Beam   13′7″ max
  Draft   7′ max (1942)
Machinery
  Main Engines   2 Caterpillar diesels
  BHP   250
  Propellers   Single
Performance
  Max Speed   14.0 kts (1942)

Logistics
  Complement   4 men (commercial)
Electronics
  Probably none
Armament
  NA
Design
  A former fishing boat.

Boulder

1942–43 assigned to the 4th District—stationed at Atlantic City, NJ, and used for patrol duty.

EMERGENCY ACQUISITION

Name	Visual Call Sign	Builder	Commissioned	Disposition
Wicomico (ex-*Catoctin*; ex-*Dupont*; ex-*Saelmo*; ex-*Kwasind*; ex-*Nokomis*)	WPYc 158	Robins Dry Dock & Repair Co., Brooklyn, NY	May 14 (private); 14 Oct 42 (CG)	*Decomm* Jun 45

Cost
    Acquisition CG Reserve; conversion $164,325

Hull
Tonnage	303 gross (1941); 206 net (1941)
Length	175' oa; 154'5" bp
Beam	23'6" mb
Draft	12'8" max (1942)

Machinery
Main Engines	Diesel
SHP	900
Propellers	Single

Performance
Max Speed	NA

Logistics
Complement	NA

Electronics
Detection Radar	None
Sonar	Probably none

Armament (1943)
    1 3"/50; 2 20mm; 3 mg; dc tracks

Design
    A former steel-hulled yacht; her name was changed from the *Catoctin* to the *Wicomico* on 16 Aug 43.

Wicomico

1942–45 assigned to CINCLANT (DESLANT)—stationed at Newport, RI, and used on patrol duty and by the CG Reserve.

The *Catoctin* prior to her name change.

EMERGENCY ACQUISITION

Name	Visual Call Sign	Builder	Commissioned	Disposition
Blackstone (ex-*Crescent III*; ex-*Alert*)	[WPYc]	Herreshoff Manufacturing Co., Bristol, RI	1929 (private); 2 Sep 42 (CG)	NA

Cost
    Acquisition $8,000; conversion $75,000

Hull
Displacement (tons)	170 fl (1942)
Tonnage	152 gross (1941); 103 net (1941)
Length	140' oa; 138'8" wl
Beam	17'6" max
Draft	6'5" max (1941)

Machinery
Main Engines	2 Cooper-Bessemer diesels
SHP	1,500

Performance
Max Speed	NA

Logistics
Complement	NA

Electronics
    Probably none

Armament	NA

Design
    A former steel-hulled yacht designed by the builder. She had been re-engined in 1940.

Blackstone

Service NA.

EMERGENCY ACQUISITION

Name	Visual Call Sign	Builder	Commissioned	Disposition
Blanchard (ex-CGR 106; ex-*Nedra B*; ex-*Alacrity*)	WPYc 369	Pusey & Jones Co., Wilmington, DE	1910 (private); 20 Aug 42 (CG)	*Decomm* 25 Nov 43

Cost
  Acquisition $1; conversion $2,390
Hull
  Displacement (tons)   213 fl (1942)
  Tonnage   101 gross (1941); 69 net (1941)
  Length   118' oa; 109'9" wl
  Beam   15' max
  Draft   5'6" max (1942)
Machinery
  Main Engines   2 Winton gasoline engines
  SHP   175
  Propellers   Twin
Performance
  Max Speed   8.0 kts (1942)

Logistics
  Complement   NA
Electronics
  Probably none
Armament
  NA
Design
  A steel-hulled yacht designed by Cox & Stevens.

Blanchard

1942–43 assigned to GULFSEAFRON—stationed at Key West, FL, and used for patrol.

EMERGENCY ACQUISITION

Name	Visual Call Sign	Builder	Commissioned	Disposition
Blanco (ex-*Atlantic*; ex-*Moby Dick*)	WPYc 343	Bethlehem Shipbuilding Corp., Wilmington, DE	1923 (private); 20 Aug 42 (CG)	*Decomm* 31 Oct 45; declared surplus 4 Nov 45

Cost
  Acquisition $1; conversion $29,502
Hull
  Tonnage   198 gross (1941); 149 net (1941)
  Length   120' oa; 101'2" wl
  Beam   24'10" max
  Draft   6'10" max (1942)
Machinery
  Main Engines   1 Krupp, 6-cyl, 4-cycle diesel
  BHP   180
  Propellers   Single
Performance
  Max Speed   14.0 kts (sail & diesels) (1942)
  Cruising   10.0 kts, 2,400 mi radius (1942)

Logistics
  Diesel Fuel (95%)   4,500 gal   Complement   26 men (1942)
Electronics
  None
Armament (1943)
  2 .50 cal mg; 2 K-guns
Design
  A steel-hulled, 3-masted schooner designed by Henry J. Gielow, Inc.

Blanco

Acquired on Great Lakes; 1942–45 assigned to GULFSEAFRON and operated in Gulf of Mexico and South Atlantic; Aug 42–May 43 stationed at Miami, FL; May 43–Oct 45 stationed at New Orleans, LA.

EMERGENCY ACQUISITION

Name	Visual Call Sign	Builder	Commissioned	Disposition
Pilgrim	[WPYc]	Reed-Cook Marine Construction Co., Boothbay Harbor, ME	1932 (private); Aug 42 (CG)	NA

Cost
  Acquisition $1; conversion $281
Hull
  Tonnage   73 gross (1941); 51 net (1941)
  Length   85' oa; 70' wl
  Beam   20'8"
  Draft   11'3"
Machinery
  Main Engines   1 Winton diesel
  BHP   270
  Propellers   Single

Performance
  Max Speed   NA
Logistics   Electronics
  Complement   NA   Probably none
Armament
  NA
Design
  A wooden-hulled yacht designed by John G. Alden.

Pilgrim

Service NA.

EMERGENCY ACQUISITION

Name	Visual Call Sign	Builder	Commissioned	Disposition
Bedford (ex-*Condor*; ex-*Carolus*; ex-*Condor*; ex-*Athero*; ex-*Gypsy Jo*; ex-*Gem*)	WPYc 346	George Lawley & Son Corp., Neponset, MA	1913 (private); 28 Jul 42 (CG)	*Trans* to Navy 22 Jan 43

Cost
  Acquisition $20,000; conversion $23,774

Hull
  Displacement (tons)   370 fl (1942)
  Tonnage   201 gross (1941); 113 net (1941)
  Length   164'6" oa
  Beam   18' max
  Draft   7' max (1941)

Machinery
  Main Engines   Steam
  SHP   2,300
  Propellers   Single

Performance
  Max Speed   NA

Logistics
  Complement   NA

Electronics
  Probably none

Armament
  NA

Design
  A steel-hulled yacht designed by Cox & Stevens.

Bedford

Acquired in Chicago, IL; 1942–43 assigned to GULFSEAFRON—stationed at New Orleans, LA.

EMERGENCY ACQUISITION

Name	Visual Call Sign	Builder	Commissioned	Disposition
Micawber (ex-*Ottilie*; ex-*Nevada*)	WPYc 159	Henry B. Nevins, Inc., City Island, NY	1926 (private); 8 Jul 42 (CG)	*Decomm* 5 Jul 45; *ret* to WSA 18 Feb 46

Cost
  Acquisition $27,000; conversion $11,605

Hull
  Tonnage   153 gross (1941); 104 net (1941)
  Length   110' oa; 103' wl
  Beam   20'6" mb
  Draft   6'6" max (1942)

Machinery
  Main Engines   2 Standard diesels
  BHP   150

Performance
  Max Speed   10.0 kts (1942)
  Max Sustained   10.0 kts, 900 mi radius (1942)

Cruising   6.0 kts, 1,175 mi radius (1942)

Logistics
  Complement   NA

Electronics
  Probably none

Armament
  NA

Design   A wood-hulled yacht designed by Tams & King.

Micawber

1942–43 assigned to GULFSEAFRON—stationed at San Juan, PR; 1943–45 assigned to the 7th District—stationed at Key West, FL.

WPR—RIVER GUNBOATS

165-FOOT CUTTER

Name	Visual Call Sign	Builder	Keel Laid	Launched	Commissioned	Disposition
Ossipee	WPR 50	Newport News Shipbuilding and Dry Dock Co., Newport News, VA	15 Sep 14 (contract awarded)	1 May 15	28 Jul 15	*Decomm* 6 Dec 45; *sold* 18 Sep 46

Cost
  $222,366
Hull
  Displacement (tons)   964 fl (1915)
  Length   165'10" oa; 150' wl
  Beam   32' mb
  Draft   11'9" max (1915)
  Block Coefficient   .585
Machinery
  Main Engines   Steam reciprocating
  SHP   1,500
  Propellers   Single
Performance
  Max Sustained   12.3 kts, 2,000 mi radius (1915)
  Cruising   7.5 kts, 4,265 mi radius (1915)
Logistics
  Coal   195 tons

Complement   6 officers, 2 warrants, 66 men (1915)
Electronics
  Detection Radar   NA
  Sonar   Probably none
Armament (1942)
  2 6-pdrs
Design
  The *Ossipee* was designed as a cruising cutter. Constructed of steel, she was reinforced for ice-breaking. She had a large bunker and tank capacity to enable her to make long cruises for derelict destruction. Her near sister *Tallapoosa* was designated a WPG (gunboat).

Ossipee

1941–45 assigned to the 9th District—stationed at Cleveland, OH, and used for ice-breaking; 2–3 Dec 42 with cutter *Crocus* and motor lifeboats, rescued survivors and recovered bodies from the barge *Cleveco*.

The *Ossipee*, 7 Aug 43, at Cleveland, OH. Two 6-pdrs are fitted abeam aft and a machine gun is mounted forward of the bridge. A number of cutters built in the early twentieth century were originally classified as derelict destroyers. At that time most coastal craft and many oceangoing ships were built of wood; when abandoned, these wooden derelicts would not sink for some time and, as semi-submerged hulks, would become serious navigational hazards. A derelict destroyer would locate such menaces and either tow them in or sink them with explosives.

158-FOOT CUTTER

Name	Visual Call Sign	Builder	Launched	Commissioned	Disposition
Pamlico	WPR 57	Pusey & Jones Co., Wilmington, DE	8 Mar 07	26 Jul 07	*Decomm* 6 Sep 46; *sold* 7 Jul 47

Cost
$167,750

Hull
  Displacement (tons)   455 fl (1907)
  Length   158′ oa
  Beam   30′ mb
  Draft   5′8″ max (1907)

Machinery
  Main Engines   Steam triple-expansion reciprocating
  Main Boilers   1 Babcock & Wilcox
  SHP   600
  Propellers   Twin

Performance
  Max Sustained   9.8 kts, 817 mi radius (1907)
                   9.4 kts, 830 mi radius (1945)
  Economic   6.5 kts, 1,420 mi radius (1907)
                   6.4 kts, 1,400 mi radius (1945)

Logistics
  Coal   50 tons
  Complement   1 officer, 2 warrants, 35 men (1907); 3 officers, 1 warrant, 33 men (1945)

Electronics
  None

Armament
  None

Design
  The *Pamlico* was designed for service in inland waters and had a very shallow draft. She was constructed of steel throughout.

Pamlico

1941–45 assigned to the 5th District—stationed at New Bern, NC.

The *Pamlico*, 26 May 44, in a floating dry dock.

UNCLASSIFIED MISCELLANEOUS (WIX)

As the name implies, this was a "catchall" category. Most of these ships had some association with training. On 1 Sep 38 the administration of the ships belonging to the U.S. Maritime Service was assigned to the Coast Guard; these vessels commissioned into the Coast Guard as WIXs and were fully crewed by the service. They remained in Coast Guard service until 1 Jul 42.

CAPTURED VESSEL

Name	Visual Call Sign	Builder	Commissioned	Disposition
East Breeze (ex-Externsteine; F-Callao)	[WIX]	P. Smit Jr. Shipyard, Rotterdam, Holland	1944 (German Navy); 15 Oct 44 (to CG as prize); 24 Jan 45 (USN)	Turned over to USN late Oct 44

Cost
Captured

Hull
Displacement (tons)   1,015 fl (1945)
Length   183′ oa; 175′ wl
Beam   30′10″ max
Draft   13′11″ max (1945)

Machinery
Main Engines   Vertical triple expansion
Boilers   1 Scotch
SHP   750
Propellers   Single

Performance
Max Speed   10 kts (1945)

Logistics
Complement   16 men plus 62 additional berths (German Navy, 1944)

Electronics
NA

Armament
German ordnance

Design
A trawler design adapted to weather-station duties.

East Breeze

15 Oct 44 captured by CG cutters as the *Externsteine*—renamed the *East Breeze* and manned by a prize crew; 30 Nov 44 collided with the cutter *Travis* while enroute to Boston, MA; turned over to USN; 24 Jan 45 commissioned in USN as the *Callao*.

The *East Breeze*, 16 Oct 44, shortly after capture. A prize crew now mans the ship. The cloth draped around the bow, bridge area, and over the deck is an attempt to camouflage the vessel.

EMERGENCY ACQUISITION

Name	Visual Call Sign	Builder	Commissioned	Disposition
Alexander Graham Bell	WIX 184	Oregon Shipbuilding Corp., Portland, OR	27 Oct 42 (commercial); 7 Oct 44 (CG)	*Decomm* and turned over to WSA 28 Dec 44

Cost
  Acquisition WSA
Hull
  Displacement (tons)   14,100 fl (1944)
  Tonnage   7,176 gross; 4,374 net
  Length   427′ wl; 416′ bp
  Beam   57′ max; 56′11″ mb
  Draft   27′8″ mean (1944)
Machinery
  Main Engines   1 3-cyl direct-acting, triple-expansion engine
  Main Boilers   2 watertube, 200 psi, 450°F. superheat
  IHP   2,500
  Propellers   Single
Performance
  Max Speed   Stationary

Logistics
  Complement   Crew assembled from available force at CG yard; 16 men on board as security watch
Electronics
  NA
Armament
  NA
Design
  The *Alexander Graham Bell* was an EC2-S-C1 Liberty ship. Builder's hull number and Maritime Commission hull number is 583.

Alexander Graham Bell

Damaged 17 Apr 44 when hit by a mine off Naples; turned over to CG by WSA and used for experimentation with lifesaving devices; scrapped in Philadelphia, PA, 1962.

EMERGENCY ACQUISITION (NAVY SC-1 CLASS)

Name	Visual Call Sign	Builder	Commissioned	Disposition
Bonneville (ex-*Islander*; ex-*Cook*; ex-SC 438)	WIX 375	Rocky River Dry Dock Co., Rocky River, OH	1 Nov 19 (CG); 5 Mar 43 (CG)	*Decomm* ?; *decomm* 22 Sep 45

Cost
  Acquisition $13,250; conversion $8,898
Hull
  Displacement (tons)   85 fl (1919); 64 fl (1942)
  Length   110′
  Beam   14′9″
  Draft   5′8″ max (1919)
Machinery
  Main Engines   1 diesel
  BHP   160
  Propellers   Twin
Performance
  Max Speed   13.0 kts (1943)
  Max Sustained   13.0 kts, 547 mi radius (1943)
  Cruising   10.0 kts, 884 mi radius (1943)
Logistics
  Complement   2 officers, 25 men (1919)
Electronics
  None
Armament
  1942   1 1-pdr.; 1 20mm/80
  1943   1 1-pdr.; 2 20mm/80; 2 Mousetraps, 2 dc tracks

The *Bonneville* armed with a 1-pdr and a 20mm/80. By 1942 her armament had been increased to include two Mousetrap ASW weapons, another 20mm/80, and two depth-charge tracks. As is often the case, her union jack is flying even though she is underway.

Design

Hundreds of these wooden craft were produced in WW I to meet the German submarine threat. This unit never commissioned in USN. The *Bonneville* was re-engined between the wars.

Bonneville

1943–45 assigned to the 3rd District—stationed at New London, CT, and used for training; 20 Jul 45 damaged in collision.

EMERGENCY ACQUISITION

Name	Visual Call Sign	Builder	Commissioned	Disposition
Bison (ex-*Beaufort*; ex-*President*)	WIX 347	Globe Shipbuilding Co., Superior, WI	3 Feb 43 (special-training status)	*Decomm* 17 Jun 46; *sold* 19 Mar 47

Cost
  Acquisition $14,000; conversion $50,000
Hull
  Displacement (tons)   1,000 fl (1942)
  Length   185' oa
  Beam   45'6" max
  Draft   7'3" max (1943)
Machinery
  Main Engines   Steam

SHP   1,000
Propellers   Single
Design
  The *Bison* is the former freighter *President*.

Bison

22 Jul 43 name changed from the *Beaufort* to the *Bison*; 1943–46 assigned to CG Headquarters—stationed at CG Yard, Curtis Bay, MD; used as a floating barracks and training vessel for machinist mates' (steam) school.

EMERGENCY ACQUISITION

Name	Visual Call Sign	Builder	Commissioned	Disposition
Resolution	[WIX]	NA	17 Aug 42	*Ret* to Navy 18 Nov 42

No details available.

EMERGENCY ACQUISITION

Name	Visual Call Sign	Builder	Commissioned	Disposition
MacNichol (ex-*David C. MacNichol*; ex-*William H. Hoyt*; ex-*Stratford*)	WIX 180	Bridgeport, CT	1891 (commercial); 5 Jul 42 (CG)	NA

Cost
  Acquisition $21,405; conversion $13,625
Hull
  Tonnage   98 gross (1941); 67 net (1941)
  Length   100'6" oa
  Beam   22'1" max
  Draft   7' max (1941)
Machinery
  Main Engines   1 steam
  SHP   1,250
  Propellers   Single
Performance
  NA

Logistics
  Complement   29 men (commercial)
Electronics
  Probably none
Armament
  NA
Design
  A former freighter.

MacNichol

NA

EMERGENCY ACQUISITION

Name	Visual Call Sign	Builder	Launched	Commissioned	Disposition
City of Chattanooga	[WIX]	Newport News Shipbuilding and Dry Dock Co., Newport News, VA	1923	1923 (mercantile service); 1 Jun 42 (CG)	*Decomm* 31 Aug 42

Cost
  Acquisition U.S. Maritime Commission

Hull
  Tonnage   5,861 gross (1942); 4,343 net (1942)
  Length   381'8" oa
  Beam   52'1" max
  Draft   20'2" max (1942)

Machinery
  Main Engines Triple-expansion, 3-cyl
  Main Boilers 4 single-ended Scotch, 200 psi
  IHP   2,900
  Propellers   Single

Performance
  Max Speed   NA

Logistics
  Coal (95%)   457 tons
  Complement   25 officers and warrants, 100 men, 400 trainees (1942)

Electronics
  Probably none

Armament
  NA

Design
  The *City of Chattanooga* was acquired by the Maritime Commission from the Ocean Steamship Co., which had operated her as a coastal passenger-cargo vessel.

City of Chattanooga

1942 used as a training vessel.

The *City of Chattanooga* fitting out. The CG ensign flies atop the mast.

EMERGENCY ACQUISITION

Name	Visual Call Sign	Builder	Commissioned	Disposition
Mayfair (ex-*Pansy*)	[WIX]	Baird & Huston, Philadelphia, PA	1878 (commercial); 13 May 42 (CG)	*Decomm* 31 Aug 42

Cost
  Acquisition loan from Navy

Hull
  Tonnage   302 gross (1941); 128 net (1941)
  Length   145' oa
  Beam   25' max
  Draft   10'4" max (1941)

Machinery
  Main Engines Steam
  Main Boilers 1 return tubular boiler
  IHP   250
  Propellers   Twin

Performance
  Max Speed   NA

Logistics
  Fuel   Coal
  Complement   NA

Electronics
  Probably none

Armament
  NA

Design
  An iron-hulled schooner rebuilt in 1941.

Mayfair

1942 used to release the cutter *Kimball* from duty at Merchant Marine Training School, Hoffman Island, NY.

EMERGENCY ACQUISITION

Name	Visual Call Sign	Builder	Launched	Commissioned	Disposition
Danmark	WIX 283	Nakskov Skibs A/S, Nakskov, Denmark	1933	1933 (Danish Gov.); 12 May 42 (CG)	*Decomm* and *ret* to Danish Gov. 26 Sep 45

Cost
  Placed at disposal of U.S. Government

Hull
  Tonnage   1,700 gross (1942)
  Length   188'6" oa
  Beam   33' mb
  Draft   14'9" max (1942)

Machinery
  Main Engines   1 diesel
  Propellers   Single

Design
  The *Danmark* was a square-rigged training ship built for the Danish Government.

Danmark

On a visit to the U.S. when Denmark fell to Germany; 8 Dec 41 Captain K. Hansen placed the crew and the ship at the disposal of the U.S. Government; 1941–45 assigned to CG Headquarters—stationed at New London, CT—used for training of CG Academy cadets.

The *Danmark*, Sep 45, just before her return to the Danish government. She was in the United States when Denmark was overrun by the Germans, so she served as a training ship for the CG throughout WW II.

EMERGENCY ACQUISITION

Name	Visual Call Sign	Builder	Launched	Commissioned	Disposition
Alleghany	WIX	Federal Shipbuilding Co., Kearney, NJ	1923	1923 (mercantile service); 21 May 42 (CG)	*Decomm* and *ret* to Maritime Commission 31 Aug 42
Berkshire	WIX	Federal Shipbuilding Co., Kearney, NJ	1923	1923 (mercantile service); 1 May 42 (CG)	*Decomm* and *ret* to Maritime Commission 31 Aug 42

Cost
  Acquisition U.S. Maritime Commission

Hull
Displacement (tons)	14,460 fl (1942)
Tonnage	5,486 gross
Length	350'7" oa
Beam	52'1" max
Draft	19' max (1942)

Machinery
Main Engines	1 4-cyl triple-expansion steam
Main Boilers	Single-ended Scotch, 200 psi
IHP	2,700
Propellers	Single

Performance
Max Speed	NA

Logistics
Fuel Oil (95%)	600 tons
Complement	25 officers, 100 men, 400 trainees (1942)

Electronics
  Probably none

Armament
  NA

Design
  The *Alleghany* and *Berkshire* were former coastal passenger-cargo ships acquired from Merchants & Miners Transportation Co. by the Maritime Commission in Dec 41. The *Alleghany* was converted to CG needs by Bethlehem Steel Corp., Baltimore, MD, in 1942.

Alleghany

1942 used for training.

Berkshire

1942 used for training.

EMERGENCY ACQUISITION

Name	Visual Call Sign	Builder	Launched	Commissioned	Disposition
Navigation (ex-*Sard*; ex-*Navigation*; ex-*Alida*; ex-*Victoria Mary*; ex-*All Alone*)	WIX 338	Boston, MA	1922	19 Jan 42	*Decomm* 29 Jul 44; *sold* 10 Jan 46

Cost
  Acquisition loan from Navy

Hull
Tonnage	212 gross
Length	134'9" oa
Beam	20' max
Draft	9'9" max (1942)

Machinery
Main Engines	2 diesels
BHP	500

Performance
  NA

Logistics
Complement	4 officers, 9 men (1942)

Electronics	Armament
NA	NA

Design
  17 Jun 35 purchased by the Bureau of Marine Inspection and Navigation from Arrow Line for $57,950, then loaned to the Navy. She was designed as a yacht.

Navigation

1942–44 assigned to the 5th District—stationed at Norfolk, VA.

EMERGENCY ACQUISITION

Name	Builder	Commissioned	Disposition
Queen of Peace	NA	14 Jan 42	*Ret* to Navy 2 Mar 42

No details available.

EMERGENCY ACQUISITION

Name	Visual Call Sign	Builder	Launched	Commissioned	Disposition
Boston	[WIX]	Bethlehem Shipbuilding Co., Sparrows Point, MD	1924	1924 (commercial); 23 Dec 41 (CG)	*Decomm* and *ret* to Maritime Commission 31 Aug 42
New York	[WIX]	Bethlehem Shipbuilding Co., Sparrows Point, MD	1924	1924 (commercial); 19 Dec 41 (CG)	*Decomm* and ret to Maritime Commission 31 Aug 42

Cost
  Acquisition U.S. Maritime Commission
Hull
  Tonnage   4,989 gross; 2,703 net (1941)
  Length   385'3" oa
  Beam   72'5" max
  Draft   17'9" max (1941)
Machinery
  Main Engines   Steam turbine
  Main Boilers   6 single-ended Scotch, 200 psi
  SHP   2,680
  Propellers   Twin
Logistics
  Fuel Oil (95%) 339 tons
  Accommodations 800 trainees (1941)

Electronics
  None
Armament
  None
Design
  These ships were designed as coastal passenger-cargo ships and operated by the Eastern SS Co.

Boston

Dec 41 assigned to be a training ship at Fort Trumbull, CT; 1 Jan–31 Aug 42 used as a station ship.

New York

Dec 41–Aug 42 used as a station ship at Hoffman Island, NY.

The *New York*, prior to WW II. The *New York* and her sister ship the *Boston* were lost in the war following CG service. (Courtesy of the Mariners Museum.)

EMERGENCY ACQUISITION

Name	Visual Call Sign	Builder	Commissioned	Disposition
Keystone State (ex-*Seneca*)	[WIX]	Newport News Shipbuilding & Dry Dock Co., Newport News, VA	6 Nov 08 (1st CG tour)	*Decomm* 21 Mar 36; *sold* 3 Sep 36
			1941 (2nd CG tour)	*Decomm* and *ret* to Maritime Commission 31 Aug 42

Cost
  $244,500 (1908)

Hull
  Displacement (tons) 1,480 fl (1908)
  Length 240' oa
  Beam 34' max
  Draft 17' max (1908)

Machinery
  Main Engines Steam plant
  Propellers Single

Performance
  Max Speed Est. 12 kts (1941)

Logistics
  NA

Electronics
  None

Armament
  NA

Design
  The former cutter *Seneca* was of steel construction. She was noted for her attempted rescue by towing of the torpedoed steamer *Wellington* in the Bay of Biscay, 21 Sep 18.

Keystone State

". . . In active service under the jurisdiction of the CG by virtue of the operation of Executive Order No. 9083"; 1941–42 used for cadet cruises for state maritime academies in Massachusetts, New York, and Pennsylvania.

The *Seneca*, the future *Keystone State*, as she appeared in WW I. This cutter had a very eventful career during her first tour in the CG. In 1914 the *Seneca* served on the International Ice Patrol (following the disastrous sinking of the *Titanic*). During WW I she was used as an escort between Gibraltar and England.

EMERGENCY ACQUISITION

Name	Visual Call Sign	Builder	Launched	Commissioned	Disposition
Delta Queen	[WIX]	California Transportation Co., Stockton, CA	1926	15 Dec 41? (received by Maritime Commission)	*Decomm* and *ret* to commercial service 31 Aug 42

Cost
  NA
Hull
  Tonnage   1,837 gross (1941)
  Length   250' oa
  Beam   58' max
  Draft   11' max (1941)
Machinery
  Main Engines   Compound, 2-cyl steam
  Main Boilers   2 watertube
  IHP   2,000
  Propellers   Single
Performance
  NA

Logistics
  NA
Electronics
  None
Armament
  None
Design
  River passenger vessel.

Delta Queen

1941–42 used for maritime training.

EMERGENCY ACQUISITION

Name	Visual Call Sign	Builder	Launched	Commissioned	Disposition
Empire State (ex-*Shaume*; ex-*Procyon*)	[WIX]	American International Shipbuilding Corp., Hog Island, PA	Jun 19	27 Aug 41 (CG)	*Decomm* and *ret* to Maritime Commission 31 Aug 42

Cost
  Acquisition U.S. Maritime Commission
Hull
  Displacement (tons)   7,500 fl (1941)
  Tonnage   5,524 gross (1941); 3,336 net (1941)
  Length   390' oa
  Beam   54'2" max
  Draft   19' max (1941)
Machinery
  Main Engines   Steam turbine
  Main Boilers   Babcock & Wilcox, 200 psi
  SHP   2,500
  Propellers   Single
Performance
  Max Speed   11.2 kts (1941)
  Max Sustained   11.2 kts, 10,000 mi radius (1941)

  Cruising   10.0 kts, 13,000 mi radius (1941)
Logistics
  Fuel Oil (95%) 2,124 tons
  Complement   450, including trainees
Electronics
  None
Armament
  None
Design
  A WW I merchantman, the *Empire State* was the training ship of the New York State Merchant Marine Academy.

Empire State

1941–42 used for training; stationed at New York, NY, and St. Petersburg, FL.

The *Empire State* operating out of New York.

EMERGENCY ACQUISITION

Name	Visual Call Sign	Builder	Launched	Commissioned	Disposition
Vema (ex-*Hussar*)	[WIX]	Burmeister & Wain, Copenhagen, Denmark	1923	26 Jul 41	*Decomm* and *ret* to Maritime Commission 31 Aug 42

Cost
Acquisition U.S. Maritime Service; conversion $25,000

Hull
Displacement (tons)   770 fl (1941)
Tonnage   533 gross; 234 net
Length   182′ bp; 202′6″ oa
Beam   33′ mb
Draft   14′ max (1941)

Machinery
Main Engines   1 Burmeister-Wain 6-cyl, 4-cycle diesel
BHP   780
Propellers   Single
Sail area   14,000 sq. ft.

Performance
Max Speed   13 kts (sail & diesel) (1941)
Cruising   8 kts, 8,000 mi radius (1941)

Logistics
Diesel Fuel   19,500 gal
Complement   100 men, including trainees (1941)

Electronics
None

Armament
None

Design
A former yacht, *Vema* was a three-masted steel auxiliary yacht.

Vema

1941–42 used for training duty at New York, NY.

The training ship *Vema* in CG service. From 14 Jul 38 to 31 Aug 42 the CG was responsible for training merchant marine personnel. Ships serving at federal and various state merchant marine academies were commissioned in the CG.

EMERGENCY ACQUISITION

Name	Visual Call Sign	Builder	Launched	Commissioned	Disposition
American Sailor (ex-*Edgemont*)	[WIX]	Skinner & Eddy Corp., Seattle, WA	1919	Apr 1919 (mercantile); 22 Jul 41 (CG)	*Decomm* and *ret* to Maritime Commission 31 Aug 42

Cost
NA

Hull
Displacement (tons)   10,000 fl (1941)
Length   409′6″ oa
Beam   54′2″ max
Draft   29′ max (1941)

Machinery
Main Engines   Steam turbine
Propellers   Single

Performance
Max Speed   11.0 kts (1941)

Logistics
Fuel Oil (95%)   2,091 tons
Complement   450 men, including trainees

Electronics
Probably none

Armament
None

Design
    Former merchantman; Jun 40–Jan 41 converted to a training ship at Bethlehem Steel, Baltimore, MD.

American Sailor

1941–42 used for training at Port Hueneme, CA.

The *American Sailor* during her CG service.

EMERGENCY ACQUISITION

Name	Visual Call Sign	Builder	Launched	Commissioned	Disposition
Annapolis	[WIX]	L. Nixon, Elizabeth, NJ	1897	15 May 41 (CG)	*Ret* to Maritime Commission 31 Aug 42

Cost
    Acquisition U.S. Maritime Commission

Hull
    Displacement (tons)   1,010 standard (1921)
    Length   203'6" oa; 168' bp
    Beam   36' max
    Draft   12' mean (1921)

Machinery
    Main Engines   Vertical, triple expansion
    Boilers   2 Babcock & Wilcox
    IHP   1,227
    Propellers   Twin

Performance
    Speed   13 kts (1921)

Electronics
    None

Armament
    1 4"/40 (1921)

Design
    The *Annapolis* was built as a gunboat; she was schooner-rigged and of composite construction. She served in the USN from 1897 until 1921, when she was turned over to the Commissioner of Navigation, Port of Philadelphia, for use as a school ship for the Pennsylvania Maritime Academy. On 11 Apr 40 the *Annapolis* was transferred to the Maritime Commission.

Annapolis

1941–42 used as a station ship at New London, CT.

The *Annapolis,* 5 Jul 43, in a very poor state.

EMERGENCY ACQUISITION

Name	Visual Call Sign	Builder	Launched	Commissioned	Disposition
Atlantic	WIX 271	Townsend & Downey S & R. Co., Shooters Is., NY	1903	1 Apr 41	''Available for disposal'' 27 Oct 47; *sold* 10 Sep 48

Cost
  Gift; est. worth $750,000 as yacht

Hull
  Tonnage   303 gross (1947); 206 net (1947)
  Length   185' oa; 134' wl
  Beam   29'6" mb
  Draft   17'6" max (1947)

Machinery
  Main Engines   1 Seaburg triple-expansion
  Main Boilers   One
  SHP   150
  Propellers   Single
  Sail Area   11,058 sq. ft.

Electronics
  None

Armament
  None

Design
  A three-masted steel schooner, the *Atlantic* gained fame in 1903 by crossing the Atlantic from Sandy Hook, NJ, to The Lizard, England, in 12 days, 4 hrs., and 1 min. In 1905 she won the Kaiser's Cup. During WW I, the *Atlantic* served as a mother ship for submarines.

Atlantic

1941–47 assigned to CG Headquarters—stationed at CG Academy, New London, CT, and used for cadet training.

The training ship *Atlantic* in CG service. In 1903 she held the Atlantic Ocean crossing record for a vessel under sail, and in 1905 she won the Kaiser's Cup. Thirteen years later, the cup's owner gave the trophy to the Red Cross so that it might be auctioned off and the proceeds used to ameliorate the suffering of American soldiers. The cup netted $125,000 at a series of auctions. At a patriotic rally in New York, the cup was intentionally broken. It proved to be base metal, thinly plated, and not solid gold as believed. (Courtesy of the National Archives.)

EMERGENCY ACQUISITION

Name	Visual Call Sign	Builder	Launched	Commissioned	Disposition
Tusitala (ex-*Sophie;* ex-*Sierra Lucena;* ex-*Inverglas*)	[WIX]	R. Steel & Co., Greenock, Scotland	1883	14 May 40	*Decomm* and *ret* to Maritime Commission 31 Aug 42

Cost
  Acquisition U.S. Maritime Service
Hull
  Tonnage   1,747 gross (1940)
  Length   261′ oa
  Beam   39′ mb
  Draft   23′ max (1940)
Machinery
  Main Engines   Diesel auxiliary
  Propellers   Single
Logistics
  Complement   200 men, including trainees (1940)
Electronics
  None
Armament
  None

Design

A square-rigged ship constructed of iron, the *Tusitala* was the last ship built by the famous R. Steel yard. She was first used in the wool trade between Australia and England, and later in the "big triangle"—Australia, South America, and England. In the 1920s, she was employed between Hawaii and the United States. She was acquired by the U.S. Maritime Service and rebuilt in 1940. She was fitted with quarters and messing facilities for 150 men.

Tusitala

1940–42 used for merchant marine training; 1940 towed to St. Petersburg, FL, by the cutter *Mohawk*.

The *Tusitala* had been built for the Australian wool trade in 1883. During WW II she was used for training.

EMERGENCY ACQUISITION

Name	Visual Call Sign	Builder	Launched	Commissioned	Disposition
Curlew	[WIX] (CG 65016)	F. F. Pendleton, Wicasset, ME	1926	1926 (as yacht); 31 Jan 40 (CG)	*Decomm* 26 May 60; *sold* 7 Nov 60

Cost
  Donated
Hull
  Displacement (tons)   27 fl (1940)
  Length   65′3″ oa
  Beam   14′2″ mb
  Draft   8′8″ max (1940)
Machinery
  Main Engines   1 Kermath diesel (installed Aug 45)

BHP   60
Propellers   Single
Design
  A wooden, two-masted staysail schooner.

Curlew

1941–45 assigned to CG Headquarters—stationed at CG Academy and used for training (*see* CG 65016).

EMERGENCY ACQUISITION

Name	Visual Call Sign	Builder	Launched	Commissioned	Disposition
Joseph Conrad (ex-*Georg Stage*)	WIX	Burmeister & Wain, Copenhagen, Denmark	1882	30 Nov 39? (CG)	*Decomm* 31 Aug 42; used at Mystic, CT, as exhibit

Cost
  NA
Hull
  Displacement (tons)   500 fl (1941)
  Length   165′6″ oa
  Beam   25′3″ max
  Draft   13′1″ max (1941)
Machinery
  Main Engines   Diesel
  BHP   160
  Propellers   Single, 2-blade
Performance
  Max Speed   11.0 kts (1941)
  Max Sustained   8.0 kts, 1,500 mi radius (1941)
  Cruising   6.0 kts, 2,000 mi radius (1941)

Logistics
  Diesel Fuel   3,500 gal
  Complement   35 men
Electronics
  Probably none
Armament (1941)
  2 2″ brass, muzzle loaders for saluting
Design
  She was designed for training boys in the Danish merchant marine. She had a hull of Swedish iron.

Joseph Conrad

1941–42 stationed at Jacksonville, FL, for mercantile training; Dec 39 training cruise in Caribbean.

The *Joseph Conrad*, photographed while going astern during a man overboard drill. (Courtesy of the Smithsonian Institution.)

EMERGENCY ACQUISITION

Name	Visual Call Sign	Builder	Launched	Commissioned	Disposition
American Seaman (ex-*Edgemoor*)	[WIX]	Skinner & Eddy Corp., Seattle, WA	1919	May 19 (commercial); 6 May 39 (CG)	NA

Cost
  NA

Hull
  Tonnage   5,194 gross (1941); 3,317 net (1941)
  Length   380'3" bp
  Beam   52' max
  Draft   30' max (1941)

Machinery
  Main Engines   Triple-expansion steam
  Main Boilers   3 single-ended boilers
  SHP   2,500
  Propellers   Single

Performance
  NA

Logistics
  Fuel Oil (95%)   1,663 tons   Complement   NA

Electronics
  Probably none

Armament
  Probably none

Design
  A freighter-type merchantman, she was converted to a school ship at Bethlehem Steel, Baltimore, MD.

American Seaman

1939–42 used for merchant marine training—stationed at St. Petersburg, FL; Dec 39 training cruise to Caribbean; mid 41 used on CG cadet cruise.

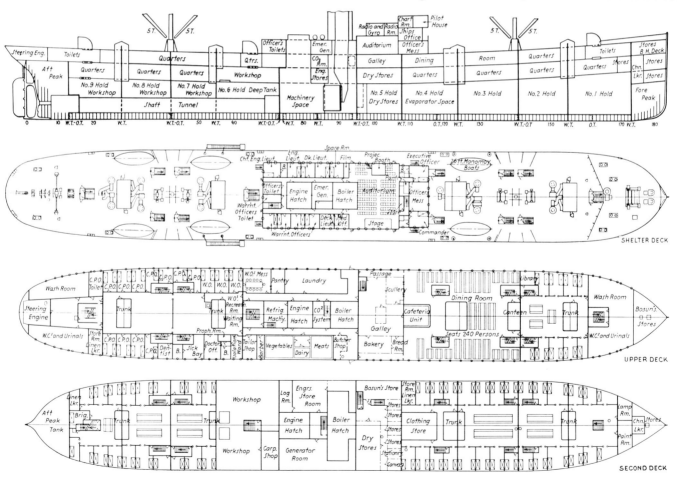

General arrangement of the *American Seaman*. (Courtesy of *Marine Engineering/Log;* copied from *Marine Engineering and Shipping Age* [June, 1939]: 262.)

The *American Seaman*. Just prior to WW II she was converted to a school ship.

EMERGENCY ACQUISITION

Name	Visual Call Sign	Builder	Keel Laid	Launched	Commissioned	Disposition
Beta (ex-*Alexander Hamilton*; ex-*Vicksburg*)	WIX 272	Bath Iron Works, Bath, ME	Mar 96	5 Dec 96 (USN)	1 Jul 21 (CG)	*Decomm* 30 Dec 44; *trans* to WSA 28 Mar 46

Cost
  NA
Hull
Displacement (tons)	1,010 fl
Length	204'5" oa
Beam	36' max
Draft	12'9" max (1942)

Machinery
  NA
Design

Constructed as the Navy gunboat *Vicksburg*, the *Beta* was little more than a hulk during WW II. Her interior had been converted into living and messing quarters for 150 men. Her weather deck from the fantail to pilot house was decked over for classrooms; and all spars and smoke stacks were removed.

Beta

18 Aug 22 name changed from the *Vicksburg* to the *Alexander Hamilton*; 1921–31 used for cadet training at CG Academy; 1931–39 employed as a receiving ship at Curtis Bay, MD; 1939–42 used as a barracks at CG Academy; 12 Jan 42 name changed from the *Alexander Hamilton* to the *Beta*; 1942–44 used at Curtis Bay as a training ship for machinists' mates and watertenders.

The *Beta*, as the *Alexander Hamilton*, prior to 1930. During WW II, she served as a station ship without masts or stack.

EMERGENCY ACQUISITION

Name	Visual Call Sign	Builder	Launched	Commissioned	Disposition
American Mariner (ex-*George Calvert*)	[WIX]	Bethlehem-Fairfield Shipyard, Inc., Baltimore, MD	1941	30 Dec 41 (CG)	*Decomm* 31 Aug 42

Cost
  NA

Hull
  Displacement (tons)   14,245 fl; 3,380 light
  Tonnage   7,176 gross, 10,865 deadweight
  Length   441'6" oa
  Beam   56'11" max
  Draft   20' max (1942)

Machinery
  Main Engines   1 3-cyl reciprocating steam engine
  Boilers   2
  Propellers   Single

Performance
  Max Speed   Est. 11.0 kts (1942)

Logistics
  Complement   525 officers & men, including trainees

Electronics
  NA

Armament
  NA

Design
  The *American Mariner* was launched as the *George Calvert* (hull no. 2007) and taken over incomplete by the Maritime Commission. This Liberty ship (Z3-EC2-SC1) is often confused with a second *George Calvert* (hull no. 2016) built by the same yard.

American Mariner

1941–42 used for merchant marine training.

EMERGENCY ACQUISITION

Name	Visual Call Sign	Builder	Commissioned	Disposition
Bay State (ex-*Nantucket*)	[WIX]	Harlan & Hellingworth, Wilmington, DE	1876 (mercantile); NA (CG)	*Decomm* 31 Aug 42

Cost
  NA

Hull
  Length   274' oa
  Beam   42' max
  Draft   16'2" max

Machinery
  NA

Logistics
  NA

Performance
  NA

Electronics
  Probably none

Armament
  NA

Design
  Acquired from the Merchants & Miners Transport Co.

Bay State

1941–42 used for training at the Massachusetts Nautical Academy.

EMERGENCY ACQUISITION

Name	Visual Call Sign	Builder	Commissioned	Disposition
El Cano (ex-*Pioneer*, ex-*Cressida*, ex-*Crimper*)	[WIX]	Friederich Krupp Germaniawerft, Kiel, Germany	1927 (as yacht); 1939 (CG)	*Decomm* and *ret* to Maritime Commission 31 Aug 42

Cost
  NA

Hull
  Tonnage   327 gross (1939), 126 net (1939)

Length   145'1" oa
Beam   28'1" max
Draft   16'7" max (1939)

Machinery
  NA

Performance
  NA
Logistics
  NA
Electronics
  Probably none
Armament
  NA

Design
  Designed as an auxiliary-motor sailing yacht, the *El Cano* was rebuilt in 1939 by General Motors Corp.

El Cano

1939–42 used for merchant marine training.

EMERGENCY ACQUISITION

Name	Visual Call Sign	Builder	Commissioned	Disposition
Felix Reisenberg	[WIX]	NA	NA	*Decomm* and *ret* to Maritime Commission 31 Aug 42

No data available

Felix Reisenberg   NA

EMERGENCY ACQUISITION

Name	Visual Call Sign	Builder	Commissioned	Disposition
Nenemoosha	[WIX]	Newport News Shipbuilding & Dry Dock Co., Newport News, VA	1925 (private); 1942 (CG)	*Decomm* and *ret* to Maritime Commission 31 Aug 42

Cost
  NA
Hull
  Tonnage   232 gross (1941); 125 net (1941)
  Length   130′ oa; 125′5″ wl
  Beam   22′3″ max
  Draft   7′4″ max (1941)
Machinery
  Main Engines   2 Bessemer diesels
  BHP   800
  Propellers   Twin
Performance
  Max Speed   NA

Logistics
  Complement   7 men (private)
Electronics
  Probably none
Armament
  NA
Design
  A steel-hulled yacht designed by Burgess, Swasey & Paine. She was acquired from Jesse Ball DuPont.

Nenemoosha

1942 used for merchant marine training.

COAST GUARD CRAFT (CG)

The Coast Guard was the leading federal agency in the development and use of small craft prior to WW II. These craft were essential tools in performing two major missions: inshore search and rescue, and law enforcement. Prohibition provided a major stimulus to the service's small craft program during the 1920s and early 1930s.

During the first six months of U.S. participation in WW II, when German U-boats were taking a heavy toll of merchantmen close to the U.S. East Coast, large numbers of pleasure craft were taken into the Coast Guard as CG and CGR boats to patrol the coastal waters. Many of these craft were propelled by sail and auxiliary engines. The use of sail both increased the time they could remain on station and afforded them the advantage of silent operations. Almost none were fitted with radar or sonar. Most were armed with a .50 cal machine gun and hand-held weapons, and a few carried a 20mm/80 and a short depth-charge track. Craft ranging between 65 and 99 feet were typically manned by a crew of seven.

Early in WW II, the Coast Guard developed a numbering system for their small craft: Coast Guard craft less than 100 feet overall (except tenders, lightships, and CGR and CGB boats) were designated by a five- or six-digit number, which was a key to the length and source of the design of the craft. The first two digits were the length; the third digit was the design source—craft designed by the Coast Guard were given the number 3 or larger, those designed elsewhere were assigned 0 through 2; the last digits were the identification numbers of the individual craft. For example,

CG 83309

Design source

Length oa   Unit number

CG 83309 was 83 feet long, was designed by the Coast Guard, and was the ninth craft within the series. If a craft were lengthened, its number would be changed. For example, CG 75002F became CG 81009F. The letters CG preceded all craft numbers, except for barges, which were preceded by CGB. In two cases letters were placed at the end of the numbers: the letter D indicated that the craft was a buoy boat, fitted with a derrick boom capable of lifting at least 1,000 pounds; the letter F following the craft's number designated a fireboat.

All CG craft are listed from B99002 through 65001. The Coast Guard considered craft less than 65 feet in length to be "miscellaneous motorboats." Only standard designs (those constructed for the Coast Guard as opposed to emergency acquisitions) from 30 feet through 64 feet are covered in this volume. No craft less than 30 feet is listed.

CG Number	Year Built	Description	Armament	District Acquired	Dates and Type of Service
B99002	—	ex-*Siesta*, # ?	none	—	May 42–Jun 45; barge, ex-CGB 18
99001	1923	ex-*Gilnockie*, #223088	small arms	1	28 Jul 42–19 Feb 46; offshore patrol
97002	—	ex-*Yankee Tar*, #224750	—	7	30 Dec 41–5 Oct 44; patrol, ex-CGC 659
96002	1930	ex-*Electra*, #230024	small arms	13	29 Aug 42–Jan 45; offshore patrol
96001F	1928	ex-*Principia*, #227176	—	13	11 Jun 42–26 Jun 46; fireboat
95005	1927	ex-*Harmony*, #226469	—	8	27 Oct 42–19 Jun 43; offshore patrol
95004	1911	ex-*Moran*, #208756	—	13	16 Jul 42–18 Jan 43; ex-whaler
95003	1912	ex-*Aberdeen*, #209852	—	13	16 Jul 42–16 Mar 44; ex-whaler

CG Number	Year Built	Description	Armament	District Acquired	Dates and Type of Service
95002	1911	ex-*Patterson*, #208757	—	13	16 Jul 42–18 Jan 43; ex-whaler
B94003	—	ex-*John K*, # ?	none	9	23 Mar 43–1 May 44; barge
94002	1927	ex-*Aeolus*, #226849	—	1	5 Sep 42–6 Oct 44; offshore patrol
94001	1931	ex-*Wanderer*, #231164	small arms	9	6 Aug 42–4 Jul 45; offshore patrol
92004	1931	ex-*Lenore II*, #230877	1 .50 cal; 2 dc tracks	9	6 Aug 42–28 Nov 45; offshore patrol, ex-CG 88004
92003	1930	ex-*Geromi*, #229492	—	9	8 Aug 42–27 Jul 43; offshore patrol, lost
92002	1926	ex-*Marilyn*, #225364	—	9	6 Aug 42–21 Aug 44; offshore patrol
92001	1931	ex-*Wasp*, #230809	—	9	6 Aug 43–8 Jan 45; offshore patrol
90007	—	—	—	—	May 42–Sep 45
90006	—	—	—	—	—
B90005	—	—	—	13	Feb 42–Oct 45; barge
90004	—	ex-*Sea King*, #225421	2 dc tracks	5	27 Aug 42–30 Aug 45; offshore patrol
90003	1929	ex-*Anstan III*, #228402	1 .50 cal; 2 dc tracks	1	11 Sep 42–30 Aug 45; offshore patrol
90002	1916	ex-*Scilla*, #21419	small arms	9	3 Aug 42–20 Sep 45; offshore patrol
90001	1912	ex-*Salvor*, #210827	1 .50 cal	13	Dec 41–Sep 45; patrol, ex-CG 657
89001F	1914	ex-*W. J. Mathews*, #212855	—	5	19 Sep 42–Aug 45; fireboat
88006	1929	ex-*Amphitr I*, # ?	—	—	Sep 43–Oct 45; ex-CGR 428
B88005	—	—	—	—	May 43–Oct 46; barge
88004 (*see* 92004)					
88002F	1926	ex-*Emma and Ruth*, #225419	—	4	6 May 42–11 Sep 45; fireboat
88001F	1923	ex-*Kathryn and Elma*, #222897	—	4	6 May 42–11 Sep 45; fireboat
B87003	1926	ex-*Peregrine II*, #225402	—	—	Sep 42–Jul 45; barge
87002	—	—	—	—	Aug 42–Oct 42 *trans;* USN as YP 569
87001	—	ex-*Manuel L. Roderick*, #240657	—	1	29 Apr 42–31 Aug 42; patrol
86004	1914	ex-*City of Southport*, #212877	1 .50 cal; 2 dc tracks	5	18 Dec 42–Aug 45; patrol
86003	1928	ex-*Cachalot*, #227703	1 .50 cal; 2 1-pdrs.	11	7 Oct 42–3 Jul 45; offshore patrol
86002F	1938	ex-*Stanley B. Butler*, #238067	—	1	29 Apr 42–14 Dec 43; fireboat
86001F	1928	ex-*A. J. Meerwald*, #227932	—	4	22 May 42–11 Sep 45; fireboat
85009	—	ex-*Army S 710*	—	5	—
85008	1928	ex-*Sea Dream*, #227175	2 .50 cal; 2 dc tracks	5	15 Jul 42–28 Nov 45; offshore patrol
85007	—	ex-*WR 1928*	—	—	—
85006	1929	ex-*Catamount*, #229192	—	3	3 Oct 42–27 Mar 43; offshore patrol, exploded
85005	—	ex-*Southerly*, #239988	—	8	5 Sep 42–15 Dec 44; offshore patrol
85004	1909	ex-*Hiawatha*, #206041	small arms	13	22 Aug 42–15 Sep 45; harbor patrol

CG Number	Year Built	Description	Armament	District Acquired	Dates and Type of Service
85003	1924	ex-*Atrebor*, #224155	small arms	9	31 Aug 42–30 Aug 45; offshore patrol
85002F	—	ex-*Reichert Brothers*, #219026	—	3	18 May 42–18 Aug 44; fireboat
85001	1940	ex-*Darmouth*, #240229	small arms	1	29 Apr 42–Jul 45; harbor patrol
84001	1930	ex-*Joan Bar*, #229662	—	9	18 Sep 42–11 Sep 44; offshore patrol

This view of a 3rd District port gives the impression that all the small craft in the country were operated by the CG. The first two digits on a CG boat were that craft's overall length. The CGR numbers, on the other hand, were given in blocks to districts, and assigned to a craft when it was acquired. Therefore, the number had no relationship to any characteristics the craft possessed. CGA numbers were similarly assigned by the districts and bore no relationship to the craft's length.

CG 95003 (ex-*Aberdeen*, a whaler), 10 Mar 43. Generally, the CG named craft 100 feet or more and numbered those less than 100 feet. Of course there were exceptions, such as the 95-foot *Pilgrim*. Whalers over 100 feet were classified as WYPs.

83-FOOTERS

Number	Builder	Commissioned	Disposition
CG 83300–83529 (CG 83300–83383 were originally CG 450–89, 491–99, 600–634, respectively)	Wheeler Shipyard, Inc., Brooklyn, NY	1941–1944	By mid 1960s all sold— *see* individual craft histories

Contract Price with Wheeler Shipyard, Inc.
(Contract price does not include armament and engines)

First Group:	CG 83300–CG 83339 (forty)	$42,450
Second Group:	CG 83340–CG 83383 (forty-four)	57,860
Third Group:	CG 83384–CG 83423 (forty)	57,860
Fourth Group:	CG 83424–CG 93523 (one hundred)	62,534
+ Supp	CG 83524–CG 83529 (six)	62,534

Cost
$125,000 approx. cost of each unit completely outfitted

Hull

Displacement (tons)	76 fl (1945); 53 fl (1946)
Length	83'2" oa; 78'0" wl
Beam	16'2" mb
Draft	5'4" max (1945); 4'6" max fl at rest (1946)

Machinery

Main Engines	CG 83343 through 83348: 2 Hall Scott Defenders, 1,200 rpm; all others: 2 Sterling Viking II
SHP	All units: 1,200
Propellers	Twin

Performance

Max Speed	15.2 kts, 215 mi radius (1945); 23.5 statute mi (trials, 1946)
Max Sustained	12.0 kts, 375 mi radius (1945)
Cruising	10.0 kts, 475 mi radius (1945)
Economic	8.2 kts, 575 mi radius (1945)

Logistics

Gasoline (95%)	1,900 gal
Complement	1 officer, 13 men (1945)

Electronics (1945)

Detection Radar	SO-2 (most units)
Sonar	QBE series (none on 83339, 83367–83369, 83427, 83476–83480)

Armament

1941	1 1-pdr, 2 .30 cal mg
1945	1 20mm/80, 4 dc tracks, 2 Mousetraps; none on CG 83302, 83312, 83335, 83342, 83367, 83387, 83388, 83392–83394, 83427, 83470, 83475, 83491, 83492, 83494, 83501, 83507, 83512, 83515, 83516, 83518–83521, 83559

Design*

83-footers were wood-hull craft; the hull form was the round bilged type, single planked. Walter J. McInnis was appointed design agent 6 Dec 40 to develop the plans for the 83-foot class. The design was completed 19 Mar 41, and 40 units were contracted to Wheeler Shipyard, Inc., Brooklyn, NY. War started before this contract was completed and subsequent contracts for 44, 40, and 106 units were awarded. A total of 230 units were eventually built for the Coast Guard.

*Cost data, design notes, and craft histories prepared and copyrighted by William D. Wilkinson.

Early units (83300–83435) were fitted with an Everdur bronze wheelhouse. These were prefabricated in Boston, MA, and shipped by rail car to the Wheeler Yard. Later units (83436–83529) had plywood wheelhouses because of a shortage of bronze. Those 83-footers operating above Cape Henry, VA, were ice sheathed. All the craft were capable of 20.6 kts full speed at time of delivery, but their performance was degraded by machinery wear as well as the increased displacement from armaments, radar, and sonar. Twelve additional units were built for the USN and transferred to Cuba (4), the Dominican Republic (3), Haiti (1), and Venezuela (4). Nineteen Coast Guard units were also transferred to Latin American navies during the war—the navies of Cuba (8), Colombia (2), Peru (6), and Mexico (3).

General Service

1941–45 used for antisubmarine patrol, coastal convoy escort, and search and rescue; spring 44, 60 units were shipped to Great Britain and became USCG Rescue Flotilla No. 1—based at Poole, England, it deployed in two 30-boat rescue groups for Normandy landings and rescued 1,500, 30 of these 60 units returned to the United States, 24 remained in Europe, 4 were transferred to the Royal Navy, and 2 were lost; Jan 45, 30 units were ordered to COMSERV7THFLEET in the PHILSEAFRON as USCG PTC Flotilla Number One and operated out of Manicani Island, just south of the island of Samar near Leyte—none of these units had served in Europe and none were returned to the United States—all were decommissioned in the Philippines and disposed of by the Foreign Liquidation Commission (an organ of the U.S. State Department); 1945, 24 additional units were transferred to the Pacific to serve in Advance Base Harbor Defense Force (ABHD) (code name LION) at bases in Okinawa and Eniwetok in the Marshall Islands, and Saipan and Guam in the Mariana Islands—4 of these units had served in Europe; following WW II most 83-footers remaining in the Coast Guard were in a decommissioned status for brief periods—only final decommissioning is cited.

83300 (ex-CG 450)

1941–44 assigned to the EASTSEAFRON—stationed at Boston, MA; 1944–45 assigned to the COM12THFLEET—stationed at Poole, England; Jun 44 assigned to USCG Rescue Flotilla No. 1, served in Normandy Invasion as USCG 1; Jun 45 assigned to the EASTSEAFRON—stationed at Boston, MA; 24 Apr 61 decommissioned; 7 Sep 62 sold.

83301 (ex-CG 451)

1941–44 assigned to the EASTSEAFRON—stationed at New York, NY; Jan 45 ordered to the COM7THFLEET—shipped 1 Jul—stationed at LION 8, Okinawa; 9 Oct 45 lost in a typhoon in Buckner Bay, Okinawa.

83302 (ex-CG 452)

1941–44 assigned to the EASTSEAFRON—stationed at New York, NY; 1944–45 assigned to SERVLANT (COM4THFLEET)—stationed at New York, NY.

83303 (ex-CG 453)

1941–45 assigned to the EASTSEAFRON—stationed at Boston, MA; 8 Jun 59 decommissioned; 4 Nov 59 sold.

83304 (ex-CG 454)

1941–44 assigned to the EASTSEAFRON—stationed at Boston, MA; 1944–45 assigned to the COM12THFLEET—stationed at Poole, England; Jun 44 assigned to USCG Rescue Flotilla No. 1—served in Normandy Invasion as USCG 2.

83305 (ex-CG 455)

1941–45 assigned to the EASTSEAFRON—stationed at Boston, MA; 11 Apr 42 rescued 11 survivors from the freighter *City of New York;* 1945 assigned to PHILSEAFRON—USCG PTC Flotilla No. 1—stationed at Manicani Island.

83306 (ex-CG 456)

1941–44 assigned to the EASTSEAFRON—stationed at South Portland, ME; Jan 45 ordered to COM7THFLEET—shipped 1 Jul—stationed at LION 8, Okinawa; 9 Oct 45 lost in a typhoon in Buckner Bay, Okinawa.

83307 (ex-CG 457)

1941–44 assigned to the EASTSEAFRON—stationed at New York, NY; Jan 45 ordered to the COM7THFLEET—stationed at LION 8, Okinawa.

83308 (ex-CG 458)

1941–45 assigned to the CARIBSEAFRON—stationed at Ponce, PR; 1 Nov 45 decommissioned.

83309 (ex-CG 459)

1941–45 assigned to the CARIBSEAFRON—stationed at Charlotte Amalie, Virgin Islands; 19 Jun 42 assisted in the rescue of 9 survivors from the schooner *Cheerio.*

83310 (ex-CG 460)

1941–45 assigned to the CARIBSEAFRON—stationed at San Juan, PR; 5 Jun 42 rescued 25 survivors from the tanker *C. O. Stillman;* 28 Jun 42 rescued 50 survivors from the tanker *William Rockefeller.*

83311 (ex-CG 461)

1941–44 assigned to the EASTSEAFRON—stationed at Newport, RI; Jan 45 ordered to the COM7THFLEET—stationed at LION 8, Okinawa.

83312 (ex-CG 462)

1941–45 assigned to the EASTSEAFRON—stationed at Norfolk, VA; 22 Mar 61 decommissioned; 28 Apr 61 sold.

83313 (ex-CG 463)

1941–45 assigned to the EASTSEAFRON—stationed at Norfolk, VA.

83314 (ex-CG 464)

1941–44 assigned to the EASTSEAFRON—stationed at Cape May, NJ; Jan 45 assigned to PHILSEAFRON, USCG PTC Flotilla No. 1—stationed at Manicani Island.

83315 (ex-CG 465)

Mar 44 transferred to Peru—became CS 1.

83316 (ex-CG 466)

Mar 43 transferred to Cuba.

83317 (ex-CG 467)

Mar 43 transferred to Cuba.

83318 (ex-CG 468)

1941–44 assigned to the EASTSEAFRON—stationed at South Portland, ME; Jan 45 assigned to PHILSEAFRON, USCG PTC Flotilla No. 1—stationed at Manicani Island; hull stripped and burned at Naval Operational Base, Subic Bay, Luzon.

83319 (ex-CG 469)

1941–44 assigned to the EASTSEAFRON—stationed at New York, NY; Jan 45 assigned to PHILSEAFRON, USCG PTC Flotilla No. 1—stationed at Manicani Island; hull stripped and burned at Naval Operational Base, Subic Bay, Luzon.

83320 (ex-CG 470)

1941–44 assigned to the EASTSEAFRON—stationed at Baltimore, MD; 1944–45 assigned to the COM12THFLEET—stationed at Poole, England; Jun 44 assigned to USCG Rescue Flotilla No. 1—served in Normandy Invasion as USCG 3; Jun 45 assigned to the EASTSEAFRON; Aug 45 shipped to the Canal Zone; 5 Jul 61 decommissioned; 31 Jul 62 disposed of by sinking.

83321 (ex-CG 471)

1941–44 assigned to the EASTSEAFRON—stationed at Cape May, NJ; 1944–45 assigned to the COM12THFLEET—stationed at Poole, England; Jun 44 assigned to USCG Rescue Flotilla No. 1—served in Normandy Invasion as USCG 4.

83222 (ex-CG 472)

1941–44 assigned to the EASTSEAFRON—stationed at Boston, MA; 17 Jun 42 rescued 14 survivors from the merchantman *Santore;* Jan 45 assigned to PHILSEAFRON, USCG PTC Flotilla No. 1—stationed at Manicani Island.

83323 (ex-CG 473)

1941–44 assigned to the EASTSEAFRON—stationed at Little Creek, VA; Jan 45 assigned to PHILSEAFRON, USCG PTC Flotilla No. 1—stationed at Manicani Island.

83324 (ex-CG 474)

1941–44 assigned to the EASTSEAFRON—stationed at Boston, MA; Jan 45 assigned to PHILSEAFRON, USCG PTC Flotilla No. 1—stationed at Manicani Island.

83325 (ex-CG 475)

1941–45 assigned to the CARIBSEAFRON—stationed at Norfolk, VA.

83326 (ex-CG 476)

1941–45 assigned to the CARIBSEAFRON—stationed at New York, NY.

83327 (ex-CG 477)

1942–44 assigned to the EASTSEAFRON—stationed at New York, NY; 1944–45 assigned to the COM12THFLEET—stationed at Poole, England; Jun 44 assigned to USCG Rescue Flotilla No. 1—served in Normandy Invasion as USCG 5; Jul 45 returned to the U.S.; 15 Jun 61 decommissioned; 28 Jan 63 sold.

83328 (ex-CG 478)

1942–44 assigned to the EASTSEAFRON (CINCLANT)—stationed at Norfolk, VA; Jan 45 assigned to PHILSEAFRON, USCG PTC Flotilla No. 1—stationed at Manicani Island.

83329 (ex-CG 479)

1942–44 assigned to the EASTSEAFRON—stationed at Norfolk, VA; Jan 45 assigned to PHILSEAFRON, USCG PTC Flotilla No. 1—stationed at Manicani Island.

83330 (ex-CG 480)

1942–44 assigned to the EASTSEAFRON—stationed at Norfolk, VA; Jan 45 assigned to PHILSEAFRON, USCG PTC Flotilla No. 1—stationed at Manicani Island.

83331 (ex-CG 481)

1942–44 assigned to the EASTSEAFRON—stationed at New York, NY; Jan 45 assigned to PHILSEAFRON, USCG PTC Flotilla No. 1—stationed at Manicani Island.

83332 (ex-CG 482)

1942–44 assigned to the EASTSEAFRON—stationed at New York, NY; Jan 45 assigned to PHILSEAFRON, USCG PTC Flotilla No. 1—stationed at Manicani Island.

83333 (ex-CG 483)

1942–45 assigned to the EASTSEAFRON—stationed at New York, NY; Jan 45 ordered to the COM7THFLEET—shipped 18 Jul—stationed at LION 8, Okinawa.

83334 (ex-CG 484)

1942–44 assigned to the EASTSEAFRON—stationed at New York, NY; 1944–45 assigned to the COM12THFLEET—stationed at Poole, England; Jun 44 assigned to USCG Rescue Flotilla No. 1—served in Normandy Invasion as USCG 6; Jul 45 returned to the U.S.; 23 Jun 59 decommissioned; 3 Mar 60 sold.

83335 (ex-CG 485)

1942–44 assigned to the EASTSEAFRON—stationed at Cape May, NJ; 1944–45 assigned to the SERVLANT (COM4THFLEET)—stationed at Cape May, NJ.

83336 (ex-CG 486)

1942–44 assigned to the EASTSEAFRON—stationed at Portland, ME; Jan 45 assigned to PHILSEAFRON, USCG PTC Flotilla No. 1—stationed at Manicani Island.

83337 (ex-CG 487)

1942–44 assigned to the EASTSEAFRON—stationed at Cape May, NJ; 1944–45 assigned to the COM12THFLEET—stationed at Poole, England; Jun 44 assigned to USCG Rescue Flotilla No. 1—served in Normandy Invasion as USCG 7; Jul 45 returned to the U.S.; 31 Jul 61 decommissioned; 28 Dec 63 disposed of by sinking.

83338 (ex-CG 488)

Mar 44 transferred to Peru—became CS 2.

83339 (ex-CG 489)

Transferred to Colombia; spring 45 returned to CG; 24 Oct 45 decommissioned.

83340 (ex-CG 491)

1942–44 assigned to the EASTSEAFRON—stationed at Southport, NC; Jan 45 assigned to PHILSEAFRON, USCG PTC Flotilla No. 1—stationed at Manicani Island.

83341 (ex-CG 492)

1942–44 assigned to the EASTSEAFRON—stationed at Southport, NC; 1944–45 assigned to the SERVLANT (COM4THFLEET)—stationed at Southport, NC; 27 Oct 45 decommissioned.

83342 (ex-CG 493)

1942–45 assigned to the EASTSEAFRON—stationed at Southport, NC; 9 Dec 60 decommissioned; 12 Jul 61 sold.

83343 (ex-CG 494)

1942–45 assigned to the EASTSEAFRON—stationed at Southport, NC; 29 Sep 47 decommissioned.

83344 (ex-CG 495)

1942–44 assigned to the EASTSEAFRON—stationed at Portland, ME; 1944–45 assigned to the SERVLANT (COM4THFLEET)—stationed at Portland, ME; 1 Nov 45 decommissioned.

83345 (ex-CG 496)

1942–45 assigned to the EASTSEAFRON—stationed at Cape May, NJ; 29 Sep 47 decommissioned.

83346 (ex-CG 497)

1942–45 assigned to the EASTSEAFRON—stationed at New York, NY; 30 Nov 60 decommissioned; 25 Aug 62 sold.

83347 (ex-CG 498)

1942–44 assigned to the EASTSEAFRON—stationed at Norfolk, VA; 1944–45 assigned to CINCLANT—stationed at Norfolk, VA; 1 Nov 45 decommissioned.

83348 (ex-CG 499)

1942–Jun 45 assigned to the GULFSEAFRON—stationed at Key West, FL; Jun 45 assigned to the 13th District—stationed at Hammond, OR.

83349 (ex-CG 600)

Aug 44 transferred to Colombia—became the *Ayacucho*.

83350 (ex-CG 601)

Mar 43 transferred to Cuba.

83351 (ex-CG 602)

Mar 43 transferred to Cuba.

83352 (ex-CG 603)

1942–45 assigned to the CARIBSEAFRON—stationed at Port of Spain, Trinidad; 1 Nov 45 decommissioned.

83353 (ex-CG 604)

1942–45 assigned to the CARIBSEAFRON—stationed at Port of Spain, Trinidad; 1 Nov 45 decommissioned.

83354 (ex-CG 605)

1942–45 assigned to the CARIBSEAFRON—stationed at Port of Spain, Trinidad; 1 Nov 45 decommissioned.

83355 (ex-CG 606)

1942–45 assigned to the CARIBSEAFRON—stationed at Port of Spain, Trinidad; 1 Nov 45 decommissioned.

83356 (ex-CG 607)

1942–45 assigned to the CARIBSEAFRON—stationed at San Juan, PR.

83357 (ex-CG 608)

1942–44 assigned to the EASTSEAFRON—stationed at Portland, ME; Jan 45 assigned to PHILSEAFRON, USCG PTC Flotilla No. 1—stationed at Manicani Island.

83358 (ex-CG 609)

1942–44 assigned to the EASTSEAFRON—stationed at Portland, ME; Jan 45 assigned to PHILSEAFRON, USCG PTC Flotilla No. 1—stationed at Manicani Island.

83359 (ex-CG 610)

1942–45 assigned to the EASTSEAFRON—stationed at Southwest Harbor, ME; 1 Jul 59 decommissioned; 4 Nov 59 sold.

83360 (ex-CG 611)

1942–44 assigned to the EASTSEAFRON—stationed at Cape May, NJ; 1944–45 assigned to the COM12THFLEET—stationed at Poole, England; Jun 44 assigned to USCG Rescue Flotilla No. 1—served in Normandy Invasion as USCG 8; Jul 45 returned to the U.S.; 6 Jan 58 decommissioned; 17 Jan 58 sold.

83361 (ex-CG 612)

1942–44 assigned to the EASTSEAFRON—stationed at Cape May, NJ; 1944–45 assigned to the COM12THFLEET—stationed at Poole, England; Jun 44 assigned to USCG Rescue Flotilla No. 1—served in Normandy Invasion as USCG 9; Jun 45 assigned to the EASTSEAFRON; late 45 assigned to COM7THFLEET—stationed at ABHD Guam (B2A5).

83362 (ex-CG 613)

1942–44 assigned to the EASTSEAFRON—stationed at Cape May, NJ; 1944–45 assigned to the COM12THFLEET—stationed at Poole, England; Jun 44 assigned to USCG Rescue Flotilla No. 1—served in Normandy Invasion as USCG 10; Jun 45 assigned to the EASTSEAFRON; late 45 assigned to COM7THFLEET—stationed at ABHD Guam (B2A5); 12 Mar 59 decommissioned; 4 Nov 59 sold.

83363 (ex-CG 614)

1942–44 assigned to the EASTSEAFRON—stationed at Cape May, NJ; Jan 45 ordered to the COM7THFLEET—shipped 18 Jul—stationed at LION 8, Okinawa.

83364 (ex-CG 615)

1942–44 assigned to the EASTSEAFRON—stationed at Cape May, NJ; Jan 45 ordered to the COM7THFLEET—shipped 18 Jul—stationed at LION 8, Okinawa.

83365 (ex-CG 616)

1942–44 assigned to the EASTSEAFRON—stationed at Norfolk, VA; Jan 45 ordered to the COM7THFLEET—stationed at LION 8, Okinawa.

83366 (ex-CG 617)

1942–44 assigned to the EASTSEAFRON—stationed at Norfolk, VA; 1944–45 assigned to the COM12THFLEET—stationed at Poole, England; Jun 44 assigned to USCG Rescue Flotilla No. 1—served in Normandy Invasion as USCG 11; Jun 45 assigned to the EASTSEAFRON; 17 Jul 61 decommissioned; 19 Apr 63 sold.

83367 (ex-CG 618)

1942–45 assigned to the EASTSEAFRON—stationed at Norfolk, VA; 24 Oct 45 decommissioned.

83368 (ex-CG 619)

1942–44 assigned to the EASTSEAFRON—stationed at Savannah, GA; 1944–45 assigned to SERVLANT (COM4THFLEET)—stationed at Savannah, GA.

83369 (ex-CG 620)

1942–44 assigned to the EASTSEAFRON—stationed at Savannah, GA; 1944–45 assigned to SERVLANT (COM4THFLEET)—stationed at Savannah, GA.

83370 (ex-CG 621)

1942–44 assigned to the EASTSEAFRON—stationed at Fernandina Beach, FL; 1944–45 assigned to the COM12THFLEET—stationed at Poole, England; Jun 44 assigned to USCG Rescue Flotilla No. 1—served in Normandy Invasion as USCG 12; Jun 45 assigned to the EASTSEAFRON; Aug 45 shipped to the Canal Zone; 1 Apr 59 decommissioned; 9 Oct 59 sold.

83371 (ex-CG 622)

1942–44 assigned to the EASTSEAFRON—stationed at Fernandina Beach, FL; Jan 45 assigned to the PHILSEAFRON, USCG PTC Flotilla No. 1—stationed at Manicani Island.

83372 (ex-CG 623)

1942–44 assigned to the GULFSEAFRON—stationed at Key West, FL; 1944–45 assigned to the COM12THFLEET—stationed at Poole, England; Jun 44 assigned to USCG Rescue Flotilla No. 1—served in Normandy Invasion as USCG 13; Jul 45 returned to the U.S.; 21 Nov 47 transferred to the USN.

83373 (ex-CG 624)

1942–44 assigned to the GULFSEAFRON—stationed at Key West, FL; 1944–45 assigned to the COM12THFLEET—stationed at Poole, England; Jun 44 assigned to USCG Rescue Flotilla No. 1—served in Normandy Invasion as USCG 14; Jul 45 returned to the U.S.

83374 (ex-CG 625)

1942–45 assigned to the GULFSEAFRON—stationed at Key West, FL.

83375 (ex-CG 626)

1942–44 assigned to the GULFSEAFRON—stationed at Key West, FL; 1944–45 assigned to the COM12THFLEET—stationed at Poole, England; Jun 44 assigned to USCG Rescue Flotilla No. 1—served in Normandy Invasion as USCG 15; Jun 45 assigned to the EASTSEAFRON; late 45 assigned to the COM7THFLEET—stationed at ABHD Eniwetok (B2A8).

83376 (ex-CG 627)

1942–44 assigned to the GULFSEAFRON—stationed at Mobile, AL; 1944–45 assigned to the GULFSEAFRON—stationed at Miami, FL.

83377 (ex-CG 628)

1942–44 assigned to the GULFSEAFRON—stationed at Galveston, TX; 1944–45 assigned to the COM12THFLEET—stationed at Poole, England; Jun 44 assigned to USCG Rescue Flotilla No. 1—served in Normandy Invasion as USCG 16; Jul 45 returned to the U.S.

83378 (ex-CG 629)

1942–44 assigned to the GULFSEAFRON—stationed at Corpus Christi, TX; 1944–45 assigned to the COM12THFLEET—stationed at Poole, England; Jun 44 assigned to USCG Rescue Flotilla No. 1—served in Normandy Invasion as USCG 17; Jun 45 assigned to the EASTSEAFRON; 8 Jun 61 decommissioned; 13 Dec 62 sold.

83379 (ex-CG 630)

1942–Jun 45 assigned to the CARIBSEAFRON—stationed at San Juan, PR; Jun 45 assigned to the 10th District; 5 Dec 52 decommissioned; 1 Oct 53 sold.

83380 (ex-CG 631)

1942–45 assigned to the CARIBSEAFRON—stationed at San Juan, PR.

83381 (ex-CG 632)

1942–Jun 45 assigned to the CARIBSEAFRON—stationed at San Juan, PR; Jun 45 assigned to the 10th District; 15 Nov 60 decommissioned; 28 Sep 62 sold.

83382 (ex-CG 633)

1942–45 assigned to the CARIBSEAFRON—stationed at Charlotte Amalie, Virgin Islands; 17 Jul 61 decommissioned; 26 Apr 63 sold.

83383 (ex-CG 634)

1942–Jun 45 assigned to the CARIBSEAFRON—stationed at Charlotte Amalie, Virgin Islands; Jun 45 assigned to the 10th District; 5 Dec 52 decommissioned; 1 Oct 53 sold.

83384

Mar 43 transferred to Cuba.

83385

Mar 43 transferred to Cuba.

83386

Mar 43 transferred to Cuba.

83387

1942–45 assigned to the CG Academy—stationed at New London, CT, and used for training; 1 Apr 58 decommissioned; 17 Feb 59 sold.

83388

1942–45 assigned to the CG Academy—stationed at New London, CT, and used for training; 29 Dec 60 decommissioned; 10 Aug 62 sold.

83389

1943–45 assigned to the GULFSEAFRON—stationed at Miami, FL; Jun 45 assigned to the 11th District—stationed at Wilmington, CA; 26 Sep 61 decommissioned; 13 Sep 62 disposed of by sinking.

83390

1943–45 assigned to the GULFSEAFRON—stationed at Miami, FL.

83391

Jan 43 delivered; 1943–45 assigned to the GULFSEAFRON—stationed at Miami, FL; 19 Jul 61 decommissioned; 17 Dec 62 sold.

83392

Jan 43 delivered; 1943–45 assigned to the CG Academy—stationed at New London, CT, and used for training; 15 Jan 61 decommissioned; 15 Feb 61 transferred.

83393

Jan 43 delivered; 1943–45 assigned to the CG Academy—stationed at New London, CT, and used for training.

83394

Jan 43 delivered; 1943–45 assigned to the CG Academy—stationed at New London, CT, and used for training; 30 Oct 59 decommissioned; 18 May 60 sold.

83395

Jan 43 delivered; early 43 assigned to the GULFSEAFRON—stationed at Miami, FL; Mar 43 transferred to Cuba.

83396

Jan 43 delivered; 1943–Dec 44 assigned to the GULFSEAFRON—stationed at Miami, FL; Dec 44–45 assigned to the 8th District; transferred to the USN.

83397

Jan 43 delivered; 1943–44 assigned to the GULFSEAFRON—stationed at Miami, FL; summer 45 assigned to the COM7THFLEET—stationed at ABHD Eniwetok (B2A8); 19 Nov 62 decommissioned; 7 Dec 64 sold.

83398

Jan 43 delivered; 1943–44 assigned to the GULFSEAFRON—stationed at Miami, FL; 1944–45 assigned to the COM12THFLEET—stationed at Poole, England; Jun 44 assigned to USCG Rescue Flotilla No. 1—served in Normandy Invasion as USCG 18; Jul 45 returned to the U.S.; 15 Oct 45 decommissioned.

83399

Jan 43 delivered; 1943–44 assigned to the GULFSEAFRON—stationed at Miami, FL; 1944 assigned to the COM12THFLEET—stationed at Poole, England; Jun 44 assigned to USCG Rescue Flotilla No. 1—served in Normandy Invasion as USCG 19; late 1944 transferred to WSA for use by the Royal Navy.

83400

Jan 43 delivered; 1943–45 assigned to the GULFSEAFRON—stationed at Miami, FL; 17 Aug 61 decommissioned; 25 May 62 disposed of by sinking.

83401

Feb 43 delivered; 1943–44 assigned to the GULFSEAFRON—stationed at Miami, FL; 1944 assigned to the COM12THFLEET—stationed at Poole, England; Jun 44 assigned to USCG Rescue Flotilla No. 1—served in Normandy Invasion as USCG 20; late 1944 transferred to WSA for use by the Royal Navy.

83402

Feb 43 delivered; 1943–44 assigned to the GULFSEAFRON—stationed at Miami, FL; 1944 assigned to the COM12THFLEET—stationed at Poole, England; Jun 44 assigned to USCG Rescue Flotilla No. 1—served in Normandy Invasion as USCG 21; Nov 1944 transferred to WSA for use by the Royal Navy; 7 Jan 46 returned to CG.

83403

Feb 43 delivered; 1943–45 assigned to the GULFSEAFRON—stationed at Miami, FL; 7 Nov 58 decommissioned; 30 Dec 59 sold.

83404

Feb 43 delivered; 1943–45 assigned to the GULFSEAFRON—stationed at Miami, FL.

CGs 83401 and 83402, wearing their invasion markings, served as rescue boats during the Normandy landings. The sloping bridge face and the rounded bridge roof are common features of the earlier series of 83-footers. CGs 83300 through 83435 had the rounded wheelhouse design of Everdur Bronze construction. As the war progressed, bronze materials became scarce and wheelhouse design was modified by the builder to one of plywood construction. Following the Normandy Invasion, these two boats were transferred to the Royal Navy.

83405

Feb 43 delivered; 1943–45 assigned to the GULFSEAFRON—stationed at Miami, FL.

83406

Feb 43 delivered; 1943–45 assigned to the GULFSEAFRON—stationed at Miami, FL.

83407

Feb 43 delivered; 1943–44 assigned to the EASTSEAFRON—stationed at Boston, MA; 1944 assigned to the COM12THFLEET—stationed at Poole, England; Jun 44 assigned to USCG Rescue Flotilla No. 1—served in Normandy Invasion as USCG 22; Nov 1944 transferred to WSA for use by the Royal Navy; 7 Jan 46 returned to CG.

83408

Feb 43 delivered; 1943–44 assigned to the EASTSEAFRON—stationed at Boston, MA; 1944–45 assigned to the COM12THFLEET—stationed at Poole, England; Jun 44 assigned to USCG Rescue Flotilla No. 1—served in Normandy Invasion as USCG 23; Jul 45 returned to the U.S.; 5 Nov 47 sold.

83409

Feb 43 delivered; 1943–44 assigned to the EASTSEAFRON—stationed at Boston, MA; 1944–45 assigned to the COM12THFLEET—stationed at Poole, England; Jun 44 assigned to USCG Rescue Flotilla No. 1—served in Normandy Invasion as USCG 24; Jun 45 assigned to the EASTSEAFRON; Aug 45 shipped to the Canal Zone.

83410

Feb 43 delivered; 1943–44 assigned to the EASTSEAFRON—stationed at Boston, MA; Jan 45 assigned to the PHILSEAFRON, USCG PTC Flotilla No. 1—stationed at Manicani Island.

83411

Feb 43 delivered; 1943–44 assigned to the EASTSEAFRON—stationed at Newport, RI; 1944–45 assigned to the COM12THFLEET—stationed at Poole, England; Jun 44 assigned to USCG Rescue Flotilla No. 1—served in Normandy Invasion as USCG 25; Jun 45 assigned to the EASTSEAFRON; Aug 45 shipped to the Canal Zone; 29 Dec 59 decommissioned; 23 May 60 sold.

83412

Feb 43 delivered; 1943–44 assigned to the EASTSEAFRON—stationed at Newport, RI; 1944–45 assigned to the COM12THFLEET—stationed at Poole, England; Jun 44 assigned to USCG Rescue Flotilla No. 1—served in Normandy Invasion as USCG 26; Jun 45 assigned to the EASTSEAFRON; 20 Mar 63 decommissioned; 4 Dec 63 transferred to USA.

83413

Mar 43 delivered; 1943–44 assigned to the EASTSEAFRON—stationed at Cape May, NJ; Jan 45 assigned to the PHILSEAFRON, USCG PTC Flotilla No. 1—stationed at Manicani Island.

83414

Mar 43 delivered; 1943–44 assigned to the EASTSEAFRON—stationed at Cape May, NJ; Jan 45 assigned to PHILSEAFRON, USCG PTC Flotilla No. 1—stationed at Manicani Island.

83415

Mar 43 delivered; 1943–44 assigned to the EASTSEAFRON—stationed at Charleston, SC; 1944–45 assigned to the COM12THFLEET—stationed at Poole, England; Jun 44 assigned to USCG Rescue Flotilla No. 1—served in Normandy Invasion as USCG 27; 21 Jun 44 sank off Normandy in a storm after sustaining damage from invasion wreckage.

83416

Mar 43 delivered; 1943–44 assigned to the EASTSEAFRON—stationed at Charleston, SC; 1944–45 assigned to the COM12THFLEET—stationed at Poole, England; Jun 44 assigned to USCG Rescue Flotilla No. 1—served in Normandy Invasion as USCG 28; Jun 45 assigned to the EASTSEAFRON; late 1945 assigned to COM7THFLEET—stationed at ABHD Eniwetok (B2A8).

83417

Mar 43 delivered; 1943–44 assigned to the EASTSEAFRON—stationed at Charleston, SC; 1944–45 assigned to the COM12THFLEET—stationed at Poole, England; Jun 44 assigned to USCG Reserve Flotilla No. 1—served in Normandy Invasion as USCG 29.

83418

Mar 43 delivered; 1943–44 assigned to the EASTSEAFRON—stationed at Charleston, SC; Jan 45 ordered to the COM7THFLEET—shipped 1 Aug—stationed at LION 8, Okinawa.

83419

Mar 43 delivered; 1943–45 assigned to the GULFSEAFRON—stationed at Miami, FL; Jul 44 assigned to the GULFSEAFRON—stationed at San Juan, PR.

83420

Mar 43 delivered; 1943–44 assigned to the GULFSEAFRON—stationed at Miami, FL; 1944 assigned to the GULFSEAFRON—stationed at New Orleans, LA; Jan 45 assigned to the 11th District—stationed at San Pedro, CA, and used for training; Apr 45 assigned to the COM7THFLEET—shipped 1 Jul—stationed LION 8, Okinawa.

83421

Mar 43 delivered; 1943–44 assigned to the GULFSEAFRON—stationed at Miami, FL; 30 Jun 44 sank in a collision with SC 1330.

83422

Mar 43 delivered; 1943 assigned to the GULFSEAFRON—stationed at Miami, FL; Jun 43 transferred to Peru—became CS 3.

83423

Mar 43 delivered; 1943 assigned to the GULFSEAFRON—stationed at Miami, FL; Jun 43 transferred to Peru—became CS 4.

83424

Mar 43 delivered; 1943–44 assigned to the EASTSEAFRON—stationed at Newport, RI; Jan 45 assigned to the COM7THFLEET—shipped 1 Aug—stationed at LION 8, Okinawa.

83425

Apr 43 delivered; 1943–44 assigned to the EASTSEAFRON—stationed at Newport, RI; 1944–45 assigned to the COM12THFLEET—stationed at Poole, England; Jun 44 assigned to USCG Rescue Flotilla No. 1—served in Normandy Invasion as USCG 30; Jul 45 returned to the U.S.

83426

Apr 43 delivered; 1943–45 assigned to the EASTSEAFRON—stationed at Boston, MA.

83427

Apr 43 delivered; 1943–45 assigned to the EASTSEAFRON—stationed at Boston, MA; Apr 45 assigned to the 1st District; 17 Jan 61 decommissioned; 30 Jun 61 sold.

83428

Apr 43 delivered; 1943–44 assigned to the EASTSEAFRON—stationed at New York, NY; 1944–45 assigned to the COM12THFLEET—stationed at Poole, England; Jun 44 assigned to USCG Rescue Flotilla No. 1—served in Normandy Invasion as USCG 31; 15 Jan 60 decommissioned; 19 Jul 60 sold.

83429

Apr 43 delivered; 1943–44 assigned to the EASTSEAFRON—stationed at New York, NY; Jan 45 assigned to the PHILSEAFRON, USCG PTC Flotilla No. 1—stationed at Manicani Island.

83430

Apr 43 delivered; 1943–44 assigned to the GULFSEAFRON—stationed at Miami, FL; 1944 assigned to the GULFSEAFRON—stationed at New Orleans, LA; Jan 45 assigned to the 11th District—stationed at San Pedro, CA, and used for training; Apr 45 assigned to COM7THFLEET—shipped 1 Jul—stationed at LION 8, Okinawa.

83431

Apr 43 delivered; 1943–44 assigned to the GULFSEAFRON—stationed at Miami, FL; 1944–45 assignd to the COM12THFLEET—stationed at Poole, England; Jun 44 assigned to USCG Rescue Flotilla No. 1—served in Normandy Invasion as USCG 32.

83432

Apr 43 delivered; 1943–44 assigned to the GULFSEAFRON—stationed at Miami, FL; 1944–45 assigned to the COM12THFLEET—stationed at Poole, England; Jun 44 assigned to USCG Rescue Flotilla No. 1—served in Normandy Invasion as USCG 33.

83433

Apr 43 delivered; 1943–44 assigned to the GULFSEAFRON—stationed at Miami, FL; Dec 44 transferred to Colombia—became the *Boyaca*.

83434

Apr 43 delivered; 1943–44 assigned to the GULFSEAFRON—stationed at Miami, FL; Sep 44 assigned to the GULFSEAFRON—stationed at New Orleans, LA; Jan 45 assigned to the 11th District—stationed at San Pedro, CA, and used for training; Apr 45 assigned to COM7THFLEET—stationed at ABHD Saipan (B2A4).

83435

May 43 delivered; 1943–44 assigned to the GULFSEAFRON—stationed at Miami, FL; 1944–45 assigned to the COM12THFLEET—stationed at Poole, England; Jun 44 assigned to USCG Rescue Flotilla No. 1—served in Normandy Invasion as USCG 34; 26 Oct 61 decommissioned; 6 Mar 63 sold.

83436

May 43 delivered; 1943–45 assigned to the EASTSEAFRON—stationed at Charleston, SC.

83437

May 43 delivered; 1943–45 assignd to the EASTSEAFRON—stationed at Charleston, SC; late 1945 assigned to PHILSEAFRON, USCG Flotilla No. 1—stationed at Manicani Island.

83438

May 43 delivered; 1943–45 assigned to the EASTSEAFRON—stationed at Newport, RI; 5 Dec 52 decommissioned; 1 Oct 53 sold.

83439

May 43 delivered; 1943–44 assigned to the EASTSEAFRON—stationed at Newport, RI; 1944–45 assigned to the COM12THFLEET—stationed at Poole, England; Jun 44 assigned to USCG Rescue Flotilla No. 1—served in Normandy Invasion as USCG 35.

83440

May 43 delivered; 1943–44 assigned to the EASTSEAFRON—stationed at Boston, MA; 1944–45 assigned to the COM12THFLEET—stationed at Poole, England; Jun 44 assigned to USCG Rescue Flotilla No. 1—served in Normandy Invasion as USCG 36.

83441

May 43 delivered; 1943–45 assigned to the EASTSEAFRON—stationed at Boston, MA; late 1945 assigned to PHILSEAFRON, USCG PTC Flotilla No. 1—stationed at Manicani Island.

83442

May 43 delivered; 1943–44 assigned to the EASTSEAFRON—stationed at New York, NY; 1944–45 assigned to the COM12THFLEET—stationed at Poole, England; Jun 44 assigned to USCG Rescue Flotilla No. 1—served in Normandy Invasion as USCG 37; 10 Sep 52 transferred to USN.

83443

May 43 delivered; 1943–44 assigned to the EASTSEAFRON—stationed at New York, NY; 1944–45 assigned to the COM12THFLEET—stationed at Poole, England; Jun 44 assigned to USCG Rescue Flotilla No. 1—served in Normandy Invasion as USCG 38; 29 Sep 47 decommissioned.

83444

May 43 delivered; 1943–45 assigned to the EASTSEAFRON—stationed at Charleston, SC; late 1945 assigned to PHILSEAFRON, USCG PTC Flotilla No. 1—stationed at Manicani Island.

83445

May 43 delivered; 1943–44 assigned to the EASTSEAFRON—stationed at Charleston, SC; 1944–45 assigned to the COM12THFLEET—stationed at Poole, England; Jun 44 assigned to USCG Rescue Flotilla No. 1—served in Normandy Invasion as USCG 39.

83446

May 43 delivered; 1943 assigned to the EASTSEAFRON—stationed at Boston, MA; Sep 43 transferred to Mexico—became CS 01.

83447

May 43 delivered; 1943–44 assigned to the EASTSEAFRON—stationed at Boston, MA; 1944–45 assigned to the COM12THFLEET—stationed at Poole, England; Jun 44 assigned to USCG Rescue Flotilla No. 1—served in Normandy Invasion as USCG 40.

83448

Jun 43 delivered; 1943–44 assigned to the GULFSEAFRON—stationed at Miami, FL; 1944–45 assigned to SERVLANT (COM4THFLEET)—stationed at Providence, RI.

83449

Jun 43 delivered; 1943–44 assigned to the GULFSEAFRON—stationed at Miami, FL; 1944–45 assigned to SERVLANT (COM4THFLEET)—stationed at Miami, FL; Apr 45 assigned to the COM7THFLEET—stationed at ABHD Guam (B2A5); 20 Jan 58 surveyed and burned.

83450

Jun 43 delivered; 1943–45 assigned to the GULFSEAFRON—stationed at Miami, FL; 31 May 62 decommissioned; 22 Mar 63 sold.

83451

Jun 43 delivered; 1943–45 assigned to the GULFSEAFRON—stationed at Miami, FL; 6 Oct 53 sold.

83452

Jun 43 delivered; 1943–45 assigned to the GULFSEAFRON—stationed at Miami, FL; 15 Mar 63 decommissioned; 19 Aug 64 sold.

83453

Jun 43 delivered; 1943–45 assigned to the GULFSEAFRON—stationed at Miami, FL; 29 Jun 62 decommissioned; 26 May 64 sold.

83454

Jun 43 delivered; 1943–45 assigned to the GULFSEAFRON—stationed at Miami, FL.

83455

Jun 43 delivered; 1943–44 assigned to the GULFSEAFRON—stationed at Miami, FL; Jul 44 assigned to the GULFSEAFRON—stationed at San Juan, PR; 3 Feb 61 decommissioned; 17 Aug 62 sold.

83456

Jun 43 delivered; 1943–45 assigned to the GULFSEAFRON—stationed at Miami, FL; 5 Dec 52 decommissioned; 8 Dec 54 sold.

83457

Jun 43 delivered; 1943–45 assigned to the GULFSEAFRON—stationed at Miami, FL; 28 Sep 61 decommissioned; 19 Feb 64 sold.

83458

Jul 43 delivered; 1943–Jan 45 assigned to the GULFSEAFRON—stationed at Miami, FL; Jan 45–1945 assigned to the WESTSEAFRON—stationed at San Pedro, CA, and used for training; 27 Sep 45 transferred to USN.

83459

Jul 43 delivered; 1943–Jan 45 assigned to the GULFSEAFRON—stationed at Miami, FL; Jan 45–1945 assigned to the WESTSEAFRON—stationed at San Pedro, CA, and used for training.

83460

Jul 43 delivered; 1943–45 assigned to the EASTSEAFRON—stationed at Newport, RI.

83461

Jul 43 delivered; 1943–45 assigned to the EASTSEAFRON—stationed at Newport, RI.

83462

Jul 43 delivered; 1943–44 assigned to the EASTSEAFRON—stationed at New York, NY; 1944–45 assigned to the COM12THFLEET—stationed at Poole, England; Jun 44 assigned to USCG Rescue Flotilla No. 1—served in Normandy Invasion as USCG 41.

83463

Jul 43 delivered; 1943–44 assigned to the EASTSEAFRON—stationed at New York, NY; 1944–45 assigned to the COM12THFLEET—stationed at Poole, England; Jun 44 assigned to USCG Rescue Flotilla No. 1—served in Normandy Invasion as USCG 42; 26 Nov 58 decommissioned; 2 Nov 59 sold.

CG 83459 running trials in 1943. The flat bridge roof and the vertical bridge face are common features of the late series 83-footers. The last ninety-four 83-footers, CGs 83436 through 83529, had the flat and angular plywood wheelhouses. This unit has not yet been fitted with radar.

83464

Jul 43 delivered; 1943–44 assigned to the EASTSEAFRON—stationed at Charleston, SC; 1944–45 assigned to the COM12THFLEET—stationed at Poole, England; Jun 44 assigned to USCG Rescue Flotilla No. 1—served in Normandy Invasion as USCG 43; 17 Nov 61 decommissioned; 31 Jan 63 sold.

83465

Jul 43 delivered; 1943–44 assigned to the EASTSEAFRON—stationed at Charleston, SC; 1944–45 assigned to the COM12THFLEET—stationed at Poole, England; Jun 44 assigned to USCG Rescue Flotilla No. 1—served in Normandy Invasion as USCG 44; 10 Sep 52 transferred to USN.

83466

Jul 43 delivered; 1943–44 assigned to the EASTSEAFRON—stationed at Boston, MA; 1944–45 assigned to the COM12THFLEET—stationed at Poole, England; Apr 44 cutter's radar was used to guide the merchantship on which she was being transported to England; Jun 44 assigned to USCG Rescue Flotilla No. 1—served in Normandy Invasion as USCG 45; 29 Sep 47 decommissioned.

83467

Jul 43 delivered; 1943–45 assigned to the EASTSEAFRON—stationed at New York, NY; 1945 assigned to PHILSEAFRON, USCG PTC Flotilla No. 1—stationed at Manicani Island.

83468

Jul 43 delivered; 1943–44 assigned to the EASTSEAFRON—stationed at New York, NY; 1944–45 assigned to the COM12THFLEET—stationed at Poole, England; Jun 44 assigned to USCG Rescue Flotilla No. 1—served in Normandy Invasion as USCG 46; 31 Jul 58 decommissioned; 2 Feb 59 donated.

83469

Jul 43 delivered; 1943–45 assigned to the EASTSEAFRON—stationed at New York, NY; 1945 assigned to PHILSEAFRON, USCG PTC Flotilla No. 1—stationed at Manicani Island.

83470

Aug 43 delivered; 1943–45 assigned to the EASTSEAFRON—stationed at Cape May, NJ; 7 Oct 52 decommissioned; 15 May 53 sold.

83471

Aug 43 delivered; 1943–44 assigned to the EASTSEAFRON—stationed at Cape May, NJ; 1944–45 assigned to the COM12THFLEET—stationed at Poole, England; Jun 44 assigned to USCG Rescue Flotilla No. 1—served in Normandy Invasion as USCG 47; 21 Jun 44 sank in a storm off Normandy, after sustaining damage from invasion wreckage.

83472

Aug 43 delivered; 1943–45 assigned to the EASTSEAFRON—stationed at Norfolk, VA; 1945 assigned to PHILSEAFRON, USCG PTC Flotilla No. 1—stationed at Manicani Island.

83473

Aug 43 delivered; 1943–44 assigned to the EASTSEAFRON—stationed at Norfolk, VA; 1944–45 assigned to the COM12THFLEET—stationed at Poole, England; Jun 44 assigned to USCG Rescue Flotilla No. 1—served in Normandy Invasion as USCG 48.

83474

Aug 43 delivered; 1943–44 assigned to the GULFSEAFRON—stationed at Miami, FL; mid 44 assigned to SERVLANT (COM4THFLEET)—stationed at Miami, FL; Jul 44 assigned to the EASTSEAFRON—stationed at Norfolk, VA.

83475

Aug 43 delivered; 1943–44 assigned to the GULFSEAFRON—stationed at Miami, FL; 1944–45 assigned to SERVLANT (COM4THFLEET)—stationed at Miami, FL.

83476

Aug 43 delivered; 1943–45 assigned to the NAOTC, 9th District—stationed at Chicago, IL; 5 Dec 52 decommissioned; 25 Sep 53 sold.

83477

Aug 43 delivered; 1943–45 assigned to the NAOTC, 9th District—stationed at Chicago, IL; 5 Dec 52 decommissioned; 25 Sep 53 sold.

83478

Aug 43 delivered; 1943–45 assigned to the NAOTC, 9th District—stationed at Chicago, IL; 25 Oct 54 decommissioned; 7 Dec 54 burned.

83479

Aug 43 delivered; 1943–45 assigned to the NAOTC, 9th District—stationed at Chicago, IL; 5 Dec 52 decommissioned; 1 Oct 53 sold.

83480

Aug 43 delivered; 1943–45 assigned to the NAOTC, 9th District—stationed at Chicago, IL.

83481

Aug 43 delivered; 1943–44 assigned to the EASTSEAFRON—stationed at Boston, MA; 1944–45 assigned to SERVLANT (COM4THFLEET)—stationed at Boston, MA; 4 Mar 59 decommissioned; 30 Dec 59 sold.

83482

Sep 43 delivered; 1943–44 assigned to the EASTSEAFRON—stationed at Boston, MA; 1944–45 assigned to SERVLANT (COM4THFLEET)—stationed at Boston, MA; Apr 45 assigned to the COM7THFLEET—stationed at ABHD Guam (B2A5); 4 Nov 59 decommissioned; 18 May 60 sold.

83483

Sep 43 delivered; 1943–44 assigned to the EASTSEAFRON—stationed at Boston, MA; 1944–45 assigned to SERVLANT (COM4THFLEET)—stationed at Boston, MA; 20 Jun 62 decommissioned; 27 Nov 63 sold.

83484

Sep 43 delivered; 1943–44 assigned to the EASTSEAFRON—stationed at Boston, MA; 1944–45 assigned to SERVLANT (COM4THFLEET)—stationed at Boston, MA; 15 Apr 63 decommissioned; 14 May 63 transferred to USN.

83485

Sep 43 delivered; 1943–44 assigned to the EASTSEAFRON—stationed at Norfolk, VA; 1944–45 assigned to SERVLANT (COM4THFLEET)—stationed at Norfolk, VA; 7 Oct 52 decommissioned; 15 May 53 sold.

83486

Sep 43 delivered; 1943–Dec 44 assigned to the 7th District—stationed at New Smyrna Beach, FL; Dec 44–1945 assigned to the 1st District—stationed at Boothbay, ME; 3 Nov 61 decommissioned; 20 Aug 62 sold.

83487

1943–Dec 44 assigned to the 7th District—stationed at New Smyrna Beach, FL; Dec 44–1945 assigned to the 1st District—stationed at Narragansett, RI; 20 Feb 62 stricken.

83488

Oct 43 delivered; 1943–45 assigned to the 7th District—stationed at St. Augustine, FL; 6 Oct 58 decommissioned; 21 Apr 59 sold.

83489

Oct 43 delivered; 1943–45 assigned to the 7th District—stationed at St. Augustine, FL; 7 Sep 62 sold.

83490

Oct 43 delivered; 1944–45 assigned to the COM12THFLEET—stationed at Poole, England; Jul 44 assigned to USCG Rescue Flotilla No. 1—served in Normandy Invasion as USCG 49; 15 Jun 61 decommissioned; 25 Apr 63 sold.

83491

Oct 43 delivered; 1943–44 assigned to the GULFSEAFRON—stationed at Key West, FL; 1944–Jul 45 assigned to SERVLANT (COM4THFLEET)—stationed at Key West, FL; Jul 45 assigned to the 8th District—stationed at New Orleans, LA; 9 Dec 60 decommissioned; 15 Mar 63 sold.

83492

Oct 43 delivered; 1943–44 assigned to the GULFSEAFRON—stationed at Key West, FL; 1944–Jul 45 assigned to the SERVLANT (COM4THFLEET)—stationed at Key West, FL; Jul 45 assigned to the 8th District—stationed at New Orleans, LA.

83493

Oct 43 delivered; 1944–45 assigned to the COM12THFLEET—stationed at Poole, England; Jun 44 assigned to USCG Rescue Flotilla No. 1—served in Normandy Invasion as USCG 50; 13 Dec 61 decommissioned; 13 Oct 62 disposed of by sinking.

83494

Nov 43 delivered; 1944–45 assigned to the COM12THFLEET—stationed at Poole, England; Jun 44 assigned to USCG Rescue Flotilla No. 1—served in Normandy Invasion as USCG 51.

83495

Nov 43 delivered; Dec 43 transferred to Peru—became CS 5.

83496

Nov 43 delivered; Dec 43 transferred to Peru—became CS 6.

83497

Nov 43 delivered; 1943–45 assigned to the 7th District—stationed at St. Augustine, FL; 6 Dec 61 decommissioned; 14 Jun 62 disposed of by sinking.

83498

Nov 43 delivered; 1943–45 assigned to the 7th District—stationed at St. Augustine, FL.

83499

Nov 43 delivered; 1943–45 assigned to CG Headquarters—stationed at Training Station, St. Augustine, FL; 1 Jul 59 decommissioned; 4 Nov 59 sold.

83500

Nov 43 delivered; 1944–45 assigned to the COM12THFLEET—stationed at Poole, England; Jun 44 assigned to USCG Rescue Flotilla No. 1—served in Normandy Invasion as USCG 52.

83501

Nov 43 delivered; 1944–45 assigned to the COM12THFLEET—stationed at Poole, England; Jun 44 assigned to USCG Rescue Flotilla No. 1—served in Normandy Invasion as USCG 53; 15 Jun 61 decommissioned; 14 Jun 62 disposed of by sinking.

83502

Nov 43 delivered; 1944–45 assigned to the COM12THFLEET—stationed at Poole, England; Jun 44 assigned to USCG Rescue Flotilla No. 1—served in Normandy Invasion as USCG 54.

83503

Nov 43 delivered; 1944–45 assigned to the COM12THFLEET—stationed at Poole, England; Jun 44 assigned to USCG Rescue Flotilla No. 1—served in Normandy Invasion as USCG 55; 29 Dec 60 decommissioned; 21 Aug 62 sold.

83504

Dec 43 delivered; 1943–45 assigned to the GULFSEAFRON—stationed at Miami, FL; 3 May 61 decommissioned; 8 Nov 62 sold.

83505

Dec 43 delivered; 1943–45 assigned to the 7th District—stationed at Fort Pierce, FL.

83506

Dec 43 delivered; 1943–45 assigned to the 7th District—stationed at Key West, FL; 15 May 61 decommissioned; 22 Mar 66 disposed of by sinking.

83507

Dec 43 delivered; 1943–45 assigned to the 8th District—stationed at New Orleans, LA.

83508

Dec 43 delivered; 1943–45 assigned to the 5th District—stationed at Norfolk, VA; summer 45 assigned to the COM7THFLEET—stationed at ABHD Eniwetok (B2A8).

83509

Dec 43 delivered; 1943–45 assigned to the 7th District—stationed at Miami, FL; summer 45 assigned to the COM7THFLEET—stationed at ABHD Saipan (B2A4).

83510

Dec 43 delivered; Mar 44 transferred to Mexico—became CS 02.

83511

Dec 43 delivered; 1943–45 assigned to the COM12THFLEET—stationed at Poole, England; Jun 44 assigned to USCG Rescue Flotilla No. 1—served in Normandy Invasion as USCG 56.

83512

Dec 43 delivered; 1943–45 assigned to the COM12THFLEET—stationed at Poole, England; Jun 44 assigned to USCG Rescue Flotilla No. 1—served in Normandy Invasion as USCG 57.

83513

Dec 43 delivered; early 44 assigned to the EASTSEAFRON—stationed at Little Creek, VA; 1944–45 assigned to the COM12THFLEET—stationed at Poole, England; Jun 44 assigned to USCG Rescue Flotilla No. 1—served in Normandy Invasion as USCG 58.

83514

Jan 44 delivered; 1944–45 assigned to the COM12THFLEET—stationed at Poole, England; Jun 44 assigned to the USCG Rescue Flotilla No. 1—served in Normandy Invasion as USCG 59; 24 Oct 45 decommissioned.

83515

Jan 44 delivered; 1944–45 assigned to the GULFSEAFRON—stationed at Miami, FL.

83516

Jan 44 delivered; 1944–45 assigned to the COM12THFLEET—stationed at Poole, England; Jun 44 assigned to USCG Rescue Flotilla No. 1—served in Normandy Invasion as USCG 60.

83517

Jan 44 delivered; 1944–45 assigned to the EASTSEAFRON—stationed at

New York, NY; 1945 assigned to PHILSEAFRON, USCG PTC Flotilla No. 1—stationed at Manicani Island.

83518

Jan 44 delivered; 1944–45 assigned to the EASTSEAFRON—stationed at Norfolk, VA; 15 Jun 61 decommissioned; 15 Mar 63 sold.

83519

Jan 44 delivered; 1944–45 assigned to the EASTSEAFRON—stationed at Norfolk, VA.

83520

Jan 44 delivered; 1944–45 assigned to the EASTSEAFRON—stationed at Charleston, SC; 1945 assigned to PHILSEAFRON, USCG PTC Flotilla No. 1—stationed at Manicani Island.

83521

Jan 44 delivered; 1944–45 assigned to the EASTSEAFRON—stationed at Charleston, SC; 1945 assigned to PHILSEAFRON, USCG PTC Flotilla No. 1—stationed at Manicani Island.

83522

Jan 44 delivered; 1944–Dec 44 assigned to the GULFSEAFRON—stationed at New Orleans, LA; Dec 44–Jun 45 assigned to the 7th District—stationed at Miami, FL; Jun 45 assigned to the 13th District—stationed at Hammond, OR.

83523

Jan 44 delivered; 1944–45 assigned to the GULFSEAFRON—stationed at New Orleans, LA; 18 Dec 62 decommissioned; 26 May 64 sold.

83524

Feb 44 delivered; 1944–45 assigned to the GULFSEAFRON—stationed at Miami, FL; 1 Nov 60 decommissioned; 26 Sep 61 destroyed by fire.

83525

Feb 44 delivered; 1944–45 assigned to the GULFSEAFRON—stationed at Miami, FL; Jan 45 assigned to the 11th District—stationed at San Pedro, CA, and used for training; Apr 45 assigned to the COM7THFLEET—shipped 29 May—stationed at ABHD Saipan (B2A4).

83526

Feb 44 delivered; 1944–Jun 45 assigned to the GULFSEAFRON—stationed at Miami, FL; Jun 45 assigned to the 11th District—stationed at San Diego, CA.

83527

Feb 44 delivered; 1944–45 assigned to the GULFSEAFRON—stationed at Miami, FL; 18 Dec 62 decommissioned; 30 Jul 64 sold.

83528

Feb 44 delivered; 1944–45 assigned to the GULFSEAFRON—stationed at New Orleans, LA; summer 45 assigned to the COM7THFLEET—stationed at ABHD Saipan (B2A4).

83529

Feb 44 delivered; 1944–Dec 45 assigned to the GULFSEAFRON—stationed at Miami, FL; Dec 44–1945 assigned to the 8th District—stationed at Pascagoula, MS; 15 Mar 62 stricken.

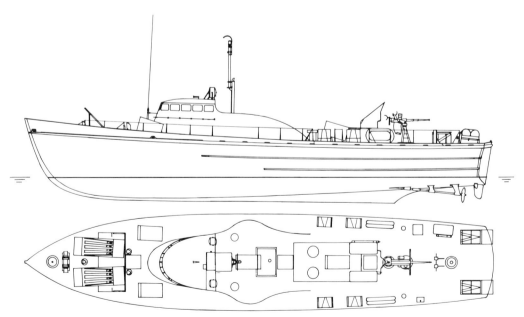

Sketch of an 83-footer in wartime configuration.

CG Number	Year Built	Description	Armament	District Acquired	Dates and Type of Service
83003	1926	ex-*Restless II*, #225998	small arms	9	29 Aug 42–Mar 45; offshore patrol
83002	—	—	—	3	Ex-CGC 490
83001	1920	ex-*Mariana II*, #?	1 .50 cal; 2 dc tracks	3	10 Feb 42–8 Oct 45; yacht, ex-CG 656
B82003	—	—	—	—	Oct 44–?
82002	1930	ex-*Sachem II*, #229595	1 .50 cal	3	30 Jul 42–28 Mar 44; offshore patrol
82001	1925	ex-*Onawa*, #234687	small arms	13	1 Aug 42–29 Aug 45; offshore patrol
81009F	—	ex-*Santa Genima*, #241159	—	1	Aug 45–May 46; fireboat, previously CG 75002F
81008	1931	—	1 1-pdr	—	Ex-83002, ex-CG 490
B81007	—	—	—	13	Barge
81006	1922	ex-*Jane Dore*, #222228	small arms	3	2 Nov 42–30 Oct 45; offshore patrol
81005	1930	ex-*Sage*, #229533	—	9	12 Aug 42–1 Jul 44; harbor patrol
81004	1938	ex-*Tamaris*, #237788	2 dc tracks	9	23 Aug 42–19 Jul 45; offshore patrol
81003	1928	ex-*Nina III*, #227340	—	9	6 Aug 42–11 Nov 43; offshore patrol
81002	—	ex-*Isabel N*, #?	small arms	4	10 Jul 42–17 Aug 45; offshore patrol
81001F	1936	ex-*Jennie & Lucia*, #235811	—	1	29 Apr 42–8 Apr 44; fireboat & harbor patrol

CG 81004 (ex-*Tamaris*) on her way out to ASW patrol. Her armament stands out clearly—a .50 cal water-cooled machine gun is mounted on her bow, and two short depth-charge tracks are fitted on the stern.

80-FOOTERS*

Number	Builder	Commissioned	Disposition
CG 80300 (ex-CG 406)	Gibbs Gas Engine Co.,	10 Mar 37	*Decomm and sold 1945–46*
CG 80301 (ex-CG 407)	Jacksonville, FL	22 Apr 37	
CG 80302 (ex-CG 408)	Walter J. McInnis of	12 May 37	
CG 80303 (ex-CG 409)	Eldredge-McInnis, Inc.,	2 Jun 37	
CG 80304 (ex-CG-410)	Boston, MA (design agent)	24 Jun 37	
CG 80305 (ex-CG 411)	Harbor Boat Building Co.,	4 Oct 37	
CG 80306 (ex-CG 412)	Terminal Island, CA	6 Nov 37	
CG 80307 (ex-CG 413)	D. M. Callis Co., Ltd.	24 Nov 37	
CG 80308 (ex-CG 414)	(design agent)	23 Dec 37	

Cost (does not include costs of radio, ordnance, supplies)

East Coast		West Coast	
Hull	$28,900	Hull	$36,250
Machinery	18,000	Machinery	18,000
Change	1,740	Change	1,060
Total	$48,640 each	Total	$55,310 each

Hull
Displacement (tons)   51.7 fl (1937); 52 fl (1945)
Length   80'9" oa; 78' wl
Beam   15'8" max
Draft   4' max (1937); 4'6" max (1945)

Machinery
Main Engines   4 Vimalert M-12 gasoline engines mounted in duplex
SHP   1,600
Propeller   Twin

Performance
Max Speed   25.87 kts on trials (1937)
   20 kts (1945)
Max Sustained   25 kts, 290 mi radius (1937)
Cruising   11 kts, 704 mi radius (1937)
   12 kts, 650 mi radius (1945)

Logistics
Gasoline (95%)   1,900 gal
Complement   7 to 9 men (1945)

Electronics (1945)
Detection Radar   80300, 80301, 80302: BK; others: none
Sonar   80300, 80301: QBE-3; 80305–80308: QBE; others: none

Armament
1937   1 1-pdr
1942   1 20mm/80; 2 Mousetraps; 2 dc tracks

*Date table, cost data, and design history prepared and copyrighted by William D. Wilkinson.

CG 80301 wearing her original numbers, shortly after commissioning, 28 May 37. Compare the size of the scuppers on the forecastle with those in the following photograph. The similarities between this design and the 83-foot design are apparent.

Design

The 80-footers were a follow-on to the 78-footers, in the continuing "design war" with rum runners, each side seeking the faster boats. The repeal of Prohibition in Dec 33 probably restricted the number built, but the Great Depression recovery plan guaranteed they would be constructed. The Coast Guard prepared preliminary plans; the builder chose which naval architects would prepare the detail plans. Architect D. M. Callis was selected to design the boats built on the West Coast; Walter J. McInnis, those built on the East Coast. The Vimalert engine was developed from the famous WW I Liberty 12 aircraft engine, but it was not gas efficient and required constant tuning. The wheelhouse was of Everdur Bronze construction. The 80-footer was the direct predecessor to the 83-footers.

Service

During WW II, used for ASW patrol and port security—high fuel consumption limited their use for convoying; 24 Jun 42 CG 80302 assisted in rescue of 25 survivors from the SS *Manuela*; Apr–Oct 43, 3 units transferred to 9th District and operated as plane guard duty for the USS *Sable* and the USS *Wolverine*; ASW armament removed Dec 44; 1 unit participated in air-sea rescue tests off Rockland, ME; 1944–45 used as rescue boats.

CG 80302 and another 80-footer astern at the Coast Guard Yard, Curtis Bay, MD, 16 Feb 44. Note the enlarged scupper in the bulwark. The 80-footer had a large well deck forward, which had a tendency to fill with water and affect the trim of the craft. These scuppers were enlarged during the war to improve drainage.

CG Number	Year Built	Description	Armament	District Acquired	Dates and Type of Service
80014	1930	ex-*Satan's Wife*, #230175	—	1	28 Oct 42–10 Feb 44; offshore patrol
80013	1933	ex-*Talisman*, #232279	small arms	3	2 Oct 42–30 Aug 45; offshore patrol
80012	1929	ex-*Compadre*, #227268	—	7	30 Sep 42–Jun 44
80011	1930	ex-*Minoco*, #229886	2 dc tracks	9	9 Aug 42–24 Sep 45; offshore patrol
80010	1927	ex-*Mary S*, #226749	—	9	31 Aug 42–1 Jul 44; offshore patrol
80009	1926	ex-*Harriet B*, #225365	small arms	9	15 Aug 42–30 Aug 45; harbor patrol
80008F	1914	ex-*John T. Lillis*, #212104	—	9	30 Jun 42–Jul 45; fireboat
B80007	—	—	—	13	22 May 42–Sep 45; barge
80006F	1918	ex-*Hourless*, #217783	—	1	6 Jul 42–8 Sep 45; fireboat
80005F	1925	ex-*Wilanna*, #225192	—	3	19 May 42–6 Sep 45; fireboat
80004	1937	—	small arms	1	Ex-CGC 415
80003	1920	ex-*Sangamo*, #219424	small arms	3	10 Feb 42–11 Dec 45; yacht, ex-CG 658
80002	1926	ex-*Rhesus*, #225605	small arms	4	5 Jan 42–30 Jul 45; yacht, ex-CG 654
80001	1930	ex-*Gomol*, #229923	small arms	3	2 Jun 42–24 Aug 45; harbor patrol
79001	1935	ex-*Florence V*, #234212	—	4	5 Jan 42–21 Aug 44; yacht, ex-CG 653

78-FOOTERS (THE "400s")

Number	Builder	Commissioned	Disposition
CG 78300–78305 (ex-CG 400–CG 405)	Southern Shipyard Corp., Newport News, VA	11 May 31–17 Sep 31	*Decomm* 4 Oct 45– 20 Feb 46; *sold* 19 Jul 46– 14 Jan 48

Cost
  $49,000 each
Hull
  Displacement (tons)   43 fl (1931, 1945)
  Length   78'9" oa; 78' wl
  Beam   14'8" max
  Draft   3'11" max (1931); 4'9" (1945)
Machinery
  Main Engines   2 Sterling Viking II, 8-cyl gasoline
  SHP   1,130
  Propellers   Twin
Performance
  Max Speed   24 kts on trials (1931)
      18 kts (1945)
  Cruising   11 kts, 500 mi radius (1945)
Logistics
  Gasoline (95%)   1,200 gal
  Complement   6 men (1931); 8 men (1945)
Electronics
  Detection Radar   None

Sonar (1945)   78300, 78303, 78304, 78305: QBE; others: none
Armament
  1931   1 1-pdr, small arms
  1945   78300: 1 .50 cal; 78301: 1 20mm/80;
      78302: 1 .50 cal; 1 1-pdr; 2 dc tracks;
      78303: 1 .50 cal; 1 1-pdr; 1 dc track;
      78304: 1 1-pdr; 2 dc tracks; 78305: 1 dc track

Design
The 78-footers were a follow-on to the 75-footers. In the upper Long Island Sound, "rummies" had developed faster craft than the 75-footers; so the 78-footers were designed to restore superiority. The Coast Guard prepared the preliminary design, and naval architect Walter J. McInnis of Boston, MA, was appointed design agent to develop the final plans. The 78-footers sacrificed crew accommodations and cruising radius in order to obtain higher speeds than the 75-footers. (*See* 75-footers and 125-foot cutters.)

Service
In October and November of 1936 all units transferred to the Pacific Coast; during WW II, used for inshore convoy patrols, air-sea rescue, and ASW patrols—high fuel consumption restricted usefulness.

CG 78303 (still wearing her original number CG 403) running trials in 1931 off Newport News, VA.

CG Number	Year Built	Description	Armament	District Acquired	Dates and Type of Service
78007	—	ex-*Hickman Sea Sled*	—	1	?–May 45
78006F	1887	ex-*Shamrock*, #116151	—	7	2 Jun 42–1 Nov 44; fireboat
78005	1927	ex-*A.F. Rich*, #226432	—	—	Dec 42–Apr 42
78004	—	ex-*Caleb Haley*, #?	—	—	Dec 42–Feb 43
78003	—	ex-*Sockeye*, #?	—	—	Sep 42–Feb 43
78002	1912	ex-*Esperanza*, #210329	—	6	27 Jul 42–7 Feb 44; offshore patrol
78001	1917	ex-*Siwash*, #224771	small arms	3	?
77003	1926	ex-*Haliglo II*, #225996	1 .50 cal; 2 dc tracks	3	23 Nov 42–22 Jun 45; offshore patrol
77002	1921	ex-*Spray III*, #221553	—	9	11 Nov 42–18 Feb 44; offshore patrol
77001	1917	ex-*Spiker*, #214929	small arms	9	25 Jul 42–13 Nov 44; harbor patrol
76005	1929	ex-*Saunterer*, #228511	—	3	17 Nov 42–17 Sep 43; offshore patrol
76004	1936	ex-*Lorine III*, #235319	—	1	2 Nov 42–6 Sep 44; offshore patrol
76003	1932	ex-*Florence Magann*, #231697	—	1	18 Sep 42–24 Aug 44; offshore patrol
76002	1929	ex-*Anhita*, #229886	2 .50 cal; 2 dc tracks	9	18 Sep 42–10 Mar 45; offshore patrol
76001F	1912	ex-*Comanche*, #210296	—	1	10 Jun 42–19 Sep 45; harbor patrol and fireboat
76000F	—	—	—	—	?–?; fireboat, 20 Oct 42 fought fire on *Surewater*
75010F	1928	ex-*George C. Henry*, #228049	—	5	5 Jun 42–26 Apr 46; fireboat
75009	1941	ex-*Beaver*, #?	—	9	13 Oct 42–16 Oct 47; offshore patrol
75008	1935	ex-*Innisfall*, #?	small arms	1	31 Dec 41–25 Sep 46; training, ex-CGR 505
75007	1921	ex-*Cesor*, #221786	—	9	22 Aug 42–24 Jan 44; offshore patrol, lost
75006	1930	ex-*Deltra*, #229575	1 .50 cal; 2 dc tracks	9	12 Aug 42–16 Mar 45; harbor patrol
75005F	—	ex-*Pioneer*, #?	—	1	Fireboat
75004F	—	ex-*Go Getter*, #222387	—	13	29 Jun 42–7 Dec 42; fireboat
75003	1923	ex-*Restless Too*, #222891	1 .50 cal; 2 dc tracks	9	15 May 42–6 Mar 45
75002F	—	ex-*Santa Gemma*, #241159	—	1	2 May 42–Aug 45; fireboat, became CG 81009F
75001F	1941	ex-*Nancy B*, #240532	—	1	2 May 42–26 Aug 46; fireboat

75-FOOTERS ("SIX-BITTERS")

Number	Builder	Commissioned	Disposition
CG 74300–CG 74301 CG 74303–CG 74310 CG 74313–CG 74316 CG 74318–CG 74319 CG 74321–CG 74326 CG 74328 CG 74330 CG 74332–CG 74335 CG 74337 CG 74339–CG 74350	Various yards	21 Oct 24 through 18 Jul 25	All sold by early 1946

75-FOOT PATROL BOAT NUMBERING*

Later Number	Original Number	Later Number	Original Number
CG 74300	CG 119	CG 74341	CG 265
CG 74301	CG 128	CG 74342	CG 270
CG 74302	CG 130	CG 74343	CG 271
CG 74303	CG 131	CG 74344	CG 288
CG 74304	CG 135		
CG 74305	CG 139		
CG 74306	CG 140		
CG 74307	CG 143		
CG 74308	CG 145		
CG 74309	CG 147		
CG 74310	CG 148		
CG 74311	CG 153		
CG 74312	CG 155		
CG 74313	CG 156		
CG 74314	CG 157		
CG 74315	CG 158		
CG 74316	CG 159		
CG 74317	CG 170		
CG 74318	CG 171		
CG 74319	CG 172		
CG 74320	CG 173		
CG 74321	CG 176		
CG 74322	CG 178		
CG 74323	CG 185		
CG 74324	CG 186		
CG 74325	CG 190		
CG 74326	CG 192		
CG 74327	CG 211		
CG 74328	CG 212		
CG 74329	CG 213		
CG 74330	CG 214		
CG 74331	CG 216		
CG 74332	CG 218		
CG 74333	CG 219		
CG 74334	CG 226		
CG 74335	CG 228		
CG 74336	CG 240		
CG 74337	CG 244		
CG 74338	CG 254		
CG 74339	CG 255		
CG 74340	CG 262		

A 75-footer, CG 159 (later CG 74316), built by T. H. Soule of Freeport, ME, returns from patrol during the Prohibition era. Two hundred and three were constructed for the CG; however, only thirty-six remained in service by the time of WW II. (Courtesy of the National Archives.)

*Numbering table, building program table, and design history prepared and copyrighted by William D. Wilkinson.

75-FOOT PATROL BOAT BUILDING PROGRAM

Original Numbers	Builder	Location of Builder	Contract Price*
CG 100—CG 114	John H. Mathis Yacht Building Co.	Camden, NJ	18,675
CG 115—CG 129	DeFoe Boat and Motor Works	Bay City, MI	20,375
CG 130—CG 139	Crowninshield Shipbuilding Co.	Fall River, MA	21,450
CG 140—CG 149	Dachel-Carter Boat Co.	Benton Harbor, MI	21,950
CG 150—CG 159	T.H. Soule	Freeport, ME	22,945
CG 160—CG 169	New York Launch and Engine Co.	New York, NY	23,600
CG 170—CG 179	Rice Brothers Corp.	East Boothbay, ME	23,950
CG 180—CG 189	Southern Shipyard Corp.	Newport News, VA	24,000
CG 190—CG 192	U.S. Navy Yard	Portsmouth, NH	24,140
CG 193—CG 202	Chance Marine Construction Co., Inc.	Annapolis, MD	24,250
CG 203—CG 212	Kingston Dry Dock and Construction Co.	Kingston, NY	24,750
CG 213—CG 222	Vineyard Shipbuilding Co.	Milford, DE	24,770
CG 223—CG 232	Colonna's Shipyard, Inc.	Norfolk, VA	25,000
CG 233—CG 242	Luders Marine Construction Co.	Stamford, CT	25,675
CG 243—CG 252	Gibbs Gas Engine Co.	Jacksonville, FL	26,900
CG 253—CG 262	A.W. DeYoung	Alameda, CA	22,167
CG 263—CG 277	Lake Union Dry Dock and Machine Works	Seattle, WA	22,800
CG 278—CG 292	John H. Mathis Yacht Building Co.	Camden, NJ	18,675
CG 293—CG 302	Gibbs Gas Engine Co.	Jacksonville, FL	19,445

*Does not include cost of engines, armament, radio equipment, etc. These items supplied by the government.

Cost

Total cost per cutter: $37,500 average; *see* Building program table

Hull

Displacement (tons)	37.5 fl (1924); 42 fl (1945)
Length	74'11" oa; 74'1" bp
Beam	13'8" mb
Draft	3'9" max (1924); 5' max (1945)

Machinery

Main Engines	2 Sterling 6-cyl gasoline (except CG 74348, 2 Lathrop gasoline)
SHP	400 (except CG 74348, 74350)
Propellers	Twin

Performance

Max speed	15.7 kts on trials (1924)

Logistics

Gasoline	1,000 gal
Complement	8 men (1924); 1 officer, 12 men (1945, combat areas); 8 men (1945, noncombat areas)

Electronics (1945)

Detection Radar	74301–74304, 74306, 74310, 74316, 74321, 74324, 74325, 74330, 74332, 74334, 74344: BK; others: none

Sonar

74308: QBE-1; 74304, 74310, 74316, 74321, 74325, 74326, 74328–74330, 74339–74341: QBE; others: none

Armament (1945)

1 20mm/80, 2 dc tracks (some units); 1 1-pdr, 1 .50 cal mg (some units); 74301, 74306–74309, 74322, 74332, 74335, 74337, 74344: unarmed

Design

To combat smuggling during Prohibition, the Coast Guard developed offshore patrol vessels for an outer coastal ring and inshore patrol craft for an inner one. The 75-footer was the first class to be developed for the inshore patrol. The Coast Guard prepared the preliminary design, and the completed plans were done by John Trumpy of Mathis Yacht Building Co., Camden, NJ. Two hundred and three 75-footers were built by 17 yards, making them the largest single type constructed for the Coast Guard up to that time. These proved to be very seaworthy units. By WW II, only 36 remained in service; 6 units that had been sold, however, were re-acquired during the war and numbered CG 74345–CG 74350. *See also* 78-footers, 83-footers, and 125-footers.

Service

During WW II, used for inshore convoy patrols, air-sea rescue, ASW patrols, and port security duties; 10 Nov 44 CG 74327 rammed and sunk by the USS *Thornback* in the sweep channel of Portsmouth, NH.

CG Number	Year Built	Description	Armament	District Acquired	Dates and Type of Service
74005	1930	ex-*Helen H*, #229507	2 .50 cal; 2 dc tracks	9	18 Sep 42–10 Sep 45; offshore patrol
74004	1932	ex-*Alrema*, #231740	—	9	11 Aug 42–12 Sep 44; offshore patrol
74003	1926	ex-*Charlotte II*, #225683	—	3	16 Jul 42–4 May 44; offshore patrol, damaged by explosion

CG Number	Year Built	Description	Armament	District Acquired	Dates and Type of Service
74002	1926	ex-*Wilmar IV*, #225692	small arms	5	27 May 42–20 Sep 45; harbor patrol
74001	1920	ex-*Rainbow*, #200074	—	11	12 Feb 42–12 Dec 44; patrol, ex-CG 651
73004	1932	ex-*Estharr*, #231990	2 .50 cal; 1 dc track	9	3 Oct 42–10 Mar 45; offshore patrol
73003	1927	ex-*Maya V*, #227032	—	1	7 Jul 42–20 Mar 43; harbor patrol
73002	1922	ex-*Elsie*, #222463	—	4	28 Jul 42–5 Nov 43; offshore patrol
73001F	1907	ex-*John Roen, Jr.*, #203853	—	9	21 May 42–16 Nov 45; fireboat

72-FOOTERS

Number	Builder	Commissioned	Disposition
72300 (ex-CG 440)	Chance Marine Construction Co., Inc., Annapolis, MD	29 Apr 37	*Decomm* Dec 44; *sold* 5 June 45
72301 (ex-CG 441)	Chance Marine Construction Co., Inc., Annapolis, MD	9 May 37	*Decomm* Sep 45; *sold* 14 Nov 47

Cost

CG 440		*CG 441*	
Hull	$24,601.14	Hull	$26,601.14
Machinery	18,000.00	Machinery	18,000.00
Changes	2,798.80	Changes	2,798.80
Total	$45,399.94	Total	$47,399.94

Hull
Displacement (tons)   27.2 fl (1937); 31 fl (1945)
Length   72′ oa; 70′ bp
Beam   14′2″ mb
Draft   3′9″ max (1937)

Machinery
Main Engines   4 Vimalert M-12 gasoline engines mounted in duplex
SHP   1,600
Propellers   Twin
Performance
Max Speed   23 kts (1945); 29.5 kts on trials (1937)
Cruising   12 kts, 640 mi radius (1945)
Logistics
Gasoline (95%)   1,500 gal
Complement   6 men (1937); 7 men (1945)

A 72-footer running trials, 1937.

Electronics
  None
Armament (1945)
  Small arms, 2 dc tracks
Design
  The 72-footers were day boats—their crews were to be billeted ashore. Originally,

these units were to have been 65-footers similar to those built by William Whiting of Long Beach, CA, but the designer, Walter J. McInnis, did not believe the desired speed could be achieved with this length craft.

Service
  During WW II, served on patrol duty; 14 Sep 44 CG 72300 damaged in hurricane. *See also* 65-footers.

CG Number	Year Built	Description	Armament	District Acquired	Dates and Type of Service
72014F	1918	ex-*Pioneer*, #216862	—	1	16 Jul 42–28 Sep 45; fireboat
72013	1900	—	—	—	
72012	1920	ex-*Night Witch*, #226155	—	1	27 Oct 42–Nov 44; offshore patrol
72011	1919	ex-*Unga*, #217701	—	13	Nov 42–14 Apr 43
72010	1936	ex-*Blue Water*, #234954	—	5	9 Sep 42–20 Sep 45; offshore patrol
72009	1928	ex-*Selarch*, #227819	—	9	3 Aug 42–16 Nov 44; offshore patrol
72008F	1901	ex-*Julian T. Bradshaw*, #130945	—	5	9 Jul 42–20 Sep 45; fireboat
72007	1930	ex-*Panzola II*, #229936	—	7	13 Jul 42–28 Apr 44; offshore patrol
72006F	—	ex-*George C. Henry*	—	5	Fireboat
72005	1932	—	1 1-pdr, 2 dc tracks	3	ex-CGC 439
72004F	1925	ex-*El Gabilan*, #224620	—	11	25 Jul 42–25 Sep 45; harbor patrol and fireboat
72003	1930	ex-*Bidgee*, #229328	—	1	15 Dec 41–Nov 44; yacht, ex-CG 655
72002	1932	ex-*Catalyst*, #231686	1 .50 cal, 2 dc tracks	13	9 Jul 14–13 Sep 45; harbor patrol
72001F	1925	ex-*Ho Toi*, #224737	—	5	15 May 42–17 May 46; fireboat
71002	1940	ex-*High Tide*, #240422	—	9	10 Sep 42–19 Jun 44; offshore patrol, ex-69002
71001	1939	ex-*Winifred M. II*, #239455	—	1	2 May 42–22 Jan 45; harbor patrol
70014	1928	ex-*Northern Queen*, #227496	—	—	Dec 42–15 Apr 43
70013	1922	ex-*Venture II*, #222134	—	5	29 Sep 43–Jan 45; offshore patrol
70012	—	?	—	5	3 Nov 42–5 Sep 44; offshore patrol
70011	—	ex-*Sunbeam*, #326577	—	13	25 Jul 42–29 Mar 44; harbor patrol
70010	1927	ex-*Who*, #226476	—	9	27 Aug 42–7 Feb 44; offshore patrol
70009	1927	ex-*Sally II*, #226356	—	1	1 Jul 42–Nov 44; offshore patrol
70008	1939	ex-*Episode*, #238637	—	9	11 Nov 42–Nov 44; offshore patrol
70007	1926	ex-*Paul L*, #225418	—	13	25 Jul 42–7 Apr 44; harbor patrol
70006	1926	ex-*Evening Star*, #225759	—	4	31 Jul 42–16 Dec 42; offshore patrol destroyed in collision

CG 72001F is the former cabin cruiser *Ho Toi*. Craft converted to fireboats were of varied configurations.

CG Number	Year Built	Description	Armament	District Acquired	Dates and Types of Service
70005	1929	ex-*Aquaria III*, #229093	—	6	29 Jun 42–11 Nov 43; harbor patrol
70004F	—	ex-*Tessler*, #201789	—	9	2 May 42–8 Sep 45; fireboat
70003	—	ex-*Niantic*, #239730	—	1	13 Jun 42–3 May 43; harbor patrol, total loss
70002F	—	ex-*Pelican*, #239049	—	1	29 Apr 42–6 Sep 45; fireboat
70001F	—	ex-*Queen of Palm Beach*, #241243	—	4	6 May 42–3 Nov 45; fireboat
69002	1931	ex-*High Tide*, #230608	—	—	—
69001	1930	ex-*Pagan*, #230148	—	13	16 Jun 42–Feb 45; harbor patrol
68011	1920	ex-*Over the Top*, #220364	—	13	Dec 42–Mar 43
68010	—	ex-*Superior*, #?	—	13	Dec 42–May 43
68009	1935	ex-*Bataan*, #254053	1 20mm, 1 6-pdr, 2 dc tracks	7	15 Nov 42–14 Feb 45; offshore patrol
68008	1927	ex-*Charmae*, #225539	—	1	28 Oct 42–Aug 45; harbor patrol
68007	1938	ex-*Edlu II*, #237137	—	3	21 Jul 42–Jul 45; offshore patrol
68006	1935	ex-*Carmelita*, #234281	—	13	31 Aug 42–Nov 44; offshore patrol
68005	1928	ex-*Off Duty*, #227451	—	4	28 Jul 42–Mar 43; offshore patrol
68004	1939	ex-*Avoca*, #238524	—	3	30 Jul 42–28 Nov 44; offshore patrol
68003F	1938	ex-*Sportfisher*, #237264	—	11	10 Jul 42–2 Aug 46; fireboat

CG Number	Year Built	Description	Armament	District Acquired	Dates and Type of Service
68002F	—	ex-*Shamrock*, #?	—	7	Fireboat
68001	1930	ex-*Pearl Necklace II*, #230190	—	1	10 Jun 42–24 Sep 45; harbor patrol
67005	1928	ex-*Katherine M*, #227732	—	13	Dec 42–May 43
67004	1929	ex-*Tamarit*, #228487	—	5	26 Oct 42–4 Feb 46; offshore patrol
67003	1931	ex-*Lady Isabel*, #230639	—	7	5 Aug 42–Nov 44; offshore patrol
67001	1927	ex-*Tom Boy*, #226804	1 dc track	4	5 Jan 42–10 Aug 45; yacht
66007F	—	ex-*Josephine P*	—	1	Fireboat
66006	1937	ex-*Nancy Ann III*, #236305	—	9	1 Aug 42–4 Dec 45; offshore patrol
66005	1926	ex-*Latouche*, #225921	—	13	—
66004	1933	ex-*Gander*, #232316	—	3	30 Jun 42–19 Jul 46; harbor patrol
B66003	—	—	—	9	Barge
66002	1929	ex-*Mohican*, #228252	—	—	1 Jul 42–16 Aug 45; harbor patrol
66001F	1922	ex-*W. E. Hopkins*, #222435	—	5	15 May 42–29 Apr 46; fireboat

65-FOOTERS

Number	Builder	Commissioned	Disposition
65300 (ex-CG 442)	William Whiting, Long Beach, CA	2 Aug 37	*Decomm* 29 Apr 47; *sold* 22 Sep 47
65301 (ex-CG 443)	William Whiting, Long Beach, CA	31 Aug 37	*Decomm* 28 Nov 45; *sold* 1947

Cost
  $27,400 each
Hull
  Displacement (tons)   26.3 fl (1937)
  Length   65' oa; 63' bp
  Beam   14'1" mb
  Draft   3'9" max (1937)
Machinery
  Main Engines   4 Vimalert M-12 gasoline engines mounted in duplex
  SHP   1,600
  Propellers   Twin
Performance
  Max Speed   27.7 kts on trials (1937 and 1945)
  Cruising   13.7 kts, 640 mi radius (1945)
Logistics
  Gasoline (95%)   1,600 gal
  Complement   6 men (1937); 7 men (1945)
Electronics
  None
Armament (1942)
  Small arms; 2 dc tracks

CG 65300 (old CG 442) running trials in 1937. The 65s and 72s were all very similar in appearance.

Design

The 65-footers were day boats. The Coast Guard prepared preliminary plans, and D. M. Callis, chosen by the builder, executed the detailed plans. Callis had designed the 80-footers built by Harbor Boat Building Co. as well. Like the 72-footers, the 65-footers were designed as day boats for high speed operation. They had a semi-round bottom, particularly sharp entries forward, and a substantial bow flare. *See also* 72-footers.

Service

WW II patrol duty on West Coast—CG 65300 was stationed at San Diego, CA, and CG 65301 at Alameda, CA.

CG Number	Year Built	Description	Armament	District Acquired	Dates and Type of Service
65023	1908	ex-*Henry W. Sawtelle*, #?	—	—	Aug 43–Feb 45
65022	—	—	—	—	Dec 42–Jun 44
B65021	—	ex-*Dootsie*, #?	—	8	Sep 42–Mar 44; barge
65020	1911	ex-*Hydah*, #208380	—	13	Nov 42–Apr 43
65019	1923	ex-*Nor'easter*, #223025	—	9	4 Nov 42–May 44; offshore patrol
65018F	1937	ex-*Hualapai II*, #237086	—	11	5 Sep 42–19 Sep 46; harbor patrol and fireboat
65017	—	ex-*Valhalla II*, #225948	—	9	1 Oct 42–9 Nov 45; offshore patrol
65016	1927	ex-*Curlew*, #153441	—	Academy	31 Jan 40–Jul 45; training—*see* WIX
65015F	1926	ex-*Nellie Crockett*, #225369	—	5	15 May 42–17 Nov 45; fireboat
65014F	1922	ex-*Transco No. 3*, #222337	—	3	18 May 42–15 Aug 45; fireboat
65013F	1922	ex-*Transco No. 2*, #222172	—	3	18 May 42–15 Apr 46; fireboat
65012F	—	ex-*Enterprise*, #232819	—	8	5 May 42–1 Aug 45; fireboat
65011F	1926	ex-*Vexeran*, #?	—	—	Sep 42–Feb 43; fireboat
65010	1924	ex-*Tara II*, #223840	—	7	30 Jul 42–16 Oct 44; offshore patrol
65009F	1938	ex-*Joseph Alioto*, #238066	—	12	11 May 42–19 Nov 45; fireboat
65008	1930	ex-*Nautilus*, #229849	—	9	14 Aug 42–18 Feb 44; offshore patrol
65007	1925	ex-*Docdeen*, #224503	—	8	30 Jul 42–20 Aug 43; offshore patrol, burned
65006F	1932	ex-*Helena G. Starn*, #222234	—	—	6 May 42–30 Jul 45; fireboat
65005	1932	ex-*Coryxa*, #231570	—	4	1 Dec 41–Oct 43; yacht
65004	1935	ex-*Zelbejan*, #234224	—	7	10 Jul 42–Aug 44; offshore patrol
65003	1941	ex-*Northwind*, #240924	—	13	29 Jul 42–26 Dec 45; harbor patrol
65002	1930	—	1 dc track	12	ex-CGC 5
65001	1925	ex-*Joe Weber*, #225183	—	7	26 Mar 42–7 Jul 45; yacht

64-FOOT HARBOR MOTORBOAT/TUG

Number	Builder	Commissioned	Disposition
CG 64300–64305	Patchogue Yacht Basin, Patchogue, NY	1944	NA
CG 64306–64311	Eiscott Boat Inc., City Island, NY	1944	NA
CG 64312–64314	Nunes Brothers, Sausalito, CA	1944	NA

Cost
  $43,591 each (1943 units)

Hull
  Displacement (tons)   65 fl (1945)
  Length   64'11" oa
  Beam   18'6" max
  Draft   6'6" max (1945)

Machinery
  Main Engine   1 Murphy diesel
  BHP   160
  Propellers   Single

Performance
  Max Speed   Est. 11 kts (1945)

Logistics
  Fuel Oil (95%)   1,120 gal
  Complement   5 men (1945)

Electronics
  None

Armament
  None

Design
  The design of these 64-foot harbor motorboats was probably based on the 63-foot AB class, small harbor tugs. Their hulls were of wood; they had round bottoms and a square stern.

Service
  During WW II, used for harbor patrol, light towing, and light ice-breaking.

CG 64312 was constructed by Nunes Brothers, Sausalito, CA, in 1944.

63-FOOT HARBOR MOTORBOAT/TUG

Number	Builder	Commissioned	Disposition
NA (28 units built?)	NA	1930s?	NA

Cost
  $57,398 each

Hull
  Displacement (tons)   69 fl (1944)
  Length   63'6" oa
  Beam   19'6" max
  Draft   5'5" max

Machinery
  Main Engines   1 diesel
  BHP   NA
  Propellers   Single

Performance
  Max Speed   11 kts (1944)

Logistics
  Fuel Oil (95%)   900 gal
  Complement   Day boat

Electronics
  None

Armament
  None

Design
  These craft were designed to inspect anchorages and to board vessels.

Service
  NA

AB 26 in 1936 after completing. These boats were used for boarding, search and rescue, and breaking thin ice around docks.

63-FOOT AIR-SEA RESCUE BOATS

Number	Builder	Commissioned	Disposition
CG 63019–63078	NA; CG 63019, CG 63020, CG 63049–63056 on loan from USA; all others on loan from USN	All prob 1944	All *decomm* prob 1946

Cost
  $75,000 each

Hull
  Displacement (tons)   23 light (1945)
  Length   63' oa
  Beam   15'3" max
  Draft   3'10" max (1945)

Machinery
  Main Engines   2 Hall Scott Defenders (except CG 63005, 2 Packards)
  SHP   1,260 (except CG 63005, 2,300)
  Propellers   Twin

Performance
  Max Speed   33.5 kts (1945); CG 63025 only, 45 kts (1945)

Logistics
  Gasoline (95%)   1,590 gal
  Complement   8 men (1945)

Electronics
  None

Armament
  None

Design
  These 63-foot craft were constructed of wood; they had a double-planked hull, a V-bottom, and a square stern. Each boat was fitted with 6 hospital berths in addition to crew spaces.

Service
  Stationed on all coasts as high-speed rescue craft.

CG 63042, Dec 44.

60-FOOT FIRE BARGES

Number	Builder	Commissioned	Disposition
CGB 60012F, 60013F, 60015F–60019F	Walter W. Johnson Co., Oakland, CA	All 1943	All *decomm* post–WW II

Cost
  NA

Hull
  Displacement (tons)   43 fl (1945)
  Length   60' oa
  Beam   18' max
  Draft   1'3" max (1945)

Machinery
  Auxiliary
  Engines   2 detachable Chrysler Marine tractors

BHP   286

Performance
  Max Speed   7 kts (1945)

Logistics
  Complement   9 men

Design
  These 60-foot fire barges were plywood construction. Each craft was fitted with 8 Chrysler pumping units.

Service
  All stationed on West Coast.

52-FOOT BUOY BOAT

Number	Builder	Commissioned	Disposition
CG 52302D, 52303D, 52305D	Coast Guard Yard, Curtis Bay, MD (later units only)	1944	NA

Cost
  NA

Hull
  Weight   70,000 lbs (1945)
  Length   52'4" oa
  Beam   15'6" max
  Draft   4'3" max (1945)

Machinery
  Main Engines   1 Buda Lathrop diesel
  BHP   120

Propellers   Single

Performance
  Max Speed   11 kts (1945)

Logistics
  Complement   3 men (1945)

Design
  Design based on a USLHS craft. Hoist capacity was 3,000 lbs.

Service
  General A/N duty.

Buoy boat CG 52302D on 13 Oct 44.

52-FOOT MOTOR LIFEBOAT

Number	Builder	Commissioned	Disposition
CG 52300 (ex-*Invincible*)	Coast Guard Yard, Curtis Bay, MD	1935	*Sank* 21 Jan 61
CG 52301 (ex-*Triumph*)	Coast Guard Yard, Curtis Bay, MD	1935	NA

Cost
   NA
Hull
   Displacement (tons)   30 fl (1936)
   Length   52' oa; 50' wl
   Beam   14'4" max (over guards); 12'8¼" wl
   Draft   6'8" max
Machinery
   Main Engines   1 Buda solid injection, 6-cyl diesel
   BHP   150
   Shafts   Single
Logistics
   Complement   4

Design*
   The 52-foot motor lifeboat originally designated as "Type F" class was a developmental design. These craft were given an improved cruising radius over the standard 36-foot class of motor lifeboats, a more powerful engine, and accommodations for crew and rescued men. The 52-footer was not self-bailing or self-righting, but her initial stability was very high. Sixty persons could be carried below in watertight compartments and an additional 100 could be carried on deck, weather permitting. She was not intended to replace the standard 36-foot class of motor lifeboats, but rather was designed to meet the need for a larger, more powerful lifeboat for use at locations with extreme sea conditions.

Service
   CG 52300 (the *Invincible*) was stationed at Point Adams, Columbia River, OR. CG 52301 (the *Triumph*) was stationed at Sandy Hook, NJ; she rescued 9 survivors from a PBY 5A on 3 Apr 43; she was later transferred to Grays Harbor, WA, and then to Coos Bay, OR.

*Design history prepared and copyrighted by William D. Wilkinson.

The 52-foot motor lifeboat *Invincible* underway. This photograph was taken while she was stationed at Sandy Hook, NJ, in 1930s. The *Invincible* was later transferred to the Pacific Northwest coast. (Courtesy of the National Archives.)

50-FOOT FIRE BARGES

Number	Builder	Commissioned	Disposition
CGB 50300F through 50313F	Various yards in Wisconsin	1942–43	All *decomm* post–WW II

Cost
   NA
Hull
   Displacement tons   42 fl (1945)
   Length   50'7" oa
   Beam   19'2" max
   Draft   2' max (1945)
Machinery
   Auxiliary   2 detachable Chrysler Marine tractors
   Engines
   BHP   286

Performance
   Max Speed   7 kts (1945)
Logistics
   Complement   8 men
Design
   The 50-foot fire barges were carvel-built. Each craft was fitted with 8 Chrysler pumping units.
Service
   All stationed on Great Lakes.

CGB 50301F with crew at fire-fighting stations.

50-FOOT HARBOR PATROL BOAT

Number	Builder	Commissioned	Disposition
CG 50017–50018	Shain Manufacturing Co., Seattle, WA	1943	NA
CG 50032–50043	Washington Boat Works, Seattle, WA	1943	NA
CG 50044–50053	Barbee Marine Yard, Seattle, WA	1943	NA
CG 50054–50057	Olsen and Winge, Seattle, WA	1943	NA
CG 50058–50061	Jensen Motorboat Co., Seattle, WA	1943	NA
CG 50062–50069	Grandy Boat Works, Seattle, WA	1943	NA
CG 50070–50081	Shain Manufacturing Co., Seattle, WA	1943	NA

Cost
  NA
Hull
  Tonnage   17 gross (1945)
  Length   50'4" oa
  Beam   12'6"
  Draft   NA
Machinery
  Main Engines   2 Chrysler Royals
  SHP   286
  Propellers   Twin

Performance
  Max Speed   17.5 kts (1945)
  Cruising   12 kts, 1,100 mi radius (1945)
Logistics
  Gasoline (95%) 500 gal
  Complement   8 men (1945)
Electronics   Armament
  None   None
Design
  Constructed of wood, with red cedar above the waterline and white cedar below.
Service
  Used for harbor patrol.

40-FOOT FIREBOATS

Number	Builder	Commissioned	Disposition
CG 40335F–40364F	Wheeler Shipyard, Brooklyn, NY	1944–45	All *decomm* post–WW II

Cost
  NA
Hull
  Weight   41,500 lbs
  Length   40′2″ oa
  Beam   14′6″ max
  Draft   4′2″ normal
Machinery
  Main Engines   1 Chrysler Royal gasoline
  SHP   143
  Propellers   Single

Performance
  Max Speed   10.3 kts (1945)
Logistics
  Gasoline (95%) 600 gal
  Complement   10 men (1945)
Design
  These 40-foot fireboats were wood construction, double planked, with a square stern and flat bottom. They were equipped with 7 fire monitors. No berthing accommodations.
Service
  Stationed on East Coast.

A 40-foot fireboat, showing water curtain used to protect craft from the heat of the fire.

40-FOOT BUOY BOAT

Number	Builder	Commissioned	Disposition
40301D series	Coast Guard Yard, Curtis Bay, MD	Early WW II	All *decomm* post–WW II

Cost
  NA
Hull
  Weight   17,995 lbs (1945)

Length   40′ oa
Beam   12′6″ max
Draft   3′8″ max (1945)

Machinery
Main Engines   1 gasoline
SHP   180
Performance
Max Speed   11 kts (1945)
Logistics
Complement   3 men (1945)

Design
The 40-foot buoy boat was constructed of wood and had her cabin aft. Hoist had a 1,500-lb capacity.

Service
General A/N duty.

40-FOOT MOTOR LIFEBOAT

Number	Builder	Commissioned	Disposition
CG 40300 (ex-CG 5357)	Coast Guard Yard, Curtis Bay, MD	Jul 1940	NA

Cost
Approx. $20,000
Hull
Weight   25,000 lbs (1945)
Length   40' oa; 36'6" wl
Beam   10'6" max; 9'8.5" wl
Draft   3'9" max (1945)
Machinery
Main Engine   Sterling PETREL 120-hp gasoline; 1951 refit GM-471 diesel
Shafts   Single
Performance
Max Speed   10.5 kts (1940)
                      8.0 kts (1945)
Logistics
Gasoline   250 gal

Complement   3 men (1945)

Design*
The 40-foot motor lifeboat was the first of her type developed by the Coast Guard. The craft was of welded steel construction with a rounded semi-dory-type stern. The advent of WW II postponed further development of this type of coastal lifeboat. Production of the standard 36-foot wood-hull motor lifeboat continued until well after the war.

Service
1940–Aug 43 CG 40300 served at a number of lifeboat stations from Maine to North Carolina to give service personnel an opportunity to evaluate the craft under a wide range of operating conditions; Aug 43, shipped to the Plum Island Lifeboat Station on Washington Island, Door Peninsula, WI—her steel hull enabled her to work in ice conditions, making her especially valuable in this assignment.

*Design history and service notes prepared and copyrighted by William D. Wilkinson.

38-FOOT PICKET BOAT*

No. Built	Year Built	Later Number	Original Number	
15	1931	CG 38301– CG 38309	CG 2385– CG 2393 CG 2394†	*Built* by Gibbs Gas Engine Co., Jacksonville, FL.; powered by a single Hall Scott, Model 168, INVADER 270 hp, 6-cyl gasoline engine, single
		CG 38310– CG 38314	CG 2395– CG 2399	screw; max speed trial runs 26.5 stat mph at 2,140 rpm on 29 Apr 1933; design agent: Walter J. McInnis of Eldredge-McInnis, Boston, MA; cost: $7,250 per boat + machinery
6	1931–32	CG 38315– CG-38319	CG 4300† CG 4301– CG 4305	*Built* by Corsair Boat Co., Trenton, MI; cost: $6,150 per boat + machinery; Hall Scott Model 168 INVADER
15	1936	CG 38320– CG 38334	CG 4306– CG 4320	*Built* by Freeport Point Shipyard, Freeport, LI, NY; Murray and Tregurtha, Model K, 6-cyl, 325-hp gasoline engine, single screw + machinery

*Builders table prepared and copyrighted by William D. Wilkinson.
†Stricken from list prior to 1940.

No. Built	Year Built	Later Number	Original Number	
6	—	CG 38335–CG 38340	CG 4321–CG 4326	*Built* by Stephens Bros., Stockton, CA; Murray and Tregurtha, Model K, 6-cyl, 325-hp gasoline engine, single screw
20	1939	CG 38341–CG 38360	CG 4327–CG 4346	*Built* by Palmer Scott & Co., New Bedford, MA
6	1940	CG 38361–CG 38366	CG 4347–CG 4352	*Built* by Robinson Marine Construction Co., Benton Harbor, MI; Sterling DOLPHIN, 6-cyl, 300-hp gasoline engine, single screw
20	1942	CG 38367–CG 38386	CG 4353–CG 4372	*Built* by Stephens Bros., Stockton, CA; cost: $6,875/boat; Hall Scott, INVADER, 6-cyl, 300-hp gasoline engine, single screw
27	1942	CG 38387–CG 38413	—	*Built* by Richardson Boat Co., North Tonawanda, NY; cost: $11,475/boat; KERMATH, 225-hp gasoline engine
20	1942	CG 38414–CG 38433	—	*Built* by Richardson Boat Co., North Tonawanda, NY; cost: $11,595/boat; KERMATH, 225-hp gasoline engine
20	1942	CG 38434–CG 38453	—	*Built* by James E. Graves, Inc., Marblehead, MA; cost: $11,595/boat; KERMATH, 225-hp gasoline engine
20	1942	CG 38454–CG 38473	—	*Built* by Henry R. Hinckley, Southwest Harbor, ME; cost: $11,652/boat; KERMATH, 225 hp-gasoline engine
20	1942	CG 38474–CG 38493	—	*Built* by Palmer Scott & Co., New Bedford, MA; cost: $11,757/boat; KERMATH, 225-hp gasoline engine
10	1942	CG 38494–CG 38503	—	*Built* by Palmer Scott & Co., New Bedford, MA; cost: $11,823/boat; KERMATH, 225-hp gasoline engine
14	1942	CG 38504–CG 38517	—	*Built* by James E. Graves, Marblehead, MA; cost: $11,767/boat; KERMATH, 225-hp gasoline engine
14	1942	CG 38518–CG 38531	—	*Built* by Henry R. Hinckley, Southwest Harbor, ME; cost: $11,663/boat; KERMATH, 225-hp gasoline engine
5	1942	CG 38532–CG 38536	—	*Built* by Palmer Scott & Co., New Bedford, MA; cost: $11,834/boat; KERMATH, 225-hp gasoline engine
70	1942–43	CG 38537–CG 38606	—	*Built* by Richardson Boat Co., North Tonawanda, NY; cost: $10,752/boat; KERMATH, 225-hp gasoline engine
30	1942–43	CG 38607–CG 38636	—	*Built* by James E. Graves, Marblehead, MA; cost: $11,156/boat; KERMATH, 225-hp gasoline engine
30	1942–43	CG 38637–CG 38666	—	*Built* by Palmer Scott & Co., New Bedford, MA; cost: $10,851/boat; KERMATH, 225 hp-gasoline engine
31	1942–43	CG 38667–CG 38697	—	*Built* by Henry R. Hinckley, Southwest Harbor, ME; cost: $10,871/boat; KERMATH, 225-hp gasoline engine
68	1942–43	CG 38698–CG 38765	—	*Built* by Ballinger Boat Works, Kirkland, WA; cost: $10,247/boat; KERMATH, 225-hp gasoline engine
71	1942–43	CG 38766–CG 38836	—	*Built* by Palatka Shipbuilding Corp., Palatka, FL; cost: $9,960/boat; KERMATH, 225-hp gasoline engine

38-FOOT CABIN PICKET BOAT

Number	Builder	Commissioned	Disposition
CG 38301–38836	*See* pages 254–55	1931–1943	All *decomm* post–WW II

Cost
(*See* Builders table)

Hull
Weight	15,700 lbs (1945)
Length	38′ oa; 37′ wl
Beam	10′4″ max
Draft	3′ max (1945)

Machinery
(*See* Builders table)

Performance
Max Speed	26.5 stat. mph at 2,140 rpm trial runs (1931)
	19 kts (1945)

Logistics
Gasoline (95%)	240 gal
Complement	2 men (1945)

Electronics
None

Armament
None

Design
The cabin-picket type of patrol boat was tailored to meet the practical requirement of policing and patrolling harbors, shallow inlets, and protected bodies of water along the coasts. The 38-footers were of carvel design and wood construction. Those operating above Cape Henry and on the Great Lakes were ice-sheathed. The lead builder of this class was Gibbs Gas Engine Co. of Jacksonville, FL, who selected as its design agent Walter J. McInnis of Eldredge-McInnis, Boston, MA. A total of 538 picket boats were built: 68 were built before 7 Dec 41, 470 after 7 Dec 41.

Service
Cabin picket boats formed an adjunct to Coast Guard lifesaving stations around large seashore resorts, and were used extensively for patrolling regattas, for customs harbor patrol and boarding duty, for emergency rescue work in harbors, and for flood relief on Western rivers.

Two 38-footers running full speed at Seattle, WA, 8 Mar 43. They had been constructed by Ballinger Boat Works, Kirkland, WA. Ballinger built a total of sixty-eight of these picket boats.

Thirty-eight-foot cabin picket boats await delivery to the CG. These units were built by Stephens Brothers, Boat Builders, Stockton, CA, and still wear their old numbers. This craft was developed to police and patrol bodies of water along the coast.

36-FOOT MOTOR LIFEBOAT*

Number	Builder	Commissioned	Disposition
Type "T" 3389–3392 3370–3677 3692(27) 3700–3710 3764–3766	U.S. Coast Guard Yard, Curtis Bay, MD	1929–31	All out of service
Type "TR" 69 constructed; numbers not known	U.S. Coast Guard Yard, Curtis Bay, MD	1931–37	All out of service
Type "TRS" 4963–4965 5078–5080 5145–5149 5174 5181–5184(50) 5186–5188 5192 5194 5948–6959 8815–8824 36479–36495‡	U.S. Coast Guard Yard, Curtis Bay, MD	1937–45†	All out of service

*This class was prepared by and the copyright is held by William D. Wilkinson.
†Fifty Type "TRS" were constructed by the end of WW II. Following the war, an additional 58 were built, with the last one constructed for CG service being completed in 1956.
‡CG 36479–CG 36495 were first 36-foot MLBs constructed under the new numbering system. Earlier boats were renumbered, but the new numbers for these boats are not known.

Cost

Type "T": total—complete per boat, $15,250 (1930)
Type "TR": total—complete per boat, $15,703 (1934)
Type "TRS": total—complete per boat, $15,099 (1941)

Type "TRS": total—complete per boat, $18,894 (1943)
Type "TRS": total—complete per boat, $18,912 (1945)

Hull	Type "T"	Type "TR"	Type "TRS"
Length	36'6" oa	36'8" oa	36'8" oa
Beam	10'4.5" max	10'8 7/8" max	10'8" 7/8" max
Draft	3'3"	3'4"	3'4"
Displacement	19,246 lbs	19,372 lbs	19,675 lbs
Machinery			
Engine	Sterling "Petrel"; 6 cyl, 4 cycle	Sterling "Petrel"; 6 cyl, 4 cycle	Sterling "Petrel"; 6 cyl, 5 cycle
Gasoline	90 HP at 1,000 rpm; 8.5 smph at 800 rpm	90 HP at 1,000 rpm; 8.21 smph at 800 rpm	90 HP at 1,00 rpm; 8.55 smph at 800 rpm
Performance			
Cruising Radius	8 kts 280 miles	8 kts 280 miles	8 kts 280 miles
Logistics			
Complement	3 men	3 men	3 men
Passengers	30 persons	30 persons	30 persons

Design

The 36-foot motor lifeboat of standard design in service at the beginning of WW II was the final design step of a type initiated in 1907–1908. She was the first 36-foot, self-righting, self-bailing motor lifeboat designed as such from the keel up. The type underwent several basic changes before 1928, when Type "T" was designed. This model and two modified versions, Type "TR" of 1931–37 and Type

A 36-foot motor lifeboat, Type "T," from Racine Station, returns from a search, 2 Mar 47.

"TRS" of 1937–56, represented the significant portion of all boats of this type in service through WW II. Although the earliest 36-foot motor lifeboat designs, which predated WW II, were built in private yards such as Electric Boat Company of Bayonne, NJ, after WW II all such craft were constructed at the Coast Guard Yard, Curtis Bay, MD.

Service

Scattered along America's coasts; rescued torpedoed merchantmen along the Eastern seaboard in early part of WW II; 36-footers rescued one survivor from tanker *Persephone* 26 May 42; assisted in rescue of 11 survivors from tanker *John D. Gill*.

A Type "A" motor lifeboat, 16 Jun 31. The first unit of this type was completed at the CG Yard, 9 Aug 29. Watertight trunk enclosures furnish shelter for the rescued and protection for the radio telephone communication equipment. Lifeboats were kept afloat at stations, or when coastal conditions permitted, launching carriages were used, in which case, a boathouse was provided. The type "TR" boats were used in flood rescue work on western rivers.

36-FOOT FIREBOATS

Number	Builder	Commissioned	Disposition
CG 36024F–36029F	Perry E. Bass Boat Works, Fulton, TX	1943	All *decomm* post–WW II

Cost
  NA

Hull
  Weight   31,400 lbs (1945)
  Length   36' oa
  Beam   13'4" max
  Draft   3'6" max (1945)

Machinery
  Main Engines   1 Universal gasoline
  SHP   83
  Propellers   Single

Performance
  Max Speed   10 kts (1945)

Logistics (1945)
  Complement   6 men (no berthing)

Design
  These 36-foot fireboats were wood construction, double-planked carvel, and had a V-bottom. They had 2 monitors and 4 pumping units.

Service
  Stationed on Gulf Coast.

30-FOOT FIREBOATS

Number	Builder	Commissioned	Disposition
CG 30032F–30131F CG 30137F–30139F	Hanley Engineering Service, Prospect, OH	1942–43	All *decomm* post–WW II

Cost
  NA

Hull
  Weight   31,000 lbs (1945)
  Length   30'6" oa
  Beam   10'7" max
  Draft   2'6" max (1945)

Machinery
  Main Engines   4 Chrysler engines, combination propulsion and pumping

Performance
  Max Speed   7 kts (1945)

Logistics
  Complement   6 men (no berthing)

Design
  The 30 fireboats were all steel-welded carvel construction. They had flat bottoms, a tubular rudder, and were self-bailing. They had 2 monitors.

Service
  Stationed on all coasts.

COAST GUARD RESERVE CRAFT (CGR)

As an emergency measure, the Coast Guard acquired hundreds of private pleasure craft. These were primarily used for harbor patrol and were mostly manned by reservists. Each district was given blocks of CGR numbers to assign to the crafts it acquired: unlike CG numbers, these had no relationship to the length of the craft. Most craft were returned to their original owners and resumed their original names. Most missing numbers in the following list were assigned to craft surveyed but not accepted by the service.

These craft were a district asset, and their records were maintained at that level. Unfortunately, neither a complete set of district nor headquarters records for these craft have been located. When, however, both district and headquarters records for a given craft were in conflict, district records were judged to be the more accurate if the conflict could not be resolved from another source. Additional characteristics concerning many of these craft may be found in the various pre–WW II issues of *Lloyd's Register of American Yachts*.

FORCE LEVEL OF COAST GUARD RESERVE (CGR) BOATS

Date	Total in Commission	Total in Decommission	Total Disposed of to Date
1941			
Dec	334	0	1
1942			
Jan	372	0	11
Feb	427	0	18
Mar	541	1	26
Apr	725	2	34
May	907	3	42
Jun	1083	3	51
Jul	1346	4	58
Aug	1577	4	71
Sep	1789	5	84
Oct	1863	9	111
Nov	1887	11	132
Dec	1843	34	168
1943			
Jan	1804	53	206

Date	Total in Commission	Total in Decommission	Total Disposed of to Date
Feb	1781	34	223
Mar	1643	171	255
Apr	1573	183	319
May	1293	389	396
Jun	1245	370	464
Jul	1206	334	539
Aug	1118	377	584
Sep	1065	367	647
Oct	1008	371	702
Nov	822	473	787
Dec	659	498	925
1944			
Jan	604	480	998
Feb	560	442	1080
Mar	509	397	1177
Apr	481	336	1267
May	464	255	1365
Jun	444	201	1440
Jul	421	163	1501
Aug	387	125	1573
Sep	353	112	1621
Oct	333	101	1653
Nov	268	94	1725
Dec	239	88	1761
1945			
Jan	195	99	1794
Feb	187	89	1812
Mar	159	77	1852
Apr	150	59	1880
May	148	45	1896
Jun	84	60	1945
Jul	80	43	1968
Aug	69	40	1982
Sep	61	34	1996
Oct	59	26	2007
Nov	3	23	2065
Dec	2	22	2067

CGR BOATS

CGR Number	District Assigned	Length	Commissioned	Decommissioned	Disposal	Notes
1	1	30'	Dec 41	Nov 43	Feb 44	ex-*Joanna Belle*, #230067
2	1	38'	Dec 41	Dec 43	Jul 44	ex-*Strebor*, #5B619
3	1	38'	Dec 41	Sep 43	Nov 43	ex-*Striker*, #4E749
4	1	29'	Dec 41	Feb 43	Jun 43	ex-*XYZ*, #4C918
5	1	37'	Dec 41	May 43	Jan 44	ex-*Defender*, #4G675
6	1	38'	Dec 41	Oct 43	Jun 44	ex-*Madclare*, #238380
7	1	34'	Dec 41	Oct 43	Mar 44	ex-*Aries*, #4H510
8	1	38'	Dec 41	May 43	Jun 44	ex-*Marmac*, #4B34
9	1	32'	Dec 41	Apr 43	Aug 44	ex-*Arrowhead*, #4J662
10	1	38'	Dec 41	Mar 43	Nov 44	ex-*Bandit*, #4F623
11	1	35'	Dec 41	Oct 43	Jan 44	ex-*Tarantula*, #4L191
12	1	27'	Dec 41	May 43	Aug 44	ex-*Sea Able*, #4H40
13	1	39'	Dec 41	Jul 43	Aug 44	ex-*Dauntless*, #1H261
14	1	35'	Dec 41	Dec 43	Jun 44	ex-*Jetty III*, #4B122
15	1	32'	Dec 41	Apr 43	May 44	ex-*Fur Trader*, #1H100
16	1	36'	Dec 41	Mar 43	Aug 44	ex-*Cyndor*, #4H741
17	1	32'	Dec 41	Mar 43	Feb 44	ex-*Sigberdean*, #4C780
18	1	61'	Sep 42	Jun 43	Feb 44	?
19	1	34'	Dec 41	Mar 43	Sep 44	ex-*Anna*, #4J204
20	1	38'	Dec 41	Sep 42	Oct 42	ex-*Caravan*, #4A361, became CG-38059
21	1	36'	Jan 42	Dec 43	Jan 44	ex-*Tancha*, #4C633
22	1	26'	Dec 41	—	May 43	ex-*Hyalis*, #1G269
23	1	38'	Dec 41	—	Oct 42	ex-*Mil-Ed*, #4B198
24	1	30'	Dec 41	Jan 43	Jul 44	ex-*Idle Hour*, #4J200
25	1	35'	Jan 42	Nov 43	May 44	ex-*Francesca*, #1J36
26	1	35'	Jan 42	Mar 43	Jun 44	ex-*Bib*, #4K760
27	1	35'	Jan 42	Apr 43	Feb 44	ex-*Yankee*, #4J647
28	1	38'	Jun 42	Apr 43	Dec 43	ex-*Black Marlin*, #4C733
29	1	32'	Dec 41	Feb 43	Jan 44	ex-*Bobby C*, #4J693
30	1	36'	Mar 42	Mar 43	Feb 44	ex-*Margo*, #4K754
31	1	32'	Mar 42	—	—	ex-*Evanlill III*, #4A311; 9 Jun 43 destroyed by fire
32	1	32'	Mar 42	Oct 43	Mar 44	ex-*Sans Souci*, #5A423
33	1	32'	Apr 42	May 43	Nov 44	ex-*Joan*, #4D958
34	1	38'	Apr 42	Dec 43	Aug 44	ex-*Esquire*, #4J990 or 229060?
35	1	38'	May 42	Jun 43	May 45	ex-*Jean III*, #?
36	1	60'	Oct 42	Mar 43	Aug 44	?
36	1	36'	Apr 42	—	Aug 42	ex-*Lena G*, #4F122
37	1	39'	May 42	—	Sep 43	ex-*Squam*, #4D708; 25 May 42 assisted in rescue of 43 survivors from the tanker *Peysander*
38	1	33'	May 42	Apr 43	Aug 44	ex-*Dancing Lady*, #4G964
39	1	36'	May 42	Apr 43	May 43	ex-*Alice A*, #4G276
40	1	32'	May 42	Oct 43	Jun 44	ex-*Alibi II*, #4C347
41	1	40'	Sep 42	Jun 43	Jun 44	?
42	1	40'	Dec 41	May 43	Jul 45	ex-*Seaboats*, #10W400
43	1	43'	Dec 41	Mar 43	Apr 44	ex-*Wanderer*, #4D944
44	1	49'	Dec 41	Oct 42	Aug 44	ex-*Helen Virginia*, #235891
45	1	47'	Dec 41	—	Oct 42	ex-*3-J's*, #4G757
46	1	46'	Dec 41	Mar 43	Dec 43	ex-*Bojest*, #4D627
47	1	46'	Dec 41	Dec 43	Feb 44	ex-*Muriel III*, #236267
48	1	42'	Dec 41	—	—	ex-*Ellie C III*, #4L342; 9 Jul 43 destroyed by fire
49	1	46'	Dec 41	Jul 44	Oct 44	ex-*Retta III*, #228351
50	1	43'	Dec 41	Nov 43	Jul 44	ex-*Wild Goose*, #1C571
51	1	46'	Dec 41	Mar 43	May 44	ex-*Visemvoe*, #231635
52	1	39'	Dec 41	Jan 44	Jun 44	ex-*Poodle Pup*, #4A82
53	1	40'	Dec 41	Oct 43	—	ex-*Doffrey*, #4C312; Dec 43 sunk
54	1	40'	Dec 41	Mar 43	Jun 44	ex-*Wanderer*, #AL222
55	1	40'	Dec 41	Mar 43	Aug 44	ex-*Ada M II*, #4C642
56	1	46'	Dec 41	Mar 43	Jul 44	ex-*Elyhson*, #226650

CGR Number	District Assigned	Length	Commissioned	Decommissioned	Disposal	Notes
57	1	42'	Dec 41	Nov 43	Sep 44	ex-*Mildred W*, #4J893
58	1	45'	Dec 41	—	Jul 44	ex-*Mermaid IV*, #4J860
59	1	43'	Jan 42	Mar 43	Dec 43	?, #4J505
60	1	41'	Jan 42	—	May 43	ex-*Sermonda*, #4A325
61	1	40'	Apr 42	May 43	Feb 46	ex-*Jean*, #229544
62	1	46'	May 42	Mar 43	Aug 44	ex-*Sabre*, #230042
63	1	36'	May 42	Apr 43	Jul 43	ex-*Truant*, #4A232
64	1	40'	May 42	Oct 43	May 44	ex-*Atalanta*, #4F992
65	1	40'	May 42	Oct 43	Mar 44	ex-*Mahal*, #4H978
66	1	32'	May 42	Mar 43	Jan 44	ex-*Valcour*, ?
67	1	31'	May 42	Oct 43	Sep 44	ex-*Joan*, ?
68	1	47'	May 42	Apr 43	Feb 44	ex-*Dixie V*, #225399
69	1	26'	May 42	—	Oct 43	ex-*Whim*, #6G487
70	1	32'	May 42	May 43	Mar 46	ex-*Lally L*, #?
71	1	63'	Dec 41	Mar 44	Sep 44	ex-*Dot III*, #232432
72	1	65'	Dec 41	Dec 43	Apr 44	ex-*Mother Goose*, #230934
73	1	67'	Dec 41	Dec 43	Aug 44	ex-*Bette Ann*, #226019
74	1	55'	Dec 41	Oct 43	Oct 44	ex-*Janice C*, #228429
75	1	51'	Dec 41	—	Dec 43	ex-*Walrus*, #229287
76	1	50'	Jan 42	—	Apr 43	ex-*Eleanor*, #231747
77	1	50'	Jan 42	Apr 43	May 44	ex-*Olympic*, #229896
78	1	50'	Mar 42	—	Nov 43	ex-*Kathryn M*, #232052
79	1	57'	May 42	Feb 45	Jun 45	ex-*Secret*, #230840
80	1	65'	May 42	Mar 43	Apr 44	ex-*Sunshine*, #226033
81	1	75'	May 42	—	Dec 43	ex-*Lions Whelp*, #229080
82	1	65'	May 42	Mar 43	Aug 44	ex-*Inishowen*, #224835
83	1	40'	May 42	Mar 43	Aug 44	ex-*Sinbad*, #?
84	1	38'	May 42	Oct 43	Jan 44	ex-*Scandal*, #?
85	1	55'	May 42	Dec 43	Aug 44	?
86	1	39'	Mar 42	Oct 43	Dec 43	ex-*B-All*, #4M356
87	1	29'	May 42	Dec 43	Jul 44	?
88	1	34'	May 42	—	—	?, #1D270
89	1	36'	May 42	Apr 43	Jun 44	ex-*Mildred G*, #5C543
90	1	34'	May 42	—	Dec 43	ex-*Carmaret*, #?
91	6–7	38'	Dec 41	—	Feb 42	?
91	6–7	38'	Feb 42	Aug 44	Aug 45	?
92	6–7	50'	Sep 42	Nov 43	Feb 44	?
93	6–7	36'	Dec 41	Aug 43	Sep 44	?
94	6–7	42'	Dec 41	Mar 43	Aug 43	?
95	6–7	32'	Feb 42	Aug 43	Jul 44	?
96	6–7	30'	Apr 42	Mar 43	Aug 44	?
97	6–7	40'	Mar 42	Jan 44	Apr 44	?
98	6–7	30'	Mar 42	Mar 43	Dec 43	?
99	6–7	32'	Mar 42	Aug 43	May 44	?
100	6–7	44'	Mar 42	May 43	Aug 44	?
101	6–7	39'	Apr 42	Apr 43	Apr 44	?
102	6–7	38'	Apr 42	Apr 43	Apr 44	?
103	6–7	30'	Apr 42	Mar 43	Aug 44	?
104	6–7	45'	Apr 42	Jul 42	Dec 42	?
105	6–7	37'	—	May 42	Nov 42	?
106	9	118'	Dec 41	—	Aug 42	ex-*Nedra B*, #207597; became *Blanchard* 3 Nov 42
107	9	42'	Dec 41	Nov 42	May 43	ex-*Dolores*, #39B964
108	9	34'	Dec 41	Jan 43	Apr 44	ex-*Archer*, #?
109	9	36'	Dec 41	Jan 43	Jul 43	ex-*Miss Joy*, #39E273
110	9	30'	Dec 41	Apr 42	May 42	ex-*Gaeli*, #39A493
111	9	46'	Dec 41	Dec 42	May 43	ex-*War Jane*, #39A446
112	9	78'	Dec 41	Dec 43	May 44	ex-*Zenith*, #212306
113	9	36'	Dec 41	May 42	Sep 42	ex-*Cag-B*, #39D609
114	9	38'	Dec 41	Jan 43	Jul 44	ex-*Leroya*, #39A909

CGR Number	District Assigned	Length	Commissioned	Decommissioned	Disposal	Notes
115	9	45'	Dec 41	Nov 42	Jun 43	ex-*Lobo*, #231862
116	9	25'	Dec 41	Jan 44	Jun 44	ex-*Seafoam*, #39F250
117	9	50'	Mar 42	May 43	Nov 44	ex-*Fifty Fifty*, #22846
118	9	30'	Mar 42	Feb 44	Jun 44	ex-*Quest II*, #39F136
119	9	106'	Sep 42	Dec 44	Oct 45	ex-*Eleanor*, #?
120	9	39'	Apr 42	Oct 43	May 44	ex-*Mileth S.*, #37C377
121	9	30'	Apr 42	Jan 43	Jun 44	ex-*Mae-Bob*, #39A239
122	9	44'	Apr 42	Jan 43	May 44	ex-*Sea Car*, #239547
123	9	50'	Apr 42	—	—	ex-*Lil Ray*, #39F433, 11 Oct 43 sunk
124	9	58'	Apr 42	Apr 44	Jul 44	ex-*Welcome*, #211540
125	9	45'	Apr 42	Dec 43	May 44	ex-*Sunset*, #236953
126	9	50'	Apr 42	Dec 43	May 44	ex-*Caroline*, #234717
127	9	47'	Apr 42	Oct 42	May 44	ex-*Goldenrod*, #237460
128	9	41'	May 42	Jun 43	Jun 44	ex-*Star Dust II*, #39B25
129	9	50'	Jun 42	—	Jun 44	ex-*Annabelle*, #225802
130	9	60'	Apr 42	Mar 45	Jun 45	ex-*Amata*, #225648
131	9	40'	Apr 42	Jan 43	Apr 43	ex-*Florence III*, #39A624
132	9	67'	Apr 42	—	Nov 42	ex-*Nancy Ann III*, #236305; 8 Oct 42 became CG-66006
133	9	65'	Apr 42	—	Nov 44	ex-*Pilgrim*, #240794
134	9	45'	Apr 42	Dec 42	Sep 44	ex-*Urchin III*, #229862
135	9	38'	Apr 42	—	—	ex-*Chimes*, #37C858; 24 Nov 42 destroyed by fire
136	9	46'	Apr 42	Dec 42	Jul 43	ex-*Hypo*, #238215
137	9	52'	Apr 42	May 44	Sep 44	ex-*Riette*, #214064
138	9	33'	Apr 42	—	—	ex-*Rowdy*, #39B361; 5 Jul 42 destroyed by fire
139	9	54'	Apr 42	Oct 44	Nov 44	ex-*Laejack*, #227086
140	9	75'	May 42	Jun 45	Oct 45	ex-*Sonom-A III*, #233187
141	9	36'	May 42	Jul 43	Feb 44	ex-*Mary-Elizabeth*, #39A436
142	9	30'	Dec 41	—	Jun 43	ex-*Footloose*, #41C128
143	9	62'	Dec 41	Apr 43	Nov 43	ex-*Lenore III*, #230762
146	9	95'	Dec 41	Sep 43	Oct 43	ex-*Desire*, #211564
147	9	49'	Dec 41	—	Jul 43	ex-*Old Timer*, #38A268 or 535656
148	9	42'	Dec 41	Sep 43	Oct 43	ex-*C Minor*, #227787
149	9	63'	Dec 41	Mar 43	May 44	ex-*Naiad*, #225744
150	9	56'	Dec 41	Mar 43	Aug 43	ex-*Janescot*, #232180
151	9	65'	Dec 41	Mar 43	Sep 43	ex-*Priscilla*, #222442
152	9	63'	Dec 41	Mar 43	Aug 43	ex-*Margaret M II*, #222978
153	9	33'	Apr 42	—	Jul 43	?, #38A907
154	9	26'	Apr 42	—	May 43	ex-*Playmate*, #38G392
155	9	31'	Apr 42	—	May 43	?, #38V937
156	9	44'	Apr 42	—	Jun 43	ex-*Red Feather II*, #227450
157	9	25'	Apr 42	—	May 43	?, #38P688
158	9	34'	Apr 42	—	Apr 43	ex-*Caruna III*, #38H853
159	9	28'	Apr 43	—	Apr 43	ex-*Shaker Girl*, #38B797
160	9	53'	May 42	Oct 43	Aug 44	ex-*Marlan C*, #236193
161	9	45'	May 42	—	Jul 43	ex-*Arturus*, #9B871
162	9	38'	May 42	—	May 43	ex-*Vagabond*, #38C92
163	9	31'	May 42	—	Jul 43	ex-*Perry III*, #9B852
164	9	32'	May 42	—	Jun 43	?, #38H778
165	9	25'	May 42	May 44	Jul 44	ex-*Hustle*, #7F441
166	9	29'	May 42	May 44	Jul 44	ex-*Swiftwater*, #7E725
167	9	25'	Jun 42	—	Jul 43	?
168	9	34'	Jun 42	—	May 43	ex-*Island King*, #41H128
169	9	38'	Jun 42	Mar 43	Jul 43	ex-*Atoz*, #41H552
170	9	30'	Jul 42	—	May 43	?
171	9	32'	Jul 42	Mar 43	Jul 43	?
172	9	30'	Jul 42	—	May 43	?
173	9	55'	Jul 42	—	Jul 43	?
174	9	29'	Jul 42	—	May 43	?
175	9	32'	Jul 42	—	Jul 43	?

CGR Number	District Assigned	Length	Commissioned	Decommissioned	Disposal	Notes
176	9	36′	Jun 42	—	Jan 43	?
177	9	25′	Jul 42	—	May 43	?
178	9	36′	Jul 42	—	May 43	?
179	9	38′	Sep 42	—	Apr 43	?
180	9	32′	Aug 42	—	—	5 Dec 42 destroyed by fire
181	9	33′	Sep 42	Mar 43	May 43	?
182	9	30′	Aug 42	Mar 43	Jul 43	?
183	9	28′	Sep 42	Mar 43	May 43	?
184	9	55′	Oct 42	Nov 43	Mar 44	?
185	9	62′	Oct 42	Nov 43	Mar 44	?
186	9	23′	Sep 42	Mar 43	Oct 43	?
187	9	51′	Nov 42	Nov 43	Nov 44	?
188	9	26′	Sep 42	May 44	Jun 44	?
196	14	25′	Jan 42	May 43	Jun 43	ex-*Seabiscuit*, #32A657
197	14	36′	Dec 41	Oct 43	Dec 43	ex-*Ipokai*, #32B546
198	14	32′	Jan 42	—	Sep 43	ex-*Kamokila*, #32B31
199	14	33′	Jan 42	—	Sep 43	?, #32A898
202	7	36′	Dec 41	—	Aug 43	ex-*Lively Lady II*, #238416
203	7	32′	Dec 41	—	Jul 43	?, #18K440
204	7	62′	Dec 41	—	May 43	ex-*Harpoon*, #221637
205	7	32′	Dec 41	—	May 43	ex-*Helen May*, #6D76
206	7	28′	Dec 41	Aug 43	Sep 43	ex-*Jeri-Bill*, #18M234
207	7	77′	Dec 41	—	Aug 43	ex-*Vahdah*, #221140
208	7	32′	Dec 41	—	Jun 43	ex-*Semper*, #18S335
209	7	46′	Dec 41	—	Nov 43	ex-*Annette R*, #234564
210	7	34′	Dec 41	—	May 43	ex-*Char-Di-Jon*, #18P159
211	7	36′	Dec 41	Feb 43	Sep 43	ex-*Mitzi II*, #239333
212	7	38′	Dec 41	—	Dec 42	ex-*Lady May*, #18R155
213	7	38′	Dec 41	—	Jul 43	ex-*Elsie B*, #18G568
214	7	32′	Dec 41	—	Jun 43	ex-*Virginia*, #180945
215	7	37′	Dec 42	Dec 43	Jul 44	ex-*Java III*, #18R729
216	7	39′	Jan 42	—	Jul 43	ex-*Murlyn*, #240244
217	7	110′	Dec 41	Sep 44	Nov 44	ex-*Jamaroy*, #227319
218	7	38′	Mar 42	Dec 43	May 44	ex-*Rascal III*, #18C498
218	7	70′	Dec 41	—	Jan 42	?
219	7	45′	Dec 41	Apr 44	Aug 44	ex-*Revere*, #240977
220	7	38′	Jan 42	—	May 44	ex-*Lady M*, #14M451
221	7	38′	Jan 42	—	—	ex-*Mary Elizabeth*, #18S324; 6 Oct 42 destroyed by fire
222	7	31′	Jan 42	—	Jul 43	ex-*Samaki*, #18N775
223	7	44′	Feb 42	—	Aug 44	ex-*Lihu*, #240818
224	7	36′	Feb 42	—	Jun 43	ex-*Trebla II*, #5B21
225	7	34′	Feb 42	—	May 43	?, #18J434
226	7	42′	Mar 42	—	Sep 43	ex-*Edna W III*, #239026
227	7	52′	May 42	Aug 43	Oct 43	ex-*Barba-Jo*, #234518
228	7	24′	Mar 42	Jun 44	Jul 44	ex-*C.B.L.*, #18S155
229	7	38′	Feb 42	Nov 43	Dec 43	ex-*Sandpiper*, #236822
230	7	38′	Mar 42	—	Mar 43	ex-*Norvad*, #18M739
231	7	40′	Feb 42	—	—	ex-*Tropic Holiday*, #18T952; 10 Aug 43 destroyed by fire
232	13	46′	Dec 41	—	Jun 43	ex-*Tuscan*, #229224
233	13	35′	Dec 41	—	May 42	ex-*Primrose II*, #?
234	13	37′	Dec 41	—	Apr 42	?
235	13	35′	Dec 41	—	Jun 43	ex-*Lois W.*, #233752
236	13	45′	Jun 42	—	Jul 42	ex-*Nohusit*, #225930, 19 Jul 42 became CG-45034
237	13		Nov 41	—		ex-*Seabanus*, #?
240	13		Dec 41	—		?
292	11	38′	Dec 41	May 43	Jul 43	ex-*Nina H*, #27A830
293	11	35′	Dec 41	—	Sep 43	ex-*Glenorchy*, #27D320

CGR Number	District Assigned	Length	Commissioned	Decommissioned	Disposal	Notes
294	11	30'	Dec 41	Jan 44	Mar 44	ex-*Phylita*, #27E203
295	11	38'	Dec 41	—	Jan 42	?
295	11	44'	Mar 42	Nov 44	Dec 44	ex-*Dundee*, #27D704
296	11	44'	Dec 41	—	May 43	ex-*Joan Henderson*, #235684
297	11	77'	Dec 41	Sep 45	Jan 46	ex-*Artemis*, #229382
298	11	38'	Dec 41	Sep 43	Dec 43	ex-*Convoy*, #27E387
299	11	47'	Dec 41	Apr 44	Jun 44	ex-*Vantuna*, #240408
300	11	42'	Dec 41	Nov 43	Apr 44	ex-*Audal*, #25A843
301	11	47'	Jan 42	Sep 45	Oct 45	ex-*Norconian IV*, #?
302	11	42'	Jan 42	—	Dec 44	ex-*Norconian V*, #?
303	11	40'	Jan 42	Mar 44	May 44	ex-*Balew*, #27D444
304	11	145'	Jan 42	Aug 45	Apr 46	ex-*Melodie*, #220556
305	11	100'	Feb 42	Jul 43	Dec 43	ex-*Los Cerritos*, #212324
306	11	90'	Dec 41	Aug 45	Mar 46	ex-*Kinkajou*, #223927
307	11	47'	Feb 42	Mar 45	Jul 45	ex-*Marlin*, #228909
308	11	52'	Feb 42	Nov 43	Jan 44	ex-*Arrow*, #222818
309	11	130'	Mar 42	—	Dec 42	Requisition by USN 24 Dec 42; ex-*Velero II*, #222419
310	11	48'	Apr 42	Feb 44	Jul 44	ex-*Weigoer*, #?
311	11	33'	May 42	Aug 45	Oct 45	ex-*Napoleone*, #?
312	11	50'	Apr 42	Aug 45	Oct 45	ex-*Zeitgeist*, #?
313	11	50'	Apr 42	Dec 44	Jan 45	ex-*Olivia*, #232441
314	11	50'	Apr 42	Aug 44	Sep 44	ex-*Gwyn Dee*, #230466
315	11	88'	May 42	Mar 45	Jul 45	ex-*Fortola*, #209943
316	11	26'	May 42	Sep 44	Oct 44	ex-*Marionette*, #?
317	11	45'	May 42	Apr 44	Jun 44	ex-*Wil-Flo*, #?
318	11	84'	May 42	Jun 43	Aug 43	ex-*Seadrift*, #224315
319	11	25'	May 42	Nov 43	Jan 44	ex-*Madra*, #27G392
320	11	38'	May 42	Sep 43	Nov 43	ex-*Paso Del Norte*, #24A1
321	11	45'	Jun 42	—	Jun 44	ex-*Cheerio III*, #229136
322	11	59'	Jun 42	Jul 44	Sep 44	ex-*Kathleen*, #N230054
323	11	31'	Jun 42	Nov 44	Dec 44	?, #27G405
324	11	62'	Jun 42	May 45	Jul 45	ex-*Peter Pan*, #21G331
325	11	43'	Jun 42	Jan 45	May 45	ex-*Dixianne*, #229818
326	11	24'	Jun 42	Sep 44	Jan 45	ex-*Miss Dorene*, #?
327	11	78'	Jul 42	Jun 43	Sep 43	?
328	11	32'	Jun 42	Sep 44	Nov 44	ex-*Flamingo*, #27G63
329	11	45'	Jun 42	Sep 45	Oct 45	ex-*Narconian II*, #235635
330	11	50'	Jun 42	Sep 45	Mar 46	ex-*Barbill*, #224691
331	11	59'	Jun 42	Sep 45	Jan 46	ex-*Vagabundo*, #235283
332	11	43'	Jul 42	Aug 43	Dec 43	?
333	11	29'	Jul 42	—	Dec 42	?
334	11	23'	Jul 42	Apr 44	May 44	?
335	11	25'	Jul 42	Sep 44	Nov 44	?
336	11	96'	Jul 42	Oct 44	Dec 44	?
337	11	26'	Jul 42	Sep 44	Oct 44	?
338	11	62'	Jun 42	Jun 43	Oct 43	?
339	11	25'	Jul 42	Sep 43	Nov 43	?
340	11	85'	Aug 42	Jan 44	Mar 44	?
341	11	37'	Aug 42	Oct 44	Nov 44	?
342	11	20'	Aug 42	Nov 43	Apr 44	?
343	11	85'	Sep 42	Aug 43	Dec 43	?
344	11	32'	Sep 42	Mar 44	Jun 44	?
345	11	28'	Sep 42	Aug 43	Nov 43	?
346	11	29'	Sep 42	Mar 45	May 45	?
347	11	62'	Sep 42	Jun 45	Sep 45	?
348	11	62'	Sep 42	Aug 43	Sep 43	?
349	11	43'	Sep 42	Apr 43	Jun 43	
350	11	48'	Sep 42	Jun 45	Sep 45	?
351	11	54'	Oct 42	Aug 45	Sep 45	?

CGR Number	District Assigned	Length	Commissioned	Decommissioned	Disposal	Notes
352	8	27'	Mar 42	May 45	Sep 45	ex-*Shan-Gri-La*, #20A251
353	8	64'	Dec 41	Sep 44	Apr 45	ex-*Cocheco*, #222574
354	8	25'	Apr 42	Oct 43	May 44	ex-*The Patrol*, #20E527
355	8	27'	Dec 41	—	Dec 43	ex-*Shan-Gri-La II*, #20K425
356	8	48'	Dec 41	Oct 43	Aug 44	ex-*Dorothy M*, #227326
357	8	25'	Dec 41	—	Mar 44	ex-*Marbob*, #19C685
358	8	65'	Dec 41	—	Jan 42	ex-*Warner*, #18P65
359	8	31'	Dec 41	—	Dec 42	ex-*Manchacon*, #20G799
360	8	24'	Dec 41	Dec 43	Apr 43	ex-*Betty Lyn*, #22G529
361	8	55'	Dec 41	Nov 43	Mar 44	ex-*Sinbad III*, #210330
362	8	39'	Dec 41	Jul 43	Apr 45	ex-*Katherine*, #21B38
363	8	23'	Dec 41	Dec 43	Jan 44	ex-*Bayvangen*, #19B96
364	8	42'	Dec 41	—	Jun 43	ex-*Chalita*, #20B509
365	8	35'	Dec 41	Sep 43	Nov 43	ex-*Hermita*, #20A852
366	8	42'	Feb 42	Dec 43	Feb 44	ex-*Jady Boy*, #18L656
367	8	25'	Dec 41	Dec 43	Feb 44	ex-*Escape*, #21B108
368	8	34'	Dec 41	—	—	ex-*Milford*, #22E679; 3 Sep 42 destroyed by fire
369	8	18'	Dec 41	Jun 43	Aug 43	ex-*Little Mick*, #21B559
370	8	32'	Dec 41	Dec 43	Apr 44	ex-*Candey*, #18K823
371	8	28'	Dec 41	Jun 43	Jul 43	ex-*Miss Irene*, #21A596
372	8	53'	Jul 42	Jul 44	Dec 44	?
372	8	30'	Dec 41	—	Jun 42	?
373	8	34'	Dec 41	—	Jan 43	ex-*Ebby II*, #20B192
374	8	50'	Dec 41	—	Jan 42	?
374	8	30'	Feb 42	Dec 45	Apr 44	ex-*Bobby Ann*, #18E757
375	8	25'	Dec 41	Jan 44	Mar 44	ex-*Mobilgas*, #1121A769
376	8	100'	Dec 41	Dec 44	Aug 45	ex-*North Wind*, #228420
377	8	42'	Dec 41	Nov 43	May 44	ex-*Sis*, #232960
378	8	71'	Feb 42	Jun 43	Apr 44	ex-*Pirate*, #218479
379	8	59'	Feb 42	Mar 43	Apr 43	ex-*Weona II*, #213797
380	8	30'	Feb 42	Dec 43	Feb 44	ex-*Elizabeth George*, #19E319
381	8	34'	Feb 42	Jan 44	Apr 44	ex-*Pirate*, #20D766
382	8	43'	Apr 42	Nov 43	Feb 44	ex-*Kerry Sue*, #236916
382	8	50'	Feb 42	—	Mar 42	?
383	8	43'	Feb 42	Jul 43	May 44	ex-*Walter Lee*, #238780
384	8	38'	Feb 42	Feb 43	May 43	ex-*Mollie Belle*, #20A653
385	8	36'	Feb 42	Nov 43	Feb 44	?, #42C968
386	8	46'	Feb 42	Nov 43	Jan 44	ex-*Rusty*, #22F387 or 297813?
387	8	37'	Feb 42	Mar 42	Jun 46	ex-*Contact*, #22H158
388	8	30'	Feb 42	Jan 44	Mar 44	ex-*Arne*, #21C94
389	8	36'	Feb 42	Jun 43	Feb 44	ex-*Mary Girl*, #19C395
390	8	60'	Jul 42	Nov 43	May 44	ex-*Mignon*, #22A392
391	8	47'	Feb 42	Jun 43	May 44	ex-*Mary Ellen*, #222683
392	8	50'	Feb 42	Nov 43	Jan 44	ex-*Sunshine*, #221028
393	8	42'	Feb 42	Jan 44	Mar 44	ex-*Sweetheart*, #227168
394	8	31'	Feb 42	Dec 43	Jan 44	ex-*Sea Robin*, #22F388
395	8	40'	Feb 42	—	Jan 44	ex-*Charlotte*, #23A374
396	8	37'	Feb 42	Jan 44	Mar 44	ex-*Tahoe II*, #20D935
397	8	46'	Mar 42	Dec 43	Jan 44	ex-*Rufnek*, #235179
398	8	47'	Feb 42	Jan 44	Mar 44	ex-*Buddy Ann*, #237846
399	8	40'	Mar 42	Feb 44	Mar 44	ex-*Hilo*, #20M416
400	8	34'	Mar 42	Mar 44	Apr 44	ex-*Brynn Marie*, #20M263
401	8	34'	Mar 42	Jan 44	Feb 44	ex-*Mary Lou*, #20C850
402	8	32'	Apr 42	Nov 43	Jan 44	ex-*Ginger*, #22F378
403	8	32'	Mar 42	—	Feb 44	ex-*Evia*, #180266
404	8	32'	Mar 42	Apr 44	May 44	ex-*Puddle Jumper*, #19C338
405	8	64'	Jul 42	Apr 43	Apr 44	?
405	8	36'	Mar 42	—	Jun 42	?
406	8	32'	Mar 42	Dec 43	Jan 44	ex-*Whemgen, Jr.*, #20M455

CGR Number	District Assigned	Length	Commissioned	Decommissioned	Disposal	Notes
407	8	33′	Mar 42	Mar 44	May 44	ex-*Lorelei II*, #19E409
408	8	38′	Mar 42	Feb 44	May 44	ex-*Flying Cloud*, #19F78
409	8	45′	Mar 42	Mar 44	Apr 44	ex-*Joanne*, #232338
410	8	31′	Mar 42	Jan 44	Mar 44	ex-*Golden Girl*, #22C236
411	8	33′	Mar 42	Nov 43	Mar 44	ex-*Respite*, #19D686
412	3	33′	Dec 41	Jul 43	May 44	ex-*Duchess*, #10H1455
413	3	35′	Jul 42	Jun 43	Mar 44	?
420	3	38′	Aug 42	—	Dec 43	?
421	3	38′	Dec 41	—	Feb 42	?
422	3	32′	Jun 42	Mar 45	Apr 45	ex-*Arcturus*, #10G49
424	3	31′	Apr 42	Sep 44	Nov 44	ex-*Nim II*, #10F1027
425	3	33′	May 42	—	Dec 43	ex-*Roamin*, #10H1729
426	3	42′	Dec 41	—	Mar 43	ex-*Talisman*, #10L292
428	3	89′	Dec 41	—	Sep 43	CG-88006; accepted as a gift
429	3	40′	Dec 41	—	Apr 43	ex-*Harriet G II*, #10A798
430	3	36′	Dec 41	Mar 43	Jul 43	?
434	3	42′	Dec 41	—	Apr 45	ex-*Roberta*, #238622
435	3	38′	Mar 42	Oct 44	Jan 45	ex-*Nipisquist*, #10E1138
436	3	52′	Dec 41	—	Dec 43	ex-*Timberdoodle*, #239153
439	3	50′	Jul 42	—	Dec 43	?
441	3	41′	Dec 41	May 43	Apr 44	ex-*Blue Marlin*, #236167
444	3	42′	Aug 42	—	Oct 44	?
445	3	31′	Dec 41	—	Aug 42	ex-*Man O'War*, #10K775
446	3	38′	Dec 41	Feb 43	Mar 43	ex-*Carrie S*, #10B75; Mar 43 dismantled
447	3	38′	Dec 41	—	Mar 43	ex-*Decibel*, #10M1102
448	3	51′	Dec 41	Apr 44	May 44	ex-*Festoon*, #10K1401
449	3	44′	Dec 41	—	Nov 44	ex-*Sly Mongoose*, #10A89
452	3	32′	Aug 42	—	Nov 44	ex-*M.S. Duchess*, #10G51
455	3	35′	Dec 41	—	Dec 42	ex-*Barbara II*, #10X137
456	3	30′	Dec 41	—	Feb 43	ex-*Alice Gee II*, #10G1557
458	3	34′	Dec 41	Mar 43	Dec 43	ex-*Dogeye II*, #10K3
459	3	35′	Dec 41	—	Mar 42	?
460	3	31′	Dec 41	May 43	Mar 44	ex-*Minmi II*, #10N839
466	3	63′	Dec 41	—	Jun 43	16 Jun 43 accepted by USN
468	3	46′	Dec 41	Jul 43	Sep 43	?
471	3	48′	Dec 41	Apr 43	Apr 44	?
472	3	38′	Dec 41	Jan 43	Feb 43	?
473	3	46′	Dec 41	Mar 43	May 43	?
477	3	32′	Dec 41	Mar 43	Mar 44	?
479	3	35′	Dec 41	—	Feb 42	?
480	3	36′	Jul 42	—	Dec 43	?
481	3	65′	Dec 41	—	Jan 42	?
482	3	38′	Jul 42	—	Oct 44	?
483	3	39′	Dec 41	—	Mar 42	?
484	3	40′	Dec 41	—	Feb 42	?
485	3	79′	Dec 41	Mar 43	Aug 43	?
486	3	69′	Dec 41	—	Jan 42	?
487	3	34′	Dec 41	Jan 43	Apr 43	?
488	3	30′	Dec 41	—	Mar 42	?
489	3	65′	Dec 41	—	Mar 43	?
490	3	54′	Dec 41	—	Apr 43	?
492	3	30′	Dec 41	—	Mar 43	?
493	3	39′	Dec 41	—	Dec 43	?
494	3	31′	Dec 41	Dec 43	Jan 44	?
495	3	38′	Dec 41	Jun 45	Jul 45	?
496	3	35′	Dec 41	Apr 45	Jun 45	?
497	3	38′	Dec 41	—	Mar 43	?
499	3	45′	Dec 41	Mar 43	Nov 43	?
500	3	44′	Dec 41	—	Jul 42	?

CGR Number	District Assigned	Length	Commissioned	Decommissioned	Disposal	Notes
501	3	50'	Dec 41	—	Feb 42	?
502	3	42'	Dec 41	Mar 43	May 43	?
503	3	39'	Dec 41	Oct 43	Nov 43	?
504	3	39'	Dec 41	Jul 43	Mar 44	?
505	3	75'	Dec 41	—	Dec 41	Became CG-75008
506	3	39'	Dec 41	—	Feb 44	?
507	3	32'	Dec 41	—	Oct 42	?
509	3	67'	Dec 41	Dec 43	Jun 44	?
510	3	35'	Dec 41	Mar 43	Oct 43	?
512	3	40'	Dec 41	Jan 43	Apr 43	?
513	3	40'	Dec 41	Dec 43	Mar 46	?
514	3	34'	Dec 41	—	Jan 42	?
515	3	38'	Dec 41	Mar 44	Apr 44	?
516	3	44'	Jun 42	Mar 43	Feb 44	?
517	3	36'	Dec 41	Mar 43	May 44	?
518	3	38'	Dec 41	—	Jan 42	1st tour
			Apr 42	Mar 43	Jul 45	2nd tour
519	3	50'	Dec 41	—	Apr 42	?
520	3	40'	Dec 41	—	Mar 42	?
521	3	37'	Dec 41	Mar 43	Nov 43	?
522	3	40'	Dec 41	Mar 43	Mar 44	?
523	3	54'	Dec 41	Feb 44	Mar 44	?
524	3	58'	Dec 41	Mar 43	May 43	?
525	3	68'	Dec 41	—	Aug 42	?
526	3	35'	Dec 41	May 43	Jul 45	?
527	3	40'	Dec 41	—	Jan 43	?
528	3	33'	Dec 41	—	Mar 42	8 Mar 42 destroyed by fire
529	3	36'	Dec 41	—	Jan 42	?
530	3	51'	Dec 41	—	Oct 44	?
531	3	65'	Dec 41	Sep 44	Oct 44	?
532	3	33'	Dec 41	Nov 43	Dec 43	?
533	3	47'	Dec 41	—	Jan 42	?
534	3	65'	Dec 41	Apr 43	May 43	?
535	3	30'	Dec 41	Apr 43	May 43	?
536	3	39'	Feb 42	—	Jan 43	?
537	3	50'	Feb 42	—	Nov 43	?
538	3	70'	Mar 42	Dec 43		1st tour
			May 44	—	Jul 44	2nd tour
539	3	73'	Feb 42	—	Jun 45	?
540	3	48'	Feb 42	Nov 44	Dec 44	?
541	3	46'	Mar 42	—	Aug 44	?
542	3	42'	Feb 42	Jul 43	Apr 44	?
543	3	37'	Mar 42	Apr 44	Jun 44	?
544	3	42'	Mar 42	—	Aug 43	Became CG-42039
545	3	38'	Mar 42	—	Dec 43	?
546	3	61'	Mar 42	—	Feb 45	?
547	3	54'	Mar 42	—	Dec 43	?
548	3	42'	Apr 42	—	Dec 43	?
549	3	62'	Apr 42	—	Apr 45	?
550	3	61'	Apr 42	—	Dec 44	?
551	3	55'	Apr 42	May 44	Jul 44	?
552	3	40'	Apr 42	Mar 43	May 43	?
553	3	42'	Apr 42	Jun 43	Oct 43	?
554	3	57'	Apr 42	Nov 44	Apr 45	?
555	3	34'	Apr 42	—	Jan 43	?
556	3	39'	Apr 42	Jul 43	May 44	?
557	3	73'	Apr 42	Jun 45	Jul 45	?
558	3	53'	Apr 42	Apr 44	May 44	?
559	3	62'	Apr 42	Mar 43	Nov 43	?
560	3	54'	Apr 42	—	Apr 43	Became CG-54016

CGR Number	District Assigned	Length	Commissioned	Decommissioned	Disposal	Notes
561	3	64'	May 42	—	Jun 42	Became CG-64005
562	5	46'	Jun 41	Jun 43	Jul 43	ex-*Moon Maid*, #13T332
563	5	49'	May 41	Dec 42	Feb 43	ex-*Naturopath*, #232967
564	5	40'	May 41	Nov 43	Jun 44	ex-*Mary-E*, #237077
565	5	48'	Apr 41	May 43	Jun 43	ex-*Olivette*, #234956
566	5	40'	May 41	Jan 43	Apr 43	ex-*Ace-Hi*, #235491
567	5	44'	May 41	—	Mar 43	ex-*Louise*, #14E957
568	5	40'	May 41	—	May 42	?
569	5	36'	May 41	—	May 42	ex-*Sarah F*, #14D572
570	5	50'	Jun 41	—	Jun 42	?
571	5	62'	Jun 41	—	Feb 43	ex-*Stewart Brothers*, #222783; 10 Feb 42 destroyed by fire
572	5	36'	Jun 41	—	Jun 42	ex-*Susie B*, #235008
573	5	40'	Jun 41	May 43	Sep 43	ex-*Sunshine II*, #13Q952
574	5	90'	Jun 41	—	Jan 43	ex-*City of Southport*, #212877; became CG-86004
575	5	57'	Jun 41	Apr 43	May 43	ex-*Marion Sue Handy*, #223650
576	5	60'	Jul 41	Apr 43	May 43	ex-*Bessie L*, #222836
577	5	48'	Jul 41	Nov 43	Feb 44	ex-*Lorelei*, #225526
578	5	48'	Jul 41	Nov 43	Jan 44	ex-*Panchax*, #231512
579	5	40'	Jul 41	Jun 42	Jul 42	ex-*Hilda*, #233186
580	5	44'	Jul 41	—	Apr 42	?
581	5	54'	Jul 41	—	Jun 45	ex-*Priscilla*, #235436
583	5	42'	Aug 41	Jan 43	May 44	ex-*Charlotte*, #232623
584	5	56'	Aug 41	Nov 43	Mar 44	ex-*Estherbelle*, #228833
585	5	42'	Aug 41	May 44	Jun 44	ex-*Empress*, #236644
586	5	53'	Aug 41	May 44	Jun 44	ex-*Max*, #15F413
587	5	48'	Aug 41	—	Oct 42	ex-*Slow and Easy*, #233609
588	5	57'	Aug 41	Jun 45	Feb 46	ex-*Repajo*, #233447
589	5	50'	Aug 41	Oct 43	Sep 45	ex-*Ellanor*, #228750
590	5	73'	Aug 41	—	Jun 45	ex-*Student Prince*, #216151
591	5	40'	Aug 41	—	Aug 43	ex-*Angler*, #236143
592	5	?	Aug 41	—	Dec 41	?
593	5	42'	Sep 41	Mar 43	Apr 43	ex-*Lida S*, #237409
594	5	40'	Sep 41	—	Jan 43	ex-*Bob Joe*, #238711
595	5	46'	Sep 41	Jun 44	Aug 44	ex-*Folly*, #13C629
596	5	41'	Sep 41	—	May 42	?
597	5	26'	Sep 41	Oct 43	Feb 44	ex-*Wingfoot*, #15E602
598	5	40'	Sep 41	May 43	Jun 43	ex-*Cecil*, #238581
599	5	65'	Oct 41	Aug 43	Oct 43	ex-*Greenhill*, #227225
600	5	40'	Oct 41	May 43	Nov 43	ex-*Pollyanna*, #11G9
601	5	41'	Oct 41	—	Apr 42	?
602	5	48'	Sep 41	Feb 44	Mar 44	ex-*Corsair*, #234355
603	5	59'	Oct 41	Mar 43	May 43	ex-*Amos*, #229946
604	5	72'	Oct 41	—	Jun 42	?
605	5	38'	Oct 41	May 43	Jun 43	ex-*Jim Dandy*, #235037
606	5	36'	Nov 41	—	Jun 42	?
607	5	?	Nov 41	—	Dec 41	?
608	5	62'	Nov 41	Sep 43	Apr 44	ex-*Petunia*, #220370
609	5	38'	Jan 42	May 44	Jul 44	ex-*Barlyn*, #14L731
610	5	64'	Jan 42	Mar 43	Apr 43	ex-*The Russell*, #225922
611	5	50'	Dec 41	—	Jun 45	ex-*Fifty-Fifty*, #228606
612	5	50'	Dec 41	—	Sep 42	ex-*Thomas*, #233380
613	5	46'	Dec 41	Sep 43	Oct 43	ex-*Chief*, #230533
614	5	40'	Dec 41	Nov 43	Feb 44	ex-*Meene*
615	5	45'	Jan 42	—	Jun 44	ex-*America*, #13P659
616	5	44'	Jan 42	Nov 43	Mar 44	ex-*Evelyn S*, #14K860
617	5	46'	Jan 42	Nov 44	Dec 44	ex-*Onda II*
618	5	38'	Jan 42	—	Sep 42	ex-*Bonita III*, #14M175
619	5	41'	Jan 42	—	Sep 42	ex-*Elf*, #214659

CGR Number	District Assigned	Length	Commissioned	Decommissioned	Disposal	Notes
620	5	42′	Jan 42	Apr 43	Feb 44	ex-*Scottie II*, #14J742
621	5	40′	Jan 42	Oct 43	Feb 44	ex-*Katherine*, #234783
622	5	41′	Jan 42	Dec 43	Feb 44	ex-*Cecil B*, #236208
623	5	85′	Jan 42	Jan 45	Mar 45	ex-*Speriamo*, #228954
624	5	45′	Jan 42	Feb 44	Dec 44	ex-*May Willo*, #230476
625	5	75′	Jan 42	Nov 43	Feb 44	ex-*Francson III*, #229574
626	5	45′	Jan 42	Feb 44	Jul 44	ex-*Mihar II*, #228846
627	5	74′	Mar 42	Apr 43	Oct 44	ex-*Claremont*, #212332
628	4	43′	Dec 41	—	Aug 42	?
629	4	42′	Dec 41	Mar 44	May 44	?
630	4	38′	Dec 41	Nov 43	Dec 43	?
631	4	54′	Dec 41	—	Dec 42	?; 2 Dec 42 sunk
632	4	68′	Dec 41	Mar 43	Jul 43	?
633	4	52′	Dec 41	Aug 43	Nov 43	ex-*Vulcan*, #234033
634	4	38′	Dec 41	Aug 43	Oct 43	?
635	4	32′	Dec 41	Jan 44	Feb 44	?
636	4	34′	Dec 41	—	Mar 42	?
637	4	40′	Dec 41	Aug 43	Sep 43	?
638	4	40′	Dec 41	Nov 43	Dec 43	?
639	4	38′	Dec 41	—	Jul 43	?
640	4	40′	Dec 41	—	Mar 44	?
641	4	40′	Dec 41	Feb 44	Sep 44	?
642	4	38′	Dec 41	Jul 43	Dec 44	?
643	4	28′	Dec 41	Apr 43	May 43	?
644	4	45′	Dec 41	Oct 43	Aug 44	?
645	4	32′	Dec 41	Apr 43	Jun 44	?
646	4	40′	Dec 41	Nov 43	Apr 44	?
647	4	45′	Dec 41	Jul 43	Jan 44	?
648	4	42′	Dec 41	Mar 43	Jun 43	?
649	4	40′	Jan 42	Apr 43	Jan 44	?
650	4	38′	Jan 42	Nov 43	Oct 44	?
651	4	46′	Jan 42	Feb 44	Jul 44	?
652	4	40′	Feb 42	May 43	Sep 43	?
653	4	38′	Feb 42	Dec 43	Jan 45	?; 12 Jan 43 exploded and damaged
654	4	35′	Feb 42	—	Nov 43	?
655	4	32′	Mar 42	Sep 43	Oct 43	?
656	4	39′	Mar 42	Jul 43	Aug 43	?
657	4	42′	Mar 42	Jun 43	Jan 45	ex-*Tot II*, #28J222
658	12	34′	May 41	Apr 44	May 44	ex-*Xenphora*, #28C586
659	12	30′	Nov 41	May 43	Jan 44	?, #28D792
660	12	36′	May 41	—	Dec 43	ex-*Nereid*, #237330; became CG-39014
661	12	39′	Jun 41	—	Jan 43	ex-*Thegra*, #28E375; became CG-44024
662	12	53′	Jun 41	—	Jan 43	ex-*Crusader*, #28B615
663	12	39′	Oct 41	—	Oct 42	ex-*Mohawk*, #28M192
664	12	40′	Dec 41	—	Oct 43	ex-*Bear*, #28R400
665	12	32′	Feb 42	—	Jan 44	ex-*Nadinot*, #28B301
666	12	36′	Apr 42	—	May 44	ex-*Spindrift*, #28B724
667	12	36′	May 42	May 43	Nov 43	?
668	12	27′	Sep 42	—	Apr 43	?
669	12	42′	Sep 42	—	Nov 44	1st tour
670	12	96′	May 43	—	May 44	2nd tour
			Sep 44	—	Nov 45	?
671	12	85′	May 43	—	Nov 45	?
672	12	126′	May 43	—	Nov 45	?
706	9	40′	Dec 41	—	Jun 43	ex-*Water Gypsy*, #25A153
707	9	26′	Dec 41	—	May 42	?
707	9	30′	Mar 42	Aug 43	Oct 43	ex-*Mar-Lee*, #39K197

CGR Number	District Assigned	Length	Commissioned	Decommissioned	Disposal	Notes
708	9–2	29'	Aug 41	Aug 43	Sep 43	ex-*Thelma III*, #41A869
709	9–2	34'	Aug 41	Aug 43	Sep 43	ex-*Spray*, #45A108
710	9–2	30'	Nov 41	Sep 43	Oct 43	?, #43D999
711	9–2	35'	Aug 41	Aug 43	Nov 43	ex-*Dictapator*, #42A105
712	9–2	31'	Sep 41	Nov 43	Feb 44	ex-*Victoria*, #45J817
713	9–2	25'	Sep 41	Aug 43	Sep 43	ex-*Eee Dee Bee*, #39G882
714	9–2	40'	Sep 41	Apr 44	May 44	ex-*Buccaneer*, #43C712
715	9–2	31'	Sep 41	May 44	Jun 44	ex-*Matey*, #45K833
716	9–2	40'	Sep 41	Aug 43	Dec 43	ex-*Toska Joyce*, #229695
717	9–2	38'	Sep 41	May 44	Jun 44	ex-*Reinie*, #45G160
718	9–2	31'	Oct 41	Aug 43	Sep 43	ex-*Cliff-Mar*, #35A980
719	9–2	32'	Oct 41	—	May 43	ex-*Laza-While*, #42B224
720	9–2	30'	Nov 41	—	Oct 44	ex-*Water Baby*, #43E241
721	9–2	36'	Oct 41	—	Jul 42	ex-*Diane*, #35A236
721	9–2	30'	Aug 42	—	Nov 44	?
722	9–2	32'	Oct 41	—	Jun 45	ex-*Freida II*, #45K924
723	9–2	46'	Oct 41	Apr 44	Aug 44	ex-*Esther*, #35B533
724	9–2	32'	Oct 41	Aug 43	Jun 44	ex-*Judy Ann*, #35D751
725	9–2	35'	Oct 41	Aug 43	Nov 43	ex-*Agnes B*, #12D98
726	9–2	38'	Nov 41	Sep 43	Oct 43	ex-*Carolarry*, #45C442
727	9–2	39'	Nov 41	Aug 43	Oct 43	ex-*Vitesse II*, #35C498
728	9–2	36'	Oct 41	—	May 43	ex-*Blue Wren*, #35A750
729	9–2	38'	Nov 41	Oct 43	Nov 43	ex-*Natalie*, #41B65
730	9–2	64'	Nov 41	Aug 43	Oct 43	ex-*Ensign*, #212346
731	9–2	32'	Nov 41	Jul 44	Aug 44	ex-*Red Heels II*, #42C483
732	9–2	24'	Dec 41	Jul 43	Aug 43	ex-*Johnnie B*, #42A811
732	9–2	35'	Dec 41	—	Aug 42	?
733	9–2	40'	Nov 41	Jan 43	Dec 43	ex-*Galliard*, #1228715
734	9–2	25'	Nov 41	Aug 43	Nov 43	ex-*Shangri-La*, #45H69
735	9–2	28'	Dec 41	Apr 43	Oct 43	ex-*Rosalind*, #45D610
736	9–2	29'	Dec 41	Aug 43	Oct 43	ex-*Rejoyce*, #42B666
737	9–2	26'	Dec 41	Sep 42	Dec 42	ex-*Euberchak*, #42A639
738	9–2	33'	May 42	Oct 43	Dec 43	ex-*Drussila*, #42D157
739	9–2	25'	Dec 41	—	Feb 42	ex-*Huck Finn*, #20M147; 1st tour
			Feb 42	—	Jun 45	2nd tour
740	9–2	54'	Dec 41	Nov 43	Mar 44	ex-*Weekenda II*, #228047
741	9–2	61'	Dec 41	Nov 44	May 45	ex-*Naldnah II*, #222644
742	9–2	28'	Dec 41	—	Nov 42	ex-*Que-Bee-Cee*, #45C702
743	9–2	30'	Dec 41	—	Nov 42	ex-*Oaklander*, #45H865
744	9–2	32'	Dec 41	Jun 44	Jul 44	ex-*Kitkins II*, #12B13
745	9–2	38'	Jan 42	Jun 44	Jul 44	ex-*Boaz III*, #12A486
746	9–2	34'	Jan 42	—	Oct 43	ex-*Nautical*, #18B897
747	9–2	33'	Feb 42	—	Nov 44	ex-*Dobesa*, #12B817
748	9–2	25'	Dec 41	—	Jul 44	ex-*Top Flight I*, #42D10
749	9–2	30'	Dec 41	Aug 43	Sep 43	ex-*Ellogene*, #42A594
750	9–2	26'	Dec 41	—	Aug 44	?, #42A388
751	13	42'	Sep 41	May 43	Aug 43	ex-*Klatawa*, #227190
752	13	41'	Aug 41	May 43	Nov 43	ex-*Una*, #233830
753	13	37'	Sep 41	—	Oct 42	ex-*Green Wing*, #222785
754	13	36'	Sep 42	Jul 43	Oct 43	ex-*Ju-Al*, #30G946
755	13	31'	Dec 41	—	Mar 42	?
756	13	41'	Oct 41	—	Oct 42	ex-*Atica II*, #?
757	13	37'	Dec 41	—	Aug 42	ex-*Lady Luck*, #501011
758	13	38'	Dec 41	—	May 42	?
759	13	36'	Dec 41	—	Feb 42	?
760	13	41'	Nov 41	Dec 42	Jun 43	ex-*Evening*, #240785
761	13	38'	Oct 41	Mar 43	May 43	ex-*Alida*, #?
762	13	36'	Dec 41	—	Apr 42	?
763	13	30'	Nov 41	Dec 42	Mar 43	ex-*Lazy Lou*, #229937
764	13	28'	Dec 41	—	Nov 42	ex-*Bunny*, #?

CGR Number	District Assigned	Length	Commissioned	Decommissioned	Disposal	Notes
765	13	42'	Dec 41	—	May 42	?
766	13	60'	Dec 41	Aug 45	Dec 45	ex-*Bob Cat II*, #?
767	13	41'	Jan 42	Mar 43	May 44	ex-*Springbox II*, #241261
768	13	44'	Feb 42	—	Feb 46	ex-*Prosper*, #221804
769	13	52'	Feb 42	—	Nov 42	ex-*Tatoosh*, #224191
770	13	36'	Jan 42	May 43	Jun 43	ex-*Martha B*, #238486
771	13	32'	Jan 42	—	Oct 42	ex-*Lady Mohr*, #?
772	13	32'	Jan 42	Apr 43	Aug 43	ex-*Pamarjo*, #302835
773	13	46'	Feb 42	Dec 44	Mar 45	ex-*Tradewinds Kingfisher*, #240649
774	13	55'	Jan 42	Dec 42	Dec 43	ex-*Blonde*, #225330
775	13	33'	Feb 42	May 43	Aug 44	ex-*Sea Queen*, #?
776	13	41'	Feb 42	Jan 44	May 44	ex-*Viking*, #236789
777	13	41'	Feb 42	—	Mar 45	ex-*Dunlin*, #220579
778	13	40'	Jan 42	—	Aug 43	ex-*Alcade*, #230967
779	13	32'	Feb 42	Nov 43	Apr 44	ex-*Rosarita*, #29N158
780	13	32'	Feb 42	Nov 44	Mar 45	ex-*Dickedan II*, #?
781	13	35'	Feb 42	Jun 43	Aug 43	ex-*Joanne*, #233653
782	13	30'	Feb 42	Sep 44	Dec 44	ex-*Leilani*, #?
783	13	63'	Apr 42	—	Oct 43	ex-*Winifred III*, #?
784	13	42'	Jul 42	—	Mar 43	?
785	13	42'	Mar 42	Aug 44	Nov 44	ex-*Gypsy*, #?
786	13	47'	Mar 42	Jul 44	Sep 44	ex-*Wanderer*, #?
787	13	31'	Apr 42	Mar 43	Jun 43	ex-*El Gave*, #?
788	13	30'	Apr 42	—	Feb 45	ex-?, #30W483
789	13	66'	Apr 42	Nov 44	Apr 45	ex-*Argosy*, #?
790	13	52'	Apr 42	—	Apr 43	ex-*Bamba*, #?
791	13	52'	Apr 42	Jan 45	Feb 45	ex-*Dickedann*, #?
792	13	32'	May 42	Dec 44	Mar 45	ex-*Sea Star*, #?
793	13	30'	Apr 42	Mar 43	Apr 43	ex-*Jeanette B III*, #29E203
794	13	36'	Apr 42	—	Mar 43	ex-*Capicua*, #?
795	13	31'	Apr 42	—	Nov 42	ex-*Marguerite*, #?
796	13	36'	Apr 42	Nov 43	Feb 44	ex-*Betty Lou*, #?
797	13	40'	Apr 42	Jan 45	Feb 45	ex-*White Light*, #?
798	13	31'	Apr 42	—	Oct 42	ex-?, #30Y259
799	13	34'	Apr 42	Nov 44	Mar 45	ex-*Valouris*, #?
800	13	35'	Apr 42	—	Mar 45	ex-*Pala Squaw*, #?
801	13	40'	May 42	May 43	Jul 43	ex-*Patrus*, #?
802	13	42'	Apr 42	Nov 44	May 45	ex-*El Dorann*, #227863
803	13	25'	Apr 42	Jan 45	Mar 45	?, #30T75
804	13	31'	Apr 42	Dec 44	Apr 45	?, #30X746
805	13	29'	Apr 42	Mar 43	Jul 43	ex-*Dermatics II*, #?
806	13	39'	Mar 42	—	Mar 43	ex-*Fish Tales*, #?
807	13	30'	Apr 42	—	May 43	ex-*Willette II*, #?
808	13	46'	May 42	—	Dec 42	ex-*Nika*, #?
809	13	34'	Apr 42	Mar 43	Jul 43	ex-*Helen S*, #?
810	13	45'	Jun 42	Jan 45	Mar 45	ex-*Margaret*, #?
811	1	129'	May 42	—	Nov 45	ex-*Pilot*, #?
812	1	94'	May 42	—	Nov 45	ex-*Roseway*, #?
813	1	38'	Jun 42	Jun 43	Jan 45	ex-*Seguin*, #?
814	1	32'	Jun 42	Oct 43	Oct 44	ex-*Saki*, #?
815	1	38'	Jun 42	May 43	Oct 43	ex-*Comewa*, #?
816	1	40'	Jun 42	Jul 44	Dec 44	ex-*Baltic*, #?
817	1	42'	May 42	May 43	Mar 44	ex-*At Last*, #?
818	1	39'	Jun 42	—	Apr 44	ex-*Eva C. Clark*, #?
819	1	23'	Jun 42	Feb 43	Feb 44	?, #4B705
820	1	46'	Jun 42	Dec 43	Jun 44	ex-*Clambo*, #?
821	1	34'	Jun 42	Oct 43	May 44	ex-*Tee-Dee*, #?
822	1	30'	Jun 42	May 43	Oct 44	ex-*Marlin*, #?
823	1	38'	Jun 42	May 43	May 44	ex-*Snark II*, #?
824	1	54'	Jun 42	—	Dec 42	ex-*Genevive II*, #?

CGR Number	District Assigned	Length	Commissioned	Decommissioned	Disposal	Notes
825	1	32'	Jun 42	Nov 43	Feb 44	ex-*Palengro*, #?
826	1	23'	Jun 42	Apr 43	May 44	ex-*Befair*, #?
827	1	48'	Jun 42	Dec 43	Aug 44	ex-*Myra Maude*, #?
828	1	34'	Jun 42	Jan 44	Oct 44	ex-*Mempat*, #?
829	1	35'	Jun 42	Oct 43	Jun 44	ex-*Shirley Louise*, #?
830	1	53'	Jun 42	Dec 43	Aug 44	ex-*Saga*, #?
831	1	33'	Jul 42	Oct 43	Dec 43	?
832	1	45'	Jul 42	Oct 43	Nov 43	?
833	1	26'	Jul 42	Oct 43	Jul 44	?
834	1	31'	Jul 42	Oct 43	Jun 44	?
835	1	36'	Jul 42	Oct 43	Nov 43	?
836	1	38'	Jul 42	May 43	Jan 44	?
837	1	37'	Jul 42	Dec 43	Jul 45	?
838	1	40'	Jul 42	May 43	Mar 46	?
839	1	42'	Jul 42	Oct 43	May 44	?
840	1	38'	Jul 42	May 43	Dec 43	?
841	1	36'	Jul 42	Mar 43	Jun 44	?
842	1	36'	Jul 42	Sep 43	Aug 44	?
843	1	41'	Jul 42	Oct 43	Jun 44	?
844	1	32'	Jul 42	Sep 43	Nov 43	?
845	1	39'	Jul 42	May 43	Jun 45	?
846	1	46'	Jul 42	Dec 43	Aug 44	?
847	1	36'	Jul 42	Mar 43	Aug 44	?
848	1	54'	Aug 42	Nov 43	Dec 43	?
849	1	34'	Aug 42	Jun 43	Aug 44	?
850	1	35'	Jul 42	—	Oct 42	?
851	1	33'	Aug 42	—	Aug 42	15 Aug 42 burned
852	1	40'	Aug 42	—	Nov 43	?
853	1	36'	Aug 42	Dec 43	May 44	?
854	1	38'	Aug 42	May 43	Jul 44	?
855	1	36'	Aug 42	Mar 43	Aug 44	?
856	1	48'	Aug 42	Aug 43	Nov 43	?
857	1	39'	Aug 42	Mar 43	Aug 44	?
858	1	48'	Aug 42	Nov 43	Dec 43	?
859	1	40'	Aug 42	Apr 43	Jan 44	?
860	1	40'	Aug 42	—	Apr 44	?
861	1	61'	Sep 42	—	Nov 42	?
862	1	35'	Sep 42	—	Jan 43	5 Nov 42 burned
863	1	33'	Sep 42	Mar 43	Apr 43	?
864	1	36'	Sep 42	Jan 43	Feb 43	?
865	1	38'	Sep 42	May 43	Mar 46	?
866	1	48'	Sep 42	Nov 43	Jan 45	?
867	1	36'	Sep 42	—	Jan 43	?
868	1	60'	Sep 42	Jul 44	Jan 45	?
869	1	38'	Sep 42	Oct 43	Dec 44	?
870	1	34'	Sep 42	Mar 43	Feb 44	?
871	4	37'	Mar 42	Aug 43	Sep 43	?
872	4	39'	Mar 42	Feb 44	Jul 44	?
873	4	36'	Mar 42	Feb 43	Jul 44	?
874	4	35'	Mar 42	Jan 44	Jul 44	?
875	4	36'	Mar 42	Mar 44	Apr 44	?
876	4	39'	Mar 42	Mar 44	Nov 44	?
877	4	38'	Mar 42	—	Dec 42	?
878	4	44'	Apr 42	Nov 43	Oct 44	?
879	4	46'	May 42	—	May 43	?
880	4	37'	May 42	May 43	Nov 43	?
881	4	71'	Apr 42	May 43	Jul 43	?
882	4	42'	May 42	May 43	Nov 43	?, 25 May 42 rescued 12 survivors from the tanker *Persephone*
883	4	35'	Apr 42	Jan 44	May 44	?

CGR Number	District Assigned	Length	Commissioned	Decommissioned	Disposal	Notes
884	4	38'	May 42	Feb 44	Apr 44	?
885	4	39'	May 42	—	Feb 44	?
886	4	39'	Jun 42	Mar 44	May 44	?
887	4	39'	May 42	Feb 44	Jun 44	?
888	4	28'	May 42	Jan 44	May 44	?
889	4	36'	May 42	—	Aug 44	?
890	4	36'	Jun 42	Mar 43	Apr 43	?
891	5	39'	Jan 42	Mar 45	May 45	ex-*Louwar*, #?
892	5	40'	Feb 42	Mar 45	May 45	ex-*Florence II*, #13M608
893	5	40'	Feb 42	Nov 43	Jun 45	ex-*Kirflem*, #?
894	5	69'	Mar 42	May 43	Sep 43	ex-*Rujopa*, #227727
895	5	56'	Mar 42	Jan 45	May 45	ex-*Javelin II*, #222999
896	5	62'	Mar 42	—	Jan 45	ex-*Gurkha*, #213100
897	5	40'	Feb 42	—	Jun 42	?
898	5	47'	Mar 42	May 43	Sep 43	ex-*Kay Hardin*, #13U937
899	5	49'	Mar 42	May 43	Apr 44	ex-*Spray*, #202396
900	5	45'	Mar 42	Mar 44	Jun 44	ex-*Walvrilou*, #234816
901	5	38'	Mar 42	Nov 43	Mar 44	ex-*Miss Washington*, #13H300
902	5	40'	Mar 42	Dec 44	Jan 45	ex-*Tommy*, #11K655
903	5	46'	Mar 42	Jun 45	Aug 45	ex-*Margret An*, #13Q87
904	5	46'	Mar 42	—	Oct 44	ex-*Pelican II*, #234528
905	5	36'	Mar 42	—	Feb 43	ex-*Ewan*, #13S782
906	5	48'	Apr 42	Nov 43	May 44	ex-*Peggy B*, #231085
907	5	85'	Mar 42	—	Jul 42	ex-*Sea Dream*, #?; 29 Jul 42 became CG-85008
908	5	40'	Apr 42	Feb 43	Jun 43	ex-*Sea King*, #234038
909	5	46'	Apr 42	Mar 45	May 45	ex-*Argosy*, #?
910	5	75'	Apr 42	Nov 43	May 44	ex-*Charbert*, #231807
911	5	42'	Jul 42	Nov 43	Jun 44	ex-*Mary Jane*, #?
912	5	38'	Apr 42	—	Jan 43	ex-*White Cap*, #?
913	5	50'	May 42	Nov 43	Mar 44	ex-*Decoy*, #?
914	5	46'	Jul 42	—	Feb 44	ex-*Rex II*, #?; 1st tour
			Apr 44	Nov 44	Dec 44	2nd tour
915	5	25'	May 42	Nov 43	Dec 43	?
916	6–7	32'	Apr 42	May 43	Aug 44	?
917	6–7	39'	Apr 42	Jan 44	Jun 44	?
918	6–7	38'	Apr 42	Aug 43	Dec 43	?
919	6–7	54'	Apr 42	May 43	Dec 43	?
920	6–7	40'	May 42	—	Mar 43	?
921	6–7	48'	May 42	May 43	Apr 44	?
922	6–7	39'	May 42	—	Apr 43	?
923	6–7	46'	May 42	Jan 44	Oct 44	?
924	6–7	47'	May 42	May 43	Mar 44	?
925	6–7	44'	Jun 42	May 43	Sep 44	?
926	7	51'	Feb 42	Nov 43	Dec 43	ex-*Marlin*, #230405
927	7	54'	Mar 42	—	Dec 43	ex-*Patsea*, #?
928	7	60'	Feb 42	May 43	Sep 43	ex-*Lenore*, #210819
929	7	30'	Mar 42	—	Nov 43	ex-*Flo*, #18R906
930	7	39'	Mar 42	May 43	Jun 43	ex-*Dormar*, #?
931	7	62'	Mar 42	Nov 43	May 44	ex-*Standeck*, #225607
932	7	57'	Mar 42	—	Nov 43	ex-*Velaim II*, #225477
933	7	52'	Mar 42	May 43	Sep 43	ex-*Sea-Bee*, #223717
934	7	48'	Mar 42	May 43	Aug 43	ex-*Mihaska*, #238103
935	7	38'	Mar 42	—	Dec 43	ex-*Fiji III*, #18L563
936	7	38'	Mar 42	May 43	Jun 43	ex-*Ida B. II*, #18B185
937	7	69'	Mar 42	—	May 44	ex-*Iorano*, #234791
938	7	40'	Mar 42	May 43	Mar 44	ex-*Bee Gee III*, #18M336
939	7	30'	Apr 42	—	Nov 43	ex-*Strange Interlude*, #18P404
940	7	62'	Apr 42	—	Nov 43	ex-*Bing*, #222998
941	7	34'	Apr 42	May 43	Aug 43	ex-*Nana*, #18K362
942	7	54'	May 42	—	Jul 43	ex-*Atlantan*, #232664

CGR Number	District Assigned	Length	Commissioned	Decommissioned	Disposal	Notes
943	7	37'	Apr 42	May 43	Jun 43	ex-*Hakasam*, #43D685
944	7	30'	Apr 42	May 43	Jul 43	ex-*Nillor II*, #4J385
945	7	63'	Apr 42	—	Jul 43	ex-*Caprice*, #228520
946	8	33'	Mar 42	Dec 43	Jan 44	ex-*Sandspur*, #19D411
947	8	37'	Mar 42	Oct 43	Dec 43	ex-*Plauen*, #20D33
948	8	40'	Mar 42	Oct 43	Nov 43	ex-*Majoheba*, #238489
949	8	34'	Mar 42	May 43	Sep 43	ex-*Picaron*, #19B978
950	8	50'	Mar 42	Mar 43	Apr 43	ex-*Jade*, #227511; 24 Apr 43 burned
951	8	35'	Mar 42	Nov 43	Apr 44	ex-*Alondra*, #22D45
952	8	44'	Mar 42	Nov 43	Apr 44	ex-*Hazel Ann*, #18T747
953	8	33'	Mar 42	Feb 44	Mar 44	ex-*King Mirth*, #19E144
954	8	47'	Mar 42	—	Nov 42	ex-*Maxine*, #229722
955	8	28'	Mar 42	Dec 43	Feb 44	ex-*Celestine*, #18L301
956	8	42'	Mar 42	Nov 43	Jan 44	ex-*Loumar*, #19E675
957	8	30'	Mar 42	—	Aug 42	ex-*Nicolangela*, #18T393
958	8	53'	Mar 42	Dec 43	Apr 44	ex-*Frances*, #225903
959	8	?	Mar 42	?	?	ex-*Mystic*, #?
960	8	47'	Aug 42	—	Dec 43	?
	8	34'	Mar 42	—	Apr 42	?
961	8	38'	Aug 42	Nov 43	Feb 44	?
962	8	32'	Mar 42	—	Apr 42	?
962	8	35'	Mar 42	Mar 44	Apr 44	ex-*Osprey II*, #20G325
963	8	55'	Mar 42	—	Jan 43	ex-*Natasha*, #21C256; 27 Jan 43 burned
964	8	45'	Mar 42	Nov 43	Jan 44	ex-*Bonita*, #20B798
965	8	30'	Apr 42	Jan 44	Feb 44	ex-*Buckeroo II*, #19A31
966	9–2	30'	Dec 41	—	Sep 43	ex-*Dade II*, #45K394
967	9–2	30'	Dec 41	—	Jun 45	ex-*Julia Ann*, #42A337
968	9–2	30'	Dec 41	Mar 44	May 44	ex-*Scottie II*, #45A9
969	9–2	30'	Jan 42	—	Apr 43	ex-*Virginia D*, #40B620
970	9–2	30'	Dec 41	Aug 43	Oct 43	ex-*Lona Jane*, #19F363
971	9–2	30'	Jan 42	Dec 42	Jul 43	ex-*Hav-One II*, #12C21
972	9–2	32'	Feb 42	Dec 44	Jan 45	ex-*Sesami*, #43D806
973	9–2	30'	Feb 42	Oct 43	May 44	?
974	9–2	38'	Mar 42	Aug 43	Oct 43	ex-*Rascal V*, #41C303
975	9–2	33'	Apr 42	Aug 43	Oct 43	ex-*Connie K*, #35E341
976	9–2	70'	Apr 42	Aug 43	Sep 43	ex-*Eugenlann*, #234271
977	9–2	30'	Mar 42	Nov 43	Mar 44	ex-*Charlotte*, #45B955
978	9–2	28'	Apr 42	Jan 43	Apr 43	ex-*Black II*, #40B627
979	9–2	30'	Mar 42	—	May 45	ex-*Franobill*, #43F114
980	9–2	30'	Mar 42	—	Jul 44	ex-*Ardar*, #43F579
981	9–2	30'	Mar 42	Nov 43	Dec 43	ex-*Duration*, #43F609
982	9–2	32'	Apr 42	Aug 43	Oct 43	ex-*J. J. Marilyn*, #45D776
983	9–2	32'	Mar 42	Jun 43	Aug 43	ex-*Aphrodite II*, #45B277
984	9–2	30'	Jul 42	—	Jun 45	?
985	9–2	30'	Mar 42	—	Jun 43	ex-*Muramar II*, #43D821
986	9–2	32'	Mar 42	—	Nov 44	ex-*Eylene*, #45B278
987	9–2	30'	Mar 42	Sep 43	Oct 43	ex-*White Lily*, #43F580
988	9–2	36'	Mar 42	Jul 43	Sep 43	ex-*Lojac II*, #45F802
989	9–2	30'	Apr 42	Aug 43	Sep 43	ex-*Cindy*, #43E377
1000	1	49'	Jun 42	May 43	Nov 43	ex-*Joann*, #224091
1001	1	50'	Jun 42	May 43	Sep 43	ex-*Essex VI*, #?
1002	1	42'	Jun 42	—	Sep 42	ex-*Yaarab*, #4G363
1003	1	50'	Jun 42	Oct 42	Dec 42	ex-*Stormsvalla*, #?
1004	1	85'	Jun 42	Dec 43	Mar 44	ex-*Mendham*, #?
1005	1	65'	Jun 42	May 43	Oct 43	ex-*Kelpie*, #?
1006	1	41'	Sep 42	May 43	Jun 44	?
1007	1	38'	Sep 42	May 43	Jun 44	?
1008	1	40'	Sep 42	—	Nov 42	?
1009	1	40'	Sep 42	—	Oct 42	?
1010	1	34'	Sep 42	Jan 44	Mar 44	?

CGR Number	District Assigned	Length	Commissioned	Decommissioned	Disposal	Notes
1011	1	35'	Sep 42	—	Jan 43	?
1012	1	33'	Sep 42	Feb 43	Mar 44	?
1013	1	42'	Sep 42	Oct 43	Jul 44	?
1014	1	39'	Oct 42	Jul 43	Nov 44	?
1015	1	40'	Oct 42	Oct 43	May 44	?
1016	1	38'	Oct 42	Jun 44	Aug 44	?
1017	1	40'	Sep 42	—	Jul 44	?
1018	1	44'	Oct 42	—	Dec 43	?
1019	1	48'	Oct 42	Jan 44	Jan 45	?
1020	1	37'	Oct 42	—	May 44	?
1021	1	47'	Oct 42	—	Oct 44	?
1022	1	42'	Oct 42	—	Dec 43	?
1023	1	60'	Oct 42	Oct 43	Apr 45	?
1024	1	34'	Nov 42	Nov 43	May 44	?
1025	1	55'	Nov 42	Dec 43	Apr 45	?
1026	1	39'	Nov 42	Nov 43	Aug 44	?
1027	1	46'	Nov 42	Dec 43	Feb 44	?
1028	1	36'	Nov 42	Nov 43	Nov 44	?
1029	1	48'	Nov 42	May 44	Jan 45	?
1030	1	50'	Nov 42	Aug 44	Feb 45	?
1031	1	56'	Dec 42	Dec 43	Aug 44	?
1032	1	32'	Nov 42	Apr 43	Apr 44	?
1033	1	40'	Nov 42	May 43	Jun 43	?
1034	1	69'	Jan 43	—	Nov 45	?
1101	3	43'	May 42	Feb 44	Sep 45	?
1102	3	43'	Apr 42	—	May 42	?
1103	3	43'	May 42	May 43	May 44	11 May 44 became CG-42040
1104	3	25'	Apr 42	—	Dec 43	?
1105	3	45'	May 42	—	Apr 45	?
1106	3	56'	Apr 42	May 43	Dec 43	?
1107	3	35'	May 42	—	Dec 44	?
1108	3	55'	May 42	—	Jan 43	18 Jan 43 sunk
1109	3	38'	May 42	—	Dec 43	?
1110	3	34'	May 42	Dec 43	Feb 44	?
1111	3	43'	May 42	Mar 45	Apr 45	?
1112	3	32'	May 42	May 43	Apr 44	?
1113	3	40'	May 42	—	Nov 44	?
1114	3	36'	May 42	Dec 43	Oct 45	?
1115	3	30'	Aug 42	—	Sep 43	?
1116	3	50'	May 42	Sep 44	Mar 45	?
1117	3	52'	May 42	—	Jun 42	9 Jun 42 destroyed
1118	3	45'	May 42	May 43	Apr 44	?
1119	3	26'	May 42	Dec 43	Mar 43	?
1120	3	50'	Jun 42	Dec 43	Mar 43	?
1121	3	32'	May 42	—	Sep 43	?
1122	3	37'	May 42	Mar 44	Apr 44	?
1123	3	39'	May 42	—	Apr 45	?
1124	3	45'	May 42	—	Mar 45	?
1125	3	42'	Jun 42	—	Apr 43	?
1126	3	53'	Jul 42	—	Sep 44	?
1127	3	45'	Jul 42	May 43	Jul 43	?
1128	3	38'	Jul 42	—	Nov 43	?
1129	3	29'	Jun 42	May 43	Jun 44	?
1130	3	48'	Jul 42	Nov 43	Nov 44	?
1131	3	43'	Jun 42	May 43	Dec 43	?
1132	3	30'	Jun 42	—	Mar 45	?
1133	3	30'	Jul 42	May 43	Feb 45	?
1134	3	25'	Jul 42	Nov 44	Mar 45	?
1135	3	29'	Jul 42	—	Mar 45	?
1136	3	50'	Jul 42	Dec 43	Mar 43	?

CGR Number	District Assigned	Length	Commissioned	Decommissioned	Disposal	Notes
1137	3	40'	Jul 42	Nov 44	Jan 45	?
1138	3	54'	Jun 42	Nov 43	May 44	?
1139	3	37'	Jul 42	Mar 45	Apr 46	?
1140	3	37'	Jun 42	—	Dec 42	?
1141	3	38'	Jun 42	May 43	Apr 44	?
1142	3	38'	Jun 42	—	Sep 44	?
1143	3	39'	Jun 42	—	Aug 43	?
1144	3	38'	Jun 42	May 43	Jun 44	?
1145	3	38'	Jun 42	—	Dec 43	?
1146	3	76'	Jun 42	Jun 44	Sep 44	?
1147	3	60'	Jun 42	May 43	Dec 43	?
1148	3	34'	Jun 42	May 43	Mar 44	?
1149	3	26'	Jun 42	May 43	Jan 44	?
1150	3	38'	Jun 42	May 43	Jul 44	?
1151	4	40'	May 42	—	Jun 43	?
1152	4	40'	Jun 42	—	Nov 43	?
1153	4	57'	Jul 42	—	Feb 43	6 Feb 43 damaged by explosion
1154	4	31'	Jun 42	—	Mar 43	?
1155	4	38'	Jul 42	—	Nov 43	?
1156	4	40'	Aug 42	—	Oct 43	?
1157	4	32'	Jul 42	—	Nov 43	?
1158	4	34'	Aug 42	—	Mar 43	?
1159	4	35'	Aug 42	—	Nov 43	?
1160	4	36'	Aug 42	Sep 43	Oct 43	?
1161	4	26'	Aug 42	May 43	Nov 43	?
1162	4	39'	Aug 42	Mar 44	Feb 45	?
1163	4	35'	Aug 42	Nov 43	Dec 43	?
1164	4	38'	Sep 42	Dec 43	Mar 44	?
1165	4	34'	Oct 42	Mar 44	Jan 46	?
1166	4	31'	Oct 42	Aug 43	Dec 43	?
1167	4	30'	Oct 42	May 43	Jun 43	?
1168	4	38'	Oct 42	Nov 43	Oct 44	?
1169	4	38'	Oct 42	—	Apr 43	?
1170	4	38'	Oct 42	Mar 44	Jun 44	?
1171	4	38'	Oct 42	Nov 43	May 44	?
1172	4	150'	Dec 42	—	Nov 45	?
1173	4	119'	Jan 43	—	Nov 44	?
1174	4	24'	Jan 43	—	Jun 44	?
1175	4	23'	Jan 42	—	Mar 43	?
1201	5	41'	Mar 42	—	Jun 45	ex-*Mary Elizabeth*, #233276
1202	5	45'	Mar 42	Mar 43	Aug 43	ex-*Horizon*, #10A1730
1203	5	46'	Mar 42	Oct 43	Aug 44	ex-*Gaynelle*, #237212
1204	5	38'	Jun 42	Mar 44	Jun 44	ex-*Dolly H II*, #15E190
1205	5	38'	May 42	Feb 44	Mar 44	ex-*Lar Mace*, #15E968
1206	5	61'	May 42	Aug 44	Sep 44	ex-*Mobjack*, #237869
1207	5	55'	May 42	—	Jan 45	ex-*Elsie Virginia*, #222566
1208	5	36'	May 42	Sep 44	Oct 44	ex-*Rummy*, #13L284
1209	5	39'	May 42	Feb 44	Jun 44	ex-*Washington III*, #13S427
1210	5	44'	May 42	Sep 44	Nov 44	ex-*Playboy*, #236626
1211	5	55'	May 42	—	Mar 45	ex-*Harold*, #224545
1212	5	?	?	—	May 42	?
1213	5	65'	Jun 42	Oct 44	Nov 44	ex-*Elsie K*, #227097
1214	5	45'	Jun 42	Apr 43	May 43	ex-*Harmattan*, #13N204
1215	5	72'	Jun 42	Sep 43	Dec 43	ex-*Westhaven*, #210110
1216	5	38'	Jun 42	May 43	Sep 43	ex-*Monterey*, #13C654
1217	5	58'	Jun 42	Jun 45	Aug 45	ex-*Fay Anne II*, #227989
1218	5	40'	Jun 42	Feb 44	Jul 44	ex-*Manderley*,
1219	5	42'	Jun 42	May 43	Jul 43	ex-*Florentine*, #229846
1220	5	38'	Jun 42	Dec 43	May 44	ex-*Suse Q III*, #13T211
1221	5	40'	Jun 42	May 43	Feb 44	ex-*Bess Ann*, #13A396

CGR Number	District Assigned	Length	Commissioned	Decommissioned	Disposal	Notes
1222	5	45'	Jun 42	May 43	Dec 43	ex-*Sea Hawk*, #13E336
1223	5	48'	Jun 42	—	Dec 42	ex-*Nellie Jane*, #239152
1224	5	48'	Jun 42	Feb 44	Mar 44	ex-*Lucille*, #239371
1225	5	47'	Jun 42	Sep 43	Jun 45	ex-*Rambler*, #?
1226	5	41'	Jun 42	May 43	Jun 43	ex-*Ricky*, #?
1227	5	64'	Jun 42	—	Mar 45	ex-*Wanda*, #?
1228	5	39'	Jun 42	May 43	Jun 43	ex-*Victory*, #?
1229	5	49'	Jun 42	Sep 43	Jan 44	ex-*Malolo*, #?
1230	5	38'	Jun 42	Feb 44	Jul 44	ex-*My Fancy*, #?
1231	5	39'	Jun 42	—	Jan 45	ex-*Bobjack II*, #?
1232	5	40'	Jun 42	Jan 43	Feb 43	ex-*Sea Breeze*, #?
1233	5	46'	Jun 42	—	Dec 44	ex-*Daisy May*, #?
1234	5	43'	Jun 42	Sep 44	Oct 44	ex-*Buzz Bee II*, #?
1235	5	43'	Jun 42	Jun 45	Aug 45	ex-*Eva May*, #?
1236	5	55'	Jun 42	—	Mar 43	ex-*Crusader*, #?
1237	5	38'	Jun 42	—	Mar 45	ex-*Terrapin*, #?; 17 Mar 43 burned
1238	5	42'	May 42	Dec 44	Jan 45	ex-*Alnan*, #?
1239	5	44'	May 42	—	Oct 44	ex-*Hobo IV*, #?
1240	5	40'	Jun 42	Dec 44	Jan 45	ex-*Meldawil*, #13U21
1241	5	44'	Jun 42	Dec 44	Jan 45	ex-*Undine II*, #238514
1242	5	46'	Jun 42	May 43	Sep 43	ex-*Tramp*, #13P462
1243	5	40'	Jun 42	Sep 43	Jul 44	ex-*Wild Goose II*, #?
1244	5	38'	Jun 42	—	Jun 45	ex-*Red Jacket*, #?
1245	5	40'	Jun 42	Sep 43	Jan 44	ex-*Larramore*, #?
1246	5	46'	Jul 42	Oct 43	Apr 44	?
1247	5	43'	Jul 42	Dec 43	Feb 44	?
1248	5	40'	Jul 42	Feb 44	Jul 44	?
1249	5	39'	Jul 42	—	Oct 43	?
1250	5	38'	Jul 42	Jun 45	Jul 45	?
1251	5	94'	Jul 42	Dec 43	Dec 44	?
1252	5	38'	Jul 42	Jun 45	Jan 46	?
1253	5	46'	Jul 42	Oct 43	Apr 44	?
1254	5	40'	Jul 42	May 43	Aug 43	?
1255	5	67'	Jul 42	Jan 43	Feb 43	?
1256	5	40'	Jul 42	—	Oct 44	?
1257	5	42'	Jul 42	Mar 43	Jun 43	?
1258	5	46'	Jul 42	Sep 43	Nov 43	?
1259	5	64'	Jul 42	Jun 45	Jul 45	?
1260	5	54'	Jul 42	Mar 44	May 44	?
1261	5	46'	Jul 42	Jan 45	Jul 45	?
1262	5	45'	Jul 42	May 43	Apr 44	?
1263	5	43'	Jul 42	Nov 43	Dec 43	?
1264	5	54'	Jul 42	Mar 44	Oct 44	?
1265	5	38'	Jul 42	Dec 43	Jun 44	?
1266	5	46'	Jul 42	May 45	Jun 45	?
1267	5	38'	Jul 42	May 43	Nov 43	?
1268	5	39'	Jul 42	May 43	May 44	?
1269	5	42'	Jul 42	May 43	Dec 43	?
1270	5	39'	Jul 42	Jun 45	Aug 45	?
1271	5	39'	Jul 42	Apr 44	May 44	?
1272	5	38'	Jul 42	May 43	Dec 43	?
1273	5	80'	Jul 42	—	Oct 42	?
1274	5	55'	Aug 42	May 43	Aug 43	?
1275	5	39'	Aug 42	May 43	Jul 43	?
1276	5	46'	Aug 42	Feb 44	Apr 44	?
1277	5	38'	Aug 42	May 43	Aug 43	?
1278	5	65'	Aug 42	Jul 44	Oct 44	?
1279	5	54'	Aug 42	Jun 45	Jul 45	?
1280	5	30'	Aug 42	Jun 45	Aug 45	?
1281	5	42'	Jul 42	—	Dec 42	?

CGR Number	District Assigned	Length	Commissioned	Decommissioned	Disposal	Notes
1282	5	68'	Jul 42	—	Aug 42	?
1283	5	46'	Jul 42	—	Sep 42	?
1284	5	39'	Jul 42	Sep 44	Feb 45	?
1285	5	44'	Jul 42	Dec 42	Jan 43	?
1286	5	46'	Jul 42	Feb 44	Sep 44	?
1287	5	22'	Jul 42	—	Dec 42	?
1288	5	36'	Jul 42	—	Nov 42	?
1289	5	77'	Jul 42	—	May 45	?
1290	5	46'	Jul 42	Jun 45	Aug 45	?
1291	5	61'	Aug 42	Jun 45	Aug 45	?
1292	5	46'	Sep 42	May 43	Apr 44	?
1293	5	46'	Sep 42	—	Feb 43	?
1294	5	40'	Sep 42	Nov 43	Feb 45	?
1295	5	46'	Oct 42	Oct 43	Apr 44	?
1296	5	40'	Oct 42	Nov 43	Mar 44	?
1301	13	34'	May 42	Dec 42	Jun 43	ex-*Lazy Lady*, #?
1302	13	36'	May 42	—	Dec 42	ex-*Liberty*, #?
1303	13	40'	Jun 42	Mar 44	May 44	ex-*Chemy*, #?
1304	13	38'	May 42	—	Dec 42	ex-*Zephyr*, #241324
1305	13	31'	May 42	Jan 45	Feb 45	ex-*Honey III*, #241135
1306	13	32'	May 42	Jan 45	Mar 45	ex-*Mary Lou*, #240761
1307	13	35'	May 42	—	May 43	ex-*Marily Jean*, #235952
1308	13	36'	May 42	Jan 43	Jul 43	ex-*Bambi II*, #241006
1309	13	65'	May 42	Dec 45	Apr 46	ex-*Marilyn*, #228841
1310	13	25'	May 42	—	Jan 45	?, #30S221
1311	13	46'	May 42	Jan 45	Mar 45	ex-*Sea Breu*, #228393
1312	13	34'	May 42	Mar 43	Jun 43	ex-*Wilmar*, #29A885
1313	13	50'	May 42	Nov 44	Mar 45	ex-*Flying Cloud*, #235095
1314	13	32'	May 42	Jul 44	Nov 44	ex-*Scorpion*, #239297
1315	13	44'	May 42	—	Dec 42	ex-*Vestone*, #224757; 1 Dec 42 burned
1316	13	42'	May 42	Jan 45	Mar 45	ex-*Aida*, #233821
1317	13	36'	May 42	Mar 43	May 43	ex-*Relax*, #29B848
1318	13	30'	Jun 42	Feb 44	May 44	?
1319	13	35'	Jun 42	Oct 43	Dec 43	?
1320	13	30'	Jul 42	Jun 43	Jul 43	?
1321	13	31'	Jun 42	Oct 43	Apr 45	?
1322	13	32'	Jun 42	Mar 43	May 43	?
1323	13	30'	Jul 42	—	Apr 43	?
1324	13	40'	Jun 42	Jan 45	Mar 45	?
1325	13	45'	Aug 42	Jan 45	Sep 45	?
1326	13	32'	Aug 42	—	Jan 43	?
1327	13	33'	Aug 42	—	Oct 42	?
1328	13	41'	Aug 42	Nov 43	Jan 44	?
1329	13	43'	Sep 42	Mar 43	Apr 43	?
1330	13	45'	Sep 42	Jan 45	May 45	?
1331	13	29'	Sep 42	Mar 43	May 43	?
1332	13	45'	Sep 42	Jan 45	Mar 45	?
1333	13	33'	Sep 42	Mar 43	Apr 43	?
1334	13	42'	Sep 42	Jan 45	Aug 45	?
1335	13	25'	Sep 42	Jan 45	Mar 45	?
1336	13	34'	Sep 42	Dec 44	Mar 45	?
1337	13	45'	Sep 42	Jan 45	Mar 45	?
1338	13	17'	Sep 42	Feb 44	May 44	?
1339	13	36'	Sep 42	Mar 43	Oct 43	?
1340	13	55'	Sep 42	Jan 45	Mar 45	?
1341	13	37'	Sep 42	Mar 43	Apr 43	?
1342	13	39'	Sep 42	Dec 43	Apr 44	?
1343	13	57'	Sep 42	Mar 43	Apr 43	?
1344	13	45'	Sep 42	—	Jan 43	?
1345	13	46'	Oct 42	Jan 45	Mar 45	?

CGR Number	District Assigned	Length	Commissioned	Decommissioned	Disposal	Notes
1346	13	46'	Oct 42	—	Apr 43	?
1347	13	38'	Oct 42	Mar 44	Jun 44	?
1348	13	24'	Oct 42	Jan 45	Apr 45	?
1349	13	45'	Oct 42	Jun 43	Sep 43	?
1350	13	38'	Oct 42	Dec 44	Mar 45	?
1401	6–7	85'	May 42	Sep 44	Nov 44	?
1402	6–7	65'	May 42	Oct 44	Nov 44	?
1403	6–7	40'	May 42	—	Nov 45	?
1404	6–7	38'	May 42	Mar 43	Oct 44	?
1405	6–7	63'	May 42	—	Nov 45	?
1406	6–7	47'	Jun 42	—	Nov 45	?
1407	6–7	78'	May 42	Nov 43	Aug 44	?
1408	6–7	36'	May 42	Mar 43	Apr 44	?
1409	6–7	40'	May 42	—	Nov 45	?
1410	6–7	31'	May 42	—	Nov 45	?
1411	6–7	45'	May 42	Apr 43	May 44	?
1412	6–7	23'	Jun 42	Nov 43	Jan 45	?
1413	6–7	65'	Jun 42	Nov 43	Apr 44	?
1414	6–7	28'	Jul 42	Mar 43	Sep 44	?
1415	6–7	30'	Jun 42	Mar 43	Dec 43	?
1416	6–7	30'	Jun 42	—	Apr 43	?
1417	6–7	38'	Jun 42	Mar 43	Jul 44	?
1418	6–7	98'	Jun 42	Mar 43	Aug 44	?
1419	6–7	85'	Jun 42	Nov 43	Apr 44	?
1420	6–7	63'	Jun 42	Nov 43	Apr 44	?
1421	6–7	47'	Jun 42	Nov 43	Dec 43	?
1422	6–7	27'	Jul 42	—	Mar 43	?
1423	6–7	35'	Jul 42	Mar 43	Apr 44	?
1424	6–7	30'	Jul 42	May 43	Oct 43	?
1425	6–7	30'	Jul 42	Mar 44	Apr 44	?
1426	6–7	30'	Jul 42	Mar 43	May 44	?
1427	6–7	34'	Jul 42	Jan 44	Feb 44	?
1428	6–7	28'	Jul 42	May 43	Oct 44	?
1429	6–7	38'	Jul 42	May 43	Nov 43	?
1430	6–7	38'	Jul 42	May 43	Jan 44	?
1431	6–7	30'	Jul 42	May 43	Aug 44	?
1432	6–7	32'	Jul 42	Jun 44	Jul 44	?
1433	6–7	26'	Jul 42	Jan 44	Jul 44	?
1434	6–7	30'	Aug 42	May 43	Aug 43	?
1435	6–7	45'	Aug 42	May 43	Oct 43	?
1436	6–7	43'	Aug 42	Mar 43	Sep 43	?
1437	6–7	60'	Aug 42	May 43	Jan 44	?
1438	6–7	36'	Jul 42	Nov 44	May 45	?
1439	6–7	43'	Aug 42	Oct 44	Feb 45	?
1440	6–7	50'	Jul 42	Oct 44	Feb 45	?
1441	6–7	19'	Aug 42	—	Feb 43	?
1442	6–7	32'	Aug 42	May 43	Jul 44	?
1443	6–7	30'	Aug 42	May 43	Dec 43	?
1444	6–7	31'	Aug 42	May 43	Dec 43	?
1445	6–7	54'	Aug 42	Jan 44	Apr 44	?
1446	6–7	37'	Aug 42	May 43	Sep 43	?
1447	6–7	26'	Aug 42	May 43	Dec 43	?
1448	6–7	34'	Aug 42	Mar 43	Feb 45	?
1449	6–7	42'	Sep 42	May 43	Jul 43	?
1450	6–7	38'	Sep 42	—	Jan 43	?
1451	6–7	40'	Apr 42	May 43	Jun 43	ex-*Gem*, #236846; 27 Jan 43 burned
1452	6–7	41'	Apr 42	Sep 44	Nov 44	ex-*Claire I*, #?
1453	6–7	50'	Apr 42	—	Dec 43	ex-*Conch*, #?; 1 Dec 43 burned
1454	6–7	49'	Mar 42	Nov 43	May 44	ex-*Gulf Stream*, #?
1455	6–7	54'	Apr 42	—	Nov 43	ex-*Tempo*, #229597

CGR Number	District Assigned	Length	Commissioned	Decommissioned	Disposal	Notes
1456	6–7	45′	Apr 42	May 43	Jul 43	?
1457	6–7	38′	Mar 42	Jan 44	Oct 44	ex-*Eleanor E III*, #18S343
1458	6–7	44′	Mar 42	Jan 44	Jul 44	ex-*Virginia III*, #?
1459	7	50′	Mar 42	—	Apr 43	ex-*Se-Ward*, #228199
1460	7	78′	Mar 42	Jan 44	Feb 44	ex-*Apelco*, #236499
1461	7	34′	Mar 42	Jun 44	Nov 44	ex-*Amigo*, #234052
1462	7	18′	Apr 42	Nov 43	Dec 43	ex-*M L M*, #18S769
1463	7	39′	Apr 42	Nov 43	Dec 43	ex-*Jay Vee*, #18M517
1464	7	26′	Apr 42	May 43	Jul 43	ex-*Snort*, #18S587
1465	7	44′	Apr 42	Jun 44	Jul 44	ex-*Silver King II*, #235963
1466	7	28′	Apr 42	Dec 43	Jan 44	ex-*Three Sisters*, #1H104
1467	7	44′	Apr 42	—	Dec 43	ex-*Natalie H*, #24006
1468	7	38′	Apr 42	May 43	Jul 43	ex-*Osprey*, #230344
1469	7	25′	Apr 42	—	Jul 43	ex-*John Lee*, #18P728
1470	7	50′	Apr 42	—	Dec 43	ex-*Silver King*, #?
1471	7	34′	Apr 42	Aug 43	Dec 43	ex-*Lindisfarne*, #18S386
1472	7	38′	Apr 42	May 43	Sep 43	ex*Voyager*, #18A545
1473	7	46′	Apr 42	Aug 43	Dec 43	ex-*Lucky Len II*, #236004
1474	7	18′	Apr 42	May 43	Jun 43	?
1475	7	46′	Apr 42	May 43	Sep 43	ex-*Matilda J*, #?
1476	7	16′	May 42	May 43	Sep 43	?
1477	7	30′	May 42	May 43	Nov 43	?
1478	7	36′	May 42	May 43	Jun 43	ex-*Serutan IV*, #180557
1479	7	51′	May 42	Apr 44	May 44	ex-*Hel-N-Bob*, #240115
1480	7	38′	May 42	Mar 44	Apr 44	ex-*Fun II*, #18G77
1481	7	130′	May 42	Aug 44	Sep 44	ex-*Black Swan*, #222385
1482	7	26′	May 42	—	Dec 43	?
1483	7	29′	May 42	Aug 43	Sep 43	?
1484	7	30′	May 42	Nov 43	Jan 44	ex-*Katy K*, #18S14
1485	7	42′	May 42	May 43	Aug 43	ex-*Emily Grace*, #18M262
1486	7	40′	May 42	May 43	Jun 43	ex-*Marie*, #233560
1487	7	38′	May 42	May 43	Jul 43	ex-*Dido*, #18S448
1488	7	38′	May 42	May 43	Jul 43	ex-*Horse Conch*, #?
1489	7	30′	Jun 42	—	Nov 45	?
1490	7	33′	Jun 42	—	Nov 45	?
1491	7	32′	Sep 42	—	Feb 44	?
1492	7	32′	Sep 42	May 43	Jul 43	?
1493	7	32′	Jul 42	May 43	Sep 43	?
1494	7	22′	Jul 42	—	Nov 42	21 May 43 became CG-24149
1495	7	32′	Jul 42	—	Nov 43	?
1496	7	32′	Jul 42	—	Nov 43	?
1497	7	38′	Aug 42	—	Mar 43	?
1498	7	36′	Jul 42	—	Jan 43	?
1499	7	30′	Jul 42	May 43	Jul 43	?
1500	7	30′	Jul 42	May 43	Jul 43	?
1501	8	30′	Apr 42	Nov 43	Jul 44	?, #19F521
1502	8	53′	Apr 42	—	Aug 44	ex-*Picayune IV*, #232070
1503	8	48′	Jul 42	Nov 43	Mar 44	?
1504	8	30′	Apr 42	—	Jul 43	ex-*Nita*, #21A150
1505	8	44′	Apr 42	Sep 43	Jan 44	ex-*Saint Elaine*, #230172
1506	8	30′	Apr 42	Jul 43	Apr 44	ex-*Tootsie Roll*, #22E628
1507	8	34′	Apr 42	Oct 43	Apr 44	ex-*Florafred*, #22A626
1508	8	80′	Mar 42	Dec 43	May 44	ex-*Mystic*, #220208
1509	8	52′	Apr 42	Mar 44	May 44	ex-*Escape*, #238052
1510	8	70′	Apr 42	—	Nov 42	ex-*Vigilante*, #206750
1511	8	65′	Feb 42	Dec 43	Apr 44	ex-*Lurline*, #232507
1512	8	62′	Apr 42	Dec 43	Feb 44	ex-*Dux V*, #228517
1513	8	85′	Apr 42	—	Oct 42	ex-*Southerly*, #239988; 7 Oct 42 became CG-85005
1514	8	42′	May 42	—	Dec 43	ex-*New Life III*, #238455
1515	8	34′	May 42	Nov 43	Feb 44	ex-*Izzard III*, #22G606

CGR Number	District Assigned	Length	Commissioned	Decommissioned	Disposal	Notes
1516	8	38'	May 42	—	Jan 44	ex-*Vega*, #14L302
1517	8	56'	Apr 42	Mar 44	May 44	?
1518	8	38'	Jun 42	Dec 43	Apr 44	ex-*Cavalier III*, #?
1519	8	65'	Aug 42	Aug 44	Sep 44	?
1520	8	39'	Jul 42	Mar 44	Apr 44	?
1521	8	70'	Aug 42	Jul 45	Sep 45	?
1522	8	45'	Jun 42	Jan 44	May 46	ex-*Chance*, #?
1523	8	22'	Jun 42	Feb 44	Mar 44	ex-*Little*, #?
1524	8	30'	Jul 42	Nov 43	Jan 44	?
1525	8	50'	Jul 42	Mar 43	Feb 44	?
1526	8	40'	Jul 42	Nov 43	Feb 44	?
1527	8	54'	Jul 42	Nov 43	Jan 44	?
1528	8	61'	Jul 42	Nov 43	Feb 44	?
1529	8	60'	Jul 42	Jun 43	Sep 43	?
1530	8	56'	Jul 42	Nov 43	May 44	?
1531	8	71'	Jul 42	Nov 43	Mar 44	?
1532	8	58'	Jul 42	Nov 43	Apr 44	?
1533	8	37'	Jul 42	Aug 43	Mar 44	?
1534	8	47'	Jul 42	Nov 43	Jan 44	?
1535	8	44'	Jul 42	Nov 43	Feb 44	?
1536	8	41'	Aug 42	Nov 43	Feb 44	?
1537	8	40'	Aug 42	Nov 43	Feb 44	25 Feb 44 became CG-40040?
1538	8	50'	Sep 42	Nov 43	Feb 44	?
1539	8	38'	Sep 42	Nov 43	Feb 44	?
1540	8	37'	Aug 42	Dec 43	Feb 44	?
1542	8	38'	Sep 42	Nov 43	Jan 44	?
1551	8	36'	Oct 42	Jun 43	Nov 43	?
1552	8	52'	Oct 42	Nov 43	Dec 43	?
1553	8	34'	Oct 42	Oct 43	Apr 44	?
1554	8	17'	Oct 42	Aug 43	Sep 43	?
1554	8	31'	Aug 42	—	Sep 42	?
1555	8	25'	Oct 42	Aug 43	Sep 43	?
1556	8	44'	Oct 42	Jan 44	Mar 44	?
1559	8	25'	Aug 42	Jan 44	Feb 44	?
1560	8	45'	Aug 42	Nov 43	Mar 44	?
1561	8	58'	Aug 42	Sep 44	Dec 44	?
1562	8	92'	Sep 42	Nov 43	Mar 44	?
1563	8	43'	Sep 42	Nov 43	Jan 44	?
1564	8	36'	Sep 42	Jun 43	Feb 44	?
1565	8	85'	Sep 42	Nov 43	Feb 44	?
1566	8	42'	Sep 42	—	Oct 42	?
1568	8	31'	Oct 42	Nov 43	Mar 44	?
1569	8	40'	Oct 42	Aug 43	Sep 46	?
1581	8	46'	Jul 42	—	Dec 44	?
1582	8	50'	Jul 42	Nov 43	Dec 43	?
1583	8	50'	Jul 42	—	Feb 45	?
1584	8	46'	Jul 42	Nov 43	Mar 44	?
1585	8	33'	Aug 42	Nov 43	Feb 44	?
1586	8	104'	Apr 43	—	Nov 45	?
1587	8	94'	Jul 42	Nov 43	Mar 44	?
1588	8	40'	Aug 42	—	Oct 43	?
1589	8	36'	Aug 42	—	Oct 44	?
1597	8	51'	Sep 42	Nov 43	Mar 44	?
1598	8	41'	Sep 42	Dec 43	Mar 44	?
1599	8	32'	Sep 42	Nov 43	Feb 44	?
1600	8	34'	Sep 42	May 43	Dec 43	?
1601	9	31'	May 42	Feb 43	Apr 43	ex-*Lark*, #37L794
1602	9	30'	May 42	Dec 42	May 43	ex-*Betty*, #37G991
1603	9	49'	May 42	May 43	Jul 43	ex-*Rex*, #37B301
1604	9	33'	May 42	—	Apr 43	ex-*Mandalay*, #39D336

CGR Number	District Assigned	Length	Commissioned	Decommissioned	Disposal	Notes
1605	9	40'	May 42	May 43	Jul 43	ex-*Loraine*, #39A603
1606	9	32'	May 42	Aug 43	Jun 44	ex-*Jer-Jac*, #39D139
1607	9	29'	May 42	Jan 43	Apr 44	ex-*Mae L J*, #39F954
1608	9	46'	May 42	Aug 43	Jun 44	ex-*Watsul*, #230637
1609	9	39'	May 42	Feb 43	Apr 43	ex-*Sylbar*, #39A497
1610	9	42'	May 42	Jan 43	May 43	ex-*Betty Gail*, #39E956
1611	9	35'	Jun 42	Jul 43	Sep 43	ex-*Betsy*, #39B474
1612	9	39'	Jun 42	Nov 43	May 44	ex-*Sue J*, #232697
1613	9	28'	Jun 42	Nov 43	May 44	ex-*Boatie*, #39A302
1614	9	29'	Jun 42	Jan 43	Apr 43	ex-*Debutramp*, #39D462
1615	9	26'	Jun 42	—	Apr 43	ex-*Ada C*, #39E195
1616	9	28'	Jun 42	Sep 43	Jul 44	?
1617	9	26'	Jun 42	Apr 44	May 44	?
1618	9	54'	Jul 42	Dec 43	May 44	?
1619	9	30'	Jul 42	Dec 43	May 44	?
1620	9	31'	Jul 42	Dec 43	May 44	?
1621	9	42'	Jun 42	Nov 43	Jun 44	?
1622	9	46'	Jul 42	May 43	Jun 43	?
1623	9	70'	Jul 42	May 43	Jul 43	?
1624	9	74'	Jul 42	Dec 42	Jun 43	?
1625	9	32'	Jul 42	Apr 43	Jul 43	?
1626	9	46'	Jun 42	Oct 43	May 44	?
1627	9	28'	Jun 42	May 44	Mar 44	?
1628	9	43'	Jun 42	Apr 43	May 43	?
1629	9	25'	Jun 42	May 43	Jul 43	?
1630	9	24'	Jun 42	Feb 44	May 44	?
1631	9	45'	Jul 42	Dec 43	May 44	?
1632	9	45'	Aug 42	Sep 43	Jun 44	?
1633	9	29'	Jul 42	Mar 43	Jun 43	?
1634	9	52'	Aug 42	Jan 43	Apr 43	?
1635	9	70'	Sep 42	Nov 43	Feb 44	?
1636	9	26'	Sep 42	Aug 43	May 43	?
1701	9–2	30'	Feb 42	Nov 43	Dec 43	?, #43F591
1702	9–2	32'	Feb 42	Nov 43	Nov 44	ex-*Hannah H. Hilbert*, #45D146
1703	9–2	30'	Mar 42	—	Apr 43	ex-*My Fortune*, #43F661
1704	9–2	40'	Feb 42	Nov 43	Jan 44	ex-*Sally H-11*, #43F41
1705	9–2	34'	May 42	Nov 44	Dec 44	ex-*Ellen O*, #45L25
1706	9–2	30'	Apr 42	—	Jan 45	ex-*Marionetta*, #43F645
1707	9–2	30'	Apr 42	Sep 43	Oct 43	ex-*Margaret Bell*, #43F634
1708	9–2	20'	Oct 42	—	Sep 44	?
1709	9–2	35'	Mar 42	Sep 43	Jan 44	ex-*Mary Kay*, #43E414
1710	9–2	30'	Mar 42	Oct 44	Jan 45	ex-*Nancy*, #43F1
1711	9–2	30'	Mar 42	—	Dec 42	ex-*Casita*, #45H715
1712	9–2	29'	Apr 42	Jun 43	Sep 43	ex-*Crescentia*, #39F610
1713	9–2	30'	Apr 42	—	Jan 43	ex-*Miss Alane*, #39G689
1714	9–2	30'	Jun 42	Aug 44	Sep 44	ex-*Lilliah D II*, #43F112
1715	9–2	32'	Mar 42	—	Jun 45	ex-*Victory I*, #45H549
1716	9–2	32'	Mar 42	—	Nov 44	ex-*Victory II*, #45H550
1717	9–2	50'	Apr 42	Dec 42	May 43	ex-*Lazy Sue*, #45J755
1718	9–2	30'	Apr 42	Nov 43	Dec 43	ex-*Fate*, #43F597
1719	9–2	31'	Apr 42	—	Jul 44	ex-*Pete*, #41E888
1720	9–2	30'	Apr 42	Aug 44	Sep 44	ex-*Queen B*, #39H593
1721	9–2	30'	Apr 42	Jan 43	Oct 43	ex-*Hildart*, #42A258
1722	9–2	30'	Apr 42	—	Aug 43	ex-*Labu*, #41F92
1723	9–2	33'	Apr 42	—	Oct 44	ex-*Skidgins IV*, #45D960
1724	9–2	30'	May 42	—	Jan 44	ex-*Francis B II*, #430850
1725	9–2	38'	Apr 42	May 43	Nov 43	ex-*Mariner*, #38F513
1726	9–2	33'	Apr 42	Sep 44	Oct 44	ex-*Apache*, #45E143
1727	9–2	30'	Apr 42	—	Jan 43	ex-*Patricia V*, #42D164
1728	9–2	30'	Apr 42	—	Jan 45	ex-*Orsalee*, #43F641

CGR Number	District Assigned	Length	Commissioned	Decommissioned	Disposal	Notes
1729	9–2	31'	Apr 42	Oct 43	Nov 43	ex-*Vanguard*, #45F410
1730	9–2	31'	Apr 42	Feb 43	Jun 43	ex-*Mae Beth*, #41J960
1731	9–2	32'	Apr 42	—	Nov 44	ex-*Corida Lee*, #45G73
1732	9–2	30'	Apr 42	Oct 43	Dec 43	ex-*Barjo*, #42C814
1733	9–2	32'	Apr 42	Jan 43	Jun 43	ex-*Amelia*, #42C921
1734	9–2	32'	May 42	—	Jun 43	ex-*Pegasus*, #43F504
1735	9–2	30'	Apr 42	Jan 43	Nov 43	ex-*Silota*, #42C788
1736	9–2	30'	Apr 42	—	Jun 45	?, #43F2
1737	9–2	33'	Apr 42	Aug 43	Nov 43	ex-*Inspiration*, #39E821
1738	9–2	30'	Apr 42	Sep 43	Oct 43	ex-*Betsey*, #41P762
1739	9–2	31'	Apr 42	Aug 43	Sep 43	ex-*Sheva*, #45E112
1740	9–2	30'	Apr 42	—	Nov 44	ex-*Mariellen*, #42B387
1741	9–2	45'	May 42	Aug 43	Nov 43	ex-*Mare Jane*, #45A394
1742	9–2	31'	Apr 42	Jul 43	Sep 43	ex-*Mary Barbara*, #42A577
1743	9–2	32'	May 42	—	Nov 44	ex-*Bee Gee Bee*, #42B132
1744	9–2	30'	Apr 42	Jan 43	Apr 43	ex-*Albatross*, #41P814
1745	9–2	32'	Apr 42	—	Nov 44	ex-*Kingfish*, #42B151
1746	9–2	32'	Apr 42	—	May 43	ex-*Vagabond*, #43B586
1747	9–2	38'	May 42	Sep 43	Oct 43	ex-*Marta*, #43F749
1748	9–2	30'	Apr 42	—	Jun 45	ex-*Lou Amelia*, #43F728
1749	9–2	30'	Apr 42	Apr 44	Jun 44	ex-*Nabinger VIII*, #45H300
1750	9–2	30'	Apr 42	Jan 43	Apr 43	ex-*Black Alice*, #42D159
1751	9–2	14'	Aug 42	—	Jun 45	?
1751	2	42'	Jun 42	—	Sep 42	ex-*Betty Jean*, #45L123
1752	2	30'	Apr 42	—	Nov 44	ex-*Beau Beau*, #42D166
1753	2	31'	Apr 42	—	Jun 45	ex-*Miss Muff*, #42B552
1754	2	32'	Apr 42	Oct 44	Nov 44	ex-*Ann IX*, #45F457
1755	2	30'	Apr 42	—	Nov 44	ex-*Beverly*, #45K978
1756	2	31'	Apr 42	Dec 42	Sep 43	ex-*Darlene Sue*, #45A770
1757	2	33'	Apr 42	—	Jun 45	ex-*Manilla*, #43D747
1758	2	30'	May 42	Dec 43	Jan 44	ex-*Orleans Lee*, #43E714
1759	2	36'	Apr 42	Aug 43	Sep 43	ex-*Sybonesa*, #41B40
1760	2	31'	Apr 42	Aug 43	Nov 43	ex-*The Senator*, #12A473
1761	2	30'	Mar 42	—	Nov 44	?, #12D728
1762	2	30'	Mar 42	Dec 42	Jun 43	?, #12D730
1763	2	31'	Apr 42	—	Aug 44	ex-*Swanee*, #12C998
1764	2	31'	May 42	Oct 43	Dec 43	ex-*Euphoria*, #12D448
1765	2	38'	Jul 42	Aug 44	Sep 44	?
1766	2	38'	Jul 42	Aug 44	Sep 44	?
1767	2	30'	Apr 42	—	Nov 44	ex-*Laddie II*, #39J225
1768	2	37'	May 42	Mar 44	Apr 44	ex-*San Souci*, #236015
1769	2	31'	Apr 42	Apr 44	Jun 44	ex-*Frank E*, #45A964
1770	2	30'	Apr 42	—	Mar 44	ex-*Independent*, #42D165
1771	2	32'	Apr 42	—	Nov 44	ex-*Mike*, #42D155
1772	2	30'	Apr 42	—	Nov 44	ex-*Kay Frances*, #43E817
1773	2	32'	Apr 42	—	Nov 44	ex-*Mac*, #45C642
1774	2	30'	May 42	—	Nov 44	ex-*Marcat*, #45D152
1775	2	31'	Apr 42	Jan 43	Apr 43	ex-*Water Blossom II*, #42C841
1776	2	30'	May 42	—	Jun 45	ex-*Nelle Grey*, #43E436
1777	2	31'	May 42	—	Nov 44	ex-*Susan Dunne*, #45L21
1778	2	37'	May 42	Nov 43	Mar 44	ex-*Grace*, #237607
1779	2	20'	Jun 42	—	Nov 44	ex-*Pal*, #45J526
1780	2	20'	Jun 42	Apr 44	May 44	ex-*Janice Lee*, #45H934
1781	2	30'	Jul 42	—	Aug 44	?
1782	2	18'	Jun 42	—	Nov 44	ex-*Sea Biscuit*, #45F400
1783	2	31'	Jul 42	Aug 43	Sep 43	?
1784	2	33'	Jun 42	—	Jun 45	ex-*El Farida*, #35C968
1785	2	61'	Jul 42	—	Jun 44	?
1786	2	31'	Jun 42	—	Nov 44	ex-*Suzy*, #45L214
1787	2	31'	Aug 42	Aug 43	Sep 43	?

CGR Number	District Assigned	Length	Commissioned	Decommissioned	Disposal	Notes
1788	2	32'	Jun 42	—	Jan 44	ex-*Florence May*, #45L215
1789	2	45'	Jun 42	Sep 44	Oct 44	ex-*Old Bets*, #25B374
1790	2	30'	Jun 42	—	Aug 43	ex-*Miss You*, #42D314
1791	2	33'	Jun 42	Dec 42	Apr 43	ex-*Rambler*, #41K394
1792	2	30'	Sep 42	Aug 43	Dec 43	?
1793	2	34'	Jun 42	—	Jan 44	ex-*Shangri La III*, #45G199
1794	2	30'	Jun 42	—	Nov 43	ex-*Victory Queen*, #41R265
1795	2	28'	Jun 42	—	Jun 43	ex-*Good News*, #45E625
1796	2	31'	Jun 42	Nov 43	Jan 44	?
1797	2	30'	Jun 42	Jan 43	Apr 43	ex-*Kip-Katz II*, #42C411
1798	2	32'	Jun 42	Aug 43	Sep 43	?
1799	2	38'	Jul 42	—	Aug 43	?
1800	2	34'	Jul 42	—	Mar 43	20 Mar 43 demolished in collision
1801	11	43'	Oct 42	Aug 45	Oct 45	?
1802	11	21'	Oct 42	Apr 43	May 43	?
1803	11	65'	Oct 42	—	Aug 43	?
1804	11	36'	Oct 42	Nov 44	Jan 45	?
1805	11	26'	Oct 42	Sep 43	Nov 43	?
1806	11	38'	Oct 42	Jul 44	Sep 44	?
1807	11	30'	Oct 42	Jan 44	Feb 44	?
1808	11	145'	Oct 42	—	Feb 43	?
1809	11	83'	Oct 42	Aug 43	Nov 43	?
1810	11	38'	Oct 42	Aug 43	Nov 43	?
1811	11	38'	Oct 42	Aug 43	Nov 43	?
1812	11	62'	Oct 42	Dec 44	Jan 45	?
1813	11	48'	Nov 42	Jan 44	Apr 44	?
1814	11	38'	Nov 42	Mar 45	May 45	?
1815	11	34'	Nov 42	Aug 45	Sep 45	?
1816	11	47'	Nov 42	Nov 43	Dec 43	?
1817	11	40'	Nov 42	Aug 43	Nov 43	?
1820	11	45'	Dec 42	Jun 45	Nov 45	?
1821	11	45'	Dec 42	Aug 45	Nov 45	?
1822	11	45'	Dec 42	Mar 45	Jul 45	?
1823	11	60'	Jan 43	Sep 44		1st tour
			Nov 44	—	Aug 46	2nd tour
1824	11	24'	Jan 43	Nov 43	Feb 44	?
1825	11	38'	Jan 43	Aug 43	Dec 43	?
1826	11	39'	Jan 43	Jan 45	Feb 45	?
1827	11	30'	Jan 43	Sep 44	Nov 44	?
1828	11	58'	Mar 43	—	Nov 45	?
1901	3	39'	Jun 42	—	May 43	?
1902	3	155'	Jun 42	—	Nov 45	?
1903	3	157'	Jun 42	—	Nov 45	?
1904	3	123'	Jun 42	—	Nov 45	?
1905	3	33'	Jun 42	May 43	Feb 44	?
1906	3	54'	Jun 42	—	Mar 43	?
1907	3	46'	Jun 42	—	Dec 44	?
1908	3	34'	Jun 42	May 43	Apr 45	?
1909	3	28'	Jun 42	Dec 43	Aug 44	?
1910	3	57'	Jun 42	May 43	Apr 44	?
1911	3	38'	Jun 42	—	Mar 45	?
1912	3	38'	Jul 42	—	Apr 43	?
1913	3	53'	Jun 42	Jan 45	Feb 45	?
1914	3	32'	Jun 42	—	Mar 43	?
1915	3	45'	Jun 42	—	Dec 43	?
1916	3	36'	Jun 42	Jan 45	Apr 45	?
1917	3	64'	Jun 42	—	Mar 44	?
1918	3	40'	Jun 42	—	Dec 43	?
1919	3	44'	Oct 42	—	Jun 45	?
1920	3	38'	Jul 42	—	Mar 43	?

CGR Number	District Assigned	Length	Commissioned	Decommissioned	Disposal	Notes
1921	3	40'	Jun 42	May 43	May 44	?
1922	3	38'	Jul 42	—	Dec 42	?
1923	3	60'	Jun 42	—	Jun 45	?
1924	3	35'	Jul 42	—	Dec 43	?
1925	3	30'	Jun 42	May 43	Nov 43	?
1926	3	38'	Jun 42	—	Apr 43	?
1927	3	68'	Jun 42	—	Jul 42	Became CG 68007
1928	3	40'	Jul 42	—	Mar 43	?
1929	3	45'	Jul 42	—	Apr 45	?
1930	3	30'	Sep 42	—	Dec 43	?
1931	3	38'	Jul 42	—	Apr 45	?
1932	3	55'	Aug 42	Mar 45	Apr 45	?
1933	3	45'	Aug 42	Jul 44	Sep 44	?
1934	3	43'	Aug 42	—	Nov 44	?
1935	3	42'	Aug 42	—	Nov 44	?
1936	3	33'	Sep 42	Oct 43	Nov 43	?
1937	3	50'	Sep 42	Jan 44	Feb 44	17 Feb 44 became CG 51023
1938	3	47'	Oct 42	—	Mar 45	?
1939	3	47'	Oct 42	Nov 44	Feb 45	?
1940	3	36'	Oct 42	Nov 44	Dec 44	?
1941	3	42'	Jun 42	—	May 43	?
1942	3	44'	Aug 42	—	Dec 43	?
1943	3	49'	Jun 42	—	Mar 44	?
1944	3	40'	Jun 42	—	May 43	?
1945	3	37'	Jun 42	—	Apr 43	?
1946	3	41'	Jul 42	—	Dec 42	?
1947	3	40'	Jul 42	Apr 43	Oct 43	?
1948	3	37'	Jul 42	May 43	—	1st tour
			Oct 43	Sep 44	Jun 45	2nd tour
1949	3	44'	Jun 42	Oct 42	Dec 43	?
1950	3	36'	Jun 42	May 43	Nov 43	?
1951	3	36'	Jun 42	—	Oct 42	Became CG 56017
1952	3	50'	Jun 42	May 43	Dec 43	?
1953	3	53'	Jun 42	May 43	Mar 44	?
1954	3	40'	Jul 42	Apr 44	Dec 45	?
1955	3	36'	Jun 42	—	Mar 43	?
1956	3	33'	Oct 42	Mar 43	May 43	?
1957	3	33'	Jul 42	—	Sep 42	?
1958	3	39'	Jul 42	—	Apr 45	?
1959	3	43'	Jul 42	Dec 43	Jan 44	?
1960	3	35'	Jun 42	May 43	Mar 46	?
1961	3	30'	Jul 42	—	Aug 42	?
1962	3	32'	Jun 42	May 43	May 44	?
1963	3	34'	Jun 42	Dec 44	Mar 45	?
1964	3	40'	Jun 42	Nov 43	Dec 43	?
1965	3	52'	Jul 42	Jun 45	Oct 45	?
1966	3	40'	Jul 42	Feb 45	Mar 45	?
1967	3	36'	Jun 42	May 43	Apr 44	?
1968	3	41'	Jun 42	—	Aug 44	?
1969	3	86'	Jun 42	—	Dec 42	?
1970	3	36'	Jun 42	—	Dec 43	?
1972	3	65'	Aug 42	—	Sep 44	ex-*Two Brothers*, #?
1973	3	42'	Aug 42	Nov 44	Jan 45	?
1974	3	43'	Jul 42	—	Apr 43	?
1975	3	47'	Jul 42	Dec 43	Apr 44	?
1976	3	38'	Jul 42	May 43	May 44	?
1977	3	36'	Jul 42	May 43	Dec 43	?
1978	3	38'	Jul 42	Jan 45	Jul 45	?
1979	3	52'	Jul 42	—	Nov 43	?
1980	3	35'	Jul 42	Dec 43	Aug 45	?

CGR Number	District Assigned	Length	Commissioned	Decommissioned	Disposal	Notes
1981	3	40'	Jul 42	May 43	Jun 45	?
1982	3	60'	Sep 42	—	Oct 42	?
1983	3	46'	Jul 42	Mar 45	Apr 45	?
1984	3	40'	Jul 42	Jan 44	Feb 44	?
1985	3	43'	Jul 42	Aug 45	Sep 45	?
1986	3	40'	Jul 42	—	Nov 42	?
1987	3	34'	Jul 42	Feb 45	Apr 45	?
1988	3	43'	Jul 42	—	Mar 43	?
1989	3	78'	Jul 42	—	Jun 45	?
1990	3	38'	Jul 42	May 43	Feb 44	?
1991	3	45'	Jul 42	—	Sep 44	?
1992	3	75'	Jul 42	—	Dec 43	?
1993	3	37'	Jul 42	May 43	Feb 44	?
1994	3	46'	Jul 42	—	Feb 45	?
1995	3	38'	Jul 42	Apr 45	May 45	?
1996	3	38'	Aug 42	May 43	Nov 43	?
1997	3	37'	Jul 42	Jun 44	Jul 44	?
1998	3	39'	Jul 42	Mar 43	Dec 43	?
1999	3	38'	Jul 42	Oct 43	Jun 44	?
2000	3	45'	Sep 42	Dec 43	Jun 44	?
2001	5	62'	Jun 42	—	Nov 44	ex-*J.C. Drewer*, #228850
2002	5	70'	Jun 42	Sep 43	May 44	ex-*Comanche*, #?
2003	5	60'	Jun 42	Apr 43	May 43	ex-*Windflower*, #?
2004	5	50'	Jun 42	—	Nov 44	ex-*Lantana*, #?
2005	5	75'	Jun 42	Sep 42	Oct 42	Became CG 74349
2006	5	154'	Jun 42	Jun 45	Jun 46	ex-*Wicomico*, #?
2007	5	90'	Jun 42	Jun 45	Aug 45	ex-*North State*, #81015
2008	5	53'	Jun 42	Nov 43	Mar 44	ex-*Night Hawk*, #224260
2009	5	59'	Jun 42	Dec 43	Mar 44	?
2010	5	45'	Jun 42	Sep 43	—	1st tour
			Apr 44	—	Oct 45	2nd tour
2011	5	45'	Jun 42	May 43	Jun 43	?
2012	5	45'	Jun 42	—	Dec 42	?
2013	5	53'	Jun 42	Jan 43	Feb 43	?
2014	5	45'	Jun 42	May 43	Jun 44	?
2015	5	58'	Jul 42	—	Aug 43	6 Aug 43 burned
2016	5	46'	Jul 42	—	Dec 43	?
2017	5	48'	Jul 42	—	Dec 43	?
2018	5	83'	Jul 42	Dec 43	Aug 44	?
2019	5	65'	Jul 42	Feb 43	May 43	?
2020	5	49'	Jul 42	Nov 43	Apr 44	?
2021	5	75'	Jul 42	Feb 44	Jun 44	?
2022	5	50'	Aug 42	Nov 43	Jan 44	?
2023	5	90'	Aug 42	Nov 43	Oct 44	?
2024	5	52'	Aug 42	Sep 43	Jun 44	?
2025	5	52'	Sep 42	Dec 43	Feb 44	?
2101	7	55'	May 42	—	Nov 43	ex-*Macson*, #230946
2102	7	45'	May 42	May 43	Jun 43	ex-*Charlene*, #239395
2103	7	38'	May 42	—	Jun 43	ex-*Billie Jane*, #233375
2104	7	40'	May 42	—	Nov 43	ex-*Girlie K*, #18J978
2105	7	48'	May 42	Nov 43	Dec 43	ex-*Phoenix*, #?
2106	7	38'	May 42	May 43	Sep 43	ex-*Judge Wag*, #18A75
2107	7	30'	Jul 42	Nov 43	Dec 43	?
2108	7	34'	Jul 42	—	May 43	?
2109	7	30'	Jul 42	Jun 43	Jul 43	?
2110	7	57'	Jul 42	May 43	May 44	?
2111	7	32'	Jul 42	Nov 43	Dec 43	?
2112	7	33'	Jul 42	Nov 43	Jan 44	?
2113	7	25'	Jul 42	—	Apr 43	?
2115	7	24'	Jul 42	May 43	Jul 43	?

CGR Number	District Assigned	Length	Commissioned	Decommissioned	Disposal	Notes
2116	7	45′	Jul 42	May 43	Jul 43	?
2117	7	25′	Jul 42	May 43	Sep 43	?
2118	7	33′	Jul 42	May 43	Jul 43	?
2119	7	15′	Aug 42	May 43	Jul 43	?
2120	7	24′	Jul 42	—	Nov 43	?
2121	7	24′	Aug 42	May 43	Aug 43	?
2122	7	24′	Aug 42	—	Nov 43	?
2123	7	22′	Aug 42	May 44	Jun 44	?
2124	7	38′	Aug 42	—	Dec 43	?
2125	7	85′	Aug 42	—	Oct 43	?
2126	7	37′	Aug 42	—	Mar 44	?
2127	7	26′	Aug 42	—	Dec 43	?
2128	7	24′	Aug 42	—	Jul 43	?
2129	7	32′	Aug 42	—	Dec 42	?
2130	7	25′	Sep 42	—	May 43	?
2131	7	26′	Aug 42	May 43	Jul 43	?
2132	7	22′	Aug 42	May 43	Jun 43	?
2133	7	30′	Aug 42	—	Jul 43	?
2134	7	30′	Sep 42	—	Dec 42	?
2135	7	30′	Sep 42	—	Dec 42	?
2136	7	31′	Aug 42	—	Aug 43	?
2137	7	32′	Aug 42	—	Aug 43	?
2138	7	39′	Aug 42	Nov 43	Dec 43	?
2139	7	31′	Aug 42	—	Apr 43	?
2140	7	25′	Sep 42	Nov 43	Dec 43	?
2141	7	30′	Oct 42	May 43	Aug 43	?
2142	7	32′	Aug 42	—	Jan 43	?
2143	7	53′	Oct 42	—	Oct 43	?
2144	7	26′	Sep 42	—	Jul 43	?
2145	7	38′	Aug 42	May 43	Jul 43	?
2146	7	19′	Sep 42	—	May 43	?
2147	7	26′	Sep 42	—	Jun 44	?
2148	7	28′	Sep 42	—	Aug 43	?
2149	7	30′	Sep 42	—	Dec 42	?
2150	7	25′	Aug 42	May 43	Jun 43	?
2151	7	22′	Aug 42	May 43	Jun 43	?
2152	7	24′	Sep 42	May 43	Jul 43	?
2153	7	22′	Sep 42	May 43	Jul 43	?
2154	7	28′	Sep 42	—	Apr 43	?
2155	7	23′	Sep 42	Jun 43	Dec 43	?
2156	7	30′	Aug 42	—	Dec 42	?
2157	7	35′	Sep 42	—	May 43	?
2158	7	25′	Sep 42	—	Sep 43	3 Sep 43 exploded
2159	7	26′	Sep 42	Nov 43	Dec 43	?
2160	7	26′	Sep 42	May 43	Jul 43	?
2161	7	24′	Aug 42	—	Dec 43	?
2162	7	33′	Oct 42	May 43	Jun 43	?
2163	7	80′	Nov 42	Apr 44	May 44	?
2164	7	24′	Oct 42	May 43	Jun 43	?
2165	7	32′	Oct 42	May 43	Sep 43	?
2166	7	22′	Nov 42	May 43	Jun 43	?
2167	7	39′	Jan 43	—	Nov 45	?
2168	7	26′	Jan 43	—	Nov 45	?
2169	7	26′	Jan 43	—	Nov 45	?
2170	7	41′	Feb 43	—	Nov 45	?
2171	7	30′	Jan 43	—	Jul 45	25 Jul 45 burned
2172	7	39′	Jan 43	—	Nov 45	ex-*Egmont*, #293193
2173	7	40′	Jan 43	—	Nov 45	?
2301	7	30′	Jun 42	Jan 43	Apr 43	ex-*Two Sons*, #42C24
2302	2	34′	Jun 42	—	Aug 43	?

CGR Number	District Assigned	Length	Commissioned	Decommissioned	Disposal	Notes
2303	2	30'	Jun 42	—	Aug 44	ex-*Gimco*, #43D978
2304	2	30'	Jun 42	Jun 44	Jul 44	?
2305	2	40'	Jun 42	—	Dec 42	?
2306	2	30'	Aug 42	—	Aug 43	?
2307	2	30'	Aug 42	—	Aug 43	?
2308	2	31'	Jul 42	Aug 44	Sep 44	?
2309	2	34'	Jul 42	—	Aug 44	?
2310	2	30'	Jul 42	Nov 42	Sep 43	?
2311	2	30'	Jul 42	—	Aug 43	?
2312	2	30'	Aug 42	—	Jul 44	?
2313	2	58'	Jul 42	Nov 43	Jun 44	?
2314	2	31'	Jul 42	Sep 43	Oct 43	?
2315	2	30'	Jul 42	Sep 43	Oct 43	?
2316	2	30'	Jul 42	—	Oct 43	?
2317	2	30'	Jul 42	—	Jul 43	?
2318	2	30'	Aug 42	—	Nov 44	?
2319	2	30'	Aug 42	—	Jun 45	?
2320	2	35'	Jul 42	Aug 43	Sep 43	?
2321	2	31'	Aug 42	—	Nov 44	?
2322	2	44'	Oct 42	—	Nov 43	?
2323	2	26'	Aug 42	Aug 43	Sep 43	?
2324	2	46'	Jul 42	Nov 43	Mar 44	?
2325	2	31'	Aug 42	—	Jun 45	?
2326	2	35'	Aug 42	—	Jun 45	?
2327	2	30'	Sep 42	—	Aug 43	?
2328	2	30'	Aug 42	—	Nov 44	?
2329	2	40'	Oct 42	Oct 43	Nov 43	?
2330	2	65'	Aug 42	Mar 45	May 45	?
2331	2	34'	Sep 42	Sep 43	Nov 43	?
2332	2	50'	Sep 42	—	Sep 43	?
2333	2	30'	Sep 42	Oct 42	Jun 43	?
2334	2	33'	Aug 42	—	Jun 45	?
2335	2	30'	Aug 42	—	Jun 45	?
2336	2	31'	Aug 42	—	Jun 45	?
2337	2	30'	Sep 42	—	Nov 44	?
2338	2	30'	Oct 42	—	Jun 45	?
2339	2	30'	Aug 42	Jun 44	Jul 44	?
2340	2	30'	Sep 42	Oct 43	Nov 43	?
2341	2	30'	Sep 42	Sep 43	Nov 43	?
2342	2	34'	Sep 42	—	Nov 44	?
2343	2	53'	Oct 42	Aug 43	Jun 44	?
2344	2	31'	Sep 42	Oct 43	Nov 43	?
2345	2	30'	Oct 42	Nov 44	Dec 44	?
2346	2	34'	Oct 42	—	Jun 45	?
2347	2	76'	Nov 42	Oct 44	Nov 44	?
2348	2	36'	Dec 42	—	Mar 45	?
2349	2	24'	Jun 43	—	Jun 45	?
2451	13	49'	Jul 42	—	Oct 42	?
2452	13	45'	Jul 42	Nov 43	Apr 44	?
2453	13	80'	Aug 42	Jun 43	Jul 45	?
2454	13	62'	Aug 42	Nov 43	Jan 44	?
2455	13	50'	Oct 42	—	Jun 43	?
2456	13	30'	Oct 42	—	May 43	?
2457	13	30'	Oct 42	Apr 43	Jun 43	?
2458	13	30'	Nov 42	Feb 44	May 44	?
2459	13	25'	Nov 42	Sep 43	Nov 43	?
2460	13	32'	Oct 42	Jan 45	Mar 45	?
2461	13	39'	Nov 42	Dec 44	Mar 45	?
2462	13	34'	Nov 42	Dec 44	Mar 45	?
2463	13	44'	Nov 42	Jan 45	Apr 45	?

CGR Number	District Assigned	Length	Commissioned	Decommissioned	Disposal	Notes
2464	13	36′	Nov 42	Mar 43	Jul 43	?
2465	13	86′	Nov 42	Jan 45	Jun 45	?
2466	13	57′	Dec 42	Mar 43	Jun 43	?
2467	13	30′	Dec 42	Aug 44	Nov 44	?
2468	13	43′	Jan 42	Mar 43	May 45	?
2469	13	113′	Nov 43	—	Feb 46	?
2500	1	58′	Jun 42	May 43	Jul 43	ex-*Venturer*, #?
2501	1	39′	Jun 42	—	Nov 42	ex-*Sea Lion*, #?
2502	1	90′	Jun 42	Dec 43	Jul 44	ex-*Duchess*, #?
2503	1	50′	Jun 42	Nov 43	Jan 44	ex-*Marneegil*, #?
2504	1	64′	Jun 42	Nov 43	Nov 44	ex-*Action*, #?
2505	1	49′	Jul 42	May 43	Aug 44	?
2506	1	48′	Jul 42	May 43	Jun 43	?
2507	1	70′	Jul 42	Dec 43	Jan 44	?
2508	1	54′	Jul 42	Jan 43	Mar 43	?
2509	1	71′	Jul 42	Sep 43	Jun 44	?
2510	1	50′	Jul 42	—	Apr 43	?
2511	1	58′	Jul 42	—	Oct 42	?
2512	1	50′	Jul 42	—	Dec 43	?
2513	1	53′	Jul 42	Dec 43	Aug 44	?
2514	1	58′	Jul 42	May 43	Feb 44	?
2515	1	45′	Jul 42	May 43	Sep 43	?
2516	1	57′	Jul 42	Nov 43	Dec 43	?
2517	1	55′	Jul 42	Oct 43	Dec 43	?
2518	1	65′	Jul 42	—	Oct 42	?
2519	1	75′	Jul 42	Dec 43	Jan 44	?
2520	1	52′	Jul 42	May 43	Jul 44	?
2521	1	58′	Jul 42	Nov 43	Aug 44	?
2522	1	65′	Jul 42	—	Dec 42	?
2523	1	60′	Aug 42	May 43	Oct 43	?
2524	1	58′	Aug 42	—	Nov 43	?
2525	1	72′	Aug 42	Nov 43	Apr 44	?
2526	1	52′	Aug 42	Mar 43	Nov 43	?
2527	1	51′	Jul 42	Nov 43	Dec 43	?
2528	1	80′	Aug 42	—	Nov 43	?
2529	1	57′	Aug 42	Sep 43	Jul 44	?
2530	1	55′	Aug 42	Jan 44	Aug 44	?
2531	1	52′	Aug 42	May 43	Aug 43	?
2532	1	50′	Aug 42	Apr 43	Aug 44	?
2533	1	56′	Aug 42	Dec 43	Aug 44	?
2534	1	62′	Aug 42	—	Nov 43	?
2535	1	52′	Aug 42	Dec 43	Jan 44	?
2536	1	56′	Sep 42	Mar 43	Aug 44	?
2537	1	59′	Aug 42	May 43	Sep 44	?
2538	1	95′	Aug 42	Nov 43	Apr 44	?
2539	1	79′	Aug 42	May 43	Nov 43	?
2540	1	62′	Aug 42	—	Dec 43	?
2541	1	65′	Aug 42	May 43	Aug 44	?
2543	1	60′	Aug 42	Dec 43	Sep 44	?
2544	1	60′	Aug 42	Dec 43	Aug 44	?
2545	1	52′	Aug 42	Mar 43	May 44	?
2546	1	56′	Sep 42	—	Dec 43	?
2547	1	63′	Sep 42	Dec 43	May 44	?
2548	1	76′	Sep 42	Dec 43	Aug 44	?
2549	1	73′	Sep 42	—	May 43	?
2550	1	68′	Sep 42	Oct 43	Jun 45	?
2551	1	58′	Oct 42	Oct 43	Nov 43	?
2552	1	78′	Oct 42	Dec 43	Dec 44	?
2553	1	50′	Oct 42	May 43	Jul 43	?
2554	1	52′	Nov 42	Nov 43	May 44	?

CGR Number	District Assigned	Length	Commissioned	Decommissioned	Disposal	Notes
2555	1	77'	Nov 42	—	Feb 43	?
3000	3	85'	Jul 42	—	Apr 43	?
3001	3	42'	Jul 42	—	Jun 45	?
3002	3	33'	Jul 42	—	Sep 44	?
3003	3	38'	Aug 42	—	Dec 42	?
3004	3	30'	Jul 42	—	Jan 45	?
3005	3	33'	Jul 42	Oct 44	Dec 44	?
3006	3	45'	Aug 42	—	Nov 44	?
3007	3	40'	Aug 42	—	Jan 44	?
3008	3	42'	Aug 42	—	Jan 43	?
3009	3	41'	Aug 42	Mar 43	May 43	?
3010	3	56'	Aug 42	—	Aug 45	?
3011	3	37'	Aug 42	—	Apr 43	?
3012	3	57'	Aug 42	May 43	Mar 44	?
3013	3	47'	Aug 42	—	Sep 42	?
3014	3	25'	Aug 42	Dec 43	Jan 44	?
3015	3	55'	Sep 42	—	Nov 42	9 Nov 42 became CG 55031
3016	3	36'	Aug 42	Mar 43	Apr 43	?
3017	3	46'	Sep 42	—	Aug 44	?
3018	3	59'	Aug 42	Nov 44	Dec 44	?
3019	3	46'	Aug 42	May 43	Apr 44	?
3020	3	62'	Aug 42	Sep 43	May 44	?
3021	3	38'	Sep 42	—	Dec 43	?
3022	3	45'	Aug 42	May 43	—	1st tour
			Dec 43	Dec 44	Jul 45	2nd tour
3023	3	44'	Aug 42	—	Dec 42	?
3024	3	39'	Aug 42	Dec 43	Jun 45	?
3025	3	39'	Aug 42	Oct 43	Dec 43	?
3026	3	39'	Aug 42	—	Mar 43	?
3027	3	59'	Aug 42	—	Dec 43	?
3028	3	46'	Sep 42	May 43	Apr 44	?
3029	3	62'	Aug 42	May 43	—	1st tour
			Sep 43	Dec 44	Jan 45	2nd tour
3030	3	52'	Oct 42	—	May 43	?; became CG 52028
3031	3	49'	Aug 42	Dec 43	Mar 44	?
3032	3	50'	Aug 42	—	Apr 45	?
3033	3	39'	Aug 42	—	Nov 42	?
3034	3	42'	Aug 42	—	Dec 42	?
3035	3	39'	Aug 42	May 43	Apr 44	?
3036	3	41'	Sep 42	Jan 45	Feb 45	?
3037	3	40'	Aug 42	—	Oct 42	18 Oct 42 burned
3038	3	41'	Aug 42	May 43	Feb 44	?
3039	3	42'	Sep 42	—	Aug 44	?
3040	3	43'	Aug 42	—	Dec 43	?
3041	3	39'	Aug 42	—	May 43	?
3042	3	56'	Sep 42	Nov 44	Dec 44	?
3043	3	51'	Aug 42	Nov 43	Mar 44	?
3044	3	25'	Aug 42	—	Feb 43	?
3045	3	38'	Sep 42	—	Apr 43	?
3046	3	41'	Aug 42	Mar 43	Feb 44	?
3047	3	25'	Oct 42	Mar 43	May 43	?
3048	3	58'	Aug 42	Nov 44	Dec 44	?
3049	3	62'	Sep 42	Nov 44	Dec 44	?
3050	3	65'	Sep 42	—	Mar 43	?
3051	3	42'	Sep 42	May 43	—	1st tour
			Oct 43	Feb 44	Mar 44	2nd tour
3052	3	60'	Aug 42	Jun 45	Jul 45	?
3053	3	54'	Sep 42	—	Nov 42	?; 14 Nov 42 became CG 53017

CGR Number	District, Assigned	Length	Commissioned	Decommissioned	Disposal	Notes
3054	3	40'	Sep 42	—	Jan 43	24 Jan 43 burned
						?
3055	3	38'	Oct 42	—	Dec 42	1st tour
3056	3	36'	Sep 42	May 43	—	2nd tour
			Oct 43	—	Jan 44	?
3057	3	59'	Sep 42	—	Jul 45	?
3058	3	41'	Sep 42	May 43	Jul 43	?
3059	3	50'	Oct 42	—	Nov 44	?
3060	3	47'	Sep 42	—	Dec 43	?
3061	3	60'	Sep 42	Nov 44	Dec 44	?
3062	3	62'	Sep 42	—	Jun 45	?
3063	3	38'	Sep 42	—	Nov 43	?
3064	3	55'	Sep 42	Nov 44	Dec 44	?
3065	3	56'	Sep 42	—	Jun 45	?
3066	3	35'	Sep 42	—	Dec 43	?
3067	3	62'	Sep 42	Sep 43	Nov 43	?
3068	3	44'	Sep 42	—	Dec 44	?
3069	3	42'	Sep 42	Nov 44	Dec 44	?
3070	3	57'	Sep 42	—	Jun 45	?
3071	3	42'	Sep 42	Dec 43	Jan 44	?
3072	3	50'	Oct 42	—	Nov 44	
3073	3	64'	Sep 42	—	Feb 44	?
3074	3	29'	Sep 42	Nov 44	Mar 45	?
3075	3	34'	Oct 42	—	Jun 44	?
3076	3	47'	Oct 42	—	Sep 45	?
3077	3	42'	Oct 42	Aug 44	Sep 44	?
3078	3	30'	Oct 42	Jan 44	Apr 44	?
3079	3	30'	Oct 42	—	Dec 42	?
3080	3	112'	Oct 42	—	Nov 45	?
3081	3	37'	Dec 42	—	Sep 45	?
3082	3	97'	Oct 42	—	Jun 45	?
3083	3	71'	Oct 42	—	Jul 45	?
3084	3	109'	Nov 42	—	Dec 43	?
3085	3	102'	Nov 42	—	Jun 45	?
3086	3	48'	Oct 42	—	Mar 43	?
3087	3	42'	Nov 42	Dec 44	Feb 45	?
3091	3	85'	Nov 42	—	Jun 45	?
3093	3	59'	Feb 43	Feb 45	Jun 45	?
3094	3	52'	Jan 43	—	Nov 45	?
3095	3	39'	Jan 43	—	Nov 45	?
3096	3	53'	Dec 41	Dec 43	Apr 44	?
3097	3	45'	Oct 43	—	Nov 45	?
3098	3	32'	Oct 43	—	Dec 44	?
3099	3	45'	Oct 44	—	Nov 45	?
3100	3	45'	Dec 44	—	Nov 45	?
4400	4	59'	Jul 42	Dec 43	Apr 44	?
4401	4	64'	Jul 42	Nov 43	Dec 43	?
4402	4	70'	Jul 42	—	Dec 42	?
4403	4	92'	Jul 42	Nov 43	Dec 43	?
4404	4	43'	Aug 42	Mar 43	Sep 43	?
4431	4	46'	Aug 42	Mar 43	Jun 44	?
4432	4	40'	Aug 42	Mar 43	Oct 43	?
4433	4	42'	Aug 42	Mar 43	May 45	?
4434	4	38'	Aug 42	Mar 43	Oct 44	?
4436	4	40'	Sep 42	Mar 43	Mar 44	?
5015	5	50'	Oct 42	May 43	Apr 44	?
5100	5	42'	Aug 42	Apr 43	May 43	?
5101	5	42'	Aug 42	Aug 44	Sep 44	?
5102	5	53'	Aug 42	Jun 45	Sep 45	?
5103	5	38'	Aug 42	Feb 44	Mar 44	?

CGR Number	District Assigned	Length	Commissioned	Decommissioned	Disposal	Notes
5104	5	45′	Aug 42	May 43	Jun 43	?
5105	5	43′	Aug 42	Apr 43	Oct 43	?
5106	5	50′	Aug 42	—	Oct 44	?
5107	5	30′	Aug 42	Mar 43	Apr 43	?
5108	5	47′	Aug 42	Mar 44	May 44	?
5109	5	37′	Aug 42	—	Sep 44	?
5110	5	45′	Aug 42	Mar 44	Sep 44	?
5111	5	45′	Aug 42	Dec 43	Jul 44	?
5112	5	35′	Aug 42	—	Jul 44	?
5113	5	42′	Aug 42	—	Oct 43	?
5114	5	41′	Aug 42	Apr 43	May 43	?
5115	5	39′	Aug 42	Dec 42	Jan 43	?
5116	5	53′	Aug 42	Dec 43	Jan 44	?
5117	5	38′	Aug 42	—	Dec 44	?
5118	5	42′	Aug 42	Dec 42	Jan 43	?
5119	5	35′	Aug 42	Dec 42	Jan 43	?
5120	5	36′	Aug 42	—	Mar 44	?
5121	5	50′	Aug 42	Jun 45	Aug 45	?
5122	5	40′	Aug 42	May 43	May 44	?
5123	5	42′	Aug 42	—	Jan 44	?
5124	5	50′	Aug 42	Oct 43	Jan 44	?
5125	5	38′	Aug 42	Mar 44	Sep 44	?
5126	5	40′	Aug 42	Sep 43	Jul 44	?
5127	5	48′	Aug 42	Sep 43	Nov 43	?
5128	5	40′	Aug 42	—	Sep 44	?
5129	5	64′	Aug 42	—	Jan 44	?
5130	5	39′	Aug 42	—	Mar 44	?
5131	5	39′	Aug 42	May 43	Mar 44	?
5132	5	40′	Sep 42	May 43	Apr 44	?
5133	5	40′	Sep 42	Dec 42	Jan 43	?
5134	5	33′	Sep 42	—	Mar 44	?
5135	5	40′	Sep 42	Oct 44	Nov 44	?
5136	5	54′	Sep 42	Feb 44	Apr 44	?
5137	5	35′	Sep 42	Dec 42	Jan 43	?
5138	5	36′	Sep 42	Dec 42	Jan 43	?
5139	5	38′	Sep 42	Dec 42	Jan 43	?
5140	5	42′	Sep 42	Dec 42	Jan 43	?
5141	5	36′	Sep 42	—	Mar 44	?
5142	5	50′	Sep 42	—	Jan 45	?
5143	5	46′	Sep 42	Oct 42	Apr 43	?
5144	5	39′	Sep 42	—	Jan 45	?
5145	5	43′	Sep 42	Feb 43	May 43	?
5146	5	40′	Sep 42	Aug 44	Sep 44	?
5147	5	40′	Sep 42	—	Mar 44	?
5148	5	40′	Sep 42	—	Mar 44	?
5149	5	36′	Sep 42	Mar 43	Apr 43	?
5150	5	64′	Sep 42	Oct 44	Nov 44	?
5151	5	39′	Aug 42	Nov 43	Dec 43	?
5152	5	53′	Sep 42	Mar 45	Apr 45	?
5153	5	40′	Sep 42	—	Aug 44	?
5154	5	36′	Sep 42	—	Jul 44	?
5155	5	36′	Sep 42	Dec 42	Jan 43	?
5156	5	42′	Sep 42	Feb 44	Jun 44	?
5157	5	40′	Sep 42	May 43	Aug 43	?
5158	5	35′	Sep 42	—	Jul 44	?
5159	5	30′	Sep 42	Dec 42	Jan 43	?
5160	5	42′	Sep 42	Aug 44	Sep 44	?
5161	5	40′	Sep 42	Apr 44	Jul 44	?
5162	5	46′	Sep 42	Sep 44	Oct 44	?
5163	5	42′	Sep 42	Feb 43	May 43	?

CGR Number	District Assigned	Length	Commissioned	Decommissioned	Disposal	Notes
5164	5	40'	Sep 42	—	Sep 44	?
5165	5	45'	Sep 42	—	Sep 44	?
5166	5	40'	Sep 42	—	Mar 44	?
5167	5	55'	Sep 42	May 43	Jul 44	?
5168	5	46'	Sep 42	Feb 43	May 43	?
5169	5	46'	Sep 42	—	Mar 44	?
5170	5	36'	Sep 42	—	Mar 44	?
5171	5	40'	Sep 42	—	Mar 44	?
5172	5	41'	Sep 42	Jun 44	Aug 44	?
5173	5	42'	Aug 42	—	Mar 44	?
5174	5	39'	Sep 42	Mar 44	Jul 44	?
5175	5	43'	Oct 42	Dec 43	Apr 44	?
5177	5	32'	Sep 42	Feb 43	May 43	?
5178	5	40'	Sep 42	—	Mar 45	?
5179	5	45'	Sep 42	Jun 45	Sep 45	?
5180	5	50'	Sep 42	Feb 44	Mar 44	?
5181	5	32'	Oct 42	—	Jan 45	?
5182	5	24'	Oct 42	May 43	Oct 43	?
5183	5	39'	Oct 42	Mar 45	Apr 45	?
5184	5	41'	Oct 42	—	Jul 44	?
5185	5	38'	Nov 42	Feb 44	Apr 44	?
5186	5	50'	Nov 42	Jan 43	Mar 43	?
5187	5	30'	Nov 42	May 43	Oct 43	?
5188	5	39'	Nov 42	Jun 44	Jul 44	?
5189	5	125'	Dec 42	—	Nov 45	?
5190	5	160'	Jan 43	—	Nov 45	?
5191	5	41'	Feb 43	—	Nov 45	?
5192	5	139'	Jan 43	—	Nov 45	?
6001	6–7	65'	Jul 42	Nov 43	Nov 44	ex-*Jonbob II*, #213242
6002	6–7	50'	Jul 42	Nov 43	Dec 43	?
6003	6–7	63'	Jul 42	—	Sep 42	?
6004	6–7	54'	Aug 42	Nov 43	May 43	?
6005	6–7	48'	Aug 42	Jun 43	Jul 43	?
6006	6–7	45'	Aug 42	—	Feb 43	?
6007	6–7	94'	Aug 42	Jul 43	Aug 43	?
6008	6–7	73'	Aug 42	May 45	Jul 45	?
6009	6–7	48'	Aug 42	Nov 43	Jul 44	?
6010	6–7	56'	Sep 42	Nov 43	Mar 44	?
6011	6–7	57'	Oct 42	Nov 43	Apr 44	?
6012	6–7	51'	Oct 42	Nov 43	Dec 43	?
6013	6–7	46'	Oct 42	Mar 43	Apr 44	?
6014	6–7	64'	Oct 42	—	Feb 43	Became CG 64031
6015	6–7	19'	Dec 42	Dec 43	Mar 44	?
6016	6–7	85'	Jul 45	—	Nov 45	?
6200	6–7	47'	Aug 42	Aug 44	Oct 44	?
6201	6–7	26'	Aug 42	May 43	Jun 44	?
6202	6–7	42'	Nov 42	May 43	Apr 44	?
6203	6–7	26'	Aug 42	May 43	Jan 44	?
6204	6–7	34'	Sep 42	May 43	May 44	?
6205	6–7	34'	Sep 42	—	Mar 43	?
6206	6–7	38'	Sep 42	Jan 44	Mar 44	?
6207	6–7	32'	Sep 42	Jan 44	Jun 44	?
6208	6–7	22'	Sep 42	May 43	Aug 44	?
6209	6–7	33'	Sep 42	May 43	Nov 43	?
6210	6–7	46'	Sep 42	May 43	Jun 44	?
6211	6–7	30'	Sep 42	May 43	Apr 44	?
6212	6–7	38'	Sep 42	May 43	Sep 44	?
6213	6–7	26'	Sep 42	May 43	Oct 43	?
6214	6–7	40'	Sep 42	Jan 44	Sep 44	?
6215	6–7	17'	Sep 42	May 43	Jan 44	?

CGR Number	District Assigned	Length	Commissioned	Decommissioned	Disposal	Notes
6216	6–7	41'	Oct 42	Jun 44	Sep 44	?
6217	6–7	38'	Oct 42	Jul 44	Nov 44	?
6218	6–7	34'	Sep 42	May 43	Jul 43	?
6219	6–7	37'	Oct 42	May 43	Dec 43	?
6220	6–7	33'	Oct 42	May 43	Apr 44	?
6221	6–7	45'	Oct 42	Apr 44	Aug 44	?
6222	6–7	43'	Oct 42	May 43	Jul 44	
6223	6–7	40'	Oct 42	Apr 44	Jul 44	?
6224	6–7	42'	Oct 42	May 43	Jan 44	?
6225	6–7	39'	Oct 42	Jan 44	Apr 44	?
6226	6–7	26'	Sep 42	May 43	Aug 44	?
6227	6–7	43'	Oct 42	Sep 44	Nov 44	?
6228	6–7	34'	Oct 42	Jan 44	Feb 44	?
6229	6–7	46'	Nov 42	Dec 43	Feb 44	?
6230	6–7	36'	Oct 42	Jan 44	Mar 44	?
6231	6–7	46'	Nov 42	Jul 43	Nov 43	?
6232	6–7	42'	Dec 42	Jan 44	Feb 44	?
7000	7	48'	Jul 42	Jul 44	Aug 44	?
7001	7	42'	Jul 42	May 43	Jun 43	?
7002	7	35'	Jul 42	May 43	Jul 43	?
7003	7	35'	Jul 42	—	Jan 43	?
7004	7	38'	Jul 42	—	Aug 43	?
7005	7	35'	Jul 42	—	Jan 43	?
7006	7	38'	Aug 42	—	May 43	?
7007	7	64'	Jul 42	—	Aug 44	?
7008	7	38'	Jul 42	—	May 43	?
7009	7	38'	Jul 42	May 43	Jun 43	?
7010	7	46'	Jul 42	—	May 43	?
7011	7	50'	Jul 42	Nov 43	Dec 43	?
7012	7	30'	Jul 42	—	Aug 42	?
7013	7	35'	Jul 42	May 43	Jul 43	?
7014	7	48'	Jul 42	Aug 43	Sep 43	?
7015	7	46'	Jul 42	—	Dec 43	?
7016	7	37'	Jul 42	May 43	Dec 43	?
7018	7	60'	Jul 42	May 43	Jul 43	?
7019	7	34'	Jul 42	May 43	Jun 43	?
7020	7	42'	Jul 42	—	Mar 43	?
7021	7	38'	Jul 42	May 43	Jan 44	?
7022	7	28'	Jul 42	Dec 43	Feb 44	?
7023	7	26'	Jul 42		Oct 42	24 Oct 42 burned
7024	7	22'	Jul 42	Dec 43	Jan 44	?
7025	7	25'	Jul 42	—	Sep 42	?
7026	7	40'	Aug 42	May 43	Jun 43	?
7027	7	38'	Aug 42	—	Apr 43	?
7028	7	38'	Aug 42	—	Apr 43	?
7029	7	38'	Aug 42	May 43	Jun 43	25 Jun 43 damaged
7030	7	38'	Aug 42	—	Jan 44	?
9000	8	43'	Aug 42	—	Nov 45	?
9001	8	22'	Sep 42	Jan 44	Mar 44	?
9002	8	62'	Sep 42	Oct 43	Dec 43	?
9003	8	61'	Sep 42	Nov 43	Mar 44	?
9004	8	61'	Sep 42	Nov 43	Mar 44	?
9006	8	63'	Sep 42	Nov 43	Jan 44	?
9007	8	25'	Sep 42	—	Nov 45	?
9008	8	80'	Sep 42	—	Nov 45	?
9009	8	80'	Sep 42	—	Nov 45	?
9010	8	25'	Sep 42	—	Dec 43	?
9011	8	33'	Sep 42	Jan 44	Mar 44	?
9012	8	57'	Sep 42	—	Nov 45	?
9013	8	38'	Sep 42	May 43	Jul 43	?

CGR Number	District Assigned	Length	Commissioned	Decommissioned	Disposal	Notes
9014	8	46'	Sep 42	—	Mar 43	?
9015	8	21'	Sep 42	—	Mar 44	?
9016	8	30'	Sep 42	May 43	Jul 43	?
9019	8	31'	Sep 42	—	Aug 43	?
9020	8	51'	Oct 42	Feb 44	Mar 44	?
9021	8	40'	Sep 42	—	Nov 45	?
9022	8	36'	Oct 42	Nov 43	Feb 44	?
9023	8	35'	Nov 42	Nov 43	Feb 44	?
9024	8	37'	Nov 42	Nov 43	Feb 44	?
9025	8	31'	Nov 42	Nov 43	Feb 44	?
9026	8	36'	Dec 42	Dec 43	Jan 44	?
9027	8	75'	Jun 42	—	Nov 45	?
9028	8	29'	Apr 42	—	Nov 45	?
9029	8	16'	Feb 43	—	Nov 45	?
9030	8	26'	Jan 43	—	Jun 45	9 Jun 45 burned
9031	8	100'	Feb 43	—	Nov 45	?
9032	8	57'	Mar 43	—	Nov 45	?
9033	8	57'	Apr 43	—	Nov 45	?
9034	8	59'	Apr 43	—	Nov 45	?
9035	8	31'	Apr 43	—	Nov 45	?
9036	8	47'	Apr 43	—	Nov 45	?
9037	8	34'	Mar 44	—	Nov 45	?
9038	8	30'	Jun 44	—	Nov 45	?
9039	8	85'	May 45	—	Nov 45	?
9040	8	43'	Jul 45	—	Nov 45	?

During WW II, Disney Studios produced hundreds of logos for the U.S. Armed Forces. The nickname ''Corsair Fleet'' was given to the thousands of CG and CGR craft that patrolled the coast watching for U-boats and saboteurs. (Courtesy of the National Archives.)

CGR craft at Chattanooga Depot, 1942. Many CGR boats used on the Great Lakes and in the inland waterways were never painted gray.

CGR 557 making full speed. Photograph not dated.

Large cabin cruisers and sailing craft were the backbone of the Coast Guard Reserve.

CGR 672, 18 Sep 43, being used as a pilot boat.

COAST GUARD AUXILIARY CRAFT (CGA)

On the eve of World War II, the Coast Guard Auxiliary was composed of approximately 9,500 boats manned by 11,500 members. At the beginning of the war, approximately 1,000 of these craft were taken into the Coast Guard Reserve, and in the majority of cases their owners and crews joined the Temporary Reserves. The total number of CGA craft to serve during World War II is unknown. Each district determined its own needs as to type and number of craft, and records concerning these craft were not preserved. More than 10,000 craft probably served in the Auxiliary during the war.

The Auxiliary was a non-military organization. It was created on 23 Jun 39 as the Coast Guard Reserve and was renamed the Coast Guard Auxiliary on 19 Feb 41, when a new Coast Guard Reserve was created. This later force closely paralleled the reserve forces in the other armed services.

NAVAL VESSELS MANNED BY THE COAST GUARD DURING WORLD WAR II*

During World War II, the Coast Guard manned 351 naval ships and craft. These ranged in size from a former transatlantic liner manned by 934 Coast Guardsmen to small amphibious craft crewed by 2 men. On VJ Day, 3,357 Coast Guard officers and 45,265 Coast Guard enlisted men were used to man naval ships.

Coast Guardsmen began to man naval vessels on 6 Jun 41. Coast Guardsmen—recently removed from cutters given to Great Britain under lend-lease—crewed three former Army transports which had been turned over to the Navy following the 1941 amphibious exercise. These three transports—the *Leonard Wood, Joseph T. Dickman,* and *Hunter Liggett*—had been manned by civilian crews, but this arrangement proved impractical. The Coast Guard's first World War II casualty occurred when the *Leonard Wood* was bombed by Japanese aircraft in Singapore on 8 Dec 41. As the war progressed and coastal danger lessened, more and more Coast Guardsmen were taken from picket-boat duty and port security and reassigned to man naval vessels.

CG Personnel Manning USN Ships and Craft

Date	Personnel	Vessels
1 Jan 43	3,547	48
1 Apr 43	8,598	118
30 Apr 44	30,192	205
31 Dec 44	46,900	273
30 Jun 45	49,283	288
1 Mar 46	21,100	185

*Many works detail the characteristics and histories of these naval ships. Among them are James Fahey's *The Ships and Aircraft of the U.S. Fleet,* editions 1 through 5, reprinted by U.S. Naval Institute Press, 1976; Paul Silverstone's *U.S. Warships of World War II,* published by Ian Allan, 1966; and the Naval History Division's *Dictionary of American Naval Fighting Ships,* 8 volumes, GPO, 1959–81.

Hull Number	Ship	Date CG Manned	Date CG Crew Removed
AGP 20	*Pontus*	15 Aug 44	5 Feb 46
AK 80	*Enceladus*	22 Aug 43	18 Dec 45
AK 82	*Hydra*	25 Sep 43	19 Nov 43
AK 90	*Albireo*	28 Mar 43	5 Jul 46
AK 91	*Cor Caroli*	15 Apr 43	30 Nov 45
AK 92	*Eridanus*	7 May 43	8 May 46
AK 93	*Etamin*	24 May 43	26 Jun 44
AK 94	*Mintaka*	10 May 43	13 Feb 46
AK 95	*Murzim*	14 May 43	8 Jun 46
AK 96	*Sterope*	15 May 43	17 May 46
AK 97	*Serpens*	28 May 43	29 Jan 45
AK 123	*Menkar*	2 Jun 44	15 Apr 46
AK 173	*Codington*	23 Jul 45	27 Feb 46
AK 175	*Craighead*	5 Sep 45	18 Jan 46
AK 212	*Somerset*	20 Sep 45	2 Nov 45
AK 213	*Sussex*	12 Jul 45	23 May 46
AK 214	*Tarrant*	13 Jul 45	21 Nov 45
AKA 16	*Aquarius*	30 Aug 43	23 May 46
AKA 17	*Centaurus*	20 Oct 43	30 Apr 46
AKA 18	*Cepheus*	19 Jan 44	22 May 46
AKA 62	*Sheliak*	1 Dec 44	10 May 46
AKA 63	*Theenim*	14 Dec 44	10 May 46
AOG 23	*Ammonusuc*	18 May 44	4 Jun 46
AOG 24	*Sheepscot*	28 Jun 44	6 Jun 45
AOG 25	*Calamus*	11 Jul 44	15 May 46
AOG 26	*Chiwaukum*	25 Jul 44	31 May 46
AOG 27	*Escatawpa*	18 Aug 44	20 Mar 46
AOG 28	*Gualala*	24 Aug 44	29 Mar 46
AOG 29	*Hiwassee*	24 Oct 44	5 Feb 46
AOG 30	*Kalamazoo*	16 Oct 44	18 May 46
AOG 31	*Kanawha*	23 Nov 44	23 Mar 46
AOG 32	*Narraguagas*	2 Dec 44	5 Mar 46
AOG 33	*Ochlockonee*	29 Dec 44	14 Jan 46
AOG 34	*Oconee*	12 Jan 45	28 Mar 46
AOG 35	*Ogeechee*	6 Sep 45	18 Feb 46
AOG 36	*Ontonagon*	12 Sep 44	27 Feb 46
AOG 64	*Klickitat*	14 Jul 45	7 Feb 46
AOG 65	*Michigamme*	10 Aug 45	23 Jan 46

Hull Number	Ship	Date CG Manned	Date CG Crew Removed
AOG 66	Nanticoke	1 Sep 45	4 Jan 46
AOG 68	Peconic	11 Jan 45	4 Jan 46
AP 21	Wakefield	10 Feb 44	15 Jun 46
AP 61	Monticello	6 Aug 45	22 Mar 46
AP 114	*General William Mitchell*	20 Jan 44	22 Feb 46
AP 115	*General George Randall*	14 Apr 44	31 Jan 46
AP 116	General M. C. Meigs	3 Jun 44	5 Mar 46
AP 117	General W. H. Gordon	29 Jul 44	11 Mar 46
AP 118	General W. P. Richardson	2 Nov 44	14 Feb 46
AP 119	*General William Weigel*	6 Jan 45	10 May 46
AP 121	*Admiral W. C. Capps*	18 Sep 44	8 May 46
AP 123	Admiral E. W. Eberle	24 Jan 45	8 May 46
AP 124	Admiral C. F. Hughes	31 Jan 45	3 May 46
AP 125	Admiral H. T. Mayo	24 Apr 45	26 May 46
AP 134	General R. L. Howze	7 Feb 44	1 Apr 46
AP 135	General W. M. Black	24 Feb 44	28 Feb 46
AP 136	General H. L. Scott	3 Apr 44	29 May 46
AP 141	General A. W. Greely	22 Mar 45	29 Mar 46
AP 142	General C. H. Muir	12 Apr 45	18 Jun 46
AP 143	General H. B. Freeman	26 Apr 45	4 Mar 46
AP 144	General H. F. Hodges	6 Apr 45	13 May 46
AP 155	General A. W. Brewster	23 Apr 45	10 Apr 46
AP 156	General D. E. Aultman	20 May 45	15 Mar 46
AP 176	General J. C. Breckinridge	30 Jun 45	10 Feb 46
APA 12	Leonard Wood	10 Jun 41	22 Mar 46
APA 13	Joseph T. Dickman	10 Jun 41	7 Mar 46
APA 14	Hunter Liggett	6 Jun 41	18 Mar 46
APA 25	Arthur Middleton	8 Sep 42	9 Feb 46
APA 26	Samuel Chase	12 Jun 42	21 Mar 46
APA 33	Bayfield	20 Nov 43	8 Mar 46
APA 35	Callaway	10 Sep 43	10 May 46
APA 36	Cambria	10 Nov 43	13 Mar 46
APA 37	Cavalier	15 Jan 44	16 Apr 46
DE 151	Poole	29 Sep 43	1 May 46
DE 152	Peterson	29 Sep 43	1 May 46
DE 249	Marchand	8 Sep 43	1 May 46
DE 250	Hurst	30 Aug 43	1 May 46
DE 251	Camp	16 Sep 43	1 May 46
DE 252	Howard D. Crow	27 Sep 43	22 May 46
DE 253	Pettit	23 Sep 43	6 May 46
DE 254	Ricketts	5 Oct 43	17 Apr 46
DE 255	Sellstrom	12 Oct 43	13 Jun 46
DE 316	Harveson	12 Oct 43	1 May 46
DE 317	Joyce	30 Sep 43	1 May 46
DE 318	Kirkpatrick	23 Oct 43	1 May 46
DE 319	Leopold	19 Oct 43	10 Mar 44*
DE 320	Menges	25 Oct 43	12 Apr 46
DE 321	Mosley	31 Oct 43	15 Mar 46
DE 322	Newell	31 Oct 43	1 May 46
DE 323	Pride	13 Nov 43	6 May 46
DE 324	Falgout	15 Nov 43	24 Mar 46
DE 325	Lowe	22 Nov 43	1 May 46
DE 382	Ramsden	19 Oct 43	13 Jun 46
DE 383	Mills	12 Oct 43	13 Jun 46
DE 384	Rhodes	25 Oct 43	13 Jun 46
DE 385	Richey	30 Oct 43	13 Jun 46

*Struck by a torpedo on 9 Mar 44 at 57°37'N. 26°30'W while in convoy CU-16—sank next day. 171 men lost.

Hull Number	Ship	Date CG Manned	Date CG Crew Removed
DE 386	Savage	29 Oct 43	13 Jun 46
DE 387	Vance	1 Nov 43	27 Feb 46
DE 388	Lansing	10 Nov 43	6 May 46
DE 389	Durant	16 Nov 43	27 Feb 46
DE 390	Calcaterra	17 Nov 43	1 May 46
DE 391	Chambers	22 Nov 43	1 May 46
DE 392	Merrill	27 Nov 43	1 May 46
IX 59	Volador	1 Jul 43	10 Aug 43
IX 61	Geoanna	2 Jul 43	28 Aug 43
IX 99	Sea Cloud	4 Apr 42	4 Nov 44
IX 131	Abarenda	26 Feb 44	28 Feb 46
IX 137	Celtic	15 Jan 44	6 Feb 46
IX 207	Big Horn	17 Jan 44	6 May 46
LCI(L) 83		23 Jan 43	8 Apr 46
LCI(L) 84		23 Jan 43	13 Apr 46
LCI(L) 85		25 Jan 43	6 Jun 44
LCI(L) 86		29 Jan 43	8 Apr 46
LCI(L) 87		1 Feb 43	20 Mar 46
LCI(L) 88		2 Feb 43	7 Mar 46
LCI(L) 89		3 Feb 43	7 Mar 46
LCI(L) 90		6 Feb 43	8 Apr 46
LCI(L) 91		8 Feb 43	5 Jun 44
LCI(L) 92		10 Feb 43	6 Jun 44
LCI(L) 93		12 Feb 43	6 Jun 44
LCI(L) 94		15 Feb 43	Mar 46
LCI(L) 95		15 Feb 43	Mar 46
LCI(L) 96		15 Feb 43	2 Apr 46
LCI(L) 319		3 Feb 43	26 Mar 46
LCI(L) 320		8 Feb 43	25 Mar 46
LCI(L) 321		6 Feb 43	2 Mar 46
LCI(L) 322		15 Feb 43	26 Mar 46
LCI(L) 323		10 Feb 43	15 Mar 46
LCI(L) 324		12 Feb 43	7 Mar 46
LCI(L) 325		15 Feb 43	31 May 46
LCI(L) 326		31 Oct 43	8 Mar 46
LCI(L) 349		26 Dec 43	2 Apr 46
LCI(L) 350		15 May 43	3 May 46
LCI(L) 520		10 Jan 45	26 Mar 46
LCI(L) 562		10 Jan 45	26 Mar 46
LCI(L) 581		10 Jan 45	21 Mar 46
LCI(L) 583		10 Jan 45	25 Mar 46
LST 16		17 Mar 43	8 Mar 46
LST 17		19 Apr 43	23 Nov 44
LST 18		26 Apr 43	3 Apr 46
LST 19		15 May 43	20 Mar 46
LST 20		14 May 43	3 Apr 46
LST 21		14 Apr 43	25 Jan 46
LST 22		16 Jun 43	1 Apr 46
LST 23		16 Jun 43	8 May 46
LST 24		14 Jun 43	26 Feb 46
LST 25		30 Jun 43	25 Aug 46
LST 26		7 Jun 43	1 Apr 46
LST 27		16 Jun 43	9 Nov 45
LST 66		12 Apr 43	26 Mar 46
LST 67		19 Apr 43	28 Mar 46
LST 68		4 Jun 43	7 Mar 46
LST 69		20 May 43	21 May 44
LST 70		28 May 43	1 Apr 46
LST 71		9 Jun 43	25 Mar 46
LST 166		22 Apr 43	3 May 46

Hull Number	Ship	Date CG Manned	Date CG Crew Removed	Hull Number	Ship	Date CG Manned	Date CG Crew Removed
LST 167		27 Apr 43	25 Sep 43	PC 590		5 Oct 42	9 Oct 45
LST 168		3 May 43	14 Mar 46	PF 3	Tacoma	25 Sep 43	11 Oct 45
LST 169		22 May 43	12 Apr 46	PF 4	Sausalito	4 Mar 44	6 Jul 45
LST 170		31 May 43	6 Apr 46	PF 5	Hoquiam	8 May 44	6 Jul 45
LST 175		19 May 43	6 Apr 46	PF 6	Pasco	15 Apr 44	6 Jul 45
LST 176		12 May 43	23 Nov 44	PF 7	Albuquerque	20 Dec 43	6 Jul 45
LST 202		9 Apr 43	11 Apr 46	PF 8	Everett	22 Jan 44	6 Jul 45
LST 203		22 Apr 43	1 Oct 43	PF 9	Pocatello	18 Feb 44	2 May 46
LST 204		27 Apr 43	23 Feb 46	PF 10	Brownsville	6 May 44	2 Aug 46
LST 205		15 May 43	2 Apr 46	PF 11	Grand Forks	18 Mar 44	16 May 46
LST 206		7 Jun 43	6 May 46	PF 12	Casper	31 Mar 44	16 May 46
LST 207		9 Jun 43	20 Mar 46	PF 13	Pueblo	27 May 44	26 Apr 46
LST 261		22 May 43	22 Feb 46	PF 14	Grand Island	27 May 44	21 May 46
LST 262		16 Jun 43	14 Jan 46	PF 15	Annapolis	4 Dec 44	29 May 46
LST 326		26 Feb 43	18 Dec 44	PF 16	Bangor	22 Nov 44	16 Aug 46
LST 327		6 Mar 43	19 Nov 45	PF 17	Key West	5 Aug 44	14 Jun 46
LST 331		11 Mar 43	20 Nov 44	PF 18	Alexandria	11 Mar 44	10 Apr 46
LST 381		25 Aug 43	19 Dec 44	PF 19	Huron	7 Sep 44	19 Apr 46
LST 758		19 Aug 44	29 Mar 46	PF 20	Gulfport	16 Sep 44	28 May 46
LST 759		25 Aug 44	28 Mar 46	PF 21	Bayonne	14 Feb 44	26 Aug 45
LST 760		28 Aug 44	24 May 46	PF 22	Gloucester	10 Dec 43	26 Aug 45
LST 761		2 Sep 44	28 Mar 46	PF 23	Shreveport	24 Apr 44	9 May 46
LST 762		5 Sep 44	29 Mar 46	PF 24	Muskegon	19 Feb 44	27 Aug 46
LST 763		8 Sep 44	29 May 46	PF 25	Charlottesville	10 Apr 44	26 Aug 45
LST 764		Sep 44	30 May 46	PF 26	Poughkeepsie	6 Sep 44	26 Aug 45
LST 765		18 Sep 44	29 May 46	PF 27	Newport	8 Sep 44	26 Aug 45
LST 766		25 Sep 44	19 Mar 46	PF 28	Emporia	7 Oct 44	28 Aug 46
LST 767		30 Sep 44	9 Mar 46	PF 29	Groton	5 Sep 44	26 Sep 46
LST 768		4 Oct 44	15 Apr 46	PF 30	Hingham	3 Nov 44	5 Jun 46
LST 769		9 Oct 44	29 Apr 46	PF 31	Grand Rapids	10 Oct 44	9 May 46
LST 770		13 Oct 44	29 Apr 46	PF 32	Woonsocket	1 Sep 44	18 Sep 46
LST 771		18 Oct 44	14 May 46	PF 33	Dearborn	10 Sep 44	5 Jun 46
LST 782		22 Aug 44	14 May 46	PF 34	Long Beach	8 Sep 43	26 Aug 45
LST 784		1 Sep 44	29 Mar 46	PF 35	Belfast	24 Nov 43	26 Aug 45
LST 785		4 Sep 44	6 May 46	PF 36	Glendale	1 Oct 43	26 Aug 45
LST 786		28 Aug 44	29 Mar 46	PF 37	San Pedro	23 Oct 43	26 Aug 45
LST 787		13 Sep 44	27 May 46	PF 38	Coronado	12 Nov 43	26 Aug 45
LST 788		18 Sep 44	16 Apr 46	PF 39	Ogden	14 Dec 43	26 Aug 45
LST 789		11 Sep 44	29 May 46	PF 40	Eugene	15 Dec 44	14 Jun 46
LST 790		22 Sep 44	27 May 46	PF 41	El Paso	1 Dec 43	30 Jun 46
LST 791		27 Sep 44	24 May 46	PF 42	Van Buren	17 Dec 43	26 Apr 46
LST 792		2 Oct 44	29 Apr 46	PF 43	Orange	1 Jan 44	28 Oct 46
LST 793		5 Oct 44	29 Apr 46	PF 44	Corpus Christi	29 Jan 44	2 Aug 46
LST 794		16 Oct 44	29 May 46	PF 45	Hutchinson	3 Feb 44	23 Sep 46
LST 795		9 Oct 44	29 Apr 46	PF 46	Bisbee	15 Feb 44	28 Apr 45
LST 796		19 Oct 44	17 Apr 46	PF 47	Gallup	28 Feb 44	28 Aug 45
LST 829		23 Oct 44	9 May 46	PF 48	Rockford	6 Mar 44	28 Aug 45
LST 830		28 Oct 44	29 Apr 46	PF 49	Muskogee	16 Mar 44	28 Aug 45
LST 831		8 Nov 44	May 46	PF 50	Carson City	24 Mar 44	28 Aug 45
LST 832		4 Nov 44	30 Apr 46	PF 51	Burlington	3 Apr 44	28 Aug 45
LST 884		30 Oct 44	15 Feb 46	PF 52	Allentown	24 Mar 44	10 Apr 45
LST 885		26 Oct 44	29 Apr 46	PF 53	Machias	25 Mar 44	10 Apr 45
LST 886		2 Nov 44	10 May 46	PF 54	Sandusky	18 Apr 44	10 Apr 45
LST 887		7 Nov 44	29 Mar 46	PF 55	Bath	9 Sep 44	10 Apr 45
LST 1148		9 Jun 45	11 May 46	PF 56	Covington	17 Oct 44	23 Sep 46
LST 1150		20 Jun 45	8 Feb 46	PF 57	Sheboygan	14 Oct 44	10 Aug 46
LST 1152		30 Jun 45	1 Jul 46	PF 58	Abilene	28 Oct 44	21 Aug 46
PC 469		13 Jul 42	Jun 46	PF 59	Beaufort	28 Aug 44	19 Apr 45
PC 545		27 Jun 42	17 Oct 44	PF 60	Charlotte	9 Oct 44	16 Apr 45
PC 556		1 Sep 42	15 Oct 44	PF 61	Manitowoc	24 Oct 44	3 Sep 46

Hull Number	Ship	Date CG Manned	Date CG Crew Removed	Hull Number	Ship	Date CG Manned	Date CG Crew Removed
PF 62	*Gladwyne*	21 Nov 44	31 Aug 46	YP 93		Feb 44	5 Apr 46
PF 63	*Moberly*	4 Dec 44	12 Aug 46	YP 98		?	28 Jul 43
PF 64	*Knoxville*	29 Apr 44	12 Jun 46	YP 114		26 Dec 41	20 May 42
PF 65	*Uniontown*	6 Oct 44	20 Dec 45	YP 115		30 Apr 43	2 Aug 45
PF 66	*Reading*	19 Aug 44	19 Dec 45	YP 116		26 Dec 41	?
PF 67	*Peoria*	21 May 45	15 May 46	YP 120		15 Dec 41	3 May 45
PF 68	**Brunswick**	3 Oct 44	15 May 46	YP 122		31 Dec 41	Jun 45
PF 69	*Davenport*	15 Feb 45	4 Feb 46	YP 127		26 Dec 41	31 Aug 45
PF 70	*Evansville*	4 Dec 44	26 Aug 45	YP 130		14 Dec 41	6 Sep 45
PF 71	*New Bedford*	18 Nov 44	24 May 46	YP 131		15 Jul 43	20 Feb 44
PF 93	*Lorain*	15 Jan 44	6 Sep 46	YP 134		15 Dec 41	?
PF 94	*Millidgeville*	16 Oct 44	16 Aug 46	YP 135		15 Dec 41	20 May 42
PF 99	*Orlando*	15 Nov 44	24 Jun 46	YP 140		15 Dec 41	?
PF 100	*Racine*	28 Oct 44	27 Jun 46	YP 142		15 Dec 41	5 Sep 45
PF 101	*Greensboro*	29 Jan 45	11 Sep 46	YP 143		15 Dec 41	?
PF 102	*Forsyth*	9 Dec 44	2 Aug 46	YP 197		5 Jan 42	2 Nov 45
PG 86	*Action*	22 Nov 42	7 Sep 45	YP 198		29 May 42	26 Oct 45
PG 87	*Alacrity*	10 Dec 42	4 Oct 45	YP 227		17 Sep 42	10 Sep 45
PG 89	*Brisk*	6 Dec 42	9 Oct 45	YP 250		29 Apr 42	Apr 44
PG 92	*Haste*	6 Apr 43	5 Jul 45	YP 251		31 Dec 41	24 Oct 45
PG 93	*Intensity*	31 Mar 43	29 Jun 45	YP 259		9 Dec 42	19 Aug 44
PG 94	*Might*	22 Dec 42	9 Oct 45	YP 260		24 Nov 42	4 Dec 43
PG 95	*Pert*	23 Jul 43	3 Oct 45	YP 316		15 Jul 43	?
PG 96	*Prudent*	14 Aug 43	11 Oct 45	YP 323		15 Jul 43	?
PYc 3	*Amethyst*	10 Mar 44	27 Feb 46	YP 324		15 Jul 43	?
SC 527		28 May 42	7 Mar 46	YP 325		15 Jul 43	?
SC 528		13 Jun 42	7 Mar 46	YP 335		26 Feb 42	13 Apr 43
SC 688		28 Nov 42	28 Nov 45	YP 339		7 Jun 43	17 Oct 44
SC 689		2 Nov 42	24 Jan 46	YP 341		2 Mar 42	13 Apr 43
SC 704		28 Sep 42	15 Feb 46	YP 361		?	20 Feb 44
SC 705		2 Oct 42	22 Jan 46	YP 362		1 Apr 44	14 Oct 44
YF 677		?	14 Jul 45	YP 370		15 Jul 43	12 Oct 44
YFB 30		24 Mar 42	Sep 45	YP 371		4 Feb 44	Apr 46
YHB 22		13 Apr 43	31 Dec 43	YP 381		15 Jul 43	25 Aug 45
YNG 40		2 Aug 45	16 Nov 45	YP 401		22 Jan 44	24 Oct 45
YP 28		28 Apr 43	6 Oct 44	YP 411		?	Mar 44
YP 70		9 Feb 42	16 Sep 44	YP 677		Aug 44	14 Jul 45
YP 75		20 Mar 42	1 Sep 44				

The *Aquarius* (AKA 16) inboard, at a harbor in the Russell Islands. She participated in the Kwajalein, Guam, Peleliu, Leyte, Lingayen Gulf, and Okinawa landings. The CG manned fifteen cargo ships (AKs) and five attack cargo ships (AKAs) during WW II.

The *Wakefield* (Apr 21) heads home after VE Day with six thousand troops on board. She was the largest ship manned by the CG during WW II. The CG manned thirty-one transports (APs) for the Navy.

The *Kirkpatrick* (DE 318) during 1944. The CG manned thirty destroyer escorts (DEs) for the Navy during the war. One of these, the *Leopold* (DE 319), was torpedoed and lost in the North Atlantic on 9 Mar 44. Only twenty-eight out of the 199-man crew survived.

The *Leonard Wood* (APA 12), 28 Apr 44. This aerial view shows the fine lines of her prewar construction. She was one of the three attack transports (APAs) manned by the CG prior to its incorporation into the Navy on 1 Nov 41. Ultimately, the CG manned nine APAs during WW II.

LCI(L) 350 plows her way through heavy seas upon return to the U.S. from a European landing. These 155-foot rough-riding craft crossed the Atlantic and Pacific under their own power. The CG manned twenty-eight landing craft, infantry (large) for the Navy. Four of these craft—numbers 85, 91, 92, 93—were lost during the Normandy Invasion.

LST 831 beached at Okinawa on D-Day. As her bow ramp is being lowered, one can see the unauthorized stenciled letters "USCG" above the bow door. The CG manned seventy-six landing ship tanks (LSTs—affectionately known as "large slow targets"). Three of these vessels—LSTs 69, 167, and 203—were lost during the war.

The *Knoxville* (PF 64) on weather station during WW II. She has been modified for this duty: note the weather balloon hangar aft the mainmast and what is missing from the aft mount. Prior to the commissioning of the patrol frigates (PFs), the CG had used old merchant ships and large yachts for this duty. The CG manned seventy-five PFs during WW II.

ARMY VESSELS MANNED BY THE COAST GUARD DURING WORLD WAR II*

On 14 Mar 44 the Coast Guard agreed to man numerous small Army Transportation Corps ships; by the end of the war, it had manned a total of 288 USA craft. Many of these vessels were already operating in the southwest Pacific, and most served in the South Pacific with no assigned permanent station or home yard.

CG Personnel Manning USA Ships and Craft

Date	Personnel	Vessels
30 Apr 44	1048	47
31 Dec 44	6851	278
30 Jun 45	6851	262
1 Mar 46	96	4

Name	Date CG Manned	Date CG Crew Removed
Duluth	15 Aug 44	20 Mar 47
James B. Houston	9 Aug 44	25 Feb 46
J. E. Gorman	5 Sep 44	20 Mar 47
J. M. Davis	27 Jul 44	4 Apr 47
William F. Fitch	14 Jun 44	3 Feb 47
W. J. Connors	4 Sep 44	16 Jun 47

*There are no readily available works that provide characteristics or histories of these ships.

Hull Number	Date CG Manned	Date CG Crew Removed
F 8	15 May 44	?
F 11	15 May 44	?
F 14	12 Oct 44	Jan 46
F 16	Oct 44	?
F 51	4 Jul 44	Oct 45
F 54	24 Oct 44	?
F 55	27 Oct 44	?
F 73	Oct 44	29 May 45
F 74	Oct 44	17 May 45
F 75	11 Oct 44	?
F 77	7 Oct 44	?
F 91	8 Nov 44	?
F 96	14 Nov 44	?
F 116	19 Nov 44	?
F 117	19 Nov 44	7 May 45
F 118	11 Oct 44	16 May 45
F 120	23 Oct 44	Oct 45
F 126	5 Oct 44	Oct 45
F 128	31 Oct 44	?
F 129	Oct 44	Dec 45
F 130	3 Nov 44	?
FS 34	22 May 45	30 Jan 46
FS 140	31 Oct 44	?
FS 141	Oct 44	Dec 45
FS 142	20 Sep 44	9 Oct 45
FS 143	?	?
FS 144	27 Oct 44	13 Oct 45
FS 145	2 May 44	Nov 45
FS 146	21 Apr 44	Dec 45
FS 147	24 Apr 44	Dec 45
FS 148	24 Apr 44	7 Oct 45
FS 149	21 Apr 44	?
FS 150	20 Sep 44	Jan 46

Hull Number	Date CG Manned	Date CG Crew Removed	Hull Number	Date CG Manned	Date CG Crew Removed
FS 151	17 Apr 44	13 Oct 45	FS 227	1 Mar 45	?
FS 152	28 Apr 44	19 Oct 45	FS 228	13 Mar 45	?
FS 153	28 Apr 44	31 Oct 45	FS 229	?	?
FS 154	21 Apr 44	Dec 45	FS 230	?	?
FS 155	10 May 44	Nov 45	FS 231	?	?
FS 156	6 May 44	4 Sep 45	FS 232	?	?
FS 157	6 May 44	Nov 45	FS 233	?	?
FS 158	17 May 44	Dec 45	FS 234	?	?
FS 159	17 May 44	2 Sep 44	FS 253	7 May 44	23 Oct 45
FS 160	17 May 44	Dec 45	FS 254	23 May 45	7 Dec 45
FS 161	?	19 May 44	FS 255	6 Jun 44	11 May 45*
FS 162	17 Apr 44	?	FS 256	16 Jun 44	14 Oct 45
FS 163	18 Apr 44	12 Oct 45*	FS 257	24 Jun 44	Dec 45
FS 164	21 Apr 44	?	FS 258	20 Aug 44	22 Oct 45
FS 165	26 Apr 44	21 Sep 45	FS 259	?	?
FS 166	28 Apr 44	9 Oct 45	FS 260	26 Jul 44	Nov 45
FS 167	1 May 44	?	FS 261	2 Aug 44	Jan 46
FS 168	4 May 44	1 Oct 45	FS 262	9 Aug 44	Jan 46
FS 169	4 May 44	5 Oct 45	FS 263	16 Aug 44	Oct 45
FS 170	8 May 44	Dec 45	FS 264	24 Aug 44	24 Sep 45
FS 171	10 May 44	22 Sep 45	FS 265	1 Sep 44	?
FS 172	19 May 44	?†	FS 266	8 Sep 44	25 Nov 45
FS 173	14 May 44	25 Oct 45	FS 267	18 Sep 44	Jul 45
FS 174	18 May 44	29 Nov 45	FS 268	22 Sep 44	Nov 45
FS 175	19 May 44	?	FS 269	2 Oct 44	?
FS 176	21 May 44	Jan 46	FS 270	6 Oct 44	10 Oct 45
FS 177	26 May 44	19 Aug 45	FS 271	13 Oct 44	27 Sep 45
FS 178	27 May 44	16 Oct 45	FS 272	22 Oct 44	Jan 46
FS 179	28 May 44	1 Oct 45	FS 273	6 Nov 44	30 Oct 45
FS 180	31 May 44	18 Oct 45	FS 274	31 Oct 44	Nov 45
FS 181	31 Aug 44	?	FS 275	6 Nov 44	Nov 45
FS 182	24 Jun 44	?	FS 276	13 Nov 44	Nov 45
FS 183	22 Jul 44	Nov 45	FS 277	20 Nov 44	Dec 45
FS 184	2 Aug 44	Dec 45	FS 278	25 Nov 44	3 Oct 45
FS 185	24 Jul 44	Oct 45	FS 279	2 Dec 44	22 Oct 45
FS 186	24 Jul 44	Nov 45	FS 280	9 Dec 44	Nov 45
FS 187	31 Jul 44	Dec 45	FS 282	27 Dec 44	Oct 45
FS 188	2 Aug 44	3 Oct 44	FS 283	2 Jan 45	25 Sep 45
FS 189	9 Aug 44	Nov 45	FS 284	12 Jan 45	12 Aug 45
FS 190	9 Aug 44	?	FS 285	22 Jan 45	Dec 45
FS 191	12 Aug 44	Dec 45	FS 286	?	1 Oct 45
FS 192	21 Aug 44	Dec 45	FS 287	1 Mar 45	23 Aug 45
FS 193	23 Aug 44	Dec 45	FS 288	10 Mar 45	?
FS 194	30 Aug 44	Dec 45	FS 289	?	?
FS 195	26 Aug 44	Dec 45	FS 290	?	9 Nov 45†
FS 196	29 Aug 44	22 Aug 45	FS 309	10 Apr 44	Dec 45
FS 197	2 Sep 44	Dec 45	FS 310	11 Apr 44	Nov 45
FS 198	5 Sep 44	Nov 45	FS 311	13 Jun 44	Dec 45
FS 200	19 Sep 44	29 Oct 45	FS 312	27 Jun 44	15 Oct 45
FS 201	30 Sep 44	Jan 46	FS 313	2 Jul 44	?
FS 202	7 Oct 44	?	FS 314	22 Jul 44	Nov 45
FS 203	17 Oct 44	31 Oct 45	FS 315	31 Jul 44	?
FS 222	31 Jan 45	18 Jan 46	FS 316	12 Sep 44	Nov 45
FS 223	6 Feb 45	10 Nov 45	FS 317	25 Sep 44	Oct 45
FS 224	?	Nov 45	FS 318	6 Oct 44	14 Oct 45
FS 225	14 Feb 45	Dec 45	FS 319	27 Oct 44	Jan 46
FS 226	17 Feb 45	Nov 45			

*Lost in a typhoon.
†Sunk off Mugil Point, Cape Croisilles, New Guinea.

*Torpedoed off Taloma Bay, Davao Gulf, Mindanao, Philippines—4 enlisted men lost.
†Lost in a typhoon off Okinawa.

Hull Number	Date CG Manned	Date CG Crew Removed	Hull Number	Date CG Manned	Date CG Crew Removed
FS 343	?	21 Sep 45	FS 547	4 Oct 44	27 Oct 45
FS 344	7 Apr 45	Jan 46	FS 548	2 Nov 44	?
FS 345	26 Jul 44	?	FS 549	29 Nov 44	24 Nov 45
FS 346	23 Aug 44	30 Aug 45	FS 550	21 Dec 44	24 Sep 45
FS 347	30 Sep 44	?	LT 1	8 May 44	4 Jan 46
FS 348	8 Nov 44	28 Sep 45	LT 20	13 Oct 44	29 Oct 45
FS 349	16 May 44	Nov 45	LT 21	13 Oct 44	Oct 45
FS 350	5 Jul 44	23 Sep 45	LT 54	?	1 Aug 46
FS 351	12 Sep 44	Nov 45	LT 57	4 May 44	Jan 46
FS 352	9 Aug 44	28 Nov 45	LT 58	22 May 44	Oct 45
FS 353	5 Oct 44	Nov 45	LT 59	16 Mar 45	Dec 45
FS 354	10 Nov 44	?	LT 128	26 Apr 44	16 Oct 45
FS 355	5 Dec 44	19 Nov 45	LT 129	11 Nov 44	Dec 45
FS 356	11 Jan 45	30 Oct 45	LT 131	10 Nov 44	6 Oct 45
FS 361	10 Apr 44	26 Oct 45	LT 132	?	?
FS 362	10 Apr 44	10 Oct 45	LT 133	10 Jun 44	29 Sep 45
FS 363	20 May 44	?	LT 134	29 May 44	17 Oct 45
FS 364	14 Apr 44	Dec 45	LT 135	4 Apr 44	Nov 45
FS 365	12 Apr 44	?	LT 217	8 Oct 44	1 Oct 45
FS 366	20 Apr 44	22 Sep 45	LT 218	8 Oct 44	Nov 45
FS 367	29 Apr 44	24 Sep 45	LT 219	17 Nov 44	Jan 46
FS 371	1 Aug 44	Dec 45	LT 220	28 Oct 44	6 Oct 45
FS 372	22 Aug 44	?	LT 225	7 Oct 44	Jan 46
FS 373	5 Oct 44	Nov 45	LT 226	7 Dec 44	Dec 45
FS 374	5 Oct 44	Dec 45	LT 227	7 Dec 44	Jan 46
FS 383	24 Sep 44	Nov 45	LT 228	21 Apr 44	Jan 46
FS 384	24 Sep 44	28 Sep 45	LT 229	30 May 44	6 Oct 45
FS 385	23 Oct 44	Nov 45	LT 230	19 May 44	Jan 46
FS 386	4 Dec 44	Nov 45	LT 231	19 May 44	Dec 45
FS 387	23 May 44	?	LT 348	17 May 44	Jan 46
FS 388	2 Jun 44	Dec 45	LT 354	17 Mar 45	17 Oct 45
FS 389	28 Jun 44	Nov 45	LT 356	?	?
FS 390	4 Jul 44	15 Oct 45	LT 357	?	Oct 45
FS 391	28 Jul 44	Dec 45	LT 358	6 Apr 45	8 Oct 45*
FS 392	8 Aug 44	19 Oct 45	LT 454	18 Apr 45	5 Jan 46
FS 393	27 Aug 44	Nov 45	LT 455	6 May 44	10 Oct 45
FS 394	14 Dec 44	Nov 45	LT 528	30 May 44	Dec 45
FS 395	1 Jan 45	Nov 45	LT 529	23 May 44	Nov 45
FS 396	18 Jan 45	18 Jan 46	LT 530	23 May 44	3 Oct 45
FS 397	20 Feb 45	?	LT 531	10 Apr 44	Dec 45
FS 398	?	?	LT 535	6 Jun 44	22 Oct 45
FS 399	1 Jan 45	?	LT 536	13 Jun 44	Jan 46
FS 400	?	?	LT 579	21 Mar 45	27 Sep 45
FS 404	24 Oct 44	31 Oct 45	LT 633	6 May 44	Nov 45
FS 405	23 Nov 44	Dec 45	LT 634	14 Jun 44	Oct 45
FS 406	30 Dec 44	8 Oct 45*	LT 635	24 May 44	23 Sep 45
FS 407	16 Jan 45	Nov 45	LT 636	29 May 44	23 Sep 45
FS 408	13 Feb 45	9 Nov 45	LT 637	13 Apr 44	Jan 46
FS 409	20 Feb 45	?	LT 643	13 Mar 45	Jan 46
FS 410	?	9 Nov 45†	LT 645	?	6 Oct 45
FS 524	1 Jul 44	11 Oct 45	LT 646	21 Apr 45	?
FS 525	16 Aug 44	Nov 45	LT 647	17 May 45	29 Sep 45
FS 526	6 Sep 44	Dec 45	LT 648	2 Mar 45	?
FS 527	14 Oct 44	?	LT 647	27 May 44	1 Oct 45
FS 528	15 Nov 44	25 Nov 45	LT 650	10 Dec 44	Nov 45
FS 529	28 Dec 44	25 Sep 45	Y 3	22 Sep 44	?
FS 546	27 Sep 44	Nov 45	Y 4	20 Sep 44	Dec 45
			Y 5	Oct 44	27 Dec 45
			Y 6	20 Sep 44	Dec 45

*Lost in a typhoon off Okinawa.
†Lost in a typhoon at Okinawa.

*Lost in a typhoon off Okinawa.

Hull Number	Date CG Manned	Date CG Crew Removed		Hull Number	Date CG Manned	Date CG Crew Removed
Y 7	Oct 44	?		Y 20	22 Sep 44	Jan 46
Y 8	23 Sep 44	28 Nov 45		Y 21	20 Sep 44	Jan 46
Y 9	24 Sep 44	29 Sep 45		Y 35	31 Jul 44	?
Y 11	20 Sep 44	18 Oct 45		Y 44	17 Aug 44	25 Oct 45
Y 13	21 Aug 44	Nov 45		Y 45	2 Sep 44	Mar 45
Y 14	20 Sep 44	12 Oct 45		Y 46	16 Sep 44	Dec 45
Y 15	20 Oct 44	Nov 45		Y 59	18 Aug 44	Dec 45
Y 18	9 Oct 44	Dec 45		Y 108	30 Aug 44	3 Oct 45
Y 19	22 Sep 44	?		Y 109	4 Oct 44	Nov 45

The repair ship *J. E. Goodman*, 3 Oct 44. The CG manned six of this type vessel for the Army. All served in the Pacific theatre; their CG crews were removed in 1946 and 1947.

FS 177 in the Southwest Pacific, 1944–45. The CG manned 188 FS (freight supply) ships for the Army. They ranged in size from 114′ to 180′ and were built between 1943 and 1945. A lot of them served in the Pacific Theatre and were known as "island hoppers." Many of this type were originally classified as FP (freight personnel). FS 177 still bears her old designator above the bridge, FP 177. Note the unauthorized CG seal adorning the stack.

COAST GUARD DISTRICTS, 1944

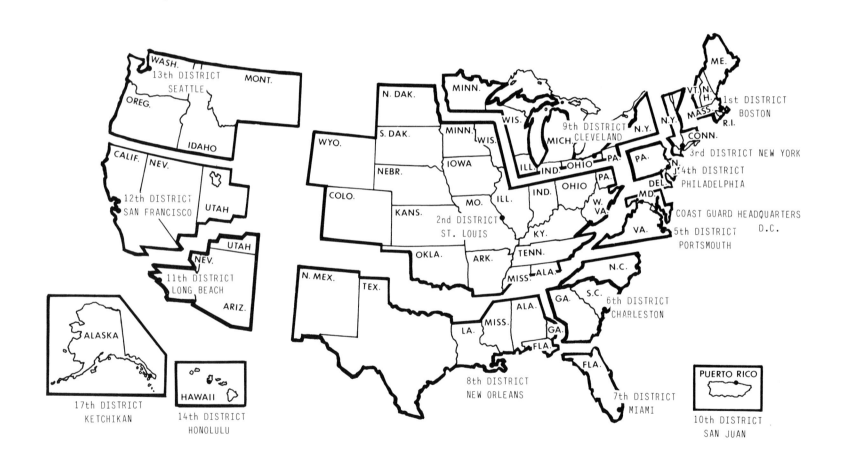

APPENDIX D

LIGHTSHIP STATIONS, 1941

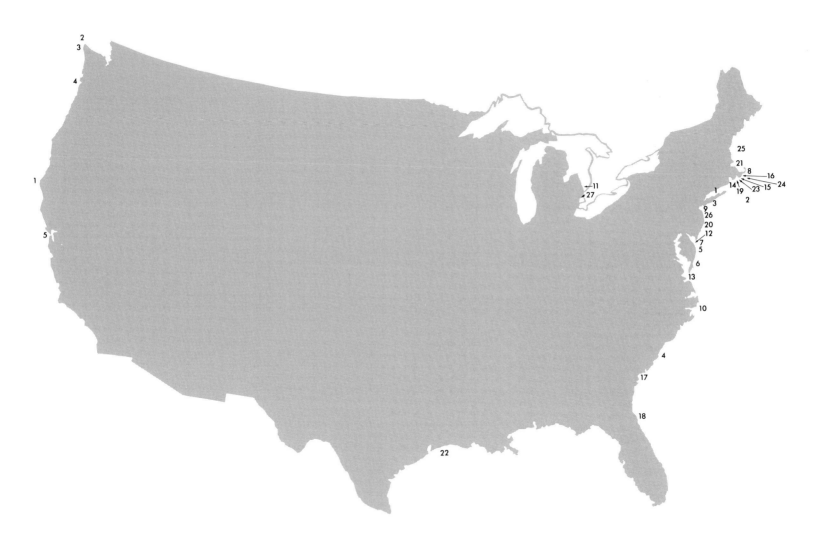

WEST COAST LIGHTSHIP STATIONS, 1941

		Latitude	Longitude
1	Blunts Reef	40°26′	124°30′
2	Swiftsure Bank	48°32′	125°00′
3	Umatilla Reef	48°10′	124°50′
4	Columbia River	46°11′	124°11′
5	San Francisco	37°45′	127°42′

EAST COAST, GREAT LAKES, AND GULF OF MEXICO LIGHTSHIP STATIONS, 1941

		Latitude	Longitude
1	Cornfield Point	41°13′	72°22′
2	Nantucket	40°37′	69°37′
3	Fire Island	40°29′	73°11′
4	Frying Pan Shoals	33°28′	77°34′
5	Fenwick Island	38°25′	74°46′

		Latitude	Longitude
6	Winter Quarter	37°55′	74°56′
7	Five Fathom Bank	38°47′	74°35′
8	Pollock Rip	41°24′	69°55′
9	Ambrose	40°27′	73°49′
10	Diamond Shoal	35°05′	75°20′
11	Lake Huron	43°03′	82°25′
12	Overfalls	38°48′	75°01′
13	Chesapeake (Cape Charles)	36°59′	75°42′
14	Brent Reef	41°26′	71°23′
15	Cross Rip	41°27′	70°17′
16	Handkerchief	41°29′	70°04′
17	Savannah	31°57′	80°40′
18	St. Johns River	30°23′	81°18′
19	Hen and Chickens	41°27′	71°01′
20	Barnegat	39°46′	73°56′
21	Boston	42°20′	70°45′
22	Heald Bank	29°06′	94°12′
23	Vineyard Sound (Sow and Pigs)	41°23′	71°00′
24	Stonehorse Shoal	41°33′	69°59′
25	Portland	43°32′	70°06′
26	Scotland	40°27′	73°55′
27	Lake St. Clair (Grosse Point)	42°28′	82°45′

SEA FRONTIERS (AREA COMMANDS)

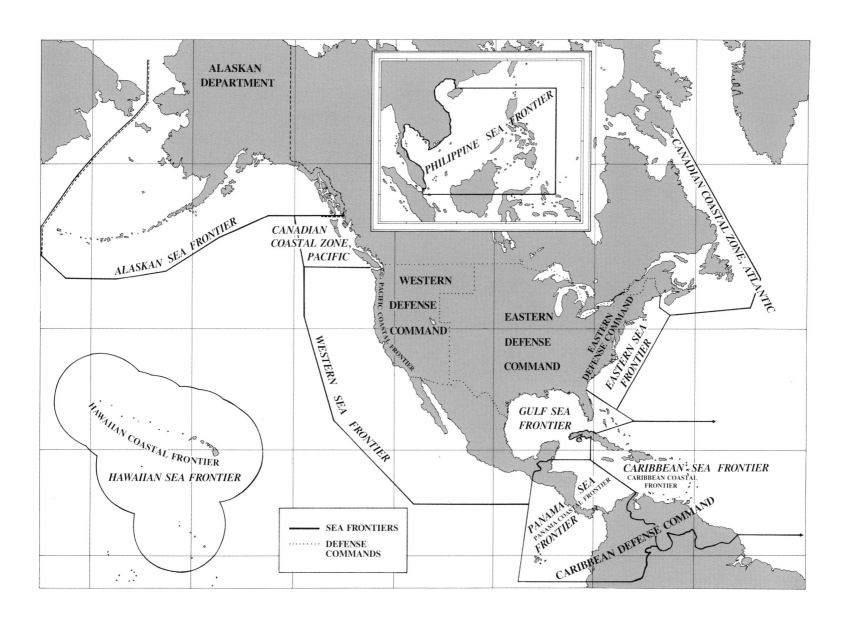

Index

References to illustrations are printed in boldface type. For ships without names see Index to Ships Identified by Length p. 332.

Pirate (CGR-378), 266
Pirate (CGR-381), 266
Pittsburgh, PA, 111, 129
Planetree (WAGL 307), 96–97
Plauen (CGR-947), 275
Playboy (CGR-1210), 277
Playmate (CGR-154), 263
Plum Island, WI, 254
Plymouth (USS), 38
Pocahontas. See EM *Pocahontas*
Pocatello (PF 9), 301
Pocomoke City, MD, 170, 172, 174, 179
Poinciana (WAGL 266), 125
Point Adams, OR, 251
Point Judith Lighthouse, 39
Point Pleasant, WV, 37–38
Pollock Rip Lightship Station, 154, 311
Pollyana (CGR-600), 269
Pol VIII. See Pol
Pol (WYP 382), 173
Ponce, PR, 223
Pontchartrain [WPG], 25–30, **29**
Pontchartrain (WPG 70), 1–3, **3**
Pontus (AGP 20), 299
Poodle Pup (CGR-52), 261
Poole (DE 151), 300
Poole, England, 222–33
Poplar (WAGL 241), 109, **109**
Portal. See West Portal
Port Angeles, WA, 14, 55, 66
Port Arthur, TX, 71
Port Everglades, FL, 156
Port Hueneme, CA, 209
Port Huron, MI, 145, 155
Portland Lightship Station, 160, 311
Portland, ME, 21, 70–71, 79, 130, 224–25
Portland, OR, 112, 151, 200
Portland Shipbuilding Co., 168–69
Port of Spain, Trinidad, 225
Portrero del Llano (tanker), 40, 74
Port Richmond, NY, 66, 144, 161
Portsmouth Navy Yard, 74, 241
Portsmouth, NH, 241
Portsmouth, VA, 72, 85, 93, 107, 124, 133, 141, 154
Port Townsend, WA, 33
Potomac. See Electra
Poughkeepsie (PF 26), 301
President. See Bison
Presidential yachts, 6, 38, 41, 47
Pride (DE 323), 300
Primrose (WAGL 316), 88
Primrose II (CGR-233), 264
Prince. See Student Prince
Prince of Wales (HMS), 33
Prince Rupert, British Columbia, 141
Prince Rupert (merchantman), 144
Principia (CG-96001F), 218
Priscilla (CGR-151), 263
Procyon. See Empire State
Prohibition, 13, 37–38, 41, 45, 48, 237–38, 240–41
Prospect, OH, 259
Prosper (CGR-768), 272
Providence, RI, 230
Provincetown, MA, 47
Prudent (PG 96), 302
P. Smit Jr. Shipyard, 199

PTC Flotilla Number One, 222–25, 228–31, 234
P-38s, 31
Public Jumper (CGR-404), 266
Public Works Administration (PWA), 21
Pueblo (PF 13), 301
Puerto Princessa landing, 15
Pulaski (WSC 149), 44–49
Pup. See Poodle Pup (CGR-52)
Pusey & Jones Co., 9, 21, 76–77, 115, 123, 150, 157, 191, 194, 198

Q ship, 64–65
Quadia. See Boca de Quadia
Que-Bee-Cee (CGR-742), 271
Queen. See Northern Queen, Sea Queen, Victory Queen
Queen B (CGR-1720), 283
Queen of Palm Beach (CG-7001F), 244
Queen of Peace [WIX], 204
Quest II (CGR-118), 263
Quincy, MA, 25, 159, 183

Racine Boat Manufacturing Co., 139, 158
Racine (PF 100), 302
Racine-Truscott-Shell Lake Boat Co., 157
Radar, fire-control used by CG, 3; training, 6
Rainbow (CG-74001), 242
Raitan (WYT 93), 71–72
Rambler (CGR-1225), 278
Rambler (CGR-1791), 285
Rambler (WAGL 298), 88
Ramsden (DE 382), 300
Ramsey. See H. A. Ramsey Co.
Randall. See General George Randall
Randolph. See Lupine
Rapids. See Grand Rapids
Rappahannock Marine Railway Co., 178
Rascal III (CGR-218), 264
Rascals V (CGR-974), 275
Rawlins (USS), 99
Reading (PF 66), 302
Redbud (WAGL 398), 92–95
Red Feather II (CGR-156), 263
Red Heels II (CGR-731), 271
Red Jacket (CGR-1244), 278
Redwing [WAT], 68, **68**
Reed. See EM *Reed*
Reed-Cook Marine Construction Co., 195
Reinie (CGR-717), 271
Reisenberg. See Felix Reisenberg
Rejoyce (CGR-736), 271
Relax (CGR-1317), 279
Reliance (WSC 150), 44–49
Rena III (CGR-49), 261
Rensseler. See Jeremiah Van Rensseler
Repajo (CGR-588), 269
Republic (tanker), 48
Rescue Flotilla No. 1, 222–33. *See also* Normandy landings
Rescues. *See Arabutan, Arletta, Atengo, Barberry, Bonneville, Buarque, C. O. Stillman, Chatham, Cheerio, Cherokee, China Arrow, Cities Service Empire, City of New York, Cleveco, Coulmore, Cristales, Dorchester, E. H. Blum, Edwin Duke, Faja de Oro, Guido, Gulftrade, Hartwelson, Henry S. Mallory, Iris, James Withycombe, Jeremiah Van Rensseler, John D. Gill, John Lind, Kalliopi, Lewis*

Case, Manuela, Marconi, Maria da Gloria, Mattawin, Matthew Luckenbach, Melrose, Mont Parnes, Neilson Alonzo, Nevada, Norness, Pan Massachusetts, Penmar, Peysander, Pipestone County, Plymouth, Portrero del Llano, Republic, Robert E. Hopkins, R. W. Gallagher, St. Augustine, San Gil, Santore, Sommeisdijk, Surewater, Suwied, Svend Foyne, Tennessee, Tiger, Tresillian, W. D. Anderson, West Portal, William C. McTarnahan, William Rockefeller. See also Air-sea rescue, Retriever method
Resolution [WIX], 201
Respite (CGR-411), 267
Restless Too (CG-75003), 239
Restless II (CG-83003), 235
Retriever method, 21
Revenue Cutter Service (RCS), 7, 78
Revere (CGR-219), 264
Rex (CGR-1603), 282
Rex II (CGR-914), 274
Reykjavik, Iceland, 14
Rhesus (CG-80002), 237
Rhodes (DE 385), 300
Rhododendron (WAGL 267), 112
Rice Brothers Corp., 149, 156, 241
Rich. See A. F. Rich
Richardson. See General W. P. Richardson
Richardson Boat Co., 255
Richey (DE 385), 300
Ricketts (DE-254), 300
Ricky (CGR-1226), 278
Riette (CGR-137), 263
River Rouge, MI, 86, 89, 118
R. L. Howze. See General R. L. Howze
RO-32 (Japanese Navy), 47
Roamin (CGR-425), 267
Roberta (CGR-434), 267
Robert E. Hopkins (merchantman), 14
Robin. See Sea Robin
Robins Dry Dock & Repair Co., 193
Robinson Marine Construction Co., 255
Rockefeller. See William Rockefeller
Rockford (PF 48), 301
Rockland, ME, 134, 185, 187–88, 237
Rocky River Dry Dock Co., 200
Rocky River, OH, 200
Roderick. See Manuel L. Roderick
Roen. See John Roen, Jr.
Roger B. Taney. See Taney
Roll. See Tootsie Roll
Romance Line, 4
Roosevelt. See Franklin D. Roosevelt
Roosevelt, Franklin, 26, 41
Roosevelt, Theodore, 6
Rosalind (CGR-735), 271
Rosarita (CGR-779), 272
Rose (WAGL 242), 138, **138**
Roseway (CGR-812), 272
Rotterdam, Holland, 199
Rowdy (CGR-138), 263
Rowe. See EM *Rowe*
Rowland H. Wilcox. See EM *Wilcox*
Roy. See Lil Roy
R. Palmer & Sons, 165–66
R. Steel & Co., 211–12
Rufnek (CGR-397), 266
Rujopa (CGR-894), 274

Index to Ships Identified by Length